Quetzalcóatl and Guadalupe

Jacques Lafaye

Quetzalcóatl and Guadalupe

The Formation of Mexican National Consciousness 1531–1813

With a Foreword by Octavio Paz

Translated by
BENJAMIN KEEN

The University of Chicago Press
Chicago and London

JACQUES LAFAYE studied at the University of
Strasbourg, received his Doctorat de l'État, and
is professor of Latin American history at the
Sorbonne and assistant director of the Musée
de l'Homme in Paris. He is the author of *Les
Conquistadores* and editor of the *Manuscrit
Tovar: Origines et Croyances des Indiens du Mexique.*

BENJAMIN KEEN is professor of history at
Northern Illinois University and served as 1974
chairman of the Conference on Latin American
History. His publications include *Life and Labor
in Ancient Mexico: The Brief and Summary Relation
of Alonso de Zorita* and *The Aztec Image in Western
Thought.*

Originally published as *Quetzalcóatl et Guadalupe,*
© 1974 Éditions Gallimard

The University of Chicago Press, Chicago 60637
The University of Chicago Press, Ltd., London

Library of Congress Cataloging in Publication Data

Lafaye, Jacques.
    Quetzalcóatl and Guadalupe.

    Translation of Quetzalcóatl et Guadalupe.
    Includes bibliographical references and index.
    1. Mexico—Civilization—History. 2. Mexico—
Religion. 3. Guadalupe, Nuestra Señora de.
4. Quetzalcóatl. I. Title.
F1210.L313   972   75-20889
ISBN 0-226-46794-5

To my wife, *Simonne*
and children,
Etienne, Jean-Jacques, and Olivier

Contents

Foreword   The Flight of Quetzalcóatl and the Quest for Legitimacy

Imagination is the faculty that reveals the hidden relations between things. It does not matter that in the poet it works upon phenomena which relate to the world of sensibility, in the scientist upon natural facts and processes, and in the historian upon the events and personages of societies of the past. In all three cases, the discovery of secret affinities and repulsions makes visible what was invisible. Poets, scientists, and historians show us the other side of things, the hidden face of language, nature, or the past. But their results are different: the poet produces metaphors, the scientist natural laws, and the historian—just what does the historian produce?

The poet aspires to a unique image which will resolve into its unity and singularity the multiple richness of the world. Poetic images are like the angels of Catholicism: each is a species in itself. They are unique and universal. At the other extreme, the scientist reduces individuals to series, changes to tendencies, and tendencies to laws. For poetry, repetition spells impoverishment; for science, repetition is the regularity that confirms hypotheses. The exception is the poet's reward and the scientist's punishment. The historian stands between the poet and the scientist. His kingdom, like that of the poet, is the kingdom of particular cases and facts which are not repeated; at the same time, like the scientist before natural phenomena, the historian operates on series of events which he tries to reduce, not to species and families, but to tendencies and currents.

Historical events are not ruled by laws, or, at least, these laws have not been discovered. The Newtons and Einsteins of history are still to be born. Yet it is perfectly clear that each society, each epoch, is something more than an ensemble of disparate facts, persons, realities, and ideas. A unity arisen from the collision of contradictory tendencies and forces, each epoch is a community of tastes, needs, principles, institutions, and techniques. The historian searches for historical coherence—a modest equivalent of the order of nature—and this search relates him to the scientist. But the form that this coherence assumes is that of the poetic fable: novel, drama, epic poem. Historical events rhyme with each other, and the logic that governs their development does not evoke axioms but a space in which echoes and correspondences combine and separate.

History is one with science in its methods and with poetry in its vision. Like science, it is a discovery; like poetry, a new creation. By contrast with science and poetry, history does not invent or explore worlds; it reconstructs, refashions the world of the past. Its knowledge is not a knowledge that transcends itself; I mean to say that history does not include any metahistory, like that which is offered by those chimerical systems which certain men of genius, a Marx or a Saint Augustine, conceive from time to time. Nor is it knowledge in the strict sense of the word. Situated between ethnology (description of societies) and poetry (imagination), history is empirical rigor and aesthetic sympathy, a mixture of pity and irony. Rather than being knowledge, it is wisdom. That is the true historical tradition of the West, from Herodotus to Michelet, from Tacitus to Henry Adams. To that tradition belongs the remarkable book of Jacques Lafaye about two myths of New Spain: Quetzalcóatl-Saint Thomas and Tonantzin-Guadalupe.

Lafaye's study belongs to the history of ideas or, more precisely, to that of beliefs. Ortega y Gasset thought that the substance of history, its marrow, was not the ideas but rather what the ideas covered up: beliefs. A man is better defined by his beliefs than by his ideas. Other historians prefer to define societies by their techniques. That is their right, but it remains true that techniques, like ideas, change more rapidly than beliefs. The tractor has replaced the cart and Marxism has replaced scholasticism, but the magic of the Neolithic and the astrology of Babylon still flourish in New York, Paris, and Moscow. Lafaye's book is an admirable description of the beliefs of New Spain during the three centuries of its existence. Complex beliefs in which two syncretisms blend: Spanish Catholicism and the Aztec religion. The first, marked by its agelong coexistence with Islam, by its crusading spirit and obsession with the end of the world; the second, likewise the militant religion of a chosen people. The mass of believers was as complex as their beliefs: the Indian peoples (each with its own language and tradition), the Spaniards (also divided in race and language), the creoles, the mestizos, the mulattoes. Against this flamboyant background unfold the two myths studied by Lafaye. Both were born in the pre-Hispanic world and refashioned in the seventeenth century by minds who joined nascent modern thought with medieval tradition (Descartes and Thomas Aquinas). The two myths, and especially that of Guadalupe, were transformed into symbols and banners of the War of Independence and have come down to our own day not as the speculations of theologians or ideologues but as images arisen from the collective consciousness. The Mexican people, after more than two centuries of experiments and defeats, have faith only in the Virgin of Guadalupe and the National Lottery.

Historical reconstructions are also archaeological digs in the historical subsoil. A society is composed of its institutions, its intellectual and artistic creations, its techniques, its material and spiritual life. It also includes all that is found behind or below those things. The metaphor which designates this hidden reality changes according to the schools, generations, and historians: historical factors, roots, cells, infrastructures, foundations, strata. . . . Metaphors borrowed from agriculture, biology, geology, architecture, all these names evoke a hidden reality, masked by appearances. Historical reality has many ways of concealing itself. A most effective way consists in displaying itself in the full view of all. Lafaye's book is a magnificent example of my point: the world that it reveals to us—the society of the viceroyalty of Mexico in the seventeenth and eighteenth centuries—is a world which we all knew but which no one had yet seen. Studies of the subject abound, yet none had shown us that world in all its uniqueness. Lafaye reveals to us an unknown world, unknown not because it remained hidden from us but, on the contrary, because its visibility blinded us. His book obliges us to rub our eyes and admit to ourselves that we have been victims of a strange historical optical illusion.

New Spain: that name describes a singular society and a no less singular destiny. It was a society that passionately denied its antecedents and its ancestors—the Indian world and the Spanish world— and at the same time formed ambiguous links with both; in its turn, that society was to be denied by modern Mexico. Mexico would not be what it is without New Spain, but Mexico is not New Spain; indeed, it is its negation. The society of New Spain was a world which was born, grew, and then expired the moment it reached its maturity. Mexico killed it. The historical optical illusion is neither fortuitous nor innocent. We do not see New Spain because, if we saw it as it really is, we would see all that we neither could nor wished to be. That which we could not be—a universal empire; that which we did not want to be—a hierarchical society governed by a church-state.

Most historians offer us a conventional image of New Spain: an intermediate stage between Indian Mexico and modern Mexico, conceived as a stage of formation and gestation. This linear perspective distorts the historical reality; New Spain was more than a pause or a period of transition between the Aztec world and independent Mexico. The official history presents it in an even more negative light: New Spain was an interregnum, a stage of usurpation and oppression, a period of historical illegitimacy. Independence closed this parenthesis and reestablished the continuity of the historical discourse, interrupted by three centuries of colonization. Independence was a *restoration*. Our defective vision of New Spain's historical reality is at last explained: not myopia but an eclipse concealed it from our view. Lafaye's book forces us to disinter the corpse which we buried in our backyard.

New Spain is the point of origin of modern Mexico, but there is a break between the two. Mexico does not continue the society of the seventeenth and eighteenth centuries; it contradicts that society, it is a different society. Although this idea does not explicitly appear in Lafaye's book, it is a conclusion that can properly be inferred from many of his pages. Viceregal society was not only a unique society but felt the need to affirm its particularity. Not content with being and feeling different from Spain, it invented a universal destiny with which it confronted and countered Spanish universalism. New Spain wished to be the Other Spain: an empire, the Rome of America. A contradictory proposition: New Spain wished to be the realization of Old Spain, and this implied the negation of the latter. In order to consummate Old Spain, the New negated it and became another Spain. The image of the phoenix appears constantly in the literature of the seventeenth and eighteenth centuries: Sigüenza y Góngora calls Saint Thomas-Quetzalcóatl the Phoenix of the West, that is, the American Phoenix. The Apostle is born from the pyre on which the Indian god consumed himself, and New Spain springs up from the ashes of Old Spain. An unfathomable mystery: it is other, yet the same. This mystery gives it life but contains a contradiction which it cannot resolve without ceasing to be; in order to be *other* it must die, it must negate both the Old and the New Spain. The contradiction which defined it possesses the ambiguous character of original sin. But by contrast with the "happy error" of Saint Augustine, New Spain is condemned: the reason of her being is the cause of her death.

Lafaye finds in the sixteenth century a desire for a total break with the pre-Hispanic civilization. The Conquest is followed by the extermination of the native sacerdotal caste, the repository of the ancient religious, magical, and political power; the subjection of the Indians was followed by their evangelization. The first Franciscans—inspired by the prophecies of Joachim of Floris—rejected all compromise with pre-Hispanic religions and beliefs. None of the ceremonies, none of the rites described by Sahagún—despite their troubling resemblance to confession, communion, baptism, and other Christian practices and sacraments—was considered a "sign" that could have served as a bridge between the old religion and the Christian religion. Syncretism appeared only at the base of the social pyramid: the Indians were converted to Christianity and simultaneously converted the angels and saints into prehispanic gods. Syncretism, as a deliberate speculation designed to root Christianity in the soil of Anahuac and uproot the Spaniards, only appears later, in the seventeenth century, and does not reach its apogee, masterfully described by Lafaye, until the eighteenth century.

The reinterpretation of the pre-Hispanic histories and myths in the light of fantastic glosses of the Old and the New Testaments coincided with the growing importance of two groups with an ambivalent attitude toward the Indian and the Spanish worlds: the creoles and the mestizos. The change in the ethnic and social composition of the country coincided with a decline of the Franciscans, replaced by the Jesuits. The Jesuits became the spokesmen of the creoles, voicing their resentments, their aspirations, and their hopes of transforming New Spain into the other Spain. The consciousness of New Spain's uniqueness appeared very early, the day after the Conquest; the transformation of this consciousness into the will to create another Spain took more than a century. It first found expression in artistic creations and speculations about sacred history, and still later in political briefs, like the famous sermon of Fray Servando Teresa de Mier in the basilica of Guadalupe, in which he affirmed, as one foundation of the Mexican right to independence, the identity of Quetzalcóatl with the apostle Saint Thomas.

Historians have interpreted all this as a sort of prefiguration of Mexican nationalism. Lafaye himself appears to accept this linear vision of the history of Mexico. From this point of view, the Jesuits, Sigüenza y Góngora, and Sor Juana de Inés de la Cruz herself were "precursors" of Mexican independence. To make a nationalist author out of a baroque poetess is no less extravagant an idea than to discover the forebear of modern Mexico in the last Aztec *tlatoani,* Cuauhtemoc. Critics as perspicacious as Alfonso Reyes and Pedro Henríquez Ureña have even discovered in the comedies of Ruiz de Alarcón and the sonnets and dizains of Sor Juana certain typical Mexican accents. It is undeniable—one's eyes and ears alone confirm it—that the poetry of New Spain during the baroque period is clearly different from that of the peninsular models. That is particularly true of Sor Juana's poems, despite the echoes of Calderón, Góngora, and other poets that one finds in her writings. The same can be said, granted they are minor poets, of Sandoval and Zapata and Carlos de Sigüenza y Góngora. We find the same phenomenon in the field of architecture: the baroque of New Spain is not reducible to the Spanish baroque, although stylistically it depends on the latter. We have here not artistic nationalism—a romantic nineteenth-century invention—but a rich and original variant of the styles dominant in Spain at the end of the eighteenth century.

The art of New Spain, like the very society which created it, did not want to be *new*; it wanted to be *another*. This ambition tied it even more firmly to its peninsular model: the baroque aesthetic sought to surprise, dazzle, go beyond. The art of New Spain is not an art of invention but of free use—more precisely: of freer use—of the fundamental elements of imported styles. It is an art that combines and mixes motifs and manners. That is why, in her great poem, "El Sueño" ("The Dream"), Sor Juana combines the visual and plastic style of Góngora with conceptism, and both with scientific erudition and neo-scholasticism. Sor Juana's originality does not consist in the rather uncommon combination of disparate elements but in the very subject of her poem: the dream of knowledge and knowledge as dream. Not a single poem in the whole history of Spanish poetry, from its beginnings to the present, has that subject for its theme. Although Sor Juana was probably the most intelligent poet of her age, with the exception of Calderón, it is not her intelligence that distinguishes her from her contemporaries but her intellectual vocation. In order to find the like, we must go to a tradition unknown to Sor Juana: that of the English "metaphysical" poets, with their mixture of brilliant images, subtle concepts, and scientific preoccupations. John Donne and Sor Juana are both fascinated by scientific apparatus, physiological processes, astronomy and physics. Science and magic: both believed that the stars ruled our passions—although, to tell the truth, Sor Juana's experience with passion, compared with that of Donne, was rather poor. The English poet is incomparably richer, more agile, freer and more sensual than Sor Juana, but I say without hesitation that he was neither more intelligent nor more subtle.

As a poet, Sor Juana marks no advance over her epoch, and her work, even in its excesses, remains faithful to the poetic syntax of the Spanish seventeenth century. What distinguishes it, I repeat, is its intellectual vision: she does not see the world as an object of religious conversion, of moral meditation, or of heroic action—the ways of Spanish poetry—but as an object of knowledge. At the end of her life she was harassed by her confessor (for two years he denied her absolution) and tormented by the powerful and neurotic archbishop of Mexico City. This personage detested women as much as heretics, as if the former were a heresy of nature. Overcome by isolation and illness, Sor Juana surrendered. She renounced literature and learning as other people renounce the passions of the senses. She gave herself up to devout exercises, sold her books and musical instruments, fell silent—and died. Her silence expressed the insoluble conflict which confronted that society.

The contradiction of New Spain is recorded in Sor Juana's silence. It is not difficult to decipher its meaning. The impossibility of creating a new poetic language was but one aspect of a greater impossibility: that of creating—with the intellectual premises of Spain and her possessions as one's point of departure—a new thought. At the moment when Europe opened its doors to the critical, philosophical, scientific, and political doctrines that were preparing the modern world, Spain cloistered herself and imprisoned her finest minds in the intellectual prisons of neo-scholasticism. We Hispanic peoples have never become truly modern because, by contrast with other Western peoples, we never knew an age of criticism. New Spain was young and full of intellectual vigor, as Sor Juana and Sigüenza y Góngora prove, but it could never invent anything or think for itself, given the intellectual premises on which New Spain's society rested. The solution would have been to criticize those premises. But there was an insurmountable obstacle: it was forbidden to criticize. Moreover, this critique would have led to the negation of New Spain, as happened in the nineteenth century. This was the predicament in which Fray Servando Teresa de Mier found himself. His argumentation, based on sacred history (and borrowed from Sigüenza y Góngora), relative to Quetzalcóatl-Saint Thomas justified not only secession from Old Spain but the destruction of New Spain. The society of independent Mexico deliberately broke with New Spain and adopted antagonistic foreign principles as its foundation: the democratic liberalism of France and England.

In the field of religion proper, the situation was the same: the Catholicism of New Spain was that of the Counter-Reformation, a religion on the defensive which had exhausted its creative energy. Here was an aesthetic, intellectual, and religious contradiction: the principles on which New Spain had been founded—the double universalism of the Catholic Counter-Reformation and the Spanish monarchy—had become impediments which were choking it. The generations which followed Sor Juana tried to pierce the wall of history: they sought to root Catholicism in the soil of Anahuac by means of syncretic speculation and to transform New Spain into the Other Spain, Mexico-Tenochtitlan—capital of the Aztec empire—into the Rome of North America. Their project culminated in independence, but independence reduced those dreams and the men who wove them to nothingness: Mexico was not creole but mestizo, not an empire but a republic. In 1847 the United States flag was planted on the palace of Moctezuma Ilhuicamina and the viceroys. The dream of a Mexican empire was dispelled; the true empire was another empire. Mexico became poorer but not wiser; a century after the war with the North Americans we still ask ourselves who we are and what we want. We mestizos have destroyed the majority of the creole works, and today we are uprooted beings among the ruins. How shall we reconcile ourselves with our past?

The contradiction of New Spain appears in all fields and on all levels, from poetry to the economy and from theology to the ethnic hierarchies. The ambiguity of New Spain vis-à-vis the Indian world and the Spanish world was the ambiguity of the two groups that composed the mass of its population: the creoles and the mestizos. The creoles were and were not Spaniards; like the Indians, they were born in America and, usually unaware of the fact, shared many of the Indian beliefs. The creoles scorned and detested the Indians as violently as they envied and hated the Spaniards. The ambiguity of the mestizo was twice as great as that of the creole but negated the creole ambiguity in the last analysis. Like the creole, the mestizo is neither Spanish nor Indian, nor is he a European who seeks to put roots down into the American soil; he is a product of that soil, a new man. The creole strives to put down roots by means of a religious and historical syncretism, but it is the mestizo who achieves it in an existential and concrete form. Socially the mestizo is a marginal being, rejected by Indians, Spaniards, and creoles; historically, he is the incarnation of the creole dream. His situation vis-à-vis the Indians reflects the same ambivalence; he is their hangman and their avenger. In New Spain he is a bandit and a policeman, in the nineteenth century he becomes a guerrilla and a *caudillo,* in the twentieth century a banker and a trade union leader. In Mexican history his ascent signifies the sway of violence; his silhouette embodies endemic civil war. All that the creole projected and dreamed of, the mestizo turned into reality but in the form of a violence that until 1910 lacked the mestizo's own historical design. For more than a century we mestizos lived off the crumbs of the intellectual banquet of the Europeans and North Americans.

In the seventeenth century the creoles discovered that they had a *patria,* a fatherland. The word appears both in the writings of Sor Juana and those of Sigüenza, and in both invariably designates New Spain. Creole patriotism did not contradict their loyalty to the empire and the church: it was a question of two different orders of loyalty. Although the seventeenth-century creoles felt intensely anti-Spanish, theirs was not a nationalism in the modern sense of the word. They were good vassals of the king and, without the slightest contradiction, good patriots of Anahuac. A century and a half later, even as they demanded independence, the creoles still wanted to be governed by a prince of the royal Spanish line. In the theater of Sor Juana and in her religious poems, Indians and blacks, whites and mestizos, speak and sing each in his own fashion. The universality of the empire extended its protection over a plurality of tongues and peoples. The patriotism of New Spain and the recognition of its aesthetic originality did not contradict this universalism:

> By means of what magic herbs
> Have the Indians of my country
> Cast their spell
> Over my writings?

The contradiction appeared later, about 1730, notes Lafaye. As the years pass, the discord grows ever sharper, and by the moment of independence it has become insoluble. An incident dramatically illustrates this contradiction: the quarrel between the two leaders of the movement for independence, Hidalgo and Allende, the former the leader of Indians and mestizos, the latter the leader of the creoles.

The need to sink roots in America and to dispute the Spanish titles to domination led the creoles to exalt the Indian past. This exaltation was simultaneously a transfiguration. Lafaye perspicuously describes the meaning of this operation: "It abolished the break with the American past that the Conquest represented and thereby endowed America with a spiritual status (and consequently a political and juridical status) that put her on a footing of equality with the tutelary power, Spain." When Sigüenza y Góngora decided to take the Aztec emperors as the theme of the triumphal arch that was built to receive the viceroy, the Count of Paredes (1680), he introduced his text with this prefatory statement: "Theater of the Political Virtues that Constitute a Prince, Observed in the Ancient Monarchs of the Mexican Empire, with Whose Effigies the Triumphal Arch Raised by the Very Noble and Imperial City of Mexico Was Ornamented...." Sigüenza y Góngora proposed to the Spanish viceroy, as an example of good government, not the emperors of classical antiquity, models of political wisdom, but the Aztec sovereigns. Noteworthy, too, is the frequency with which, in all the texts of this period, there appears the adjective "imperial," applied indifferently to the Aztec state and Mexico City.

The exaltation of the dead Indian past coexisted with hate and fear for the living Indian. The same Sigüenza y Góngora relates that, when a canal of the city was being cleaned, there was found "a considerable number of small fetish objects..., many clay figurines and dolls, all representing Spaniards and pierced with lances or knives of the same material, with necks painted red as if their throats had been

cut . . . , irrefutable proof of the hatred that the Indians have for us
and the fate they wish for the Spaniards." Sigüenza y Góngora emphasized that the canal in which these objects of black magic were
found was the one in which many Spaniards had perished during the
Noche Triste. Admiration, hatred, fear—and friendship. Among the
great friends of Sigüenza y Góngora was a pure-blooded Indian, Don
Juan de Alva Ixtlilxochitl, a descendant of the ancient kings of Texcoco. They were such good friends that Ixtlilxochitl, who had no
heirs, bequeathed to Sigüenza his rich collection of Indian chronicles,
documents, and antiquities. We recall the comment of Gide, who
wrote: "Only simple minds can say that there are simple feelings."

From the second half of the sixteenth century to the end of the
eighteenth century New Spain was a stable, peaceful, and prosperous
society. There were epidemics, attacks by pirates, shortages of maize,
risings of nomadic Indians in the North, but New Spain also knew
abundance, peace, and frequently good government. Not that all the
viceroys were good, although some were, but because the system was,
in effect, one of a balance of powers. The authority of the state was
limited by that of the church. The viceroy's power was balanced by
that of the Audiencia, while the archbishop's power was countered by
that of the religious orders. Although the masses exercised only an
indirect influence in this hierarchical system, the division of powers
and the plurality of jurisdictions obliged the government to seek a sort
of public consensus. In this sense, the system of New Spain was more
flexible than the present presidential regime. Under the mask of
democracy, our presidents are constitutional dictators in the Roman
style. The only difference is that the Roman dictatorship lasted six
months, while ours lasts six years. New Spain was incapable of creating a science or a philosophy, but its artistic creations, particularly in
the fields of poetry, urbanism, and architecture, are admirable. In
1604, Bernardo de Balbuena published a long poem on Mexico City
and entitled it *La Grandeza Mexicana* ("The Mexican Grandeur"). The
phrase may seem hyperbolic, especially when we recall the authentic
grandeur of Teotihuacan, a thousand years before, but not if we consider the disaster that the modern Mexico City represents on the
urban, social, and aesthetic levels.

The most complex and original creation of New Spain was not
individual but collective, not an artistic but a religious creation: the
cult of the Virgin of Guadalupe. If the fecundity of a society is meas-
ured by the richness of its mythical images, New Spain was very
fecund; the identification of Quetzalcóatl with the apostle Saint
Thomas was no less prodigious an invention than the creation of
Tonantzin-Guadalupe. Lafaye's study of the birth and evolution of

these two myths is a model of its kind. It would be difficult for me to add anything to it, so I will offer only some marginal remarks.

The myth of Quetzalcóatl-Saint Thomas was never truly popular. From the first, it represented an effort at historical and theological interpretation rather than a religious mystery. That is why it preoccupied historians, jurists, and ideologists. Tonantzin-Guadalupe, on the other hand, conquered the heart and the imagination of all. She was a true apparition, in the sense of the divine *numen:* a constellation of signs come from all the skies and all the mythologies, from the Apocalypse to pre-Columbian manuscripts, and from Mediterranean Catholicism to the pre-Christian Iberian world. In this constellation each epoch and each Mexican has read his destiny, from the peasant to the *guerrillero* Zapata, from the baroque poet to the modern poet who exalts the Virgin with a sort of sacrilegious passion, from the seventeenth-century scholar to the revolutionary Hidalgo. The Virgin was the standard of the Indians and mestizos who fought in 1810 against the Spaniards, and a century later she became the banner of the peasant armies of Zapata. She is the object of a private, public, regional, and national cult. The feast day of Guadalupe, December 12, is still the feast day par excellence, the central date in the emotional calendar of the Mexican people.

Mother of gods and men, of stars and ants, of maize and agave, Tonantzin-Guadalupe was the imaginary compensation of the Indians for the state of orphanage to which the Conquest had reduced them. The Indians, who had seen the massacre of their priests and the destruction of their idols, whose ties with their past and their supernatural world had been severed, took refuge in the lap of Tonantzin-Guadalupe, the lap of the mother-mountain, the mother-water. The ambiguous situation of New Spain led to a similar reaction: the creoles found in the bosom of Tonantzin-Guadalupe their true mother. A natural and supernatural mother, composed of American earth and European theology. For the creoles, the brown Virgin represented the possibility of striking roots in the soil of Anahuac. She was both womb and grave: to strike root is to bury oneself in the earth. In the creole cult of the Virgin there is the fascination with death and the vague hope that this death will be a transfiguration: to be the Virgin's children may mean to obtain American *naturalization.* In the mestizos the sense of being orphaned was and is more total and profound. For the mestizos the question of origins is the primordial question, a question of life and death. In the imagination of the mestizos, Tonantzin-Guadalupe was her infernal replica: *la Chingada.* On the one hand, the violated mother exposed to the outside world, ravaged by the Conquest; on the other, the Virgin

Mother, intact, invulnerable, who carries a child in her womb. The secret life of the mestizo oscillates between *la Chingada* and Tonantzin-Guadalupe.

Like the phoenix of the baroque poet Sandoval y Zapata, Quetzalcóatl is "the winged eternity of the wind." His name is Nahuatl but he is a very ancient god, earlier than the name under which we know him. He was a coastal divinity, associated with the sea and wind, who reached the central plateau, established himself at Teotihuacan as a great god, then, after the destruction of the city, reappeared at Tula centuries later, henceforth bearing the name that he bears today. At Tula he duplicated himself: he was the creator and culture god Quetzalcóatl, whom the people of Tula inherited or stole from Teotihuacan, but he was also a priest-king whose ritual name is that of the god (Topiltzin-Quetzalcóatl). Tula was devastated by a religious war which was also a mythical combat between the warlike divinities of the nomads and the culture god from Teotihuacan. Quetzalcóatl—the god or the priest-king?—flees and disappears to the place "where the water joins the sky": the marine horizon on which Evening Star and Morning Star alternately appear. The date of the disappearance and transfiguration of Quetzalcóatl into the morning star was a year *ce acatl* (one reed). The year of his return, said the prophecy, would also be *ce acatl*.

The fall of Tula and the flight of Quetzalcóatl ushered in an interregnum in Anahuac. Centuries later the Aztec state arose, created like that of Tula by newly civilized barbarians. The Aztecs founded Mexico-Tenochtitlan in the image of Tula, which had been founded in the image of Teotihuacan. In ancient Mexico, legitimacy had a religious character. It is not surprising, therefore, that the Aztecs, wishing to establish the legitimacy of their rule over the other Indian peoples, proclaimed themselves the direct heirs of Tula. The Mexican *tlatoani* governed in the name of Tula. The appearance of Cortés on the Gulf shore precisely in a *ce acatl* year seemed to close the interregnum: Quetzalcóatl had returned, Tula had reclaimed its heritage. When the Aztecs, or a fraction of their ruling caste, discovered that the Spaniards were not the envoys of Tula, it was too late. The historians who minimize this episode do not perceive its true significance: the arrival of the Spaniards demonstrated the falseness of the Aztec claims. Even before the walls of Mexico-Tenochtitlan crumbled, the religious foundation of its hegemony had collapsed.

Quetzalcóatl, or legitimacy: by demonstrating with every kind of proof the identity of Quetzalcóatl and the apostle Saint Thomas, Don Carlos de Sigüenza y Góngora and the Jesuit Manuel Duarte only repeated the operation of religious legitimation performed by the

Aztecs several centuries before. As Lafaye says: "If the American *patria* was to take root in its own soil, it must develop a sense of its identity, and it could only find the foundations it sought in the grace of God, not in the disaster of a Conquest that strongly resembled Apocalypse. For Mexicans Quetzalcóatl was the instrument of a change in spiritual status."

Quetzalcóatl disappeared from the historical horizon of the nineteenth century, except in the case of those writers and artists who, without much success, chose him as the subject for their works. He disappeared but did not die; he was no longer god or apostle but a national hero. He was called Hidalgo, Juarez, Carranza: the quest for legitimacy has continued down to our own time. Each of the great official figures of independent Mexico, and each of the capital moments of its history, have been manifestations of this aspiration, ever renewed. For the majority of Mexicans, Independence was a restoration, that is, an event which closed the interregnum established by the Conquest. A curious conception, this, which made New Spain little more than a parenthesis. Juarez, in his turn, represented the national legitimacy against Maximilian, significantly dubbed *el Intruso* (the Intruder); Maximilian's empire is another historical parenthesis. Finally, the victorious party in the Mexican Revolution took the name of "Constitutionalist" and rose against the usurping reactionary general Huerta. Independence, the liberal revolution of 1857, the popular revolution of 1910: all these movements, so ran the current interpretation, had reestablished legitimacy. But the quest for this legitimacy continues, and for some even the regime which has governed us for half a century has usurped the Mexican revolutionary legitimacy. The interregnum opened by the flight of Quetzalcóatl in 987 has not yet ended.

For a Mexican it is an extraordinary intellectual adventure to follow Jacques Lafaye in the analysis of these two myths, in the exposition of the historical logic which governed their evolution, and to contemplate his reconstruction of the beliefs on which they were grafted. At the end of this journey, the reader confronts two constants of the history of the Mexican people: its obsession with legitimacy and its feeling of being an orphaned people. Do we not have here two manifestations of a single historical and psychic problem? The myths of New Spain and those of modern Mexico, like all the great myths, are efforts to answer the question of origins. From this point of view, they are not the exclusive property of Mexicans: the sentiment of being orphaned and the search for legitimacy appear, under other names, in all human societies and in all epochs. Lafaye's book shows us the two faces of history: he describes universal situations which are at the same time particular and irreducible to others. Lévi-Strauss thinks that myths, by contrast with poems, are translatable. They are, in fact, but each of these translations, like that of a poem, is also a transubstantiation: Quetzalcóatl-Saint Thomas is not Topiltzin-Quetzalcóatl.

Each historical situation is unique and each is the metaphor of that universal fact that consists in the fact of being men. In Lafaye's work—the work of an ethnologist, a poet, a thinker—there appears the ambiguity of history, which always oscillates between the relative and the absolute, the particular and the universal. If it is no longer metaphysics but history that defines man, then we must put at the center of our meditations, in place of the key word *to be*, the key word *between*. Man between heaven and earth, between water and fire; between the plants and the animals; at the center of time, between the past and the future; between his myths and his acts. All this comes down to a single proposition: man among men.

Octavio Paz

Acknowledgments

As a child, I was taken by my mother to see a film based on the heroic life of Pancho Villa. It was my first contact with Mexico, and I was simultaneously fascinated and terrified. To this day my feelings toward that country bear the stamp of that initial ambiguity.

Much later, two meetings decided my turn toward Mexico. A meeting with Marcel Bataillon convinced me that the course I had chosen was the right one for me. In 1952 I began my first Mexican study under the direction of a teacher whose work I continue to regard as a model—a model as fruitful as it is inimitable.

My second decisive meeting was with Paul Rivet, whose acquaintance I made through Marcel de Coppet. Thanks to Rivet, who opened up to me his library and the immense treasury of his knowledge and memories, and who invited me to come Sunday afternoons to that "roof of America" that was his apartment in the Musée de l'Homme, I had my first living contact with the New World without leaving Paris. The name of Rivet, who guided my first steps as an Americanist, simultaneously gave me access to the men and books without which my study of Mexico would have remained a youthful dream. Robert Ricard and Jacques Soustelle, both Paul Rivet's disciples, later gave me a masterful preparation for undertaking the research which resulted in this book.

I could not have completed this book without the help of institutions, both French and foreign, which made it possible for me to visit repositories of books and archives and become acquainted with the Mexican geographical and human milieu, and which gave me the leisure needed for research and writing. This book could not have seen the light without the help of the Centre National de la Recherche Scientifique (C.N.R.S.); the Institut des Hautes Études de l'Amérique Latine of the University of Paris; the Direction Générale des Affaires Culturelles et Techniques of the French Ministry of Foreign Affairs; the Universidad Nacional Autónoma de México; the Consejo Superior de Investigaciones Científicas (C.S.I.C.) of Madrid; and, last but not least, the Casa de Velázquez (École Française des Hautes

Études Hispaniques) in Madrid. I express my sincere gratitude to officials of those institutions for their efforts in my behalf.

I must also acknowledge my debt to all those persons whose personal assistance lightened my labors, and first of all to archivists and librarians: the personnel of the Bibliothèque Nationale de Paris, the Musée de l'Homme, the Institut des Hautes Études de l'Amérique Latine, the Bibliothèque Nationale et Universitaire de Strasbourg.

The Institut des Hautes Études de l'Amérique Latine and the Musée de l'Homme were my workshops. The steady and friendly support of the director of the Institute, Pierre Monbeig, Directeur des Sciences Humaines at the Centre Nationale de la Recherche Scientifique, proved invaluable. At the Casa de Velázquez, François Chevalier, its director, placed his personal library of Mexican historical works at my disposal; the librarian of the Casa, Mlle Françoise Cotton, assisted me daily. My colleague, Mlle M. C. Gerbert, and Mme M. A. Sauvé helped me in the last stages of the book's preparation, the former as paleographer, the latter as cartographer. I recall with special gratitude the persons in charge of other great Americanist libraries in Europe, Latin America, and the United States: E. de la Torre Villar, Guastavino, J. de la Peña, R. P. Egaña, L. Vázquez de Parga, the late Howard F. Cline, Doña Matilde Lopez-Serrano, Thomas R. Adams, N. L. Benson, A. Pompa y Pompa. I cite these names as they come to mind. The list could be much longer; to all I express my thanks.

Let me say that I have learned from discussions as much as from books. I must not fail to mention the names of the late Dr. Ángel María Garibay K., Wigberto Jiménez Moreno, R. P. Zubillaga, J. P. Berthe, Ernest J. Burrus, Silvio Zavala.

Finally, I acknowledge a special debt to Guy Stresser-Péan; his courses and his incomparably rich library in Paris, his hospitality at the Mission Archéologique et Ethnologique Française in Mexico, greatly enriched my knowledge of pre-Columbian Mexico, the historical background of the period studied in this book.

A Summary Chronology of Mexican History

c. 900   Foundation of Tula (Central Mexico).
987   Exile of Quetzalcóatl Topiltzin, high priest of Tula.
1156   Fall of Tula.
1325   Foundation of Mexico-Tenochtitlan.
1502   Accession of Moctezuma II Xocoyotzin, at Tenochtitlan.
1517   Accession of Charles V to the throne of Spain, under the name of Charles I.
1518   Grijalva discovers the Gulf coast of Mexico.
           Arrival of Cortés in Tenochtitlan.
1520   Luther's schism.
1521   Cuauhtemoc assumes leadership of the Aztec resistance.
           Cortés besieges and conquers Tenochtitlan.
           Cuauhtemoc is made prisoner.
1522   Charles V names Cortés "Captain General and Governor" of New Spain.
1523   "The Twelve" (first Franciscan missionaries) land at Veracruz.
1527   Establishment of the first audiencia of Mexico City.
1528   The Franciscan Fray Juan de Zumárraga becomes bishop (later archbishop) of Mexico City and "Protector of the Indians."
1530   Foundation of Puebla (La Puebla de los Angeles).
1531   Apparitions of Our Lady of Guadalupe to the Indian Juan Diego and to the archbishop of Mexico City, Juan de Zumárraga, according to the pious tradition.
1535   Installation of the first viceroy of New Spain, Antonio de Mendoza.
1536   Inauguration of the Indian college of Santa Cruz de Tlaltelolco by the Franciscans.
1537   Vasco de Quiroga becomes bishop of Michoacán.
           Trial of the cacique of Texcoco for idolatry.
           Introduction of the printing press in Mexico City.
1542   Publication in New Spain of the New Laws of the Indies.

1666   Inquiry of the chapter of the cathedral of Mexico City into the pious tradition of Our Lady of Guadalupe.

1669   First conversion of Sor Juana Inés de la Cruz.

1681   *Manifiesto filosófico contra los cometas* of Carlos Sigüenza y Góngora.

1692   Riot in Mexico City, caused by food shortages.

1693   Publication of the first Mexican periodical, the *Mercurio volante* of Carlos de Sigüenza y Góngora.

1725–28   Epidemic of measles.

1729   Construction of a mint (Real Casa de monedas) in Mexico City.

1730   A. de Vizarrón y Eguiarreta, creole archbishop of Mexico City, is installed in his diocese.

1735   Inquisitorial edict issued against Manuel de Bahamón, a seditious and illuminist naval officer (February 26).

1736   Epidemic.
    Construction of a new and imposing tribunal of the Inquisition in Mexico City.

1737   Our Lady of Guadalupe is solemnly sworn "principal Patroness" of Mexico City.

1746   Installation of Viceroy Revillagigedo.

1747   Edict of the Inquisition of Mexico City confiscating all licenses to read books on the Index of forbidden works.

1748   The printing press of the Jesuit college of San Ildefonso of Mexico City begins to operate.

1752   The council of professors of the University of Mexico City takes a solemn oath of allegiance to its new patron, Saint Luis de Gonzaga.

1753   The printing press of the Bibliotheca mexicana of J. J. de Eguiara y Egurén begins to function in Mexico City.

1754   Bull of Pope Benedict XIV (April 24) recognizing the Mexican Guadalupan tradition by a canonical office.

1758   Eruption of the volcano of Jorullo.

1759   Accession of Charles III in Spain.

1762   Taking of Havana by the English.

1766   Open letter from the Inquisitors of Mexico City denouncing the revolutionary ideas that circulated among soldiers of foreign origin.

1767   The decree of Charles III, expelling the Jesuits from his states in Europe and America, is put into effect in New Spain, June 25.
    Riots at Mexico City, Guanajuato, Pátzcuaro, San Luis Potosí, etc., in support of the expelled Jesuits.

1768   Edicts of the Inquisition of Mexico City (May 20 and June

	15) ordering the seizure of libels against the king, written in support of the Jesuits and the image of Saint Josaphat. Codification of military privileges (*fuero militar*) in New Spain.
1770	Convocation by Archbishop Lorenzana of the Fourth Mexican Council.
1770–78	Crisis of the "Communal Life," bringing the viceroy into conflict with the religious orders (especially in Puebla).
1778	Crisis of ecclesiastical privilege (*fuero eclesiastico*) in the internal provinces of New Spain.
1780	Proclamation of martial law (*estado de guerra*) in New Spain.
1782	The congregation of Our Lady of Guadalupe adopts new constitutions and new rules.
1791	Revolt of the black slaves in Santo Domingo.
1792	Inauguration of the Royal School of Mines (Escuela de Minas) of Mexico City.
1794	Sermon of the Dominican Fray Servando Teresa de Mier (December 12) in the collegiate church of Our Lady of Guadalupe, criticizing the pious tradition and associating the "prodigious image" with the evangelization of the Mexicans by the apostle Saint Thomas-Quetzalcóatl.
1795	Inquisitorial trial of Fray Servando Teresa de Mier.
1800	Trial of the creole conspirators (*Los Guadalupes*) of Mexico City.
1804	Royal order regarding the alienation of the property of pious foundations (Cédula de consolidación), with the proceeds to be transferred to Spain.
1805	Publication of the first Mexican daily, *El Diario de México*.
1808	Rising of the people of Madrid against the army of Napoleon (*Dos de mayo*).
1810	Hidalgo launches an appeal for Mexican independence (*grito de Dolores*) and rallies the insurgents about the banner of Guadalupe (September 16).
1811	The bishop of Michoacán, Abád y Queipo, excommunicates the parish priest Hidalgo.
	Hidalgo, captured by the regular army, is tried by the court of the Inquisition and executed (July 30).
1812	Viceroy Venegas suspends ecclesiastical immunity (*fuero eclesiástico*) (June 25), requisitions the University of Mexico City and the convents for quartering troops and suspends the exemption from military service for students.

Publication of an ordinance establishing freedom of the press.

Establishment of a constitutional monarchy in Spain by the cortes of Cádiz.

1813   Proclamation by Morelos of *The Sentiments of the Nation* and the order requiring all Mexican patriots to wear the emblem of Guadalupe.

Proclamation of Independence by the Congress of Chilpancingo (November 6).

Abolition of the Inquisition in Spain by the cortes of Cádiz.

Publication at London of the *Historia de la Revolución de la España* of S. T. de Mier, in exile (the work includes a long appendix designed to prove the evangelization of Mexico by Saint Thomas Quetzalcóatl).

1814   Promulgation by the Mexican Congress of the Constitution of Apatzingan (October 22).

Reestablishment of the Inquisition in Spain by a decree of Ferdinand VII.

1815   Morelos, captured by the regular army, is tried by the court of the Inquisition and executed (December 22).

1817   Francisco Javier Mina, a Spanish revolutionary, disembarks in Mexico in the company of S. T. de Mier; after a brilliant foray he is captured by the regular army and executed (November 11).

1821   Historic meeting between the revolutionary chief Vicente Guerrero and General Iturbide and proclamation of the "Plan of the Three Guarantees" (Independence, Union, and Religion) (February 24).

Entry into Mexico City of the "Army of the Three Guarantees," achieving Mexican independence (September 27, Independence Day).

Death of Juan O'Donoju, last viceroy of New Spain.

1822   General Iturbide proclaims himself emperor with the name "Agustín I" (May 18), and dissolves the Constituent Congress.

Decree of Agustín I, creating the national Order of Guadalupe and the imperial Order of the Aztec Eagle.

Pronunciamiento in support of Congress by Generals López de Santa Anna and Guadalupe Victoria.

1823   Abdication of Iturbide (March 19) and proclamation of the Republic.

Apotheosis of the martyrs of Mexican Independence

(September 16) celebrated especially at the collegiate church of Our Lady of Guadalupe of Tepeyac.

1824   Iturbide, outlawed by Congress, is captured and executed (July 19).

Representation to the Constituent Congress by the chapter of the collegiate church of Our Lady of Guadalupe.

1831   Solemn celebrations (processions, poetic games) of the tricentenary of the apparitions of the Virgin of Guadalupe of Mexico.

Some Statistical Estimates

1519   25 million Indians (approximately) in Mexico, with 1,500,000 in the valley of Mexico.

end of 16th. cent.   Approximately 70,000 Indian survivors in the valley of Mexico.
10,000 Spaniards, creoles, and immigrants of European stock.

1545   800,000 Indians died in the course of the epidemic.

1736   40,000 dead in Mexico City
50,000 dead in Puebla
20,000 dead in Querétaro   } in the course of the epidemic (*peste*).

In the course of the eighteenth century twenty-three viceroys governed in New Spain.

In the course of the colonial period there were eight great epidemics; five great earthquakes or volcanic eruptions; nineteen important revolts (in the northern part of the country).

A Historian's Profession of Faith

To search for the meaning of the cult of Guadalupe and the belief in Saint Thomas-Quetzalcóatl, preacher of the Gospel in Mexico, is primarily to seek an answer to the question—a historical question—posed by the evolution of culture in Mexico (New Spain) between the first quarter of the sixteenth century and today.

As Wilhelm Mühlmann has shown, significant analogies and correlations certainly exist between religious and political manifestations (contemporary and past) in different parts of the world.[1] But my aim is more limited: to shed light on the formation of Mexican national consciousness with the aid of its religious components.

The convergence of the eschatological hopes of the Aztecs, expressed in the hope for a return of Quetzalcóatl, and the millenarianism of the Catholic missionaries, became one of the roots of the creole national mystique. That mystique assumed the features of the Virgin of Guadalupe before it found secular expression in the device of a people who, like the Aztecs, came to believe that they were a chosen people: "No country can compare with Mexico" (*Como México no hay dos*).

When Marcel Bataillon, who had dealt with Quetzalcóatl as one of the original manifestations of the creole mind in the New World in a course he taught at the Collège de France, suggested that I undertake a study of the god's traces, it was understood that I would limit my research to the Quetzalcóatl myth in Hispano-Mexican missionary literature. This intriguing quest, which was to lead me from the Olmecs to the sources of the Bible, gradually revealed to me the link connecting the Quetzalcóatl myth to the development of the Mexican national consciousness. Marcel Bataillon had already perceived that link, just as he had grasped the central role of the cult of Guadalupe, first revealed by the late Francisco de la Maza in his famous essay *El guadalupanismo mexicano*.[2] As my research progressed, it became ever more apparent that a dialectical relation existed between a series of questions which today seem alien to each other because they belong to different disciplines: physical anthropology, history, natural theology.

1

The questions of the origin of the Indians, of the evangelization of America by an apostle of Christ, and the foreknowledge of God by the gentiles of the New World were, in the sixteenth century, the complementary facets of a single agonizing problem, that of the supernatural destiny of mankind.

These concerns with regard to the native peoples of an America that had been recently discovered by the Europeans corresponded to a first phase in the formation of an American consciousness; they were inseparable from the search for a way of spiritual salvation for the Indians. The protection of the Indians against the abuses and violence of conquistadors, colonists, slave-hunters, depended on the juridical status granted to them, and that status flowed from the place they should be assigned in the economy of salvation. The identification of the hero-god Quetzalcóatl (the plumed serpent) with the apostle Saint Thomas, evangelizer of the Indies, was one of the principal means of the spiritual redemption of the Indians and consequently of achieving recognition of their full humanity. Meanwhile the favor dispensed to Mexico by the prodigious appearance to an Indian convert of the Virgin Mary in her image of Guadalupe at Tepeyac offered new hope of Indian salvation. The effort of the Dominican Mier at the end of the eighteenth century to merge into one royal road to national independence these two ways of liberation accented the functional link between Quetzalcóatl-Saint Thomas, the first sally of the Mexican national consciousness, and Tonantzin-Guadalupe, its decisive sortie. This joining by the creole intellect of New Spain of the mythical figures of Quetzalcóatl (the "good jinni" of the Indians) and Tonantzin (their mother-goddess) is all the more remarkable because the couple Quetzalcóatl-Tonantzin appears to have been one of the avatars of the universal dual principle, Ometeotl, in the Aztec theogony. However, only the late metamorphoses of the old Indian beliefs in the creole thought of colonial Mexico interest us here.

In view of the intellectual strangeness of the region which readers must traverse, they should at least know my points of departure. Granted that history is unitary, I nevertheless agree with Bloch when he writes that the historian must "frankly admit the subordination of the perspective to the angle of the inquiry."[3] Ideas and beliefs are related to all the other manifestations of the cultural and material life of a society. The geographic milieu, the economic infrastructure, the demographic evolution, and the administrative organization of colonial Mexico influenced the development of millenarian hopes and messianic movements. These beliefs and their manifestations in turn modified ethnic and social relations and contributed to the unleashing of the political crisis which gave birth independence—an independence which in its turn generated important socioeconomic and political transformations. However, for the study of myths, the weight of secular, age-old traditions is relatively superior to that of economic and political factors. The history of states of mind has its own rhythm; in the society which interests us here, that history has known significant *moments*—moments which are not homogeneous among themselves. The metamorphosis of ideas and beliefs takes place over periods of time that are dead and others that are quick with life; from this point of view there are long and short generations.

These remarks require a revision of the customary use of chronology in history. I have deliberately chosen a "false" date, 1531, as the point of departure of my study of Guadalupe. This date does not correspond to any established fact in an objective chronology; it appears for the first time in a work published in Spanish in 1648; this work seems to have borrowed the date from a Nahuatl manuscript whose authenticity is doubtful, but which was probably written between 1558 and 1572. According to a pious tradition which goes back to 1648, extraordinary appearances of the Virgin of Guadalupe took place in 1531. Viewed from the perspective of the history of beliefs, whether the date 1531 is correct or not is less important than its retrospective "truth" in the minds of its devotees of Guadalupe beginning in 1648. Inversely, the fact that the pious legend took shape in 1648 allows us to consider the latter date as that of the real "appearance" of the Mexican cult of Guadalupe. At the other end of the chronological sequence that I have chosen as my field of study, the date 1813 does not mark the end of the evolution of the myths of Quetzalcóatl and Guadalupe (the latter still lives in present day Mexico), but it dates their last avatar, their patriotic secularization. In 1813 the creole Dominican Mier published in London his *Historia de la* *_ución de Nueva España antiguamente Anahuac*.[4] In a long appendix, __thor summed up the arguments he had advanced in his famous __n of 1794, which revised the Guadalupe tradition by associating __rgin of Guadalupe with Saint Thomas, called Quetzalcóatl by __dians, the first Christian missionary in Mexico. That same year, __erator Morelos launched from his camp of Ometepec a procla-__on in which he denounced as traitors to the nation all those who __led to wear a cockade with the colors of the Virgin or who did not __rform the customary devotions to the Virgin.[5] We recall that the previous year Hidalgo had chosen the banner of the Virgin as the __blem of the insurgents. Consequently it seems appropriate to re-__this date of 1813 as marking the last step in the evolution of __efs which blend with the Mexican national consciousness.

The two great mythical figures of Quetzalcóatl and Guadalupe would be incomprehensible outside the society in which they developed, itself part of a vaster whole, the Spanish Empire, the last form of political unity of the Christian West. We are not dealing here with a parallel evolution of Mexican creole society and its myths but with a unique growth whose different facets illuminate each other as in a set of mirrors. Even as I focus attention on the historical function of those myths in the coming-to-be of the Mexican nation, I hope to make my readers vividly aware of the presence of the Mexican nation in that process. The function I assign to the myths has nothing to do with a "functionalism"[6] that stands opposed to a "structuralism";[7] this function forms part of a dynamic that evolved together with the society whose aspirations over time it expressed. "Listening to the texts,"[8] in the happy phrase of Marcel Bataillon, deliberately effacing myself so as to allow my mental images of the men of the past and their mode of thought and being, their *vividura,*[9] as Américo Castro would say, to emerge more clearly, I have adopted a phenomenological posture. This choice does not imply an uncritical attitude toward sources.

My book will give a better idea of my conception of history than a long theoretical exposition could do. The intent of this essay on Quetzalcóatl and Guadalupe is to show the movement in progress, to demonstrate that today's history is not condemned to the alternatives of evaporating into abstraction ("structuralist" history)[10] or relapsing into chronicle (the history of "events"). Serial and quantitative methods will never be anything more than aids; valuable though they may be, there will always be something more. That "more" I regard as the essential thing in the history of beliefs; it corresponds to what Marc Bloch once defined as the "human climate."[11] If the notions of "spiritual moment" and "human climate" acquire in the course of the pages that follow some solidity and appear better adapted to the study of states of mind and of that "intra-history" whose riches Miguel de Unamuno foresaw than the notions (borrowed from the econom[ic] sciences) of "structure" and "conjuncture," my time shall have be[en] well spent.

There are historical topics which the present quickens and oth[er] which it leaves to their sleep. History, Marc Bloch wrote in a cru[el] time, "must endlessly join the study of the dead to that of the living[.]" The work which I offer my readers is never free from concern with the present, the present of Mexico and of mankind.[12]

Part 1

New Spain from the Conquest to Independence 1521–1821

1 Brothers and Enemies: Spaniards and Creoles

The political life of New Spain was in the hands of a white minority of European origin. This minority included others than Spaniards and descendants of Spaniards. From the first days of the Conquest, despite restrictive measures, persons who were not subjects of the states ruled by the Castilian monarchy passed over to the Indies. Among the missionaries we find Flemings, Italians, and, later, Czechs. John H. Parry notes the presence of Italian laymen at Zacatecas from the beginning of the seventeenth century. Robert Ricard calls attention to the presence of Portuguese in the viceregal court and in Mexico City. Many of the Portuguese were Jewish converts who fled the rigors of the Inquisition when Portugal was united to Spain (1580). Castilian Jews had already preceded them. French names also occasionally appear in the records of the Inquisition of New Spain as blasphemers or freethinkers. It seems that aside from the English and the Dutch, excessively suspect of heresy, Europeans from all countries could establish themselves in New Spain but were never numerous or powerful enough to play a significant role in Mexican life in general. The minority of European stock, then, was relatively homogeneous by virtue of its Hispanic origin.

One of the internal tensions of this ruling class—a tension which emerges whenever one attempts to grasp the meaning of a political episode in New Spain—is the opposition between Spaniards and creoles, called respectively *españoles* and *españoles americanos*. In practice, the terms *americanos* and *criollos* designated the latter, while the Spaniards were given the perjorative or downright insulting nickname *gachupines* (the origin of the term has not yet been explained). The creole-Spanish antagonism appeared from the first years of the Conquest, merging with the hostility felt by the conquerors toward the *licenciados* (lawyers) sent by Spain to impose over them a power which from the first they regarded as alien. The "creole spirit" preceded the birth of the first true creole; consequently we will see "creolized" Spaniards, come from the Peninsula, who allied themselves with creole families, identified mentally with Mexican creole

7

society, and espoused its local loyalties and even its hatred for the *gachupines*. It was knowledge of the country and, above all, loyalty to the colonial ethic of creole society, rather than place of birth, that defined the *criollo*.

In practice, the supreme power, that of the viceroy, was virtually always entrusted to a peninsular Spaniard, but some viceroys, yielding to the country's pull, "mexicanized" themselves to a considerable degree. Whereas the viceroys were Spaniards, the archbishops of Mexico were often creoles; in any case, the long duration of their ministry facilitated the process of naturalization. Among the religious orders, whose relative importance (numerical, spiritual, and economic) in society may appear to modern eyes overwhelming, the rivalry between creoles and Spaniards early attained a troubling sharpness. Efforts were made to reduce this tension by instituting a system of "alternation" or *ternas* in the selection of priors of convents and in the recruitment of religious. Under the system of "alternation," the prior was alternately a Spaniard and a creole; in the system of *ternas*, a distinction was made between Spaniards, on the one hand, Spaniards who had taken the habit in New Spain, on the other, and finally between these and natives of New Spain; this latter system allowed the "real" creoles to govern two years out of three. Higher posts in the civil administration were reserved almost exclusively to Spaniards, totally in the army. The creole elite formed in the University of Mexico (whose student body was almost entirely creole from an early date) and in the colleges of the Company of Jesus was thus deprived of job opportunities or restricted to inferior employment. For many young Mexicans of wealthy family, exclusion from public employment did not signify economic misery; but the bar to official honors inflicted a deep wound, continually reopened, on the nascent national consciousness.

From a very early date the Spaniards who came from the Peninsula affirmed their superiority over the creoles and displayed distrust of them.

In law, the creoles were regarded as Spaniards without any qualification. In the authoritative work on such matters, the *Política Indiana,* the royal councilor Solórzano wrote of the creoles: "There can be no doubt that they are true Spaniards, and by this title they should enjoy the rights, honors, and privileges of Spaniards and be judged like them."[1] In practice, the creoles were denied public posts in the Peninsula as well as in the Indies, and, twenty years after the appearance of Solórzano Pereira's work, one of them wrote a memorial "in favor of the Spaniards who are born in the Indies";[2] the memorial brought together and expressed for the first time the complaints of

American creoles against the discrimination to which they were subjected. The charges and countercharges on this subject were endless; in reality the quarrel involved more than a simple question of interest or ambition. It appears that in one area, about which the documents are inevitably reticent, there was a vital rivalry between creoles and *gachupines*. If we may believe foreign witnesses, the creole women (revealing a trait of *malinchismo* of considerable interest for the historian of attitudes) preferred to marry a *gachupín* rather than a creole, provoking the jealous hatred of the latter.

This rivalry on all levels quickened as the creoles became numerically and economically preponderant, and in the eighteenth century they passed over to the offensive. The *Representación vindicatoria* of the Mexican creoles in 1771, in an address to the king, sought to prove point by point that the American creoles were in no respect inferior to peninsular Spaniards. Beginning in the sixteenth century, the dispute assumed the character of an anthropological question. Doctor Juan de Cárdenas was the first to raise the issue, destined to have a great future, in his book *Problemas y secretos maravillosos de las Indias*, which appeared in Mexico City in 1591. Although born in Spain, Cárdenas did not hesitate to write: "in what concerns capacity to understand and explain, it seems to me that they [the creoles] surpass us in all that they attempt to do," and he added, in the style of the Arab physicians, that the creoles were of "sanguine choleric" humor, the most favorable of the nine possible humors.[3] All the criticisms and defenses with regard to the creoles invoked arguments of this kind, stressing the effects of the American climate on men of European stock.

In the eighteenth century, in connection with the publication of Cornelius de Pauw's *Recherches philosophiques sur les Américains* and the polemic which followed its appearance in Europe, the creoles found a brilliant champion in a Mexican Jesuit who had been exiled to Italy, Francisco Javier Clavigero. Clavigero published in Italian a *Storia antica del Messico* to which he joined a series of "Dissertations" designed to rehabilitate the Americans in all respects. The climate, the fauna, the Indian, the creole, were each in turn found innocent of the accusations made without much basis by de Pauw, who had borrowed them from Buffon.

The creoles, however, did not present a united front. Between the *ricos hombres,* the mine owners or *hacendados* of the "provincias internas," and the friars of the towns; between the latter and the religious of the missions; between the doctors of the University of Mexico City and the artisans or petty municipal officials existed profound differences. Creoles from noble and wealthy families who dreamed of

forming alliances with families of Spanish grandees, or even with high
gachupín officials, displayed a sincere loyalist attitude and adjusted to
their position. The viceregal court divided the creoles into camps, the
privileged creoles who were admitted there, and the others.

One of the most striking aspects of the mentality which Spain had
transmitted to New Spain was its parochial spirit. If a Mexican national consciousness did not arise earlier, it was partly because of the
exclusive and almost mystical attachment to one's local "fatherland"
(patria chica). Doubtless the most significant example of this spirit,
throughout the colonial period, was the rivalry between Mexico City
and Puebla. Although Puebla had only one-fourth the population of
Mexico City and the latter was the seat of the viceroys, Puebla was one
of the secondary centers of New Spain's life; to ignore this fact is to
misread Mexico's colonial history. Puebla was, to begin with, a
spiritual center, for Puebla de los Angeles was above all others a
Spanish town, founded in the Tlaxcalan region at the request of
Franciscan religious in order to relieve pressure on Mexico City,
which was becoming overpopulated by Europeans, if we may believe
Fray Agustín de Vetancurt. Different traditions report the marvelous
events that attended the city's founding: according to one such tradition, the bishop of Tlaxcala had a vision in which angels defined for
him the boundaries of the future city; others attributed this dream to
Isabella the Catholic. It is certain that one of the most venerated early
missionaries, Fray Toribio de Motolinia, said the first mass in Puebla.
According to one tradition, doubtless of later origin, it was in 1531
(the same year in which, according to another tradition, the miraculous image of Guadalupe appeared), that the archangel Saint Michael
appeared to an Indian in a remote spot between Puebla and Tlaxcala.
The bishopric established in Puebla in 1526, its numerous and important convents, the prestige of an origin linked to the Franciscan
pioneers, the role which the Jesuits later played there (in Vetancurt's
time they already had three colleges), the brilliant career and memory
of Bishop Palafox, in the seventeenth century, all endowed Puebla
with a moral grandeur which enabled it to challenge the capital. The
town itself, at the end of the seventeenth century, was superior to
Mexico City (then an object of much bragging) in symmetry and appearance, according to Gemelli Carreri, who wrote: "almost all the
buildings there are built of stone and lime and are not at all inferior to
those of Mexico City. Although the streets are not paved, they are
much cleaner. . . . The square of the Cathedral of Puebla is much
more beautiful than that of Mexico City."[4] Agustín de Vetancurt
added: "Persons born in this city are resolute in character . . . ; those
who apply themselves to study have subtle intellects and, inspired by a

praiseworthy zeal, become learned men. The town is inhabited by many gentlemen of recognized nobility, and some are members of the great military orders; there are coaches and riding horses and (although it has no viceregal court) both men and women display a courtly elegance and refinement."[5]

Humboldt tells us that in his time, "Puebla de los Angeles [was] more thickly populated than Lima, Quito, Santa Fé de Bogotá, and Caracas," and, with the exception of the mining complex of Guanajuato (which had more than 70,000 inhabitants), Puebla with its 67,000 inhabitants was far ahead of all the other towns of Mexico (except for Mexico City). Guadalajara, Antequera de Oaxaca, Valladolid de Michoacán had about 20,000 inhabitants each, while Vera Cruz, Durango, Mérida de Yucatán had populations of between 12,000 and 15,000 inhabitants. New Spain, or Mexico, then, possessed an "imperial" capital (where the majority of the Spaniards lived), and a series of towns of middling importance, each of which regarded its bell tower with pride; that of the cathedral of Puebla was not quite as high as the towers of the cathedral of Mexico City; on the other hand, the bishop of Puebla, as Gemelli Carreri recalled, did not have to share honors with the viceroy. Each of these cities was the center of a diocese, and each diocese was a citadel of Mexican *criollismo*.

2   Irreconcilable Enemies: Indians, Mestizos, Mulattoes

The opposition between Spaniards and creoles was a fratricidal struggle, but both groups formed a ruling caste that dominated the real Mexico, whose population at the beginning of the nineteenth century was still Indian in its great majority.

The makeup of Mexican society, as calculated by Alexander von Humboldt at that time, offers a good point of departure for reflecting on the evolution of New Spain:

Natives, or Indians	2,500,000
Whites, or Spaniards	1,095,000
Creoles 1,025,000	
Peninsulars 70,000	
African blacks	6,100
Castes of mixed blood	1,231,000
Total	4,832,100 inhabitants

Out of a total population of about 5 million inhabitants (note the very weak density per square mile), one-half was composed of Indians, one-quarter of various mixed-bloods, and one-quarter of whites (creoles in the vast majority). These facts suggest that after three centuries of Hispanic colonization the population was indeed "Mexican." In effect, only the 70,000 Spaniards born in Spain and the 6,100 African slaves were alien to the country. Keep in mind, too, that of the creoles described as "whites" a certain number, difficult to estimate but certainly high, were biologically mixed-bloods.

The role of the mestizos in Mexican society very early became a source of instability; they began to multiply from the first days after the Conquest, becoming a source of concern to the political authorities. These first mestizos, born of Spanish fathers and Indian mothers, had no home, no definite place in the society of their time. The Mexican *pícaro* type, the *lépero* whose traits J. J. Fernández Lizardi captured in *The Itching Parrot* in the nineteenth century, had appeared by the middle of the sixteenth century: the mestizo rejected by the Indian world and by Spanish society. *Hijos de la chingada,* fruits of the violation of Indian women by Europeans, their aspect soon acquired new tints, especially due to the Negroid contribution after the introduction of African slaves into Mexico. A series of pictures from the colonial period present all known forms of mixture (from the lightest to the darkest), together with their names; some of these, like the *saltatrás,* are truly picturesque.

The totality of these mixed-bloods constituted the *castas.* Gemelli Carreri, who probably echoed ideas then widely held in contemporary Mexico, explains the origin of some mixed-bloods in this way: because creole women preferred Spanish men, he writes, creole males "formed unions with mulatto women, their nurses, who together with their milk passed on to them their evil customs."[1] The widespread use of mulatto nurses in creole households no doubt gave this numerically negligible group a very real influence. The children born of creole men and mulatto women seem to have been left to fend for themselves (by contrast with what happened under the Brazilian rural patriarchate, for example). The same observer writes that "Mexico City may have one hundred thousand inhabitants, but the majority are blacks and mulattoes."[2] The vision of Mexico City in the writings of Sor Juana Inés de la Cruz, Gemelli Carreri's contemporary, tends to confirm the Neapolitan traveler's observation.

The countryside presented a very different aspect. Save in the hot lands (*tierra caliente*), where an effort was made to establish tropical monoculture (sugar cane), the black element in the population was unimportant. As a result of the collapse of the native organization produced by the Conquest, and the subsequent ravages of epidemics, Indian communities often disintegrated, setting the uprooted Indians in motion. These Indians, joined by veterans of the Conquest ruined by gambling or other circumstances and by European adventurers of later arrival (unemployed soldiers, defrocked friars or false religious, escaped criminals), composed from the first half of the sixteenth century the Mexican embryo of Spain's *hampa,* that milieu of rogues described by Cervantes in *Rinconete y Cortadillo.* Naturally, these marginal groups of the nascent colonial society were ideally suited for biological and cultural mixture at its lowest level. Despite the prohibition "that no Moor, Jew, person condemned by the Inquisition, son or grandson of an individual sent to the stake by the Holy Office may depart for the Indies,"[3] a mingling of races and beliefs took place in America from the first. Throughout the Mexican colonial period successive decrees forbade Spaniards (other than officials required to reside in Indian *pueblos*), blacks, and other persons fitting the legal definition of *castas,* to reside in Indian villages or "even to be seen in the company of Indians"—but in vain.

From the first decades of New Spain, the Indian was victimized by the mixed-blood. The climate of violence which to this day remains one of the most striking aspects of Hispanic-American life, had its origin in this fact. Caste feeling, inherited from the Spanish passion for "purity of blood" and very strong among the creoles, was no less powerful among the Indians; the mixed-blood was rejected alike by the creoles and the Indians. Thus there arose a floating, chaotic society; the fact that its relative importance steadily grew made it a serious threat to the equilibrium of a social body that was itself composite and dispersed in geographic space. New Spain had a social frontier which could not be traced on a map but whose importance was nevertheless decisive. In the long run this social frontier was to prove more of a threat than the northern "frontier." Whereas much was said in New Spain about the Apache peril, not enough was made of the danger posed by the *pardos* (a term originally applied to mixtures of blacks and Indians, but eventually a synonym for the *castas*); their incorporation in the army, beginning in the reign of Charles III, was to make them arbiters of the national destiny during the Wars of Independence. The whole history of Mexico is a history of the growing role of the *castas,* who, before their assimilation into a society that had achieved a new equilibrium, could only express themselves in violence that plunged the country into interminable convulsions and handed it over to the *caudillos* who emerged from the anarchy. The history of the progressive insertion of the *léperos* into an evolving society, whether in the private militias of the *hacendados,* in the army, or as professional gamblers (*tahures,* "tricksters"), or as *pistoleros* (instruments of political or personal vengeance), is a history of many obscure but far from insignificant aspects of Mexican reality.

The Indians have always been Mexico's vanquished; as such they have been permanent victims of a system that exploits their labor. We must first note the great diversity of the Indian condition in New Spain. In this connection, we must distinguish between the "useful Mexico" and the zones roamed by nomads. The latter clearly constituted a much greater surface area, but the density of the population was much weaker there, since in general it consisted of steppes or deserts (Chihuahua) or tropical forests difficult to penetrate (the Huasteca). The Indians of these regions had escaped conquest by the Aztecs; against the frontiers of the sedentary creoles they continued the war of harassment they had conducted in the past. Whereas the Aztecs had only sought to discourage their incursions, the Spaniards tried to reduce them to sedentary life in order to protect their lines of communication and to convert them—in short, to integrate them into New Spain. These two enterprises, defense of the frontiers and expansion of the faith, were carried on in a parallel way on the military level by colonizing the frontier areas with soldiers (*presidios*), and in the missionary realm by the mendicant orders, later by the Jesuits. Both enterprises suffered a partial failure, on the military level because the authority of the caciques who submitted or agreed to make a treaty did not extend over an entire region, and from the missionary point of view because the converts were rarely divorced from the influence of the priests (shamans) of their ancient polytheistic religion. The latter, called *dogmatizadores* in the technical language of the struggle against idolatry, periodically incited Indian revolts. The *Historia* of Alegre abounds in tales of Jesuits martyred in the Pimería, in the Tarahumara region, in Lower California. In these Indians, then called "savages" (*bravos*), we perceive a stubborn determination to defend their territories from encroachers and to maintain their cultural identity. However, the missionary effort, carried out systematically, left enduring traces in the cultures of numerous peoples in the north and the west of Mexico. Modern ethnological researches, even among peoples who had a minimum contact with Christian influence, always reveal a syncretic religious reality.

We know much more about the fate of the sedentary Indians, Otomí or Nahua farmers of Central Mexico, former subjects of the lords of Mexico-Tenochtitlan or of Tlaxcala. On the other hand, much obscurity surrounds the fate of Michoacán, Oaxaca, the Huasteca, transitional areas whose peoples were sometimes tributaries of the Aztecs but not assimilated into their empire. Each regional linguistic group was in reality unique, both from the point of view of its cultural heritage and with respect to the forms of its integration into the colonial regime. The Mexican Indians experienced in common the shock of military conquest, but this was the blow they were best prepared to withstand, having a past full of wars. The true trauma was the destruction of the traditional social organization and the eradication of the religious beliefs which formed its foundation. The pillage of Axayacatl's treasure by Cortés' comrades, the distribution (*repartimiento*) of the commoners (*macehuales*) among Spanish masters (*encomenderos*), were the immediate results of the Conquest for the Indians. The image of the Apocalypse is the more relevant because the Indians believed in great periodic catastrophes in which humanity perished; the year 1519 coincided precisely with the end of one such era or "Sun."

Other disasters struck the Indians of central Mexico, notably a series of epidemics (*pestes*). At least some of these, called *cocoliztli* in Nahuatl, were smallpox. Between the Conquest and the end of the sixteenth century the population of the valley of Mexico fell, according to the estimates of Woodrow Borah and Lesley Simpson, from about 1,500,000 Indians to 70,000. The chronicles of the Franciscan pioneers are replete with lamentations about the "disappearance" of the Indians. The principal cause of the drastic demographic decline was the epidemics; others were the disorganization of the preconquest regime of water use in the valley of Mexico by the enterprises of the conquerors-colonists and the overthrow of the native system of labor. Charles Gibson has studied these aspects in *The Aztecs under Spanish Rule;* here I only wish to sketch the main lines of historical development which made possible the spiritual phenomena to be discussed in this book.

The system of the *encomienda,** borrowed from Spain and from the first imposed on the Indians, was gradually liquidated by legal restraints (the New Laws) and by the numerical decline of the Indians given in *encomienda.* The native labor force, the target of the conquistadors' greed once booty in the form of precious metals had become exhausted, consequently suffered such a decline that the colonists had to seek new sources of wealth. The first was the land itself, which they began to occupy and exploit; a corollary of this process was the expropriation of Indian agrarian communities. Beginning in the middle of the sixteenth century, the Indian who was deprived of his land or fled from his *encomendero* often became a peon, tied to a hacendado not only by his debts but by the security that the hacienda offered him in a chaotic world. At the same time the "natural lords" (the old native aristocracy), whose prerogatives had been preserved and whom the new rulers utilized, especially as tribute collectors, suffered even worse impoverishment than the commoners. Burdened with debts, forced to make good the tribute deficits of their subjects, who had been drained dry, the only solution for the Indian caciques was to become functionaries under the new order; appointed "governors," they hastened the integration of the Indian world whose masters they had been into the system of colonial exploitation. The discovery of silver mines in the North, with its new labor demands, led to new uprootings of Indians who were torn away from their traditional communities. This phenomenon probably affected the Indians of the valley of Mexico less than the work levies required by the draining of the lagoons.

Gradually, about the middle of the sixteenth century, there arose a repressive administrative-fiscal organization which, with some changes in name, continued until Independence. The Spanish system of the *cabecera* (chief town of a district) with a *corregidor* at its head and

---

*Grant to a Spaniard of an allotment of Indians who were to serve him with tribute or labor. (Tr.)

a curate as its spiritual leader, was the base of Indian administration. The parish and the religious brotherhood devoted to the cult of a tutelary saint, on the one hand, and the *caja de comunidad* (community treasury), on the other, were the socioeconomic and spiritual expressions of Indian reality in New Spain. In both cases we observe adaptations of ancient traditional institutions. The *comunidad* (which remains to this day the cell of Indian society) was a degraded form of the *calpulli;* the Spanish corregidor was the colonial heir of the traditional cacique.

In the course of three colonial centuries Spain's Indian policy, like the prosperity of the mining districts, was subject to fluctuations; in the course of those centuries, also, the demographic decline of the first half-century was reversed. The recovery began slowly at the end of the seventeenth century, then accelerated in the eighteenth century, but at the end of the colonial period the Indian population of the valley of Mexico (according to Charles Gibson) was still only about 275,000. The process of recovery from the disasters of the terrible three decades that followed the Conquest seems to have been very slow.

The Spanish administration, especially under the influence of the religious, adopted numerous measures to protect the Indians. The majority of these measures tended to establish a legal segregation, seemingly the only practicable course. An effort was also made to foster the rise of an Indian elite in conformity with the prevailing aristocratic criteria of contemporary Europe. This effort led to the establishment of colleges and convents designed to admit and train in an assimilative spirit the descendants of the Indian aristocracy. In the linguistic field, the work of the early mendicant missionaries contributed to diffusion of the Nahuatl language, used as a vehicle of Christian doctrine. The Crown also approved efforts to stimulate and make general the teaching of Spanish to the Indians, with small success.

The contradiction between the policy of segregation, rendered necessary by the need to protect the surviving Indians against the aggressions of Spanish society, on the one hand, and a policy of assimilation which envisioned the complete integration of the Indian aristocracy, on the other, was a major cause of the failure of Spain's Indian policy as a whole. The material and cultural condition of the Indians of New Spain rapidly fell to the lowest possible level. The occupation of Indian community lands by hacendados, the forced labors imposed by local functionaries (corregidores), the abuses—fiscal, civil, and ecclesiastic (tithes)—the violence and outrages inflicted by the mixed-bloods: these were the daily lot of the former masters of Anahuac. For the rest, the spiritual climate of an Indian society completely adrift hardly favored a thorough Christianization.

3   The Inquisition and the Pagan Underground

The spiritual atmosphere of New Spain underwent profound changes in the course of its history, changes which reflected the concerns and aspirations of society. Some preliminary remarks are in order. The first, of a general nature, is that there is usually a lag in response to structural crisis, and consequently the spiritual restlessness which is the result of such crisis finds its ideological or religious expression with a certain delay. The second observation is that each of the ethnic groups whose coexistence was to lead to the formation of the Mexican nation was a bearer of original beliefs intimately tied to its history. Finally, given the historical conditions summarized above—conquest, epidemics, forced labor—none of these spiritual heritages could be transmitted to succeeding generations without important alterations. Iberian Christianity, the official religion, methodically introduced to the native peoples by the mendicant orders, maintained in creole society by the secular clergy and the friars, and protected in its orthodoxy by a tribunal of the Inquisition and all the repressive apparatus at the disposal of the viceroys, did not form an exception to this rule. Just as it became impossible to unravel the complicated skein of biological mixture, so it is often difficult to establish the origin of a rite or superstition amid the syncretic jumble of beliefs.

With these reservations, one can nevertheless distinguish constants and tendencies—more precisely, a constant tendency toward heterodoxy. The phenomenon is by no means original; Spain herself offers an example, but in the case of New Spain this phenomenon merits emphasis, for there it corresponded to a particular spiritual climate. In Mexico, a country where the printing press remained in its infancy and in the hands of the temporal and spiritual powers, heterodox writings were not published before the Cortes of Cádiz in the nineteenth century. We know that at that period the work of the Chilean ex-Jesuit Lacunza, *La venida del Mesías en gloria y majestad*, already diffused through manuscript copies which circulated clandestinely, had a great success in New Spain. The work represented a belated resurgence of the millenarianism of the pioneer missionaries and an audacious effort to reconcile Judaism and Christianity.

The beginnings of heterodoxy in New Spain took place on a much more modest level, as indicated by the archives of the tribunal of the Inquisition of Mexico City, officially established in 1570, that is, a half-century after the Conquest. But inquisitorial activity was not neglected before that date; one could even argue that it was ever one side of a medal whose other side was the "spiritual Conquest." The struggle against idolatrous survivals or their revival resembled in its ends and methods the combat waged by the inquisitors of the Peninsula against heresy. The first bishop of Mexico, the Franciscan Fray Juan de Zumárraga, seems to have given priority to his task as inquisitor; he regarded it as a necessary complement to his work in favor of the Indians. At the same time that he created the Colegio de Santa Cruz de Tlatelolco to instruct the sons of Indian caciques in Christian doctrine and European knowledge, Zumárraga prosecuted apostate caciques who had relapsed after baptism into their native idolatry. Thanks to this fact, we possess the official record of the declarations of Indians accused by this first tribunal of the Inquisition, which began to function in 1536. The faith of the Indian neophytes and their observance of the commandments of the church were suspect. But Zumárraga's zeal inspired excesses which caused, after he sent to the stake the cacique of Texcoco in 1539 and that of Yanhuitlan in 1545, the disappearance of the tribunal until 1570.

The instructions of the inquisitor general to the second tribunal expressly provided: "You must not institute suits against Indians."[1] The historian thus has a space of about ten years, coinciding with Zumárraga's ministry, for the study of the more or less clandestine manifestations of Mexican polytheism in New Spain. For the long period that follows, we are reduced to hypotheses based on occasional literary testimony, on the writings of missionaries, or on the clues provided by modern ethnological and folkloric research. However, the period of activity of the first tribunal of the Mexican Inquisition seems to have coincided with a decisive moment in the spiritual and the general history of colonial society; the fate of the Indians was decided about the middle of the sixteenth century. Thus the records of the first inquisitorial trials of Indians are especially valuable documents. Let us examine some typical examples.

The accusations inquisitors leveled against the Indians (generally caciques) were usually multiple but boiled down to two principal charges: infractions of the commandments of the church and fidelity to ancestral divinities, joined with anti-Christian propaganda. In order to understand this state of affairs, we must recall the circumstances of the Conquest and its crusading spirit. It seems that Cortés' first action after he reached the summit of the great temple of Tenochtitlan was to overthrow the idols. After the military victory of the

Spaniards the Aztec priests, if not exterminated, were annihilated as an organized body. The idols were burned in solemn autos-da-fe by Bishop Zumárraga; the temples became quarries used for the construction of the cathedral, the churches, and the houses of the new Mexico City. The Indians, especially the caciques and their children, were hastily baptized and received summary religious instruction from the few Franciscan religious who were on hand.

It is not surprising, therefore, that some ten years later an incipient renaissance of the ancestral polytheism became evident. Because of the surveillance of the missionaries, it often took the form of furtive, clandestine activities, such as the sacrifices made every twenty days to celebrate the new month, staged in forests and mountains. The vacuum created by the disappearance of the Mexican priestly class allowed degraded forms of the old polytheism, combined with popular superstitions, to emerge and pass themselves off as the spiritual heritage of the past. This circumstance, a direct consequence of the Conquest and the process of conversion, is essential for an understanding of the Mexican religious sentiment. The elimination of the Aztec priests left the field to sorcerers (*nigrománticos*) who could profess to express the traditional beliefs safe from the possibility of an authoritative disavowal. Such was the case of an Indian named Martín Ocelotl of Texcoco, baptized in 1525 by the famous Twelve (the pioneers of the Franciscan missionary army in New Spain), and tried by the Inquisition in 1536 for a series of offenses involving idolatry and sorcery. These two terms covered some very diverse activities.

Martín Ocelotl was accused of polygamy (*amancebamiento*, that is, concubinage), although he had been publicly married in a church in the presence of the guardian of the Franciscan convent of Texcoco, who had received his confession and recorded his sincere repentance.

He was accused, on the testimony of several witnesses of Tepeaca and Acacingo, of having summoned all the caciques of the region to celebrate propitiatory rites for Camaxtli, in order to combat a drought that threatened famine.

Finally, the former governor of Texcoco, Cristóbal de Cisneros, declared "that he had heard two religious say they held it certain that the said Martín was a serious obstacle to the conversion of the Indians."[2]

These different accusations were combined in the deposition of the above-cited Franciscan witness: "He regarded this Martín"—a name given in Nahuatl as Telpucle—"as a demon, the greatest demon adored by the Indians; this Martín was a sorcerer and foretold the future, transformed himself into a cat and a tiger, incited the Indians to revolt, and induced hallucinations and other effects of his idolatrous practices in them; moreover, he had a great number of con-cubines."[3] For the historian, the interest of this local sorcerer consists in the fact that he was one of the first of those petty native messiahs who sporadically appeared in the course of the colonial centuries and even later. Martín Ocelotl already presents the typical traits of the Indian messiah, a mixture of skillful impostor and savior inspired by an impoverished religious heritage, that assimilated elements bor-rowed from the victorious faith of the Europeans. In effect, Martín Ocelotl, by the testimony of the Indian *principal* of Huaxtepec, claimed to be one of those diviners who visited Moctezuma before the appearance of the Europeans in Mexico to warn him prophetically of their coming. After such disturbing revelations, Moctezuma sup-posedly had put these sorcerers in a cage; the other diviners died in that dismal condition, only Martín Ocelotl having managed to escape.

Questioned on this subject, the accused denied that he had claimed to have returned to life after being cut in pieces on Moctezuma's orders, but confirmed that he had transmitted to the Mexican *tlatoani* a prophecy of the Conquest, made by a lord of Chinantla who had seen "signs." We have here the record of the appearance of one of the great syncretic Hispano-Mexican legends, presented by all the histo-rians of New Spain, Cortés first of all, as a historical fact. What credit can one really assign to the accounts of Martín Ocelotl and the wit-nesses of this inquisitorial trial in 1536? Wonders surround the whole affair. One witness related "that one day the people of Texcoco had trapped this Martín, but while they were preparing to cut him in pieces he had escaped from their hands and later reappeared nearby to mock them."[4] Just as certain sorcerers assigned to themselves the attributes of Catholic priests in the hope of capturing the super-natural power of the priest of the victorious religion, Martín Ocelotl knew enough Catholic doctrine to try to make the Apostles play his game: "He also told them to say to Don Luis, their lord, that recently two apostles, sent by God, had arrived, that they had long claws and great fangs and other frightful features, and that the missionaries would be reduced to pulp—*chichemicli*—a very horrible devilish thing."[5]

Thus, less than twenty years after the capture of Tenochtitlan by the Spaniards, ten years after the conversion of the Indians of the valley of Mexico, anaclitic reinterpretations of the Christian tradition had already emerged. Clearly, the Apostles of Christ, with whom the Franciscan religious had identified themselves, were assimilated by Martín Ocelotl to those devouring monsters which, in the Mexican cosmogony, cyclically annihilated humanity at the end of each era or "Sun." What Martín Ocelotl had announced to Moctezuma was the

end of the Aztec "Sun"; what he now announced to the peoples of
Anahuac was the end of the Franciscan "Sun." This obscure Texcocan
messiah, unknown to himself, was a sort of Joachim of Floris in reverse; faithful to the cyclical and apocalyptic conception of the Mexican religion, he sought to integrate within it two Apostles of Christ
(unfortunately we do not know which ones, for that information
could directly illuminate the origins of Saint Thomas-Quetzalcóatl),
but in order to make them more familiar to the Indians he vested
them with the attributes of traditional divinities, with claws and fangs,
like the jaguar-god, his totemic name (*ocelotl*). Over the centuries that
followed, the Indian eschatological hope was nourished by memories
of a cosmogony in which apocalypse, the final catastrophe of an era,
had always constituted the human horizon. That explains, at least in
part, the enthusiastic adherence of the Indians to the cult of the
Virgin of Guadalupe, protectress and guarantor of salvation.

Two brothers of Martín Ocelotl, especially one named Andrés Mixcoatl, were denounced to the Inquisition the next year, 1537. This
man went from village to village, and pretended to be a god; a witness
related that Andrés had a homologue, named Uiztly, in a nearby
region. What did they do? They preached: "This Andrés passed
through the ward of Atliztaca and asked the Indians for incense and
paper to prepare sacrifices and rites of sorcery, and they gave him
these things at once; then, in the evening, he summoned all the
people, preached to them, and said: 'Have no fear, your maize will not
frost; all that you have sown will come up well.' Therefore all the
Indians [*maceguales*] had faith in him, for he had made his conjura-
tions and had preached."[6] In other words, he had gained the Indians'
support because he made ritual sacrifices to Tlaloc to bring the fruitful rain. In exchange the faithful had given him the customary tribute
of mantles (*mantas*) and the hallucinogenic mushrooms whose inges-
tion induced prophetic visions. Moreover, his brother Martín Ocelotl
had charged Andrés Mixcoatl with collecting 3,600 arrow heads to
fight the "Christians," as they called themselves, rather than the
Spaniards. The last efforts at armed resistance by Anahuac, fifteen
years after the fall of Tenochtitlan, were a magic war led by sorcerers
like Ocelotl and Mixcoatl. Such men constituted a sort of network
which was broken up by the arrest of the most visible leaders, and
their punishment was exemplary. Led on muleback in ignominious
attire, whipped in public in the squares of the villages where they had
"dogmatized," shaved of their hair, and, in the case of Martín Ocelotl,
finally sent to the Inquisitors of Seville for final disposition of his
person—in a word, assimilated to the sorcerers (*hechiceros*) of the
Peninsula—these Mexican patriots were eliminated as heretics.

After them, the polygamists, the blasphemers, and the healers continued to proliferate in the valley of Mexico, but the living memory of Aztec power receded toward a horizon that became ever more mythical, and the hope of a military revenge was repressed into the deep recesses of consciousness, whence it would emerge solely in the form of *gritos*, "cries," on the occasion of riots like the one which took place in Mexico City in 1692. Pitiless repression did not prevent the old beliefs and traditional rites from surviving and blending with the Christian religion, especially because indoctrination had been very rapid and the number of priests was always inadequate to ensure control of Indian orthodoxy, even in the region most favored in that respect, Anahuac. In the other regions of New Spain, more remote from the central authority and even more scantily provided with religious and priests, native messiahs appeared frequently; we do not know them all. The ancient beliefs did not lose their strength as regards their most essential aspect, that of propitiatory agrarian rites. It is suggestive that, in order to discredit Christianity, Andrés Mixcoatl accused the missionaries of lacking power to bring the rain. It was on this terrain that the missionaries had to struggle, and we shall see the Virgen de los Remedios replacing Tlaloc in this specific role, while the Virgin of Guadalupe will be assigned the complementary role of guarding against floods.

This last point turns our attention to an important aspect of the Mexican spiritual climate. If the Indians, who preserved their ancient religion on the routine level of ritual and in the degree that it guaranteed their subsistence, were persuaded to borrow from the new religion its symbols and supposed magic efficacy, Christianity in its turn was also contaminated, above all in the realm of morality. There are some startling individual cases, like that parish priest of Ocuytuco, named Diego Díaz, tried by the tribunal of the Inquisition in 1542 for having had intercourse with some twenty Indian women, of whom half were married, one being the wife of the cacique. Moreover, he had murdered the son of an Indian *principal* or noble whose body he had buried under the staircase of his rectory. He had also tortured many Indians, over the protests of a Franciscan named Fray Jorge. This priest, a native of the region of Calahorra in Spain, ordained in Logroño, sponsored in Mexico by no less a figure than Fray Julián Garcés, was finally condemned to perpetual imprisonment. This example, even if regarded as extreme, is illuminating; it was not an isolated case.

One of the reasons why the Jesuits refused to station missionaries among the Indians was their fear that the priests might abandon their conventual way of life. The curates of Indians, in New Spain as elsewhere in the Indies, were largely assimilated by their milieu. Some closed their eyes to idolatrous practices in exchange for a supplementary tribute; others, feeling powerless to oppose it, agreed to sprinkle holy water on offerings presented by their parishioners to the agrarian divinities. If this could happen to the secular clergy, one can imagine what might happen to laymen, more or less isolated amid an Indian society stubbornly faithful to its customs and ancestral beliefs. A curious example is that of the son of the chronicler Bernal Díaz del Castillo, who in his capacity of corregidor of a village in Guatemala was accused, in 1568, of encouraging the Indians whom he administered to allow the churches to fall into ruin, to scorn the pope and the archbishops, to mistreat the priests . . . ! The anticlericalism of the colonists culminated in a few cases in atheism, pure and simple; indirectly it contributed to the survival of beliefs which the church at first sought to extirpate, but which eventually, in the most difficult cases, she had to assimilate.

An Indian by the name of Don Balthazar, cacique of Culuacan, questioned by the tribunal of the Inquisition, in 1539, revealed that idols were buried in all the villages of the region: "in a court called Puxtlan is buried an idol named Macuil Masiciual . . . and in a place called Yluycatitlan is buried the statue of another demon named Yzmain—this place is situated near Suchitlan; and in another place called Tetenmapan are immersed four demons; and in a place called Tecanalcango are buried other idols called Chalmecatl and Ecinacatl; and in another place called Yluycatitlan is found the Heart of Heaven; and at Ecanago is buried the statue of the wind; and at Suchicalco there is Macuyl Tunal, who is five demons; nearby is a cave where is the heart of the demon; and at Tlachico is buried the statue of Ochilobos and that of Quetzalcóatl; and he has heard it said that in the pyramid of Uchinabal is a golden drum and stone trumpets that belong to the demons."[7] Despite the picturesque deformations to which the interpreter subjected the Aztec toponymy and the names of the divinities, we recognize the principal figures of the Mexican pantheon: Macuilxochitl, Chachalmecatl, Ehécatl, Huitzilopochtli, Quetzalcóatl, as well as the accessories of the ritual festivals, the drum (it is uncertain whether the reference is to a *huehuetl* or a *teponaxtli*) and the shell trumpets. The gods missing from this roll call must have been preserved in that sealed grotto which the inquisitors imprudently caused to be opened in order to inventory its contents. From this cave of Aeolus (and a number of others) escaped the "demons" of the ancient beliefs, demons whose breath sent winds of messianic revolt blowing throughout New Spain, a movement as messianic as the storm of Independence itself would be.

The Indians, even those of the valley of Mexico, were never

thoroughly Christianized. As concerns the other ethnic elements of New Spain, to whose diversity I have called attention, the situation may appear much more favorable, at least among the urban creoles. The number of clergy among them, regular and secular was truly remarkable. Nevertheless, an inspection of the records of the tribunal of the Inquisition of Mexico City, after 1570 (the date when the Holy Office ceased to have jurisdiction over the Indians), inspires strong doubts concerning the orthodoxy of a population which included so many friars. Limiting our inquiry, for reasons of convenience, to the first period of the tribunal, which extended from 1573 to 1600 and corresponds to the *Libro primero de votos de la Inquisición de México,* we observe that the majority of cases tried by the inquisitors fall into the following categories.

Commoners charged with bigamy or living in concubinage; fornicators or blasphemers (the majority of these were black slaves or mulattoes).

Priests and especially religious (mostly Franciscans in this period); confessors (*solicitantes*) accused of having seduced penitents.

Portuguese Judaizers.

French or Flemish artisans; English pirates cast away on Mexican coasts and accused of Lutheran heresy.

The treatment accorded by the tribunal to the various types of offenders differed greatly. Individuals of humble background were condemned to do penance (*reconciliados*) in a convent, then were set free with a threat of heavier penalties in the case of relapse. Unbaptized heretics, English or French, were reeducated in the Catholic faith; the same was done with the blacks. On the other hand, the inquisitors were pitiless toward unworthy confessors and Judaizers. Two dates, 1589 and 1600, are noteworthy in this respect. The first marks the trial of a Judaizer, Luis de Carvajal, a native of Mogodorio, on the borders of Spain and Portugal (near Benavente, home of Motolinia), and at the time governor of the province of Nuevo León (Monterrey). Because of the accused man's position, the affair caused a great stir. Together with his brother Gaspar, who was a Dominican, and with the rest of his family, men and women, he was put to the rack; some were reconciled, others were handed over to the secular arm. The sentence of the governor was as follows: "In the course of a public auto-da-fe let it be declared that he has incurred the penalty of major excommunication, and he will have the sentence read to him, which sentence he will hear as a penitent, candle in hand, and he will abjure his errors *de vehementi,* and shall be exiled from the Indies for six years."[8] The case of Carvajal was the most celebrated, but it was not unique. There was the affair of a rabbi by the name of Antonio Machado, who clandestinely celebrated Jewish religious ceremonies;

and there were many others whose names of Andrada, Almeida, Matos, Paiva (most of them were relatives of Carvajal), leave no doubt concerning the Portuguese origin of these Mexican Judaizers. As concerns the forms of this Judaism, one may safely conclude, in the light of what is known about Iberian crypto-Judaism in general, that it was a religion which derived its main traits from the cabalism of Isaac Luria. If the Judaizers of New Spain presented special features, they probably reflected a relative doctrinal impoverishment caused by their isolation from the living sources of European Judaism.

In 1600 there took place the trial of a priest-*solicitante* that has an interest far beyond the moral aspects of the affair. The accused, named Juan de la Plata, was chaplain of the nunnery of Santa Caterina de Siena, at Puebla; his offense was much more serious than that of the many debauched priests whom the tribunal had punished before him, not to count the many whose act had never come to light. Juan de la Plata might have been one of the latter group, given his privileged position, if he had not seduced a visionary nun, Agustina de Santa Clara. For this pair of religious their carnal intercourse was a source of revelations, as we gather from this comment of the inquisitors: "We have not reported concerning the offense that he committed by seducing in the course of confession, before and after the confession (but very close to the moment of the confession), Agustina de Santa Clara, a professed nun of the monastery of Santa Caterina de Siena";[9] and from the sentence itself, which stipulated that "henceforth he will have nothing to do with any kind of revelations."[10] The nun's sentence contained, among other penalties, a similar prohibition: "She must not discuss revelations, either in writing or orally."[11] Although rarer than cases of priests-*solicitantes,* instances of nuns or *beatas* who infringed the vow of chastity were not unusual. The seriousness of the affair consisted not in this but in the "revelations." We would like to know more about their nature, for the atmosphere that surrounds them strangely recalls the case of a Peruvian religious, Fray Francisco de la Cruz, tried in Lima a decade earlier. Fray Francisco professed to be both a religious and political messiah; it seems that Juan de la Plata was more modest. One of his colleagues, also a *solicitante,* revised dogma to suit his pleasure by casting doubt on the virginity of the Virgin Mary.

Whatever the nature of our nun's "revelations," her case and that of her confessor shed a troubling light on Mexican convent life at the beginning of the seventeenth century. No doubt some saintly men and women lived there. What can safely be said is that illuminist tendencies were as strong there as in Spain of the previous century. Given the preponderant influence of religious on the appearance and development of pious traditions in New Spain and the fact that the convergence of these traditions was the focal point of the national consciousness, the religious deserve more study than they have received. The convents of New Spain were the principal sites of spiritual activity within the framework of Catholic orthodoxy. The impact of the friars on society, their geographical and social origins, their family ties, their life outside the convent, have not yet been studied systematically. We know them chiefly through the menologies contained in the official histories of their respective religious provinces, indispensable sources, to be sure, but suspicious on account of their hagiographic spirit. Yet that very spirit is a document that illuminates the spiritual climate of New Spain.

We cannot completely divorce from the Mexican spiritual ferment—a ferment that had to be political as well in a society like that of New Spain—an episode that took place in 1642, the inquisitorial trial of Don Guillén de Lampart. This individual had arrived in Mexico two years earlier in the retinue of the viceroy Escalona (who, suspected of disloyalty to the king, was arrested and replaced by Bishop Palafox). Lampart had hatched a plot which aimed at the independence of New Spain. It was the second great plot of this kind, the first being that of Martín Cortés in 1566. Lampart was arrested too soon for us to know whether his project had numerous accomplices in the country, or who they were. But his governmental and reform program is highly revealing of the inner tensions of Mexican society in the middle of the seventeenth century; I do not find it so "extravagant" as does José Toribio Medina. We must note, to begin with, that his project had its origin in the conviction, derived from reading the Scriptures, that the rulers of Spain were illegitimate possessors of the Indies. Lampart rediscovered the arguments of the opponents of the bulls of Pope Alexander, and invoked their claim that the popes had no temporal power. Disregarding certain extravagances, we must center attention on the following points of his program:

1. Suppression of tributes and taxes.
2. Freedom for all slaves.
3. Preference to be given to descendants of conquistadors.
4. Promise of habits of the military orders to Indians who rallied to his cause.
5. Restitution of Indian parishes to the religious, in perpetuity.
6. Assignment of revenues to the convents.[12]

To shake off the Spanish yoke was clearly the crowning point of Lampart's demagogic program. This pretender to the Mexican crown, proclaiming the great service that he rendered to God, claimed for himself the patronage of all the convents of the country, the right of presentation of bishops, the grant of ecclesiastical prebends and benefices. Evidently the rancor of the despoiled conquistadors (or rather, at this date, of their descendants) was still strong enough for Lampart to use as a trump card in his separatist game. It is even clearer that he regarded the clergy, the canons, and especially the religious as indispensable allies in his enterprise. Lampart therefore spared nothing to assure the cooperation of the religious; the essential thing was to promise them the restitution of the Indian parishes, an open wound in the side of the religious for the past half-century. (We should note that the economic situation of many crowded convents was poor, sometimes tragic.) Finally, Lampart himself would present the bishops, a proposal that offered an additional guarantee against return of the disliked secular bishops, exemplified by the bishop of Puebla, Palafox (at that precise moment *visitador* and interim viceroy, later invested with full powers). To the creoles who should help him to take power, Lampart offered titles of nobility and the creation of Mexican grandees. Although his program may appear utopian in certain respects, it was perfectly coherent. It corresponded to the aspirations of the most discontented elements of society: the friars, the creole aristocracy, the slaves, and the Indian caciques. The Mexican nation is already present in Lampart's program; the program of Independence already exists there in outline form.

Less than a century after Lampart, there disembarked at Veracruz a captain of a frigate of the royal navy, by the name of Manuel de Bahamón, who was soon arrested and brought before the tribunal of the Inquisition "as a seditious person, as harmful to the spiritual government and conscience of the faithful as he was to the temporal government."[13] This mystic had announced the birth of the Antichrist and prophesied the early coming of the Last Judgment. First, however, there must take place a radical revolution which would put an end to the Kingdom of Evil and install the Reign of Justice. We recognize here the old millenarian dream, which in New Spain could always draw for support on nostalgic memories of the first great missionary crusade and the early *Iglesia Indiana*. When the hour struck for the first revolution of Independence, Hidalgo and Morelos (two priests, we recall) appeared to their followers as messiahs, or at least as providential men. The royalist authorities regarded them in the same light; after their capture they were turned over to the tribunal of the Inquisition, Hidalgo in 1811, Morelos in 1815. Accused of heresy and apostasy, the two liberators consistently protested their submission to the Roman, Apostolic, Catholic Church.

The few soundings I have made by way of examples into the spiritual history of New Spain suggest, I believe, the following conclusions.

1. Beliefs in New Spain were the unstable product of heterogeneous religious contributions, made by ethnic groups of unequal importance and influence.

2. As a result of prolonged contact with other religions, the religion of each minority group underwent important changes (losses, borrowings, substitutions).

3. By contrast with Catholicism, the official religion, the other religions of New Spain (Judaism, Mexican polytheism, African animism) had a residual character due to their remoteness from their spiritual homes and the pressure of Catholic orthodoxy (persecutions, prohibitions).

4. In the Indian communities of the countryside, in the convents in creole society, in the milieu of the slaves and the *castas* in the towns, there seem to have appeared syncretic beliefs that were specifically Mexican, together with magical practices.

5. Messianic hope and an apocalyptic conception of history were the common denominator of these religions.

6. To retie the broken thread of a supernatural history was a common aspiration of Indians, Jews, and Christians, heirs of the first Franciscan missionaries. (Let us not forget that at the time of the Conquest Spain had known more than ten centuries of coexistence of Christians, Jews, and Moslems).

7. The encounter between the divinities of the Mexican pantheon, each with its defined role, and the cult of local tutelary saints, so vital in Spanish society, gave rise to substitutions and assimilations.

8. Although only the friars and bishops could officially give a spiritual impulse to the society of New Spain, the majority of the rural population (the Indians) and the urban population (the *castas*) were attached to their own beliefs.

The friars elaborated pious legends, more or less compatible with orthodoxy, but it was the *castas* and the Indians who made them live or let them die. The dominant creole minority needed the decisive support of the rest of the population in order to free itself from Spanish tutelage; it had to elaborate an ideology capable of integrating the subjugated ethnic groups, first utilized as a labor force, later as a combat force. The oppressed state of the majority of the nation—a majority composed of the Indians and the *castas*—created a propitious terrain for the continual appearance of messianic movements of spiritual, political, and social liberation. As mythical responses destined to fulfill these aspirations, there appeared and developed the beliefs in a pristine evangelization of Mexico by the apostle Saint Thomas, under the name of Quetzalcóatl, and in the miraculous apparition of the Virgin Mary of Guadalupe on the hill of Tepeyac, the former sanctuary of Tonantzin, mother-goddess of the Aztecs.

The Indian:
A Spiritual Problem
(1524–1648)

The Providential Faith and the Millenarian Hope

The fortunes of the messianic myth of Quetzalcóatl and the flowering of the cult of the Virgin Mary in the form of the miraculous image of Guadalupe will become comprehensible only if we can recapture the great moments in New Spain's spiritual history. The first moment still belongs largely to old Spain; the Old World projected its millenarian hope upon the New in the first half-century which followed the conquest of Mexico by Cortés and his comrades-in-arms. That moment corresponds almost exactly in ecclesiastical and missionary history to the period studied by Robert Ricard in a book with the suggestive title *La Conquête spirituelle du Mexique,* a period which the subtitle defined more precisely as "the missionary apostolate of the mendicant orders."[1] Without exaggeration, one may say that this first missionary wave was dominated by the spirit of the reformed Franciscans, or Friars Minor. Thus it is possible to assign chronological limits to this phase, which opened with the arrival in Mexico of the "Twelve," the first Franciscans sent by Charles V at the request of Cortés, in 1524. The passage to a different spiritual situation coincides almost exactly with the arrival of the first Jesuit missionaries in 1572, a year marked by another event decisive for the evolution of the Mexican church, the start of the long and active spiritual magistracy of Don Pedro Moya de Contreras, archbishop of Mexico, later viceroy.

This chronology, let me note, can be disputed. I follow Robert Ricard in thinking that the date of 1572 is the turning point, but in his study of *The Millenial Kingdom of the Franciscans in the New World,* John Leddy Phelan assigns the date of 1564 as the end of the Golden Age of the Indian church. The question is unimportant as concerns the essential point, on which historians are agreed; namely, the existence among the first Franciscan missionaries of Mexico of a millenarian hope, inherited through Saint Francis of Assisi from Joachim of Floris. It is remarkable that the prophetic work of Joachim, a Calabrese monk of the twelfth century, *Divini abbatis Joachim Concordie Novi ac Veteris Testamenti,* was first published in Venice in 1519, the same year that Hernán Cortés landed on the shore of the Mexican land he was to conquer.[2] Since Mexico was the first great continental conquest in the New World, and the scene of the first contact between Spanish conquerors and a large native population, the event made a large impact on peninsular opinion, as shown by the enthusiastic crowds that greeted Cortés on his return to Spain. For contemporary historians, notably for the Franciscan Fray Jerónimo de Mendieta in his *Historia eclesiástica indiana,* it was Hernán Cortés (and not Christopher Columbus, traditionally so regarded) who was a truly providential man assigned by the Lord to this great mission of discovery of the New World. This notion suggests that the most important aspect of the discovery was not the finding of new lands but the revelation or unveiling of a new part of humanity, the promise of a rich harvest of souls to reward the zeal of the missionaries. In effect, although the great American discoveries transformed geography, this result, so important in our modern eyes, seemed much less significant at that time than the support they gave to eschatological hopes for the coming of the Kingdom. In the genesis of those hopes the ideas of Joachim of Floris, dear to the Franciscans, played a great role. Joachim's theory, the first theory of history developed in the Middle Ages, not only gave its full meaning to the concept of a "middle age" but allowed for an advance beyond it.

For Joachim of Floris, the supernatural destiny of mankind, its history, was divided into three successive stages: "the time of the letter of the Old Testament, the time of the letter of the New Testament, the time of spiritual understanding."[3] In the "book of the concordance," he shows the precise correspondence between the events of the three successive stages of mankind as it advanced toward its goal. Each stage in turn divides into periods, each having its counterpart in the two other stages; these periods bear the name of "seals." The seals of history are seven in number. It is significant that Joachim, speaking of the fifth seal, wrote: "Babylon was mentioned for the first time. Thus in our days a multitude of Christians who once thought that the church, by reason of all the good she has done, had some right to be called Jerusalem, now believe that because of all the evils she has caused she should be called Babylon."[4]

Imagine the sensation that reflections of this kind, published in 1519, just before the consummation of the Lutheran schism, could create. Indeed, the Lutherans shared with Joachim the preoccupation with the Antichrist, whose coming was supposed to precede that of the "Lord in the glory of His Father, escorted by all the Saints."[5] The heretics did not hesitate to identify the Antichrist with the pope himself, while the Judaic tradition calls him Gog. We recognize here a verse of the Book of Revelation. It was on an interpretation of Revelation of Judaic origin that Joachim founded his millenarian theory, as shown by this passage from the *Liber in expositionem in Apocalipsim*: "The third [stage] was established by Saint Benedict, whose excellence will not be fully understood until almost the end of time, when Elijah will reappear and the unbelieving Jewish people will return to God. Then the Holy Spirit will arise and will clamor with a loud voice: 'The Father and the Son have acted until now. And now, I will act.'"[6] Those last days—the days of the Holy Spirit—correspond to the eternal Gospel, a term which remains attached to the doctrine of Joachim of Floris: "And what is this Gospel? That of which Jesus speaks in Revelation: 'I saw an angel flying in the midst of heaven, and he had the eternal Gospel. And what is in this Gospel? All that goes beyond the Gospel of Christ. For the letter kills and the spirit gives life.'"[7] It is at the outer bounds of Christianity, or even beyond it, that the renovation of spiritual life in the sixteenth century manifested itself, notably in the mendicant orders, called by the prophet Joachim to abolish the carnal church and prepare a new revelation. The political corollaries of the wait for the millennium were portentous: "Under the sixth seal of the second stage the New Babylon will be destroyed. And just as in this same period of the first stage the Assyrians and the Macedonians attacked the Jews, so today we see the Saracens attacking Christendom, and soon we shall see the rise of false prophets. . . . Once these tests have ended, the faithful shall see God face to face. This will be the third stage, reserved for the reign of the Holy Spirit."[8] The Turkish victories in Europe, the decadence of the Roman church, the appearance of the false prophet Luther (regarded by some as the Antichrist), the spiritual harvest promised and, it seemed, reserved by providence for the Franciscan pioneers of the conversion of the New World, were so many converging signs of the approach of the millennium and the accomplishment of the prophecies of the abbot Joachim. Therefore we see the Franciscans of New Spain trying to found the *Iglesia Indiana,* the "Indian Church," belonging to the third stage in which the friars were to play a preeminent role.

In this climate of providential exaltation and messianic expectation was born a Franciscan current which nourished the creole mentality of New Spain. In the conception of the Franciscan pioneers, this New Spain was to be as radically new in relation to traditional Spain as the new church was to be in respect of the Roman church. The first missionaries of Mexico were certainly "creoles" in the measure that they wanted to create a new world, which implied a rupture with the Old. For the rest, more than one of their number gave lyrical expression with his pen to their attachment to the American earth and their affection for its peoples.

The wait for the millennium (no passive wait but a feverishly active preparation on the part of the evangelizers of Mexico) was the first manifestation of the creole spirit of America, for the missionary impulse nourished and placed an indelible stamp upon that spirit. We note the very extensive privileges conferred on the Franciscan missionaries by successive popes—Leon XI in 1521, then Adrian VI in 1522; privileges that in effect entrusted the destiny of the new church to their hands. The feeling prevailed in Rome, as in America, that the church was at a critical moment of her existence and that its great opportunity consisted in the reserve of New World souls, ready for conversion. According to the conceptions of that time, such an important moment in history must be announced in Scripture, source of all truth; this gave rise to efforts at scriptural exegesis designed to elucidate obscure aspects of this event and to justify the construction of the *Iglesia Indiana*. This church, whose first faithful were Spanish friars, was the first ideal model of a possible creole society. We have here a utopia, closely related in its inspiration to the Utopia of Thomas More, which a bishop of Mexico, Don Vasco de Quiroga (perceptively studied by Silvio Zavala), tried to realize with imperfect success.

Throughout the long colonial centuries, continuing down to the present, the American societies (notably that of Mexico) were to bear the seal of the millenarian hope and original grace which presided over their birth. The New World was first conceived as a world free from the tares of the Old; it was born under the sign of the Holy Spirit and the Woman of *Revelation* "clothed with the sun, having the moon under her feet."

Divinely inspired workers in the vineyard, the Franciscan missionaries of New Spain described the conquistador Cortés, who had cleared the way for their coming, as a "new Moses," in conformity with the system of concordances of Joachim of Floris. They regarded the native beliefs which they sought to extirpate as idolatrous. Faithful to a biblical and Jewish tradition, they viewed the native divinities as demons; Fray Bernardino de Sahagún calls them "devils" in his *Historia general de las cosas de la Nueva España*. This conviction of the missionaries caused them to reject any compromise with the ancient beliefs, inspired their determination to wipe the slate clean, a policy which Robert Ricard describes as "the policy of rupture." On the question of how to interpret Scripture and Jesus' precept to his Apostles to go preach the gospel to *all* the peoples, Sahagún takes an implicit position when he cries out: "Why, Lord God, have you permitted the Enemy of mankind to rule so long over this poor helpless people?.... I pray your Divine Majesty to see to it that there, where crime and darkness abounded, Grace and Light may abound."⁹ This is to interpret Christendom as *history*. In effect, taken literally, the verse can be understood as a mission given to the Apostles to preach the Gospel during their own lifetimes to all the peoples of the world. Since this was not done, the Franciscan Twelve who arrived in Mexico in 1524 could just as legitimately as the companions of Jesus be called "Apostles"; to them fell the task of preaching the faith to the last peoples not yet reached by the Word.

Correspondingly, it was the mendicant orders that were preparing the advent of Christ by seeing to the conversion of the last gentiles— the last, that is, save for the "hidden Jews" whose conversion was to precede by a little space the coming of the new Messiah, Elijah. How, asks Sahagún, can one explain the injustice (*la injuria,* he writes) done by God to such a numerous (indeed, the most numerous, he believed) portion of mankind, handed over to Satan for fifteen centuries? Here the Augustinian spirit confronted the impenetrable mysteries of God. The Franciscan pioneers thus expressed their love for the Indians of the New World through their fervent prayers that God should make grace abound and above all by their apostolic zeal, a zeal which drew inspiration from the African missions of the fourteenth and fifteenth centuries. Augustinians on this point, the friars contradicted in other respects the author of *The City of God,* for, as Norman Cohn has justly remarked, Augustine believed this city had already been founded, while for Joachim of Floris and his epigones its coming must still be prepared. These examples indicate that the eschatological hope for the coming of the Kingdom was not free from doubts and uncertainties; the temporal preeminence of the friars was soon threatened by the secular prelates, and the Golden Age of the mendicant orders evaporated with the first generation, that of the Twelve. As for the millennium, that hope was deferred as a result of the rise of a new spiritual climate, to be discussed below; that climate constitutes the second spiritual moment of Mexican creole society in process of gestation.

The millenarian hope thus implied a certain vision of the discovery of the New World and of the providential mission of its Spanish conquistadors. This sense of mission is expressed in the great historiographic works of the Conquest, works which reflect the spirit of the Spanish *Reconquista*. In the dedication to Charles V which precedes his *Historia general de las Indias,* Gómara, Cortés' chaplain, wrote that "the Conquest of the Indians began when the conquest of the Moors had ended, in order that Spaniards may always war against the infidels."¹⁰ No doubt this comment faithfully expressed the Conqueror's own feeling. The intervention of providence in the history of Spain, or rather of Spaniards who regarded themselves as the arm of Christendom in its struggle against heretics, Jews, and Moslems, was not new; it was not born with the conquest of the New World. An understanding of the miraculous appearances of the Virgin, with which I shall deal at length, requires that they be viewed against the same charismatic background. The anonymous Mercederian who composed one of the first histories of the appearance of the Virgin of Guadalupe of Estremadura wrote as early as 1440: "After the Moorish dagger had passed through almost the whole body of Spain, it pleased our Lord God to console the hearts of the Christians, that they might find the strength which they had lost. That is why the appearance of the Virgin gave them such great comfort."[11]

The apparent confusion of the worlds of religion and politics flowed naturally from the eschatological conception of history which had prevailed for centuries in Europe and which Dante had defined with special clarity. For the average man, broadly speaking, humanity included the Christians, the Jews, the Moslems, and the gentiles. The Christians par excellence were the Spaniards, a new Chosen People, whose mission was to conquer the Moslems, convert the gentiles, and lead the straying Jews back into the bosom of the church. Then Christianity would become at last truly *Catholic*, that is, universal, and the Messiah would come in glory, surrounded by all the saints, to reign over the world. The "soldiers of Christ" were in the first place the missionary friars, who could also be inquisitors like Zumárraga or even combatants. The unfolding of history according to the impenetrable designs of God could be deciphered in Scripture, particularly in the Prophets and in *Revelation*. Undoubtedly no one ever carried as far as Joachim of Floris the task of elucidating Scripture in the sense of an interpretation of medieval history, corresponding end to end to ancient history.

Nevertheless, although large use was made of the Prophets and the Old Testament in general, the apocalyptic conception of history which prevailed in medieval and Renaissance Europe deviated from the Judaic tradition and presented typically Pauline traits. The history of humanity merged with the history of sin, of a world delivered to Satan (whence arose a Manichean vision in which the forces of Good opposed those of Evil without achieving victory over the latter); this history would extend till the last days, the establishment of the reign of God. The task of the Christians was to hasten the coming of this "reign." It was the will of God that where sin abounded, grace should abound. Christendom was periodically seized with a millenarian fever. Saint Hippolytus had calculated that the millennium would come in 600 A.D.; Joachim of Floris thought it would be in 1260. But each time the wait had to be resumed. In this respect the Franciscans formed no exception. Despite the multiplication of anticipatory signs—the decadence of the Roman church, the Moslem victories, the rise of the Lutheran heresy in northern Europe, the mass conversion of the American gentiles—the wait was in vain.

One might well conclude that the Joachimite interpretation of Revelation, capable of reconciling the Judaic Messiah and the Christian Messiah, had encountered resistance. For Christendom (that is, mankind, from the viewpoint of contemporary European thinkers), it was a question of knowing whether the Middle Ages, that long period intervening between the resurrection of Jesus after the Passion and his return in glory, was to end. The springtime of the world, whose flowering was announced each time that conditions became intolerable on account of wars or epidemics, appeared to all the oppressed as a sort of final revenge. To the damnation of the earth would succeed the reign of justice. The temporal powers and the church as well had always viewed the millennium with reserve. Even the advocates of millenarianism encountered internal difficulties at each step. In the present instance, several difficulties appeared in relation to a complex of problems whose solution would either confirm or weaken the millenarian hope.

The sudden irruption of an unknown but numerous portion of mankind into a world organized according to the cosmography of Hellenic antiquity, which the Church had done little to revise, inevitably provoked serious questions. In the minds of the missionaries of that time, who represented the most advanced tendency in the Spanish church, the search for truth must in the first place be an effort at exegesis. Consequently men began to scrutinize Revelation and the Prophets, in the hope of finding there the announcement of the discovery of the New World, of which Gómara wrote: "The greatest event since the creation of the world (if we except the incarnation and death of Him who created it) is the discovery of the Indies; that is why they are called the New World."[12] This sentence (the first in the dedication to Charles V which I cited above) conveys perfectly the meaning which contemporaries assign to the discovery of America and to the expression "New World." This world, that is to say, its inhabitants, above all, was a new stage in the history of Christendom as that history moved toward its goal. The task of theologians, then, was to interpret correctly, in the light of Scripture, this event, which in view of its eschatological importance, must be *written* in the sacred texts. The prevailing idea that the history of humanity was cryptically (*en cifra*) written in holy Scripture, permitted the most audacious hypotheses. Was not Columbus foretold in the Old Testament, and was not his given name "Christoforo" (the Christ-bearer) a sign of the designs that providence had for him? Modern rationalists may smile at such explanations, but for minds impregnated with the esoteric doctrines of sixteenth-century Europeans, this was but one more sign of the designs of God.

The Question of the Origin of the Indians

Upon the response given to this question depended whether the coming of the millennium was near or distant, whether Jews and Christians would or would not be reconciled, whether Christendom was solvent or bankrupt, and whether the interpretation of Scripture must be drastically overhauled. Here was cause for permanent disquiet on the part of the temporal and spiritual powers at a time when Islam was in full process of expansion and when the Lutheran heresy was growing; at stake was the preservation of mankind, the church, and the empire. Since man's natural rights were of transcendent importance, and since Spain's sole true title to America rested on the bulls of Pope Alexander VI, which granted Spain the right to rule over the Indies and levy tribute from their peoples in return for the expenses borne by the Castilian monarchy for their conversion, it was necessary to prove the validity of this enterprise. We must not forget that papal infallibility did not become dogma until the nineteenth century (and applies only to points of faith, in particular circumstances) and that theologians and jurists of the sixteenth and seventeenth centuries could contest, without incurring ecclesiastical sanctions, the validity of the Alexandrine bulls. A certain regalist tradition of the Castilian monarchy soon encouraged them to do this; since the French kings, in particular, had declared the bulls null and void, it was important to lay a more solid foundation for Spanish rule in the New World. This was the special intent of the *Relectiones de Indis,* the lectures on the Indies presented by Francisco de Vitoria at the University of Salamanca.

Modern rationalism, of Kantian origin, has invalidated problems of origins and ultimate ends, relegating them to metaphysics and concentrating all its efforts on problems of cause and relation; that is, we are at the antipodes from the religious men and women of the Renaissance, for whom that renaissance was primarily one of eschatological aspiration. Since the supernatural destiny of mankind was a seamless robe, the fate of Christianity depended on that of the Indians, and the fate of the Indians must have been written for all eternity. The problem, then, was one of identifying the inhabitants of the New World with the descendants of one of the patriarchs of the Bible, of some-how joining them to the line of Adam (or, contrariwise, of excluding them from that line, a possiblity which was also envisaged). Here, again, our surprise is due to the weight of a Rousseauistic tradition of which we moderns are only half-conscious. For men of the Spanish sixteenth century, nourished on medieval marvels, antique humanism, and Judaizing exegesis, the radical novelty of America offered an inviting field of action. The search for Amazons, Cyclops, Sirens, or descendants of the Jews exiled by King Salmanazar was quite frequent in the time of the contest of America. We need not be sur-prised if we recall that medieval humanity, restricted to the Mediter-ranean basin and its Germanic and North African marches, regarded itself as complete and finished (with the exception of a vague East whose marvelous image the accounts of Marco Polo had diffused). As Edmundo O'Gorman has shown, the contemporary world com-prehended three continents—a symbolic correlation with the Holy Trinity and the three crowns of the pontifical tiara.

There was no place, literally speaking, for this fourth and new world, come too late into a cosmology inherited from Ptolemy and incorporated into dogma by the church. Men did not know what to do with the Indians, of whom Columbus had written that they were neither Negroes nor Canary Islanders. If Vasco de Quiroga saw in them the happy subjects of Saturn told of by Lucan, others might find it as economical and reassuring to cut them off from humanity and identify them with those "monsters" with which the ancient legends were filled and which no one had hitherto found. Certain engravings from the end of the fifteenth century, and even later, graphically convey this interpretation. Such a posture posed the danger of mak-ing vain all efforts at conversion, a danger well understood by the missionaries, fishers of souls who became champions of the "human-ity" of the Indians. On the other hand, the conquistadors saw in this position the possibility of justifying a pitiless exploitation of the in-habitants of the New World. The problem of the nature of the Indians was one battleground of the confrontation which took place, espe-cially during the first generation, between religious and colonists.

This debate transcended the conflict between conquistadors and religious for control of the New World, for the monarchy took an official position, soon followed by Pope Paul III. The brief *Cardinali toletono,* addressed to the primate of the Spains, followed by the bull *Sublimis Deus,* dates, however, from 1537; that is, these texts came after the great continental conquests of Mexico and Peru. As long as the Indians apppeared under the aspect of the nomadic hunters and collectors of Darien, Europe could still believe there were Cyclops and

Amazons among them; but this became improbable after Cortés' revelations about the Aztec empire and those of Pizarro about the Incas. The New Laws of the Indies, in effect summed up, five years later, the ideas expressed by the Roman pontiff in the bull *Sublimis Deus*. We recall, however, that as early as the end of the fifteenth century Isabella the Catholic had liberated the Indians brought by Columbus as slaves to the Peninsula and had demanded their repatriation; the young Bartolomé de Las Casas was a direct witness of this intervention, for his father possessed a slave brought from Española. Whatever doubts some may have entertained about the humanity of the Indians, the Spanish monarchs never appear to have questioned it.

Recognition of the humanity of the Indians made them fellow creatures, souls capable of salvation. The grant of a human nature to the Indians was a prerequisite of decisive importance, but it opened up a new battleground, one on which exegetes and historians were to clash for more than two centuries. To summarize here, one by one, the different positions, would be to compose a boring catalogue; besides, this task was accomplished at the beginning of the seventeenth century by a Dominican, Fray Gregorio García, in a book published in Valencia, *Origen de los Indios del Nuevo Mundo e Indias Occidentales* (1607). The genesis of the book, and how García went about writing it, are revealing. Having originally planned to write a history of ancient Peru (that is, of the Inca empire), he temporarily gave up the idea as a result of a stay in New Spain, where he acquired a considerable mass of information on pre-Columbian Mesoamerica. Since the problem of the origin of the Indians was a matter of "opinion" rather than information, he chose to publish first what was to have been the second part of a triptych (I shall speak at more length of the third part in the next chapter). Fray Gregorio remembered in the nick of time, at the very beginning of the first chapter, that "the first foundation is an article of faith, namely, that all the men and women who have lived since the beginning of the world descend and take their origins from our first forebears, Adam and Eve."[13]

This statement of orthodoxy is important; to the best of my knowledge, all the sixteenth-century authors who expressed hypotheses regarding the origin of the Indians accepted it, and one must wait until the seventeenth century to find Isaac La Peyrère coming out with the hypothesis that the Indians were "preadamites," exempt from original sin (a hypothesis vigorously combatted by the Benedictine friar Jerónimo de Feijóo). However, even granting the link of the inhabitants of the New World to Adam's line, many divergent opinions remained possible. Let us note here the second great principle of Gregorio García: "The second foundation which we must postulate is that the peoples of the Indies, whom we call Indians, came there from one of the three parts of the known world: Europe, Asia, and Africa."[14]

The idea, still largely accepted by modern paleontologists, that America had no native population and that all its peoples had a foreign origin, goes back to the sixteenth century; it may be regarded as relic of a primitive anthropology and an abandoned cosmology.

These two principles left a wide margin for hypotheses, all compatible with Catholic orthodoxy, relating to the origin of the Indians. I shall call attention here only to several of the more significant examples. In reality, all the solutions proposed for the question of the origin of the Indians derived from two sources: the pagan science of Roman and Greek antiquity, on the one hand, and the Judeo-Christian tradition, on the other. In the third chapter of the first book of his work, Gregorio García refers to Aristotle, who "in a book which he wrote on the marvels of nature, reports the voyage of a Carthaginian ship, which departing from the pillars of Hercules (that is, Gibraltar), or from Cádiz, and driven by a strong wind from the east, touched at a hitherto unknown island. This island, judging by his description was doubtless the island of Española discovered by Columbus. . . . It may be, however, as some have observed, that this land discovered by the Carthaginians was what is now called Tierra Firme, which they took for an island."[15] In the next chapter, Fray Gregorio refers to Seneca: "Of the Prophecies of Seneca about the Indies."[16]

Most interesting of all is the exegetic effort which appears in the sixth chapter of the same first book, entitled: "That Mention is Made of the Indies in Holy Scripture." I shall cite a somewhat long passage that reveals the mode of thought of the missionaries of the New World: "The Prophet Isaiah, according to the version of the Septuagint, says: 'Woe to the land which sends ships beyond Ethiopia' (Isaiah 18). This whole chapter is applied to the Indies by grave and knowledgeable authors, in particular by Master Fray Luis de León, who with the aid of this chapter and the Prophet Obadiah (in the conclusion of his prophecy), proves that the conversion of the Indians by the Spaniards had been foretold many years ago by these Prophets. (Luis de León, *Commentary on Obadiah and the Song of Songs,* chap. 8.)" Here the overlap between several questions which we now regard as distinct, but then were inseparable, is clear; those questions are the knowledge of America by the ancients, the peopling of America by immigrants come from one of the three regions of the known world, the conversion of the Indians to Christianity, and above all the explication of the content of biblical prophecies by the course of history. It was important to accumulate the greatest possible number of authorities on each of these points; consequently the seventh chapter deals with "the opinion of Origen and Saint Jerome about the New World," where the author reminds us that "Clement of Alexandria, disciple of the Apostles, also mentions the peoples that the Greeks call the Antipodes." The convergence of testimony taken from classic Greek philosophers, Prophets of the Old Testament, Fathers of the Church—testimony that was often cryptic (especially that of the Prophets)—weighed more in the matter of proof than observations made on the spot by missionaries or administrators.

However, appeal to the experience of the New World and its peoples was not rejected, as we see in the second book, where the authority of Aristotle concurs with the vision of America to support the Carthaginian hypothesis: "Of the Fourth Foundation, Where Mention Is Made of Ancient and Monumental Ruins Which Appear to Be the Work of Carthaginians."[17] The cyclopean ruins of highland Peru reminded the Spaniards of the ramparts of Carthage. We see here for the first time mention of pre-Columbian antiquities (*antigua-llas*); they were to play an ever increasing role in the American consciousness. Anthropological data were no barrier to the joint authority of the ancients, the Prophets, the church Fathers, and modern doctors of the church; "and the opinion of the Indians that these peoples were different from them does not prevent them from having been Carthaginians, the first colonizers of this country . . . , for the color of their skin and their physical structure changed in this foreign land, becoming those of the present Indians."[18] The author moved without difficulty from Mexico to Peru, from Yucatan to Tiahuanaco, where more "Carthaginian" ruins had been found that the Indians assigned to "other bearded peoples with white skin like ours."[19]

With the same conviction and honesty which he brought to the defense of the thesis of the Carthaginian origin of the Indians, Fray Gregorio García now undertook to combat it: "Of the First Doubt Relative to This Opinion." Here he developed the linguistic argument: "If the Indians descended from the Carthaginians they would speak their language . . . , but instead we confront a multitude of languages."[20] This objection inspires another in reply, namely, that "the Devil, who is so shrewd, knew by conjecture that the evangelical Law would be preached in these kingdoms, and therefore persuaded the Indians to invent new languages."[21] We should not be surprised by use of arguments of this kind by a Spanish friar formed in the sixteenth century, for whom the history of humanity was explained by the incessant struggle between the redeeming designs of Providence and the perverse efforts of the Enemy. The *Apologética historia de las Indias* of the Dominican Las Casas includes a considerable number of chapters devoted to the enterprises of the Fiend, and Las Casas seems obsessed with damnation, both of the Indians and the Conquistadors. The work of the Jesuit José de Acosta reflects similar concerns.

The history of America's past could only be conceived as an episode in the struggle which, ever since the resurrection of Christ, had locked in battle God and the Devil, in that intermediate age which was to end with the millennium. We must not be deceived, therefore, by the apparent confusion in works which at first glance seem a jumble of fantastic lucubrations based on a plethora of patristic and classical citations. In reality we have in these works a coherent conception of the history of mankind, a history into which it was necessary to integrate the inhabitants of the New World. Their novelty, their strangeness, must be assimilated into a truth which, if it had not been made totally clear, had in any case been long before revealed by Scripture.

One of the most interesting hypotheses with regard to the origins of the Indians is set forth by Gregorio García in the third book of his work, whose first chapter is entitled; "Of the Fifth Opinion, Wherein It Is Proved That the Indians Are the Descendants of the Hebrews of the Ten Lost Tribes." This thesis could hardly have caused a stir in the Spain of Philip III, also ruler of Portugal. Gregorio García, like Menasseh ben Israel after him, only repeated traditions which went back to the first discoveries in the New World. André Neher informs us that the appearance at Ferrara of a certain Reubeni, come from the Indies, had inspired a messianic movement, described in 1524 by Abraham Farisol. This author gives a fantastic description of the ten "lost tribes," found by Reubeni in "India." One naturally asks, what "India," or what "Indies"? In Spain, meanwhile, the Inquisition persecuted the converted Jews accused of crypto-Judaism; we recall the trial of Juan de Carvajal, governor of Nuevo León, in New Spain itself. Numerous Jews had gone to Peru and New Spain despite the legal obstacles to settlement in the New World of individuals who were not "Old Christians." If the Judaizers of the Old World should find their brethren in the New, might they not join together to organize a secessionist movement? If the mendicant orders continued to bring in their harvest of souls, would not the massive conversion of the Indians, descendants of the Jews, be the prelude to the Advent announced as near by Joachim of Floris and awaited by his Franciscan disciples?

These circumstances suffice to show that the problem of the origin of the Indians was not a pedantic problem, a sterile question of paleontology, at a time when that science was not even in its infancy. It involved, I repeat, a grave eschatological problem which could have political implications, as the opening of Gregorio García's first chapter suggests: "It is a very widely held opinion, and the Spaniards of the common sort who live in the Indies are convinced of it, that the Indians descend from the ten Jewish tribes lost at the time of the captivity, under the Assyrian king Salmanazar. The basis of this opinion is the character, the nature, and the customs which they observe among those Indians and which are very similar to those of the Hebrews."[22] I will not discuss the frailty of such arguments, for my role is not to judge but to understand and explain.

We note here the dialectical relationship between the eschatological concerns of the clergy and the daily experience of the common man, the *gente vulgar*. The soldiers of Cortés, according to the testimony of Bernal Díaz del Castillo, similarly and spontaneously described the Mexican temples as mosques (*mezquitas*), thus assimilating all non-Christian religions to each other and reviving the ardor of the wars of the Reconquista to combat the pagans of the New World. By means of a similar simplification, the American colonists were persuaded that the Indians were Jews, discovering the same pattern of conduct which they had assigned to the Jews of Castile or Aragon. In both cases, it was a matter of overcoming the strangeness of the New World by assimilating its peoples and their culture to others, more familiar to Spaniards through contact and historical tradition. Fray Gregorio informs us in the next chapters of the traits that the Spaniards of the Indies assigned to both Jews and Indians, traits whose similarity constituted "the second foundation of the fifth opinion."[23] Here is the common opinion: "All those who have lived or live today among those Indians believe that they are timid and fearful, ceremonious, intelligent, liars, and inclined to idolatry, all these being Jewish traits."[24] Naturally, in the last sentence the cleric comes to the support of popular opinion to confirm the common idolatrous tendency of Jews and Indians; the Mexicans adored several serpents, the Xiuhcoatl and the Quetzalcóatl, especially, with which I shall presently deal at length.

A text of this kind, weak as concerns its "proofs," nevertheless shows us how in the moment of formation of Mexican creole society the antisemitic sentiments of the "Old Christian" society of the Peninsula were transferred to the Indians, to their detriment. The scriptural foundation of this attitude was thus partly responsible for the system of *castas* which none dreamed of questioning before the nineteenth century, and which constituted an adaptation to American creole society of the principle of "purity of blood," dominant in Spain at the time of the American conquests. Similarly, we see in the third chapter of the same book of Gregorio García how the Aztec tradition of ancient migrations reinforced Spanish-creole prejudices and corroborated the Old Testament: "Who can deny that this departure and this tribulation of the Mexicans resembles the flight into Egypt?"[25]

The Apostolic Evangelization and the Foreknowledge of God

In conjunction with the preceding question (that of the origin of the Indians) there appeared the problem of the evangelization of the Indians by the Apostles. It is noteworthy that the Dominican Gregorio García, whose study on the origin of the Indians I have just cited, considered that an examination of the hypotheses relative to apostolic evangelization was a complementary question. This theologian wrote: "But there are three points in particular which have interested me more than others. The first is: which kings have governed this realm, what wars have they waged, and who were their successors until the coming of the Spaniards. The second point is the question of whence came the first inhabitants of this land and other regions of the Indies. The third point is the question whether the Gospel has been preached in these countries in the time of the Apostles. I formed the project of writing three books joined into one volume about all this."[26] The very idea of joining the three works in a single volume cannot be due to chance and emphasizes the unity of the three subjects in the mind of the author. Indeed, it is perfectly clear that no historian of the Indies in the sixteenth and seventeenth centuries attempted to evade any of these questions: the political history of the pre-Columbian period (*poliza y modo de gobierno*), the biblical connection, beginning with the patriarchs (*origen de los indios*), the evangelization by the apostles or in the time of the apostles (*viviendo los Apóstoles*). The Indian past had to flow from the nature of the Indians and from the destiny which God had reserved for them in this world and the next. The evidence of a political life and of remarkable architectural and artistic achievements led quite naturally to comparison with the most developed peoples of pagan antiquity of the Mediterranean basin, such as the Phoenicians and the Carthaginians. But the practice of human sacrifice and other barbaric customs suggested that the Indians of the New World descended from European barbarians, from the Iberians, for example. This last hypothesis offered some political advantages to the Castilian Crown.

Generally speaking, the contrast between an efficient political and social organization, on the one hand, and the practice of sanguinary rites, on the other, disconcerted the missionaries and the theologians. Men sought explanations for this apparent contradiction. The simplest solution consisted in recalling the example of the Greeks, simultaneously "civilized," having produced intellects like Aristotle, and yet pagans, because God, mysteriously, had decided it should be so. Thus, the Indians could be gentiles like the Greeks and Romans in the time of Saint Paul. But the problem was different, for Jesus had sent his apostles to preach the Gospel throughout the whole world; this could be interpreted as a mission they had to accomplish during their lifetimes. The obstacle of oceanic distance was not real, for (according to Augustine) the apostles could have been transported to the New World on the wings of angels. The question thus became one of interpreting a verse of the Bible literally or allegorically. In the first case the meaning was clear and in the second it must mean that the apostles of Christ, that is, the apostles or their spiritual sons (which could refer to the sixteenth-century Franciscans) must carry everywhere the Word of God. Interpreted literally, the mission entrusted to the apostles implied that one of them at least had evangelized among the Indians about fifteen centuries before the Spaniards. This gave rise to several questions: Who was the Apostle of the Indies? What traces had this pristine evangelization left? How had the Indians deformed the divine message? The first question was simultaneously one of exegesis and archaeology. I must deal with it at length in connection with Quetzalcóatl; consequently here I shall consider the two others. I shall only note here that several native divinities of ancient America have been identified with the apostle Thomas.

To find the apostle was in the last analysis a matter of playing the detective, of scrutinizing the beliefs of the Indians in order to find there the traces of an ancient monotheism or of the Holy Trinity. This search was the work of a lifetime for religious like the Franciscan Juan de Torquemada. There was general agreement, however, that in those cases where images of the Lord or of the Virgin Mary had been claimed to be found, they were found disfigured. The religious practices of the Indians, especially the human sacrifices used by the Aztecs, which the first Franciscans could still witness, led those religious to believe that the Word had never resounded in those regions. "We know for certain that our Lord God by design kept this half of the world hidden until our time, and that by a decree of His divine providence he has deigned to unveil it to the Roman Catholic Church, so that the Indians may receive the Light amid the darkness of the idolatry in which they have lived."[27] We see here one of the expressions of the "policy of rupture," or of *tabula rasa,* practiced by the reformed Franciscans in their missionary work. Sahagún and his companions interpreted Christianity as history; they had come to the Indies to fulfill the Word and thus achieve the prelude to the last days. I need hardly point out that this belief was perfectly consistent with the millenarian expectation discussed above. In the eyes of the Twelve, they themselves were the true apostles of the Indians. In their eyes, everything in the Indian beliefs that had a distant resemblance to the true faith was a devilish parody, invented by the Enemy in order to further lead astray the Indians; thus they regarded the Indians as gentiles of the sixteenth century.

To choose the solution of a prior evangelization of the Indians by one of the apostles, on the other hand, inevitably tended to moderate the millenarian fever of the Franciscans. That solution, however, allowed of a more rational explanation for a fact which was difficult to square with the mysterious designs of the Lord. The Peruvian Augustinian friar Antonio de la Calancha, one of the firmest adherents of the theory of the evangelization of the Indians by an apostle, recalled a verse of the Vulgate: "And this Gospel of the kingdom shall be preached in all the world for a witness unto all nations; and then shall the end come" (Matt. 24). Against the opinion of Origen and in agreement with "scores of holy and grave doctors," Calancha maintained that the *consummation* should be understood to be "not the end of the world, but the destruction of Jerusalem, which took place seventy-two years after the birth of Christ."[28] John Chrysostom and Jerome attested to this, and the universal evangelization had been very rapid, if the Gospel of Mark could be believed: "From the words of the last chapter . . . it is clear that the preaching of the Apostles was universal and that the Gospel of Our Lord was preached in our Western Indies before the destruction of Jerusalem."[29] To suppose that God could have left the Indians without his light during the many centuries that separated the coming of Christ from the dispatch of Spanish missionaries to the New World "violates the natural, divine, and positive laws, and is an insult to the mercy and justice of God."[30] It is clear here that Calancha's intellectual point of departure is the realm of moral theology, whence flows his interpretation of Matthew; in a third and final phase, the search begins for the signs, the material and ritual traces, of the original evangelization.

If the Gospel had been preached to the Indians in apostolic times, it became easy to explain by its light those aspects of Indian culture which the missionaries regarded with favor, and by the suggestion of the Devil all those which appeared perverse. On the other hand, the role of the missionaries sent in the sixteenth century by the Spanish monarchs could thereby suffer a considerable diminution, at least from the eschatological perspective, which was that of the Friars Minor. Accordingly, at the same time as they put off indefinitely the coming of the millennium, the partisans of the apostolic evangelization of the Indies figured out another means of saving the providential mission of the new apostles of the Indies. Among the prophecies attributed to the pseudo-Saint Thomas of America, was one of the coming of a second wave of evangelizers; the vagueness of the description permitted them to be identified now as Dominicans, now as

Augustinians, now as Jesuits. Thus we find that Francisco de Vera, expressing his opinion (*parecer*) as censor on the very official and classic *Historia de la Compañía de Jesús de la Nueva España* of Francisco de Florencia, did not hesitate to offer a daring interpretation of Joshua; let the reader judge for himself: "Wherein it appears clearly indicated that the holy duke Saint Francis Borgia, the Joshua of our Company of Jesus . . . delivered the land of the New World to the Caleb who explored and conquered it. *Hebron,* as appears from a reading of Saint Jerome and from the interpretation of the Hebrews which are at the end of the Bible, signifies *society,* the Company; in other words: he entrusted the Indies to the care of the first provincial, Father and Doctor Pedro Sánchez, rector of Alcalá, a new Caleb."[31]

This must not be regarded as merely a rhetoical game; rather is it another example of the tendency (already observed in Joachim of Floris and still widespread in the seventeenth century among the religious) to decipher Scripture, to find signs everywhere, to establish correspondences between the historical ages. For the early chroniclers and historians of the New World biblical analogies are not stylistic ornaments or scholarly reminiscences; they express a feeling of reliving antique exploits or moments of the history of Israel. Prophecies are invoked, and Father Florencia proclaims that "the entrance of the Society of Jesus into India was prophesied at Mylapore by the apostle Saint Thomas; it was he, also, according to the sign which he gave thereof, who prophesied the entrance of the apostolic sons of the Company into Paraguay."[32] In this way a connecting bridge was laid between the apostolic evangelization and the new evangelization by the Jesuits.

In this great debate, nourished with borrowings from the Prophets and the Gospels, in which Fathers of the church were sometimes cited against each other according to the needs of the case, the Jesuits firmly dissented from the Franciscans on one essential point. Whereas for the Franciscans the Indians had been deprived of grace and kept in darkness for long centuries in order to be at last enlightened on a day chosen by the Lord, the Jesuit theologians had a different understanding of the matter. In the view of the majority of these theologians, an invincible ignorance of God was impossible or very rare; this optimistic belief was perfectly consistent with the notion that Indian idolatrous beliefs were, so to speak, "teething rings" of the true faith. This is the exact opposite of the Franciscan doctrine of the *tabula rasa.* We note that the Jesuits entered the missionary field later than the others; it would be interesting to attempt to explain the genesis of this drastic shift in missionary doctrine, coming after the first great American missionary efforts.

If there is not invincible ignorance of God among the gentiles (and particularly among the Indians of the New World), resort to an original apostolic evangelization becomes unnecessary, for grace has already revealed itself; it is innate. Such, at least, could be the conclusion drawn from a broad interpretation of verses 18 to 23 of the Epistle to the Romans. On this last point the leading theologians of the Society of Jesus were divided; some believed that no philosopher could have an invincible ignorance of God; others thought that Paul's words applied also to the common people. Father Pedro de Achútegui has called attention to a remarkable example of evolution in the case of Suárez, whose thought on the subject, more particularly under the influence of José de Acosta and his American missionary experience, seems to have wavered. According to Father Achútegui, Suárez affirms on the one hand that many were ignorant of God, and on the other that the more normal case (*frequentius*) was knowledge of God without the aid of evangelization. This wavering on the part of one of the greatest Jesuit theologians (referring here expressly to the Brazilian Indians) suggests the oscillations in the spiritual status of the Indian (with corresponding fluctuations in his social and juridicial status) in the Spanish Empire in America.

The passionate stands assumed by a Las Casas or a Sepúlveda, and the more moderate posture of Vitoria, are also inseparable from the replies made to the questions that I have briefly set forth—questions whose solutions were sought in biblical exegesis (source of all orthodox truth) rather than in missionary experience or in observation of Indians. In the controversies relating to the nature, origin, history, and evangelization of the Indies, divergent interpretations of Scripture, that is, different philosophies, confronted each other. At stake, in the time of Charles V, was the destiny of Christendom, and more immediately the welfare of the Roman church and that of the Spanish monarchy, united under one head with the Holy Roman Empire. In this debate the Indian only played the role of object, a sign of conflict, an intruder who had not been foreseen in the organon of Judeo-Hellenic knowledge. A source of embarrassment by virtue of the intellectual problems which he posed, the Indian was nevertheless a precious prize for the fishers of souls, who vied with each other in show of zeal and disputed his eternal welfare. In the temporal order, the missionaries struggled with little success to protect their Indian converts against slave-hunters and colonists, and even against parish priests.

To what degree did theological and exegetic reflection influence the daily practice of the missionaries? It is difficult to measure. Father Achútegui writes: "The fact that the majority of our theologians were partisans of the impossibility of invincible ignorance of God is due principally to their sincere adherence to the doctrine of Saint Thomas Aquinas. But the fact that thirteen out of nineteen of them did not hesitate to concede at least a limited possibility of invincible ignorance, is due, I believe, to the attention they paid to missionary experience."[33] It is certain, in any case, that the legislation of the Indies was strongly influenced by the reports of religious to their superiors. The image of the Indian, his anthropological status, depended on the participation of the inhabitants of the New World in revelation and their role in the completion of Christendom; they were defined accordingly. The divergences of jurists in these matters were based on exegetic disputes. The place finally assigned to the Indian in the Old World, so abruptly enlarged to its present limits, was a product of the religious disquiet of the European sixteenth century. It was the need to resolve theological problems that sometimes led religious thinkers of this period to assign to the Indian (and sometimes to his origin, past, and beliefs) a spiritual worth which, despite all the evils, guaranteed his survival in the colonial society of the Indies over three centuries.

The work of Juan Solórzano Pereira, *Política indiana,* which may be regarded as the official synthesis of the most authoritative views on the Indies in the first quarter of the seventeenth century, reflects all the aspects which I have just discussed. A part of the first book of this treatise on colonial law and administration is devoted to the problem of the origin of the Indians (chap. 5), and to the prophecies of the discovery of the New World and to the possibility of an apostolic evangelization of the Indians (chap. 6). The positions taken on these issues by Solórzano Pereira (who was both a member of the Council of Castile and the Council of the Indies), reveal the political importance of these metaphysical problems. The councilor expresses surprise that great contemporary minds could entertain a belief in the Judaic origin of the Indians: "It is astounding to see such great minds take for certain what is so doubtful." He maintained on the contrary that most of the Indians had their origin in Eastern India, as was claimed by Arias Montano. He expressed the same surprise at the belief that the Jews of the twelve tribes "are today in the same captivity as before, and will remain there till the end of the world."[34]

We shall encounter again, at a bend in the road taken by the American creole consciousness, this debate inspired by the infiltration of Judaic messianism into Christian thought. As concerns the will of providence, Solórzano breaks out with a provoking assurance: "I have said, and I repeat, that this preaching and this conversion of the Indians were reserved for our time, for our sovereigns, for their ministers, and for their vassals. . . . Before our entry, the holy Gospel had not penetrated the New World."[35] From these certainties he easily deduced a Castilian policy for the Indies. "Let us march full of courage and with an assured step in this enterprise of conversion, for we see that God announced and reserved it for us, and we should let the Indians know this."[36] Here the eminent right of the Spaniards to America appears not as a result of the Alexandrine bulls but as a divine grace, a grace which promises the approach of salvation for all mankind through the instrumentality of the *Reyes Católicos*, rightly so named, for their empire was universal. The Spaniards, writes Solórzano, "as saviors and announcers of the Gospel will become masters of the cities of the West, which are those of the New World . . . , and thus, once the Gospel has been preached throughout the earth, the Day of Judgment will come, God having placed his throne on the mountains and being surrounded by the saviors."[37]

Here the Spaniards clearly appear as the new chosen people, according to the New Covenant; we will presently see Mexican creoles of the eighteenth century annexing this prophetic certitude and applying it to their own national advantage. What importance should be assigned to the political ambitions of the Castilian Crown, and especially of the Emperor Charles V, in the solutions imposed upon the spiritual and anthropological problems described above? What part did political calculation, religious faith, and eschatological concerns play in the thinking of the emperor and his spokesmen? My only intention has been to show the interplay between exegesis, science, theology, law, and politics. In other words, none of the problems raised by the discovery of the American Indian and formulated in spiritual terms was gratuitous. One of the guiding threads that helps us see the connections between missionary policy, the laws of the Indies, and colonial exploitation—a thread that also illuminates the contemporary historiography—is the anxious expectation of the last days. In this climate the Indian appeared primarily as a spiritual question. He was soon to appear as an element in the answer—known, according to the Dominican Maluenda, one of the great authorities of the time, only to "God the Father Himself"—to the most decisive question of all; that question was the date and the hour of the coming of the Messiah in glory to deliver the world and install the millennial Kingdom. In the precise measure that this question once again came to be regarded as meaningful and the last days imminent, the terms in which American questions were formulated in the first half of the sixteenth century regained their relevance at the end of the Mexican colonial era in the nineteenth century.

5

The Creole Utopia
of the "Indian Spring"
1604–1700

The "Grandeur of Mexico"
According to Bernardo de Balbuena (1562[?]–1627)

The year 1604 is a beacon for the historian who wishes to find his way in that long Mexican seventeenth century during which, the nineteenth century believed, nothing had happened. From this obscurity only ephemeral profiles, cardboard arches of triumph, and catafalques erected on the occasion of the arrival of a viceroy or the death of a prince seem to emerge. In reality, it was thanks to a long period of peace (at least in the capital and the large towns of New Spain) that the values and beliefs around which the Mexican nation was to rally in the nineteenth century, when the hour of Independence struck, assumed consistent form. Such aspirations were still remote at the beginning of the seventeenth century, when the Mexican creoles, having dissipated the odors of the bivouac and replaced the Aztec ruins with palaces of Renaissance style, luxuriated in the refined pleasures of those postwar years. Such, at least, is the tableau of the "Grandeur of Mexico" that the poet Bernardo de Balbuena, born in the Peninsula but spiritually a creole beyond the shadow of a doubt, offers us. Written two years earlier, the book was published in Mexico City in 1604. The event coincided with the passing of a Franciscan religious, Fray Jerónimo de Mendieta, who had been a champion of the millenarian utopia and had died without having been able to publish his lifework, the *Historia eclesiástica indiana*.[1] He was the last survivor of the pioneers of evangelization (although he had come after the Twelve); with him disappeared one of the great founders of a militant, evangelical New Spain. I have already noted the change, if not an immediate drastic shift of direction, which the arrival of the first Jesuits, followed by that of Archbishop Moya de Contreras, signified in this respect. But by 1604 that revision of missionary policy also belonged to the past. After the wounds of the great epidemic (*matlatzauatl*) of the years 1576 to 1579 had been healed, Mexico City blossomed amid fiestas whose luxury reflected the burgeoning wealth

51

of the silver mines, a luxury displayed without restraint by the horse-
men (the image of the *charro* dates from this period) to whom Bernardo de Balbuena devotes almost a hundred verses in octaves:

> Spirited brave horses frisky and proud;
> Houses with haughty facades in sumptuous streets;
> A thousand riders, light of hand and foot;
> Sporting rich harnesses and costly liveries,
> Embroidered with pearls, with gold, and precious stones,
> Are common sights in our city's squares.[2]

The compact description evokes a society whose tastes and aspirations had nothing in common with the militant asceticism of a
Motolinia or his ideal of charity. A generation without wars or
epidemics, the prosperity of the mines, and the urban development
had mightily contributed to this revolution in manners, which deserves a more careful examination.

In this new Florence (some would call it Venice on account of its
canals), literary culture did not lag behind, if one may believe the
descriptions of Bernardo de Balbuena in his *Grandeza Mexicana* and in
the *Siglo de Oro en las selvas de Erífile*, two titles that suggest the author's
enthusiastic mood. One could say of Balbuena that he was "the anti-
Guevara," imitating the author of *Menosprecio de Corte y alabanza de
aldea* in reverse, for his poetic letter "describing the famous city of
Mexico and its splendors" is a eulogy of the city. Yet the *Siglo de oro en
las selvas de Erífile* is a pastoral in the purest tradition of the Italian
Renaissance. The *Grandeza Mexicana* itself, a work sometimes ponder-
ous with classical allusions, reaches its pinnacle in chapter 6, entirely
devoted to singing the praises of nature:

> Here one hears a pheasant, there a nightingale
> snared in the foliage of an alder tree,
> Bathes the tremulous air with its sweet sounds.[3]

One might think he is listening to Garcilaso. It may be more fitting,
however, to speak of Lope de Vega, who also loved a city, Madrid,
whose praises he preferred to sing in preference to all gardens. There
is no contradiction, therefore, between imitation of the pastoral in
Mexico in the manner of Montemayor and love for a city whose
charm consisted in its walks (*paseos*), notably *la Alameda* (which still
exists), the *paseo de Jamaica*, which the Neapolitan traveler Gemelli
Carreri described at the end of the century, and the flowery suburbs,
which we dare not call Mexican *cigarrales*—the name given to the
gardens of Toledo. Yet those flowery floating gardens (*chinampas*) of
Xochimilco were as evocative of the Toledo of Tirso de Molina as of
the Madrid of Lope de Vega.

Thus was Spain reborn in New Spain, although the latter had been established as a utopian Spain which would break with the vices of the old Spain. The Franciscan missionaries had represented an evangelical current, a true spiritual dissident movement which emerged after the liquidation of Erasmianism. The great number of convents in Mexico City does not prove that it was dominated by a monastic spirit. The spiritual distance between the religious who lived in the urban convents of Mexico City during the first years of the seventeenth century and their predecessors in the monasteries of Actopan, Tzintzuntzan, or even of Santiago Tlatelolco, was very great. The human environment was totally different, and these convents were wide open to the outer world. Sor Juana Inés de la Cruz (half a century later) found it necessary to impose a limit on visits because Mexican conventual life was cluttered with parties, concerts, and the like. Humanistic culture, with its train of references to Hellenic polytheism, was a field cultivated, indeed almost exclusively, by ecclesiastics (regular as well as secular clergy).

Bernardo de Balbuena is a notable example of the confusion between the lay and the ecclesiastical state in Mexico. His case recalls the similar cases of Lope de Vega and Tirso de Molina (the former especially) in contemporary Spain. Balbuena addressed his great lyric poem, the *Grandeza Mexicana*, as an "epistle" (*carta*) to a lady of illustrious family, Doña Isabel de Tovar y Guzmán. The history of love affairs sometimes illuminates history, especially when we seek to re-create the atmosphere of an epoch. When he wrote the *Grandeza Mexicana*, Balbuena was just forty years old. A student of theology, he had already won some poetic competitions in Mexico City; ordained, then provided with a prebend, chaplain of the Audiencia of Guadalajara, he seems not to have spent much time in Nueva Galicia, preferring the charms of the capital. It was in a remote town of his administrative province, Culiacan, however, that he made the acquaintance of the addressee of the "Letter Concerning the Splendors of Mexico City." It is certain that Balbuena loved Isabel de Tovar with a very human love; lovers of poetry must rejoice that Isabela's entry into a convent allowed Balbuena to publish the *Grandeza Mexicana*. Its lyricism gives Balbuena away; it was with a woman, not a city, that he was smitten. This did not prevent him from dedicating the poem to the archbishop of Mexico in the hope of obtaining some advantage, which he soon was given, becoming an abbot in Jamaica before being promoted to bishop of Puerto Rico. The profane life and sacerdotal career of Bernardo de Balbuena seem to thumb their noses at the founders of the Mexican church.

Economic prosperity, which caused the eclipse of the evangelical utopia of the mendicant orders, and the advent of a literary renaissance favored by peace, played a more decisive part than the muted repression of the writings of Sahagún, Mendieta, and Durán in transforming the Mexican spiritual climate. The *Grandeza Mexicana* reflects this transformation in all its aspects. The Indian, the central figure in the writings of the first missionaries, is absent from the poem. In Mexico City, in 1602, the Indian was neither a warrior to be feared nor a soul to be saved; he was simply ignored, although his physical presence could not pass unperceived among the mulattoes and mestizos who lived in the capital. The rubble of the great temple of Mexico-Tenochtitlan had served to build an imposing cathedral. A European city had been founded on the ruins of the Aztec capital; it was an entirely new city, in the style of the Italian Renaissance, a sort of Salamanca of the New World. Balbuena's enthusiasm for its architecture is one with his admiration for the city's society, which he found completely worthy of its splendid milieu. The beauty of the women, the wit of the men, the elegant speech of both, inspired in the poet some of his best verses, such as this:

Indies of this world, Heaven on earth[4]

In this work, pervaded with amorous lyricism, the imitation of nature in the tradition of Horace does not fully explain a peculiarly Mexican element of the marvelous, an element which suggests to me one of the first "sallies" (in the Quixotic sense) of the Mexican national consciousness.

When Balbuena entitled chapter 6 of the *Grandeza Mexicana* "Eternal Spring and Its Signs," he explicitly laid the foundations of a new Mexican utopia, called to replace the evangelical utopia of the *Iglesia Indiana*, which had collapsed. The Spanish friars of the preceding century had projected their eschatological hopes upon their Indian flock; the Mexican creoles would now exhume the Edenic myth in order to apply it to their American *patria*. What this involved, to be sure, was not really exhumation but rather a new borrowing from Scripture, not from the apocalyptic texts this time, but from Genesis. Adoption of the Edenic theme could also imply a patriotic rebuff to those who claimed to recognize in the design of the lagoons of Mexico the Beast of the Apocalypse, identified with the ancient Aztec dynasty. Gemelli Carreri, writing in the last years of the seventeenth century, mentions this allegorical hypothesis.

What I have called "the creole utopia of the Indian Spring" found its finished expression in the *Grandeza Mexicana,* written more than half a century before the famous works of Carlos de Sigüenza y Góngora, which marked that utopia's flowering. Reading Balbuena's *Eternal Spring,* one cannot help comparing it with the *Indian Spring,* a "sacred-historical poem" dedicated to the Virgin of Guadalupe and published sixty-four years later by Sigüenza y Góngora. If we reflect on the Spanish literary tradition, on the mysticism of Boscán, on the technique of sacred exegesis applied by Juan de la Cruz to poetry of purely erotic aspect in the tradition of the Song of Songs (translated and glossed at the same period by Luis de León), the differences between the two poems should cause no surprise. Balbuena, a belated continuator of Petrarch, sings the unattainable love of a Laura found in Culiacan; Sigüenza y Góngora (a very different sort of man, incidentally) sees in the winter miracle of the roses of Tepeyac "the powerful arm" of God. Profane poesy in Balbuena, sacred poesy in Sigüenza y Góngora, one may conclude; but the problem does not lend itself to such simple solutions.

By way of Spain of the past century, to which Navagero had brought the vogue of Petrarch and Sannazaro, New Spain (I speak of the educated class) had assimilated a poetic heritage characterized by a constant exchange between amorous lyricism and spiritual poetry, a heritage whose common denominator was its Petrarchian vocabulary and metaphors, borrowed especially from Garcilaso, Montemayor, and Gil Polo. Reading the *Eternal Spring* of Bernardo de Balbuena, J. Rojas Garcidueñas has observed, the modern reader experiences the same impression that he receives on looking at Botticelli's *Primavera*. Indeed, the capital of New Spain in the seventeenth century was the scene of cultural phenomena which recall astoundingly the Florence of the Quattrocento. One might almost think that the Europeans, or rather their creole descendants, having failed to achieve in New Spain their aspirations of a mystical tendency (embodied in Florence by Savonarola, in New Spain by Mendieta) had deliberately chosen an aesthetic derivative.

This explanation, however, overlooks the absence of design in such great collective choices. We must return to a more prosaic level of explanation and reaffirm that peace, following a period of wars and epidemics, was propitious to the rise of a sybaritic climate in Mexico in the last quarter of the sixteenth century. The wait for the last days, maintained for half a century, could not be prolonged indefinitely. This tension sought release; and as the promise of the Kingdom receded to an ever more indefinite future the attitude of expectancy inevitably wore off. The Italian Renaissance was in its beginning a double current: a renovation of evangelical spirituality on the one hand, a resurgence of the ancient culture, Greek and Latin, on the other. In view of the epic climate of the initial Mexican decades and the transcendent role of conversion, it was the first aspect of the Renaissance that first manifested itself in New Spain. Savonarola, mediated by Cortés and his Franciscan inspirers; Erasmus, mediated by the first bishop of Mexico, Zumárraga; later Thomas More, interpreted by Vasco de Quiroga, gave to the Renaissance in New Spain its original aspect. The other aspect, the imitation of the Ancients, which required stability and tradition, took three-quarters of a century to establish itself. The Latin *Dialogues* of a professor of rhetoric, Cervantes de Salazar, published in 1554, represent a first faltering effort to create Platonic dialogue on the plateau of Anahuac. It would be interesting to know exactly when the first copy of the *Cortigiano* reached Mexico, if it was not preceded there by the *Dialoghi d'Amore* of Leon Hebreo in the translation of an illustrious son of creole culture, the Inca Garcilaso de la Vega. In New Spain, the renaissance of classic culture makes its first appearance in the work of Bernardo de Balbuena. Even that work gives only a pastoral and mythological reflection of the classic heritage assimilated through the medium of Italian literature and its prolongations in the Iberian peninsula.

The works of Leon Hebreo and Balthazar Castiglione probably became known in Mexico in the first decade of the seventeenth century. The question of when the *Dialoghi d'Amore* and the *Cortigiano* first appeared in the Mexican book trade or at least in some private libraries is not an idle question; the spirit of New Spain certainly changed together with its reading tastes. At that period the printed word was surrounded with a prestige and an authority comparable to those of Holy Scripture itself (that is why Cervantes attacked the romances of chivalry). Throughout the colonial era of Mexican history, Scripture and the various catechisms remained the very basis of culture, oral and written, the permanent frame of reference which shed an ultimate light on the past, the present, and the individual and collective future. On the other hand, belles lettres—the books one read for pleasure—underwent important changes in the course of successive generations. Thanks to Irving Leonard's splendid study of *The Books of the Brave,* we know about the atmosphere of fantasy in which the expeditions of an Orellana in quest of the Amazons or that of Ponce de León in search of the Fountain of Youth could be undertaken. Enrique de Gandía has catalogued all those fascinating myths of the Conquest. It is safe to say that from the time of the very first discoveries in the New World, the pagan sense of the marvelous, a heritage of classic antiquity, was present. Irving Leonard's statistical inventories, however, reveal a massive domination of reading tastes by romances of chivalry. The chronicler of the conquest of Mexico, Bernal Díaz del Castillo, related in his old age how the first vision of Tenochtitlan appeared to Cortés' comrades like the "enchanted palaces of the book of Amadis."

The medieval literature of the marvelous, which had haunted the dreams of the first discoverers, was rapidly succeeded by a Christian literature of the marvelous, a product of the millenarian fever which inspired the revival of the missionary enterprise. We note a systematic distrust of reports of miracles on the part of the first mendicant chroniclers. However, prodigious events which were regarded as confirming the saintliness of certain religious (tongues of fire, rains of blood, and the like) were readily accepted. The most incredulous friars with regard to miracles and prodigies undoubtedly were the Franciscans. The Augustinians, on the contrary, seem to have contributed from the very beginnings of the missionary movement to the diffusion of pious traditions. With the arrival of the first Jesuits in Mexico, in 1572, a new mentality arose that was quite favorable to assimilations—sometimes quite daring—of local polytheistic beliefs with Scriptural traditions. The Jesuits also introduced into their colleges profane Latin authors: Ovid, Horace, Virgil, who served as vehicles of the ancient mythology. Thus the marvelous elements found in 1604 in a book as secular as the *Grandeza Mexicana* of Balbuena, were not particularly novel. Men knew whence they came; only after the passage of sixty years would their ultimate drift become clear. A purely aesthetic commentary on the *Eternal Spring* (chap. 6 of the *Grandeza Mexicana*) would leave us in the dark about its essential content.

Bernardo de Balbuena, having wreathed vernal garlands about several figures of Hellenic mythology in the first octave, went on to evoke Mexico City in these terms:

> Although in general the world be such,
> In this Mexican paradise it is,
> That verdure has placed its seat and court.[5]

The notion of a "Mexican paradise," appearing here for the first time since its mention in the *Apologética historia* of Las Casas, directly prefigures the *Paraíso Occidental* of Sigüenza y Góngora. The idea that "verdure" has placed here "its seat and court" acquires special force in the light of the verses that directly follow:

> Here, Señora, Heaven with His own hand,
> It seems, has chosen hanging gardens,
> Whose gardener He Himself wished to be.[6]

God himself, who "wished to be the gardener" of this new Eden— an Eden which diminished the luster of that Vale of Tempe vaunted by the ancients—spread April flowers in profusion over Anahuac:

> Here are a thousand beauties and advantages,
> All these the sovereign hand dispensed,
> Here is His seat, and these His fallow fields,
> And this is the eternal Mexican spring.[7]

The eternal Mexican spring, which found in Balbuena's work its first poetic expression, already appears there with its transcendent correlatives: the identification of Anahuac with the terrestrial Paradise and the election of Anahuac as the divine abode. Literary historians could doubtless find the ancient or peninsular literary sources of these images, but I see more here than elegant stylistic figures. Even today one need only look about him to confirm the floral luxuriance of the valley of Mexico and the admirable ornamental use that the Indians (or their mestizo descendants) make of the flowers. The theme of the flowery spring in Balbuena is a faithful rendering of Mexican reality. The halo of the marvelous which rings the description in the *Grandeza Mexicana* directly prepares the way for the transmutation "into the divine" which the inspired pen of the "first evangelist" of Guadalupe was to accomplish in 1648. Balbuena, unknown to himself, to be sure, had created the marvelous universe needed for the prodigious appearance of the Virgin of Guadalupe. To complete the plenitude of this Edenic landscape the seal of the miracle was required, the *sign* which should confirm the divine election of the valley of Mexico; Guadalupe, the ancient mother-goddess of the Indians (herself transmuted into "Our Lady" was to be that sign.

Of course, the alliance of the divine (or divinized) woman and the city was not new; coming after Virgil and Joachim du Bellay, who sang:

> La bérécynthienne couronnée de tours,

Balbuena could present Mexico City as an offering to his "lady" without any poetic license. If we consider the matter more closely, however, we perceive the intimate bond linking Mexico City and its women in the sensibility of the poet:

> The least part of their being is their beauty,
> A beauty which Venus might well envy.[8]

I should really cite the whole passage, but will only quote these additional verses:

> As many roses has April, as many stars the sky,
> Cyprus, white lilies, and summer, flowers,
> So many lovely women are born and admired here.[9]

Let me pass quickly over the grace of the first octave, altogether reminiscent of Lope de Vega, noting only that the roses from which Guadalupe will be created and the stars of her mantle are already related here to the women of Mexico City. Doubtless the poetic arrangement of these notions is different, but only the spark of the "miracle," which transmutes everything, will be needed to transform the Mexican beauty from a rival of Venus into the new Eve, Mary. Balbuena was the first Mexican writer to associate exaltation of Mexico City with adoration of the Mexican woman when he wrote, after the manner of the Spaniard Sánchez de Badajoz: "It is a new Rome in its courtly manners and shapely figure."[10] After an enumeration which recalls that India produced ivory, Peru silver, and Japan silk, he concludes:

> Mexico produces beauties rare,
> And brilliant minds of soaring flight
> By reason of the stars or by some virtue divine.
> In fine, if beauty is a part of heaven,
> Then Mexico is the heaven of this world,
> For here grows the greatest beauty that the world has seen.[11]

These four last distichs reveal the influence of the neo-Platonic ideal (probably transmitted through the poets of the Quattrocento) on Balbuena, but a new aspect, destined to play a great role in the Mexican creole mentality, is the "divine virtue" dispensed to Mexico by its grace of beauty, and the hyperbolic description "heaven of the world" applied to Mexico City. However, it is still a profane grace that is accorded to Mexico in Balbuena's poem, which we leave regretfully:

> Here, amid winding limpid streams,
> The spring her treasures does enjoy,
> Her beauty time can never efface,
> Around her skirts all pleasures sport,
> And in the watery currents clear,
> That are her mirrors, she renews her youth.
>
> . . . .
>
> And this is the Mexican spring.[12]

A Mexican Petrarch,
Don Carlos de Sigüenza y Góngora (1645–1700)

The century which had opened with the gallant pastorals of Bernardo de Balbuena revealed its true face during its last four decades.

Two personalities dominate this period: Carlos de Sigüenza y Góngora, professor of mathematics at the University of Mexico, and a Jeronymite nun, Sor Juana Inés de la Cruz. Don Carlos de Sigüenza is linked more directly than Sor Juana to the questions I pose. His universal curiosity has led his biographer, Irving Leonard, to compare him with Petrarch, with whom he shared the distinction of never having offended orthodoxy. This circumstance, occurring at the end of the seventeenth century, a century which saw a crisis of European culture, may seem to confirm the traditional judgment which portrays the colonial culture of New Spain as "provincial." No doubt geographical remoteness caused a certain lag in the evolution of thought in Mexico.

However, we must revise the common nineteenth-century view that the ban on European books, and the activity of the Inquisition, had literally asphyxiated Hispanic America. Oppressive regulations certainly existed, but the thesis that those rules were rigorously applied is no longer tenable. We should note, to begin with, the dispensations and exemptions enjoyed by certain individuals by reason of their official or religious capacities, specifically by the friars, the ideological guides of that society. Incidentally, when I speak of society, the expression has a very restricted meaning. The lovely ladies and brilliant intellects of whom Balbuena brags came from some tens of noble families and those of their members who had chosen the church or university teaching (the two were generally the same) for their careers. Within this society there gradually took form a Mexican national consciousness whose components, it seems, Sigüenza y Góngora first brought together in his writings.

Nephew on his mother's side of the great Andalusian poet Góngora, through his father he was connected to a family of officials and great servants of the monarchy; his father himself had been tutor of the prince Balthazar Carlos. Sigüenza y Góngora entered the Society of Jesus and took his first vows, at Tepotzlan, at the age of seventeen; perhaps because of uncertainty about his vocation he was "dismissed" (*despedido,* or *expeditus*) at the end of seven years, for reasons that remain obscure. But his unsuccessful efforts in 1668 to be readmitted to the Society suggest, at least, that his thought, however original, did not deviate too far from the Jesuit mentality, which then dominated New Spain.

The Jesuits did not achieve their supremacy immediately; indeed, their beginnings were very modest. But I cannot agree with Wigberto Jiménez Moreno when he writes that the spirit of the mendicant orders dominated New Spain until 1624. The Mexican scholar rightly draws attention to the appearance at that date of an architecture of

Herreresque style, on the initiative of Bishop Palafox; therein he sees the sign of the triumph of secular-minded bishops. It is a revealing indication, to be sure, but not conclusive testimony, and I prefer to follow Jiménez Moreno when he calls attention to the role of Bishop Montúfar in the first Mexican council of 1555. For the rest, we know that the last quarter of the sixteenth century saw the appearance, in large part under Jesuit inspiration, of aspects of cultural revival hitherto unknown in New Spain. The Latin *Dialogues* of Francisco Cervantes de Salazar already testify to imitation, on a fairly school-boyish level, to be sure, of the Ancients. A more important happening in the intellectual history of the first half of the seventeenth century in New Spain, from the point of view that concerns us here, is the flowering in Mexican sensibility and literary expression of the "American marvelous." We saw its dual origin, an antique paganism inherited from the Italian Renaissance, on the one hand, and the physical reality of the valley of Mexico, on the other, in Balbuena's *Grandeza Mexicana*.

The other aspect of the creole sense of the marvelous—an aspect which was to flower in the course of the second half of the century—was as ambiguous as the preceding one; it resulted from the confluence of the Christian sense of the marvelous with ancient Indian beliefs. Because the mendicant orders had failed to eradicate idolatry, a half-century later Christian images had been substituted for Indian idols at the sites to which Indian pilgrimages were made. Along with these material substitutions there developed syncretic beliefs and pious legends. Jiménez Moreno has called attention to the rise of new centers of pilgrimages and the attachment of the mestizo and creole elements, as well as the Indians, to these cults. The new cults, including that of the Virgin of Guadalupe at Tepeyac, thus took shape in an atmosphere of unanimous hope, an amalgam of creoles, Indians, and the *castas*. The national (or more frequently regional) character of the images generally regarded as miraculous hastened formation of a consciousness of the American *patria chica* ("little fatherland"). On a broad base of popular support, the clergy were to elaborate a new ideology that broke not with the ancient Indian beliefs but with those of the first missionaries. A man who played a key role in this spiritual revolution, which at the time appeared so innocuous from the viewpoint of both political and religious orthodoxy, was Sigüenza y Góngora.

The political-religious messianism of the missionaries had made Spain, represented by the friars, the home of a Chosen People and the Indians an object of spiritual salvation. The wealth and power of the creoles, confirmed by the splendor of a capital which vied with that of

Spain, soon made them regard the spiritual tutelage of the gachupines as intolerable. Every assertion of national dignity on the part of New Spain's creoles implied the need to revise their status of spiritual dependence. Consequently the Spanish historiography of the Indies, founded on the postulate of a providential mission, triumphantly expressed by Solórzano Pereira, had to be attacked. Since Spain's evangelical mission had been justified by reference to the Indian idolatry, it became necessary, in the first place, to cleanse the Indians of the gravest of sins.

The nascent creole culture (which included, in its second phase, a mythology borrowed from Hellenic antiquity) was in all respects, in its values and their means of expression, the result of what today we call "transculturation." The forms of life, the administration, the church, and the faith itself were imported products; the American world, on which creole eyes had just begun to gaze with wonder, was denied. Such a lack of cultural authenticity could not long remain viable, particularly in a country whose fascinating beauty turned a good Castilian in a few years into a creole in spirit. The process of "Mexicanization" (one is tempted to write "re-Mexicanization") of New Spain, thanks to a devout consensus which developed in a syncretic climate of the marvelous, had already won over all the strata of the population when Sigüenza began his studies of ancient Mexico in 1668. That same year he published the *Primavera Indiana. Poema sacro-histórico, idea de María Santíssima de Guadalupe*. The vast output of this polygraph, apparently dispersed, in large part unpublished and today lost, is essentially homogeneous.

With a sure sense of the spiritual problems that underlay the controversies relative to the ancient history of the Mexican Indians, Sigüenza y Góngora concentrated on two great Mexican beliefs, Quetzalcóatl and Guadalupe. Like an augur, Sigüenza scrutinized the throbbing entrails of his injured fatherland, but his vision was not dimmed. When Sigüenza wrote his *Poema sacro-histórico* on the Virgin of Tepeyac, just twenty years had passed since Miguel Sánchez wrote what Francisco de la Maza had felicitously called "the first Gospel of Guadalupe." I have already called attention, in connection with Balbuena, to the phrase "Indian Spring," or more precisely, the "eternal spring" of Anahuac, which Sigüenza y Góngora revived; this phrase, derived from antique pastorals by Balbuena, who was still a prisoner of his literary sources, was to acquire a thoroughly native ring in Sigüenza.

The adjective "Indian" (*indiana*) is rich in implications. We find it in the title of a work by Mendieta which did not see the light until long after the achievement of Mexican independence. Thus its use by

Sigüenza, who knew well the old histories of Mexico, who had anno-tated Torquemada (who borrowed extensively from Mendieta), can-not be explained by simple chance. At this period the name *indio* or, patronizingly *indito* (a name still used in the majority of Mexico's rural areas), was applied to Indians, while the name *Indiano* was reserved (in Spain) for the creole. For these reasons I see in Sigüenza's use of it a resurgence of the early aspirations of a Mendieta. But with Sigüenza the content changes; it is no longer a question of erecting a new church, but of recognizing its existence. Although the second coming was still deferred, the "wait" had been rewarded by the "prodigious" appearance of the Virgin Mary at Tepeyac. The *Primavera Indiana* of Sigüenza y Góngora was none other than the "springtime of the world," anxiously awaited for centuries by millenarians. Thus the broken Joachimite thread of the Franciscan missionaries was secretly reknit. The fact is that the Mexican atmosphere, charged with a spiritual fluid of high tension, called for the coming of Guadalupe. It was Miguel Sánchez who launched the fecund idea of a bond between the image of Tepeyac and the Woman of Revelation, but to Sigüenza y Góngora must be given credit for having grafted the new cult on the living old trunk of millenarianism:

> If among the crags was found the sacred fatherland
> of this prodigy of both worlds
> . . . .
> All of a springtime the lovely image expressed
> on that coarse cloak.[13]

Beneath the Gongoresque inversions surges the Mexican patriotic spring, bathed in a supernatual light which will aureole it long after the coming of Independence. The redemptive design of the Mexican *patria,* redeemed from the darkness of idolatry and made by divine grace the bearer of mankind's hope for salvation, appears in one of the loveliest octaves of the poem:

> I am Mary, of omnipotent God
> the humble Mother, Virgin sovereign,
> A torch whose eternal light
> is the splendid North Star of mankind's hope;
> Let a perfumed altar in a holy temple
> be installed for me in Mexico, once Pluto's
> profane dwelling, whose horrors
> my foot dispels in a storm of flowers.[14]

We still feel the spiritual weight of the phrase "North Star," which the Jesuit Florencia was to use twenty years later in the title of a book which strongly influenced the development of the Mexican cult of Guadalupe: *La estrella del Norte de México, historia de la milagrosa Imagen de María Stma. de Guadelupe*. If the *Primavera indiana* was a creole manifestation of the "springtime of the world," the "North Star," the spiritual pole of Mexican national consciousness in search of itself, was Guadalupe. At the very source of the keywords of the cult of Guadalupe stands Carlos de Sigüenza y Góngora.

The subtitle, *poema sacro-histórico*, may surprise a modern reader; at first glance we perceive only its character of a sacred poem. In the light of what we already know, however, it is clear that it is a historical problem above all with which the poem deals, in the first place because history merges with the history of the salvation of mankind, in whose unfolding the apparition of Tepeyac was a sign of the first importance. More especially, the poet is concerned with the salvation of the Indian and the divine election of his country, which is promised a redemptive historical destiny:

> May the crystalline dwelling place of light
> glorify thee, because with love thou rises,
> O Mexico, to be the preeminent throne
> gilded by the rays of ardent Love.[15]

The history of the Mexican people appears sanctified by the rays of divine love which gild its dwelling place. The Mexican "preeminence" is a notion which is formally due to the pen of Sigüenza y Góngora; it will become one of the dominant ideas of Mexican religious-patriotic faith in the eighteenth century.

We shall have the opportunity to consider in more detail Sigüenza's book, *Fenix del Occidente, San Thomas Apóstol, hallado con el nombre de Quetzalcóatl entre las cenizas de antiguas tradiciones conservadas en piedras, en teomoxtles tultecos y en cantares teochichimecos y mexicanos*. Here I shall only observe that the logical requirement of a project for the redemption of the Mexican people made the figure of Saint Thomas-Quetzalcóatl, already sketched by the Dominican chronicler Diego Durán, as indispensable to Sigüenza y Góngora as the prodigious image of Tepeyac. The latter promised a future of divine election; the former washed from the past the sin of idolatry. That is why Don Carlos de Sigüenza diligently assembled notes on the subject of Quetzalcóatl; he did this not with any Machiavellian design but with the scrupulous care of a scholar and the humility of a Christian—a humility which inspired this exclamation: "May God grant that the hypothetical preaching of Saint Thomas in Mexico really took place." Sigüenza's sincere patriotism did not cloud his critical sense but inspired research projects all of which converged toward exaltation of New Spain's past.

A scholar with a profound knowledge of Mexican history has written: "In 1680, when—on the initiative of Sigüenza y Góngora—there appeared for the first time over the triumphal arches which greeted the arrival of a new viceroy figures drawn from pre-Hispanic history instead of the traditional figures taken from classical mythology, it became clear that the Indian past had conquered the creoles."[16] In effect, it was in connection with preparations for receiving the Conde de Paredes that Don Carlos wrote the *Teatro de virtudes políticas que constituyen a un Príncipe: advertidas en los monarcas antiguos del Mexicano Imperio, con cuyas efigies se hermoseó el arco triunfal que la muy noble, imperial Ciudad de México erigió . . . .*[17] It was nothing less than a revolution to substitute for the traditional and quasi-sacred Greco-Latin mythology the mythology of the Mexican Indians. What was more, Sigüenza offered the Aztec emperors as models to the new viceroy who had just arrived from Spain. Considered in its context, this creole initiative could be regarded as a challenge. After the theoretical jousts in which Erasmus, Ribadeneyra, and Saavedra Fajardo had disputed how to define the virtues of a "Christian prince," the entrance on the scene of uninvited "barbarian princes" of ancient Mexico might well have provoked a viceroy's protests. In the sequel, he did not protest, for the commentary on the triumphal arch, written by Sigüenza y Góngora, was published in Mexico City soon after.

The allegorical audacity of Don Carlos and the viceroy's silence are equally eloquent. If Mexican creoles began to display interest after 1650 in the Indian past, in the exemplary virtues of Aztec rulers, and in the literary dignification of the divinities of ancient Mexico, this was due to several reasons. We are struck, to begin with, by the sudden appearance, together with Don Carlos's work, of what may be called "indigenist sentiment." The Indian, we noted, was remarkably absent, three-quarters of a century earlier, from the *Primavera Mexicana* of Balbuena, that Arcadia transposed almost unchanged from Greece to Mexico. In 1604 the creoles enjoyed a newfound peace; they saw a reflection of their own prosperity in the brilliant advance of their capital city. The Indians had occupied an essential place in the life of New Spain. Now that they were truly conquered, more than decimated, and catechized only in a routine manner, the creoles of Balbuena's time tended to dismiss them from their minds. The Indian who was reborn in 1680 thanks to Don Carlos' pen was not the Indian of Sahagún and Motolinia—a soul to be saved, a man to be taught and feared. Sigüenza's Indian is a dead Indian; we could even say that Don Carlos' work is a certified report of the decease of the Aztec empire. If it was possible to erect effigies of the emperors of Anahuac along the route of the viceroy's procession, it was because these giants no longer inspired fear; they had gone to join those *Moros* who were brought out at the Spanish fiestas of "Moors and Christians." A new era had opened in which the Indian past and the Indian beliefs had lost all their subversive potential in Mexico City; the time was ripe for a process of mythification of the Indian past. In Mexico, it was long believed that Clavijero was the first to compare the Aztec ruler with Roman emperors; in reality he only revived the ideas of Sigüenza y Góngora, whose work he had read carefully. Again we find Sigüenza blazing one of the paths along which Mexican creoles would march toward the goal of spiritual emancipation.

The Conde de Paredes would have had to possess exceptional perspicacity and political sense to discern the true meaning of those cardboard emperors that had been erected for his reception. New Spain was peaceful save for sporadic Indian uprisings; there was absolutely no reason to fear the restoration of an Aztec empire. The viceroy (a newcomer, besides) had no reason to suspect the subversive protential that creole annexation of the Indian past and a literary restoration of the Aztec empire might some day have. Don Carlos himself was a loyal subject, assiduously attendant upon viceroys, and a harmless scholar, besides.

The constancy with which this scholar labored to endow his country with a past worthy of the gift of election that the apparition of the Virgin at Tepeyac had conferred upon it, his efforts as poet and writer to achieve for Mexican mythology the literary dignity of Hellenic mythology, were the very expression of creole society's will to power. Sigüenza's glorification of the conquistador Cortés in *La piedad heróyca de Don Fernando Cortés,* which he wrote a dozen years later, only appears to contradict his eulogy of the Aztec emperors; the book deals with Cortés as founder of the Hospital del Amor de Dios, which gave the author the opportunity to write a history of Mexico City since the conquest. We should not be surprised by such digressions as the following: "and this offers me the opportunity to tell where the image of the sainted Mary of Guadalupe appeared to the illustrious Bishop Don Fray Juan de Zumárraga. May this digression be permitted to a man whose only aim in his writings has been to glorify his country."[18]

Don Carlos openly presents himself as a Mexican patriot. He makes no effort to hide it, for he harbors no hidden thoughts of political separation. On the other hand, like his contemporaries—Miguel Sánchez, Florencia, Siles—he was fully conscious of the rivalry with old Spain on the level of divine grace, and his championing of the preeminence (*solío preeminente*) of Mexico City was deliberate. The process of rooting colonial society in the American soil, landscape, and historico-mythical background accelerated from the moment the Indian ceased to appear as a vital threat to creole society. Intoxicated with its development, that society could indulge with impunity in dreams of victory whose dominant note emerges from a simple enumeration of the titles of Sigüenza's writings: "The Indian Spring," "Glories of Querétaro," "Parthenic Triumph," "Western Paradise," "Heroic Piety," "Trophy of Justice," "Phoenix of the West." All Mexican literature of the second half of the seventeenth century (we shall see this climate continuing well into the eighteenth, until the expulsion of the Jesuits) gives the impression of an interminable thanksgiving, a unanimous hosanna.

The great alchemist who presided over the mythological and historiographic transmutations that produced a new mentality, the mentality of a colonial minority proud of its newfound roots in the Mexican soil, was Don Carlos Sigüenza y Góngora. Thanks to the rise of the cult of Guadalupe, especially, and to those who, like Don Carlos, gave it a literary expression, the Mexican creoles were able to achieve their historical, if not their eternal, salvation. Incapable of establishing a mixture of the races on viable socio-juridical bases, incapable of creating an Indian clergy, they achieved with the help of Sigüenza y Góngora (among others) a spiritual hybridization without which they must have remained a group of exiles in a country which rejected them. Unable to discover or recognize the America which had opened up before them, the creoles had to invent it anew after they had frightfully mutilated it.

In counterpoint, the two faces of Don Carlos' historical work evoke the marvelous milieu and its reverse:

Mexico City: a truly glorious city, which richly merits that the sound of its fame should reach the most remote limits of the universe, not so much for the delightful amenity of its situation, the incomparable beauty of its spacious streets, the wealth and courage of its ancient kings, the number and the gravity of its tribunals, the qualities which Heaven has dispensed to its illustrious children, the privileges which ever since its Christianization have made it the capital and metropolis of America, not on account of all that, but because one might well confound it with the Empyrean.[19]

Along the street where I was came bands of men, jostling each other. The Spaniards had drawn their swords and, seeing the spectacle that held my attention, also stopped; but the blacks, the mulattoes, and all the plebeian rabble yelled: "Death to the Viceroy

and all who would defend him!" And the Indians cried out:
"Death to the Spaniards and the gachupines (the name they give
to those who come from Spain), for they eat our maize!"....
"Come, ladies," said the Indian women to each other in their
language, "let us gladly join this war, for as long as every
last Spaniard is killed it does not matter if we die with confession.
Is not this our land? Then what are the Spaniards doing here?"[20]

And Don Carlos concluded: "I had the feeling I had nothing to gain
by staying there."[21]

These two texts of Sigüenza y Góngora (written only a few years
apart) give us an exact measure of the distance separating the creole
sense of the marvelous from Mexican reality; they afford a glimpse into
the abyss that separated the beribboned Indians perched on the
baroque triumphal arches from the hungry Indians who stoned the
archbishop and the Holy Sacrament before they burned the viceroy's
palace. With a lack of perspicacity that is remarkable in that great intellect, Don Carlos (his case is typical) identified himself totally with the
anti-Indian prejudices of his social milieu, attributed all the trouble to
the effects of pulque (a liquor made from the agave cactus), and
thought that new riots could be effectively prevented by an absolute
prohibition of pulque in New Spain. This learned man, so competent
in reviving the Indians of the past, preferred to turn his eyes from the
Indian of his own times. Perhaps the creole utopia of the "Indian
Spring" was a dreamy flight from the daily spectacle of the "Indian
hell," and the "miraculous roses" of Tepeyac a metamorphosis of that
"bed of roses" which Cuauhtemoc, martyred on the orders of Cortés,
had evoked with a bitter derision.

Sor Juana Inés de La Cruz,
the New Phoenix of Mexico (1648–95)

The unreal light of Botticelli again comes to mind when we think of
Sor Juana. The diaphanous light of the "Indian Spring" rendered
beings of flesh and blood evanescent in those closing years of the
seventeenth century, and the reverend Mother Juana Inés de la Cruz
did not escape this process of "spontaneous dematerialization." This
young woman, unquestionably a genius, became a myth (today we
would say a "sacred monster") to her countrymen in her own lifetime.
The name of "phoenix" which men gave her links her to her predecessor, the Spanish poet Lope de Vega, called the "Phoenix of intellects," but we perceive immediately that the two examples are not
reducible to each other. Juana de Asbaje, born in the valley of Mexico,
having spent her adolescent years in the entourage of the viceroy, the
Marqués de Mancera, was the Phoenix of America, and therefore
above all one more flower in the crown of the triumphant creole. We

recall the enthusiastic eulogy that Bernardo de Balbuena had made at the beginning of the century of the intellect of Mexican women; thus Sor Juana was foreseen, expected. What was more, she appeared to dazzle the court and the university, and her glory quickly spread to Europe. If Guadalupe, the miraculous Virgin of Tepeyac, was Mexican, Sor Juana was reciprocally divine, or almost divinized by the idolatrous admiration of her Mexican contemporaries. Between the "Phoenix of the West," Saint Thomas-Quetzalcóatl, whom Sigüenza y Góngora tried to refloat, and the "Phoenix of America," or "of Mexico," as Sor Juana was described, the difference is slight.

The collective verbal debauch to which the *arte de ingenio* tended, a debauch to which the Mexican creoles gave themselves up in those last decades of the seventeenth century, erased the boundaries between dream and reality. It is tempting to find confirmation of this assertion in the fact that what is perhaps Sor Juana's most original work, the only one which was not done to order and whose richness has frustrated all efforts at interpretation, was precisely a "dream." Now the *Sueño*, which belongs to the Alexandrine tradition, also constitutes an effort, new at that period, to elucidate dream life. In the poem it is only a step from the dream of sleep to the waking reverie. In neither case, however, is there any suggestion of the collective creole dream, projecting toward the empyrean the exalted image of their *patria*. In this erudite work (a *silva* in form), inspired stylistically by Góngora, the divinities of classical antiquity are present everywhere; a reader might think that he has returned to the times of Bernardo de Balbuena, to that renaissance of antique paganism whose presence in the *Grandeza Mexicana* I have noted. The absence, justly remarked by Robert Ricard in his commentary on the *Sueño*, of references to God, the saints, and the church fathers, corresponds to the excess of Greco-Latin mythology. Of Mexican mythology, which Sigüenza had just elevated to a position of honor, there is no trace.

Perhaps as a result of these observations, a literary historian whose vision has also been clouded by what must appear to a modern reader as a mere academic exercise (the imitation of the ancients and the borrowing from their mythology), has claimed that Sor Juana was above all a poetess of the Spanish Golden Age and that Mexico left no trace in her work or in her sensibility. The reality is very different. Otherwise it would be very difficult to explain the devotion that her countrymen felt for Sor Juana, a devotion to which she herself refers in her sprightly way:

> I was the object of worship
> of all my country.
> . . . .
> The popular superstition

> reached such a pitch
> that they adored as a goddess
> the idol they had made with their own hands.[22]

It was not modesty alone that dictated the last two lines; the "Phoenix of Mexico" (alone among the Mexican writers of her time, to my knowledge) grasped the "mythopoetic" tendency of the Mexicans, whether creoles, mestizos, or Indians. From the adoration (erotic rather than Petrarchan) of the creole woman as expressed by Bernardo de Balbuena to the divinization of Juana de Asbaje, then to the cult of the prodigious image of an Indian Virgin, there is a long process of sacred transmutation, a progressive sublimation of the Mexican *patria* incarnated in a Mexican woman. From this point of view, Sor Juana was a sort of relay; a woman of genius reputed superhuman, I see her as a human replica of the image of Tepeyac; like the latter she was the object of an enthusiastic Mexican cult, and her renown leaped over frontiers, achieving a reconquest of Spain by New Spain, a magic revenge of the creole consciousness upon the tutelary nation. A posthumous homage, published in Madrid in 1714 through the efforts of Dr. Castorena y Ursúa, consecrated the creole success and involuntarily recalled in its title the intimate bond linking the two glories of New Spain, two tutelary women, in the public consciousness: *The Fame and Posthumous Works of the Phoenix of Mexico, the Tenth Muse, the American Poetess, Sor Juana Inés de la Cruz, a Professed Nun of the Convent of Saint Jerome of the Imperial City of Mexico. . . . Dedicated to the Sovereign Empress of Heaven and Earth, Mary Our Lady.* Although the Virgin mentioned here is not expressly the one of Guadalupe, it suffices to refer to the literature of the Guadalupe cult to satisfy oneself that she is most often described as "empress" and "queen" of the Mexicans. In the title given above, Empress Mary is clearly correlated with the "imperial city," Mexico City; we behold here a Mexican imperialism, an imperialism which can be described as "magical" or simply "spiritual" but which cannot be ignored without depriving Mexican independence of one of its essential driving forces. In the degree that her person, and later her memory, became the object of Mexican national pride, with its creative implications of tutelary myths, Sor Juana Inés de la Cruz was fully Mexican. As I have shown, she was also conscious of this fact.

In an occasional work dedicated to *Doña María de Guadalupe Alencastre, la única maravilla de nuestros siglos,* the great poetess expressed in six sprightly quatrains a vision of her country that could have been borrowed from the *Grandeza Mexicana,* but was spiced with the roguish spirit characteristic of the "Tenth Muse":

> Señora, I was born
> in America, land of plenty,
> Gold is my compatriot,
> and the precious metals my comrades.
>
> Here's a land where sustenance
> is almost freely given,
> to no other land on earth
> is Mother Earth so generous.
>
> From the common curse of man
> its sons appear to be born free,
> For here their daily bread
> costs but little sweat of labor.
>
> Europe knows this best of all
> for these many years, insatiable,
> She has bled the abundant veins
> of America's rich mines.[23]

The preceding verses suffice to show that Sor Juana's work reflects all aspects of the Mexican national consciousness of her age. Let me review them in the order in which they appear above or, better still, let me present them in their proper order.

The earth-mother (creole revival of the ancient *Chicomecoatl?*), identified with America (that is, "North America" or Mexico), is presented as generous and sustaining; she was, in fact, the telluric and mythical support of the "Western Paradise." Although Sor Juana does not borrow this expression from her contemporary, Sigüenza y Góngora, the notion of Eden is implied by the evocation of a Mexican people exempt from original sin (*la común maldición*), in other words "Immaculate"—like the Virgin Mary herself! This notion, heterodox, to say the least, was bound to make easier the "naturalization" of Mary in her image of Tepeyac.

The belief in the divine election of Mexico and her people had as its corollary a feeling of humiliation and injustice, of rancor against the greedy Europeans who exhausted the nation's silver mines. But in the closing lines of the poem it is the woman who speaks—the fascinating woman that Sor Juana must have been—evoking the seductive traits (which Bernardo de Balbuena had already recounted in more detail) to which the gachupines succumbed:

For in all those who have seen her
clearly she inspires passions:
Love in all the men who stay here,
despair in all those who must leave.[24]

About the time of the Mexican poetess's premature death, the
Neapolitan traveler Gemelli Carreri described Mexico City in these
terms: "In its buildings and the pomp of its churches Mexico City
compares with the finest that Italy can show; but its surpasses Italy
with respect to the beauty of its women."[25] Sor Juana thus explicitly
shared the sentiments of her countrymen, who rightly recognized in
her one of the first great voices of "their America."

For the rest, America is everywhere present in the extensive and
varied body of Sor Juana's writings. We must not be dazzled or put off
by the excess of classical reminiscences and the conceptism of certain
poetic compositions. The majority of the writings of her Mexican
contemporaries are forgotten because they were nothing more than
artifice, ingenious plays on words. Sor Juana's sensitivity and vivacity,
added to the easy flow of her writing, doubtless saved her works from
that misfortune, but their specific national character also deserves our
attention. America appears especially in the *loas*, a traditional Spanish
genre which Sor Juana utilized as a prelude to the sacramental *autos*,
directly inspired by the contemporary Spanish theater in which the
great Calderón de la Barca then shone. The curtain to *El Divino
Narciso* rises on this vision:

Scene I
    Enters Occident, a handsome Indian, with crown, and America,
at his side, dressed as a lovely Indian woman. . . . On both sides of
the stage, Indian men and women dance, with feathers and rattles
in their hands, the customary way of dancing the *tocotín*, and while
they dance the music plays.[26]

We recognize the Indians of the theater, the same Indians that
ornamented the triumphal arches invented by Sigüenza y Góngora.
In the work of Sor Juana, as in that of her illustrious contemporary,
these Indians could only arise from the ashes of the real Indian,
exterminated physically or pushed aside by the emerging national
community. America appears here only in allegorical form, in an
edifying dialogue in which, together with Occident, she opposes the
true faith. In several scenes the meeting of two civilizations, that of the
great god of seeds and that of Christianity, is presented in stylized
form. Considering the limitations of the genre, Sor Juana's American
loa proceeds at a brisk pace. The scenic use of the *tocotín*, a folk dance
which the little Juana de Asbaje may have seen in a setting quite

different from that of the viceroy's court, during her childhood at Amecameca, introduced the reality of contemporary Mexico into the conventional dialogue.

It is in traditionally popular verse forms, above all, that Sor Juana portrays contemporary Mexican society, notably in the religious *villancicos* and in a special variant of the *villancico* called *ensaladilla*. In these verses she depicts with genius the ethnic medley of the Mexican capital in the seventeenth century. In her "linguistic salads" in the form of *villancicos,* Sor Juana lets each of the *castas* speak in turn; listen as she evokes an anticipation of the oath to the Virgin of Guadalupe, installing her as Protectress of the Mexican fatherland; the Indians sing:

> Gaily the Mexicans
> enter according to their customs
> ....
> and in the tender phrases
> of the Mexican language,
> In a sonorous *Tocotín*
> they say with gentle voices
> *Tocotín*
> Tla ya timohuica
> totlazo zuapilli
> maca ammo, Tonantzin
> titechmoilcahuiliz.

Sor Juana, herself a musician, appreciated the discreet music of the Nahuatl language, and in the chorus of Mexican Marian devotion she gave a place to each of the choral masses of Mexican society: creoles, mestizos, mulattoes, Indians. The next year, 1677, on the occasion of the festival of Saint Peter Nolasco, the poetess composed another *tocotín* in a pidgin Spanish-Nahuatl which certainly reflected the prevailing linguistic reality.[27] Ending a burlesque dialogue between a black and a student who shows off his atrocious latinity, she makes an Indian intervene and have the last word—just as race mixture was to have the last word in Mexican history:

> They were reconciled by an Indian
> who, accompanying himself on a guitar
> with discordant sounds,
> Sang a *tocotín,* a mixture
> of Spanish and Mexican.[28]

I cannot improve on Robert Ricard's comment: "A rapid look at her work may lead to the idea that Sor Juana is only a creole. . . . But this idea runs the risk of superficiality, for her *criollismo* is not exclusive. By reason of the role that she assigns to the Indians, the mestizos, the blacks, and to the Nahuatl language, Sor Juana is a Mexican, in the largest sense of the word, and her work represents an essential link in the progressive formation of Mexican national consciousness."[29]

I could mutliply examples, but one will suffice. Columbus appears in a *loa* which serves to introduce an *auto* dealing with Saint Hermenegild, and the hero exclaims: "There are other worlds, there is a *plus ultra.*"[30]

There is another, specifically Mexican aspect of the poetic corpus of Sor Juana to which I wish to turn my attention, that of the cult of the Virgin, particularly in her image of Tepeyac. It was only in 1648, the year of Juana's birth, that the cult of Our Lady of Guadalupe really arose among the creoles of Mexico City, thanks to the publication of Miguel Sánchez' book. It should cause no surprise, therefore, that a body of poetical work as abundant as that of Sor Juana contains only one sonnet expressly devoted to Guadalupe. It is an occasional composition, designed to celebrate the "poetic genius of Father Francisco de Castro of the Company of Jesus," who had written a heroic poem about the appearance of the prodigious image. The work remaining unpublished, Sor Juana hoped to interest some Maecenas in bringing it to light. This unpretentious sonnet reveals the nature of the Mexican cult of Guadalupe after the publication of Miguel Sánchez' work, at the beginning of the second half of the seventeenth century, before the phenomenon had attained its full development (toward the middle of the eighteenth century.)

> This Marvel composed of flowers,
> Divine American protectress
> who from a rose of Castile,
> is transformed into a Mexican rose;
> She whose proud foot made the dragon
> humbly bend his neck at Patmos. . . .[31]

I need not quote the sonnet's closing lines devoted to praising the talent of the Jesuit, whose heroic poem was proclaimed a second miracle of Guadalupe! What is worthy of note is that Sor Juana, like Father Francisco de Castro and Sánchez, identifies the prodigious image of Tepeyac with the vision of Saint John at Patmos. Guadalupe is the Woman of the Apocalypse, she who tramples on the Dragon (or the Beast of the Apocalypse) and thus promises salvation to humanity. We shall presently see the spiritual implications of this prophetic foundation of the Mexican cult of Guadalupe.

The first quatrain is interesting because of its intimate fusion of conceptism and a symbolism of flowers which is used to work a true transubstantiation. The Virgin of Guadalupe is a marvel composed of flowers; one cannot help thinking of a field flower that abounds in Mexico and that is literally a "marvel" (the *mirabilis jalapa*). The association is all the more tempting because the Indians had and still have the custom of composing pious tableaux or images with flowers. In a village of the modern state of Hidalgo there exists the tradition of a "Lord of Marvels"; according to the tradition this Christ saved an adulterous woman from the vengeance of her husband by miraculous transformation of the food that she was carrying to her lover into flowers, making her a rival of Saint Elizabeth of Hungary. In the light of this legend (did it precede the apparition of Tepeyac? It seems of later origin), the word *Maravilla* in the sonnet appears charged with a double sense. The same is true of a later work associated with the Guadalupe cult, by the painter Miguel Cabrera, *The American Marvel and Collection of Rare Marvels.*[32]

In this "sonnet of flowers" of Sor Juana we observe another transubstantiation, that of roses, which the Indians called "flowers of Castile" (*castilan xochitl*), into Mexican flowers; the image conveys most forcibly the transformation of Spaniard into creole. The symbolic richness of this quatrain, a cryptic expression of the "mystery" of Guadalupe, a theological mystery, perhaps, but also a crucible of the Mexican soul, represents a climactic achievement. The expression *Protectora Americana* which Sor Juana applies to the Virgin of Guadalupe anticipated by a century the official oath acknowledging the Virgin as Protectress of Mexico. The verses that the great Mexican poetess devoted to the Assumption lent definite support to the cult of Guadalupe, whether they be popular poems in the form of *tocotín*, through which Sor Juana indirectly revealed the religious solidarity of different ethnic and social groups, or Latin poems like this refrain composed in 1676 for the feast of the Assumption:

> *Quae est Ista? Quae est Ista,*
> *quae de deserto ascendit sicut virga,*
> *Stellis, Sole, Luna pulchior?–Maria!*
> (Who is she? Who is she,
> Who rises from the desert like a flowering branch,
> Lovelier than the stars, the sun, or moon?—Mary![33]

On the occasion of Sor Juana's death a knight of the Order of Santiago wrote a sonnet: "On the Incomprehensible Elevation of the Miraculous Genius and Unique Muse, Sor Juana Inés de la Cruz."[34] I see more here than a hyperbole in the style of the time. Sor Juana gave lucid testimony, with matchless sensitivity and literary grace, about the Mexico that surrounded her. More profoundly, she kneaded the symbolic dough which would soon rise into a hybrid national consciousness. In her work the alliance of the eagle of Patmos and that in the Mexican coat of arms, the roses of Castile changed into Mexican roses, the metamorphosis of the "Divine Narcissus" (which doubtless owes a debt to Ovid), are a literary transposition of the metamorphoses of Mexican society itself. In the measure that this birth of a nation was in the first place a utopian renaissance of the Indian past and the prophetic spirit of the first missionaries, one can say, even today, that Sor Juana Inés de la Cruz was "the Phoenix" of Mexico.

6

The Spiritual Emancipation 1728–1759

The Generation of 1730 and Its Books

The spiritual ambience and the intellectual interests of a generation result from the interplay of a common education and a common experience. The Mexican creoles born about 1700, who embraced a professorial career or took vows in a religious order (the two careers often went hand in hand), or who joined the ranks of the secular clergy, formed a remarkably homogeneous group. To the extent that one can speak of a collective consciousness and opinion in a society so different from ours, that consciousness and that opinion found expression in their pronouncements and writings. Their eschatological unrest, their devout fervor, their patriotic aspirations achieved a historical triumph less than a century later. This creole elite marched in unison with the Mexican nation, if by "nation" we mean that silent multitude which expressed itself in its pilgrimages, its great fears, and its solemn rejoicings.

More than two centuries of ineffective creole efforts to achieve their aspirations preceded the thirty years that ended in the spiritual emancipation of New Spain and its official consecration. No upheaval, no sharp break with the past, separates those years from those that went before. On the contrary, we observe a perfect continuity with a past in which there slowly germinated a Mexican national consciousness. The years between 1730 and 1760 precede the impact of the Enlightenment on the traditional ideology of the Hispanic realms; they correspond to the mature years of men educated in the first quarter of the century. These clerics basically had the same intellectual formation as their seniors of the previous century; they cite the same authors, take part in the same Scholastic disputes, share the same aspirations.

Despite the sway of tradition in basic principles, there were important factors making for spiritual instability, factors that sharpened the creoles' devout fervor and revived the eschatological unrest of the "Americans," as, following the example of Fray Benito Feijóo, they liked to call themselves to distinguish themselves from the

77

"Spaniards" or, more pejoratively, the *gachupines*. The vacancy in the archiepiscopal see of Mexico City in 1728, followed by the appointment as the new archbishop of a Mexican creole, a former student of the Jesuit Colegio de San Ildefonso, the gala reception accorded to him by the city authorities and by the people, the long duration of his spiritual magistracy (seventeen years, including six during which he substituted for the viceroy), were all circumstances which gave a certain unity to the years 1730 to 1747. The period opened with the setting up of triumphal arches (one in front of the Jesuit church, the other in front of the cathedral); under these arches the new prelate, dressed in his cope, passed, followed by a brilliant procession, amid the cheers of the crowd. This baroque decor, indispensable accompaniment of such an event in New Spain, only merits our attention because it symbolized the entrance on the scene of a triumphant new generation. The death of the creole archbishop Juan Antonio Vizarrón y Eguiarreta in 1747 did not check that generation's élan, for his Castilian successor, Manuel Rubio y Salinas, took to heart creole spiritual interests, caused the new collegiate church of Guadalupe to be built, and interceded with the Holy See to obtain papal approval of the patronage of Our Lady of Guadalupe over North America. Pope Benedict XIV approved the "universal patronage" of Guadalupe in 1757, and the archbishop died in 1765, sixteen years after his consecration.

The spiritual consensus and apostolic peace to which I referred above were occasionally troubled by violent Scholastic disputes, notably by disputes over the problem of grace. In these debates the Dominicans and the Augustinians, champions of efficacious grace, opposed the Jesuits, partisans of the *scientia media**. I shall not dwell on this aspect of the intellectual and spiritual life, though we must not underestimate its importance. Given the perspective I have chosen— the study of manifestations of faith in their relationship to the growth of a national consciousness—I attach more importance to the élan of a generation destined to free its Mexican *patria* from spiritual dependence on Spain. Whatever their Scholastic disputes, the creole religious were ready to sing in unison the supernatural glories of "their America," North America; they were united by a common aspiration for an immediate grace which should free their people from sin and destine them to be a Chosen People. To obtain papal and royal recognition of heaven's favor for the Mexicans, a new Chosen People, was

Scientia Media ("Middle Knowledge"). A concept originated by the Spanish Jesuit theologian Molina (1535–1600) and usually defined as that knowledge by which God, without any predetermining decree, knows from all eternity what each and every creature endowed with free will would do in any determined circumstance. (Tr.)

the aim of the creole generation with which we are concerned; that recognition would be their triumph. This victory was decisive for the subsequent political history of Mexico and above all for its independence. I shall attempt to recreate the stages of this victory and to set them within the spiritual atmosphere of that historical "moment."

When certain historians say that the history of ideas has not yet found its methodology, what they mean is that ideas are not yet subject to quantitative measurement. Certainly "quantitative approaches" will long remain a crude instrument for assessing devout fervor or patriotic enthusiasm. The *spiritual moment*, on the other hand, can be identified with the aid of certain touchstones, although one can never grasp it entire. We can capture a reflection of the ideas and aspiration of *encomienda* Indians or the independent Indians of the northern part of the country only through their collective conduct (flights, uprisings, massacres of missionaries). The *castas*, composed of different mixtures of whites and Indians, with a black element that was relatively unimportant in most regions of New Spain (save for Veracruz), are not much easier to know from this point of view. To be sure, traces in modern folklore, administrative and parish records, and the archives of the Inquisition above all, where they exist, can give us revealing glimpses of the collective aspect of the men and women who represented in fact "the population" of New Spain. If I have preferred to study the spiritual life at the summit of the social pyramid, it was not from scorn or ignorance of its base, much less of the importance of that base. My choice was based on several considerations: first, the fact that sources of information regarding the creoles, or at least their guides, the clergy, are abundant; second, the richness of the subject-matter; third, these topics have not hitherto had the attention that they deserve. But the decisive factor was the primordial role of the creole religious, beginning in the sixteenth century and continuing throughout the history of New Spain, in the evolution which was to lead the Mexican people to its spiritual emancipation, the prelude to political independence.

To be sure, the Mexican patriots of the years 1730 to 1760 never dreamed of winning by force of arms the political independence of a country whose administrative autonomy they sought to achieve by all means in their power. Many clergy aspired to a complete administrative autonomy with respect to Spain, to which New Spain should be linked only by common loyalty to the same monarch. Others, more timid, doubtless only sought the appointment of creoles to half the decision-making posts in the administration, the army, and the church of the viceroyalty (the other half to go to the European Spaniards). For the rest, the idea of a "fatherland," which is our unconscious modern frame of reference, was a product of the French Revolution and the awakening of nationalities in nineteenth-century Europe and Latin America; consequently, the notion is irrelevant for a study dealing with eighteenth-century Mexico. The Mexican creoles, and most notably the clerics (ecclesiastics, religious, professors) clearly expressed in their writings, as even a superficial reading of their texts reveals, the image of the Mexican *patria* that they carried in their hearts. I have made every effort to collate these texts and bring out all their meaning from the point of view that I have chosen, but I have abstained from all interpolations that might tend to perfect the unfinished image of a *patria* that only the future could complete.

Printed texts alone—books, gazettes, regulations, proclamations, and the like—cannot give us a total account of the intellectual and spiritual life of a society; but their informative value is nevertheless of the first order. Private diaries, ledgers, and other autobiographical materials, in which certain periods are rich, are not available for New Spain of that epoch, or else have disappeared doubtless for good. In this area, only the secret correspondence of the viceroys, the secret instructions of those viceroys to their successors, the secret memorials addressed by some bishops to the king, or to the pope by the superiors of convents, all being relatively rare documents, complement or refute (depending on the given case) the published sources. Indirectly, the account books of vestries or congregations, the incomes of canons, testamentary legacies, and the like, revealing the penury or prosperity of pious foundations, cast some light on group behavior. The mass of Mexican published works, principally works of devotion, which José Toribio Medina inventoried, appeared to provide a sufficiently large documentary base for an effort to sketch the spiritual life of New Spain and, more especially, to illuminate those aspects which bear on the growth of national consciousness.

Clearly, it is impossible within the space of this chapter, to analyze, even taking a period of only thirty years, all the books listed by José Toribio Medina in his classic work, *La Imprenta en México*. I have therefore limited my attention to those works whose relationship to patriotic feeling, especially as expressed in the cult of a pious image, is patent from the title. Even with this restriction, the field remains immense. Accordingly, I have cited for purposes of illustration only some of the most representative works at my disposal.

Let me first settle the question of how representative are works which were subjected to four or five censorships before their publication and diffusion and which even afterwards ran the risk of confiscation. Two comments come to mind, one general and the other based on the results of research into the functioning of the censorship in

New Spain during the years under consideration. It is well known that our age has highly perfected the means of repressing thought, yet ideas regarded as most subversive by very dictatorial governments have always managed to find expression in printed form. It is true that printing establishments were much fewer, and the cost of books relatively much higher, in New Spain in the eighteenth century than in a modern industrial country, but controls, on the other hand, were appreciably less rigorous. The existence of a censorship accustoms authors to engage in previous self-censorship, to adopt a code, and accustoms readers to a routine decoding. In the present instance, the historian has no need to engage in the ever dangerous exercise of decoding (all the more dangerous if done two centuries after the text under study was written). In effect, the creoles displayed their patriotic aspirations in broad daylight, veiled only by exuberant rhetoric and the abuse of biblical citations and parables. I find no evidence of systematic dissimulation of patriotic fervor on the part of Mexican authors of the thirty years under study. This statement may raise questions; let me limit myself for the moment to the objective conditions of publishing in New Spain during this period.

The printing press was introduced into New Spain as early as 1542, at least. We may therefore say, without risk of error, that two centuries later it enjoyed the experience of a long tradition. However, two important obstacles hindered its flowering: first, the establishment of a printing establishment required previous authorization from the king through his Council of the Indies; second, printing costs were so high that the market for books in New Spain was necessarily very small, while their sale in Spain or other American viceroyalties was almost impossible. For these reasons, there were very few printers in New Spain. In 1730 there were only two printers who published regularly and had a respectable volume of publications: Joseph Bernardo de Hogal, and the widow (succeeded by her heirs) of Miguel de Rivera, Doña María de Rivera. In 1748 arose the printing shop of the Colegio de San Ildefonso, whose output grew in 1755 and again about 1760, making it an important instrument of Jesuit influence. In 1753 Don Juan José de Eguiara y Egurén established the "New Printing Press," which issued two years later the first and only published volume of the *Bibliotheca Mexicana* (in Latin); it had been preceded by a pious exercise celebrating the mystery of the conception of Mary and the *Stupendous Miracle of Her Prodigious Apparition in Her Sovereign and Divine Image of Guadalupe, in This Fortunate Kingdom of New Spain*. Thus the thirty years under study were marked by an impressive development of the printing press in Mexico; by 1753 there were four large printing shops instead of the two that existed in 1727.

We must be cautious in estimating the size of editions. Medina informs us that the famous essay of Cayetano Cabrera y Quintero, *Coat of Arms of Mexico City: Celestial Protection . . . Very Holy Mary, in Her Prodigious Image of the Mexican Guadalupe*,[1] published by the widow of J. B. de Hogal in 1746, had a printing of 900 copies. This was certainly a maximum figure, explained by two facts: Cabrera had written his book on the order of his bishop; and the municipal council of Mexico City had assumed the costs of printing the work, which was dedicated to the king. The stock must have been disposed of partly by giving copies away, the rest through obligatory purchase of copies by the libraries of convents and colleges and by civil servants. Despite the book's subject, of large interest to many contemporaries, it is difficult to judge its "success" on the basis of the facts at our disposal. From a commercial point of view, the question is meaningless.

Many of the works which claim our attention were published under similar conditions: the size of their editions is generally unknown; their printing costs were borne by a religious brotherhood or some private patron. It is safe to say that these publications had to enjoy large official favor. Before a book could be published it had to be approved by two or three religious censors belonging to different orders (hence to different schools of thought), by the civil authorities, by the ordinary, and finally by the order to which the author often belonged. The patron, in the case of private individuals, was generally a mine-owner (*minero*), a landowner, a lord, sometimes an official. For the historian, the donor's gesture symbolizes the approval of civil society for the ideas the clerics developed in their books. If the patron is an ecclesiastical chapter, a convent, or a lay brotherhood, the point is even more obvious.

A different problem, but one related to the problem of the size of first editions, is that of reprints or posthumous publications. Leaving aside commercial considerations (in numerous cases the printer turned over the finished books to the patron who was footing the bill), it is difficult to conceive, in the case of books for which the demand must have been relatively small, that a reprint was undertaken before the initial printing had been exhausted. A reprint may be explained by a very small first edition, dictated by caution or lack of means. In other cases the reprints were books originally published in a provincial capital (Puebla, as a rule) or another viceroyalty or captaincy general (Santiago de Guatemala, Havana, and the like; or even in Spain or Rome) and reprinted in Mexico City in order to make the books available more rapidly or in greater quantity (if not more cheaply) to the readers of the "Imperial City."

By way of example, I cite the devotional tract of Alonso A. de Velasco, *The Self-Renovation of the Sovereign Image of Our Crucified Lord*

Jesus of Itzmiquilpan,[2] whose fifth edition appeared in Mexico City in 1729. The Christ of Itzmiquilpan was the object of a great cult among educated Mexicans of the generation under study here. Buyers and readers of the book must in the first place have been the religious (convent libraries) and the families of the mining, landed, and administrative aristocracy. We already know the importance assigned by creole religious feeling to all signs of divine grace bestowed on the Mexican *patria*. The "prodigious renovation" of the Christ of Itzmiquilpan was one of those pious traditions that were transmitted from generation to generation and served to intensify the creole charismatic sentiment.

It was no accident that in 1733 there were reprinted a novena *In Honor Of The Very Miraculous Image of Holy Mary, Our Lady of Zapopan*;[3] in 1738 an *Exercise to Increase Devotion to the Miraculous Image of Holy Christ Venerated in the Parish of the Holy True Cross of Mexico City* was reprinted by J. B. de Hogal.[4] In 1743 a sermon by the former rector of the University of Mexico City, J. Fernández de Palos, entitled *Obsidional Triumph . . . By Means of the Virgin Mary, Our Lady, in Her Prodigious Image of Guadalupe*,[5] first printed by Doña María de Rivera, was reprinted by the widow of J. B. de Hogal. Three years later a minor printer, Joseph Ambrosio de Lima, reprinted a novena *To the Great Mother of God and Sovereign Queen, Our Lady of Salvation, of the Town of Pátzcuaro*.[6] In 1749, the printing establishment of Doña María de Rivera issued (without indication of a patron, and therefore with expectations of sufficient sales to cover printing costs and yield a profit) the second edition of a book by the priest Juan José M. Montúfar, *The Marvel of Prodigies and the Flower of Miracles, Which Appeared at Guadalupe, Giving A Clear Witness of the Conception in Grace and of the Glory of Mary Our Lady*.[7] (Its title alone deserves a theological commentary, but here I want only to show the taste of Mexican readers for miraculous traditions and prodigious images.) In 1750 the *History of the Very Miraculous Image of Our Lady of Ocotlan Which Is Venerated Outside the Walls of Tlaxcala*,[8] written (as was usually the case) by the chaplain of the sanctuary, was reprinted by the widow of J. B. de Hogal; the same publisher issued the following year a reprint of the *Novena in Honor of the Very Miraculous Image of Holy Mary, Our Lady of San Juan, Situated in the Valle de los Lagos, of the Bishopric of Guadalaxara*;[9] a third edition appeared three years later, in 1754, published by the same house. Should we conclude that it took longer than two years to sell out the second edition? Or was the delay caused by slowness in securing permission to reprint? It is difficult to say. The same novena was one of the first works printed the following year, 1755, on the presses of the Bibliotheca Mexicana.

Continuing our inventory of reprints, we note the appearance in

1753 of a novena and *Brief Relation of the Origin of the Miraculous Image of Our Lady of Consolation, Which Is Venerated in the Sacrarium of the Convent of the Recollects of Our Holy Father St. Francis, Called Saint Cosmae, Outside the Walls of this Imperial City of Mexico,*[10] issued by Doña María de Rivera. In 1755 the new printing house of the Bibliotheca Mexicana reprinted another novena in honor of the Holy Cross of Querétaro. The same publisher, Don Juan José de Eguiara y Egurén, whose devout spirit we already know, published a second edition of the work of the Jesuit Escóbar y Mendoza, *New Jerusalem, Our Lady Mary, A Heroic Poem . . .;*[11] yet another edition was published by the Bibliotheca Mexicana in 1759. In 1758 from the presses of the Jesuit Colegio de San Ildefonso issued a novena composed by a religious to celebrate the mystery of the Immaculate Conception.

The Creole Charisma

How can one deny a representative character to these pious writings, reprinted several times at intervals of a few years, or several years in succession? In the case of titles which do not carry the name of a patron (if there was a patron he was anxious to see his arms appear on the cover and his name over the colophon), we are dealing with books which were sold out in a short time. Their titles alone offer valuable information about the society of that time. The practice of novenas was frequent, a fact which can be easily proven from other sources. Above all, the taste for the marvelous, the passion for miraculous traditions concerning holy images, so characteristic of the Mexican people, emerge from these works as essential aspects of creole devotion, so that we see the different provinces of New Spain pass successively before our eyes, each with its own "prodigious protective image." In this respect, the Virgin Mary enjoyed particular favor, followed by the Christs of Querétaro and Itzmiquilpan. Among reprinted works which deserve mention because of their significance for the spiritual history of New Spain, let me mention another novena, a work of Father Antonio de Paredes of the Company of Jesus in New Spain, whose title evokes the climate of those decisive years of the middle of the eighteenth century: *Novena of the Triumphant Company of Jesus, Saint Ignatius Loyola and His Fortunate Sons* (reprinted at the Colegio de San Ildefonso in 1756).[12]

The publication and numerous reprints of novenas dedicated to local cults is a fact of capital importance. But its full significance becomes clear when we consider the publishing record of New Spain as a whole. The leading place among published works is held by devotional tracts and panegyrical sermons; the latter give us the authentic flavor of sacred eloquence, one of the principal aspects of public life in New Spain. It was from the pulpit, a genuine tribune, that ideas and news most frequently emanated and were diffused among the population. A breakdown of the authors listed by Beristain gives the following results:

Mendicant orders	925	Laymen	829
Secular clergy	900	Anonymous	470
Jesuits	375		
Total number of ecclesiastics	2,351	Total number of laymen	829

These proportions, established for the entire history of the viceroyalty, probably hold for the period under consideration. We should note that a number of the anonymous writers were religious, including some women, like Sor Juana Inés de la Cruz.

The complementary genre of the funeral oration, usually of edifying tendency, also occupied a fairly large place in contemporary publishing. The public life of New Spain was punctuated by fiestas, funerals, and preachings. These events had their respective counterparts in publishing: descriptions of the triumphal arches and speeches of greetings to the new authorities, funeral orations, and sermons. The celebration of the patron saint or founder of a religious order, of the miraculous image of a parish or a city, was attended by solemnities whose memory was kept alive the following year by publication of a book or pamphlet, once the necessary authorizations had been obtained. In this period sermons and devout exercises were most frequently devoted to the Virgin Mary, in her images of Our Lady of Light, of Carmen, of Guadalupe, of Los Remedios, and the like, and also to Our Lady of Loreto. The cults of Our Lady of Loreto and Our Lady of Light were promoted by the Jesuits; the same was true of the cult of the rosary (Dominican in origin) and the cult of the Sacred Heart of Jesus. The same may be said of the cult of the Virgin in general and of her Immaculate Conception, but the cult of the Immaculate Conception (originally Franciscan, properly speaking) was shared by the whole Hispanic world, in which it had become an article of faith long before the promulgation of the dogma by the Holy See.

Saint Ignatius of Loyola, founder of the Society of Jesus; Saint Francis Xavier, the missionary; and Saint Aloysius Gonzaga, the student, frequently appear as the themes of sermons or spiritual exercises. Titles like that of a sermon preached at Puebla on the feast day of Saint Ignatius, "Heaven Placed in Our Hands by the Hands of Ignatius and His Company,"[13] are in themselves eloquent; the sermon was followed by a pontifical mass celebrated by the auxiliary bishop of Puebla. We see that times had changed considerably since the quarrel of Bishop Palafox with the Jesuits of his diocese. Only the lightning that in 1747 twice struck the chapel of Saint Ignatius of Loyola in the cathedral gave a portent of the expulsion of the Company. In 1752, the royal and pontifical University of Mexico City acknowledged Saint Aloysius Gonzaga as its patron by a public oath of allegiance; this action was very significant, for it meant that the Jesuits had forged ahead of the Dominicans and Franciscans in higher education; they now had a majority in the "college" of the professors.

Besides the cult of the Virgin under her various invocations, and that of the new Jesuit saints, we note the special place held by the cults of the Holy Trinity, the apostle Peter, and Saint Joseph (the latter linked to the Marian cult). Saints Bernard, Francis, and John of the Cross were regarded with special fervor by their own religious orders; other leading cults were those of Saint Jerome and Saint Philip Neri (the latter was especially cherished by the Oratorians). Popular devotion to Saint James, a heritage of the conquistadors, seems to have been constant. Finally, the cults of Saint Gertrude and Saint Catherine of Siena deserve mention. But the information we possess concerning the number of titles, reprints, and the size of printings establishes the primacy of the cult of the Virgin Mary and of her Mexican images in particular. Among these, the "prodigious image" of Guadalupe clearly won first place in the course of those thirty years.

The causes of the belated flowering of the Guadalupe cult (tradition assigns the apparition to 1531, and its bicentenary was brilliantly celebrated in 1732) are complex, but the stages of its rise are very clear. In this respect, the date of 1737 is very important; an epidemic (*peste*) ravaged the country and the people of Mexico City decided to carry in procession the image of Our Lady of Loreto, who had conquered the measles (*sarampión*) ten years before. This act of devotion had no effect, and appeal was made to Nuestra Señora de los Remedios, then to all the holy images of the city in turn, but the supplications addressed to them were equally unsuccessful. "However, the Lord reserved this glory for His Very Holy Mother, in her miraculous image of Guadalupe, under whose protection He wished the whole kingdom to be placed." No sooner was the decision taken to acknowledge by a solemn oath the patronage of the Virgin of Guadalupe at Tepeyac, adds the chronicler of the Company, than "one might think that the exterminating angel only waited for this decision to sheath his sword."[14] Our Lady of Guadalupe thus gained a firm advantage in the pious competition which ranged the different prodigious images (not only those of the Virgin but those of the Christs) against each other. Later, San Luis Potosí, followed by the city of Valladolid in Michoacán, installed Guadalupe as the principal protectress against epidemics.

However, a dissenting voice was raised. We find evidence of this in a tract whose author preferred to remain anonymous, but which sought to refute the opinion of an adversary of Guadalupe. In 1741 the printing establishment of María de Rivera published *The Patronage Contested, Apologetical Dissertation in Favor of the Vow, the Election, and the Oath of Allegiance to Holy Mary, Venerated in Her Image of Guadalupe of Mexico City*;[15] this pamphlet was directed against the master of ceremonies of the cathedral of Puebla, who refused to draw the consequences of the patronage of Guadalupe in the services and gave great publicity to his decision. We are not surprised to hear a dissenting voice raised in Puebla, rather than in any other Mexican city, against the patronage of Guadalupe of Tepeyac, which consecrated on a transcendent level the supremacy of the "Imperial City of Mexico" in New Spain.

But this was a rearguard action, and the same publisher issued the next year a sermon pronounced in the sanctuary of Guadalupe de Valladolid of Michoacán by an Augstinian religious, *Eclipse of the Divine Sun, Causd by the Interposition of Our Lady, Immaculate Mary, Venerated in Her Holy Image of Guadalupe*.[16] This title is the baptismal act, so to speak, of the Mexican cult of the Virgin Mary. The sun is God himself, and Mary, identified by contemporary exegetes with the Woman of the Revelation, of whom the image of Tepeyac is a replica, is heiress to the Greco-Roman lunar tradition, reinforced in the present instance by a tradition having its distant origin in Qumran but transmitted through the Old Testament. The two pyramids of the ancient holy city of Teotihuacan (the two largest in the new World with the exception of that of Cholula), the Pyramid of the Sun (Tonatiuh) and the Pyramid of the Moon (Teteoinnan), still testify to the importance of the sun and the moon in the ancient Mexican pantheon. Father Sahagún informs us that in the time of the Aztec empire, the goddess Toci, double of Teteoinnan, had a sanctuary on Mount Tepeyac (only several leagues from Teotihuacan) where the Indians came on pilgrimages in great numbers. The image of Our Lady of Guadalupe of Mount Tepeyac thus concentrated in itself a variety of beliefs, some derived from the Judeo-Christian tradition and the others from Mexican polytheism. This varied content of the image of Guadalupe was to endow it with a spiritual radiance that would soon eclipse all the other "miraculous" images.

This last avatar of the old Toci of the Aztecs casts a curious light on the spiritual universe of the Mexican eighteenth century. The Virgin Mary in her image of Guadalupe, who first appeared to the native Mexicans represented by a humble Indian convert, had endowed the "Americans" with charisma. The identification of Mary with the Woman of Revelation made it possible by reference to prophecies attributed to the apostle Saint John to see in the Marian cult of Tepeyac the announcement of the last times, or at least the end of the church of Christ, to be replaced by the church of Mary, the church of the last days. Just as God had chosen the Hebrews in order to incarnate himself in Christ his son, so Mary, the redeemer of the last times, she who was to triumph over Antichrist, had chosen the Mexicans.

This last idea finds unequivocal expression in a sermon pronounced December 12, 1749, and entitled "The Celestial Conception and the Mexican Birth of the Image of Guadalupe."[17] Guadalupe, that is, the Virgin Mary, mother of Christ, *is* Mexican. One of the great defenders of Guadalupe, the *maestro* Ita y Parra, could explain in the cathedral of Mexico City, in the presence of the Blessed Sacrament, the viceroy, the audiencia, the chapter, the tribunals, and the orders: "In this respect, the American people [*pueblo indiano*] surpasses not only Israel but all the peoples [*naciones*] of the world and leaves them far behind";[18] the term *indiano* should not be understood here in its ethnic sense but in the transcendent meaning which it had in the expression *Iglesia Indiana,* already used in the sixteenth century by the Franciscan Jerónimo de Mendieta. In reality, the old eschatological hope of the pioneers of the "spiritual conquest," the Joachimite Franciscans, achieved a belated triumph in the eighteenth century under the aspect of the cult of Guadalupe, so energetically fought in its beginnings by these same Franciscans. The "Indian church" (read "creole" for "Indian") was a church in which the cult of Guadalupe eclipsed that of Jesus. Where, then, were the feared inquisitors and what were they doing? They were in accord with the common devotion; Ita y Parra was himself a censor of the Holy Office, and the censors of sermons shared fully the patriotic enthusiasm of the bold preachers for Guadalupe.

Bishops and viceroys pushed on by the clergy, professors, confessors, creole preachers, encouraged in their course by an unanimous popular support that united Indians, *castas,* and creoles, paid tribute to Guadalupe. In 1750 a new collegiate church was founded at Tepeyac, and in 1754 the initiatives of the archbishop of Mexico and the campaign waged by the Jesuits at the Holy See culminated in pontifical recognition of the patronage of Guadalupe over New Spain or, as it then was often called, "North America." An office of the first class of December 12 translated into canonical terms the famous reference to Psalm 147, which would remain attached like a legend to the image of Guadalupe: *Non fecit taliter omni nationi* (He has not done the like for any other nation).

Leaving aside for the moment the figure of Guadalupe and its eschatological implications, I should like to stress the patriotic significance which is one of its essential aspects. The "translation" of the

Virgin Mary in her aspect of the image of Tepeyac, "not from Nazareth to Juda, but from the Empyrean itself to this fortunate place [Tepeyac],"[19] was the transcendent guarantee of the Mexican national aspirations. I would even say more precisely that the apparition of the Virgin Mary of Guadalupe at Tepeyac was a creole *response* to the translation of the Virgin Mary to Pilar de Zaragoza (this would be understood in the sense of Américo Castro's writing that the Spanish cult of Saint James Matamoros was a response to Mohamed). The subject of the "translation" seems to have been a stereotype; in a devout tract published in Mexico in 1731 we read that the pope had granted a plenary indulgence "the day when our Holy Mother Church celebrates the descent of the Very Holy Virgin Mary from the skies to found on earth her order of the Redeemers [the Mercedarians], under the invocation of the Virgen María de la Merced."[20] The rivalry in the quest for grace between Spain and New Spain during the years under study is associated with certain names: the creole Franciscan Agustín de Bengochea, cited above; Ita y Parra, professor of sacred theology at the University of Mexico; and many other Mexican preachers. Against these champions a solitary voice was raised, that of a Catalan Dominican, in the name of the congregation of Pilar de Zaragoza; he had a forerunner in the Augustinian Fray Pedro de San Francisco, who had preached at Mexico City a panegyrical sermon on "The Queen of America, Our Lady of Pilar de Zaragoza."[21] But that was in 1739, and the celestial-terrestrial rule of Guadalupe over North America had not yet been indisputably established.

When Pope Benedict XIV yielded to creole pressure in 1754, the Mexican cult of Guadalupe gained new power and audacity. Not content with having freed their *patria* from its spiritual debt to Spain ("America no longer fears that her idolatry will be thrown up to her," Ita y Parra preached as early as 1747),[22] the creole religious transformed their devotion into a victorious messianism. The Jesuit Carranza, one of the great artisans of the Guadalupe cult, had not even waited for the papal benediction to prophesy "the translation of the Church to Guadalupe."[23] Nothing but that consecration was lacking to fulfill the glory of Mexico City; only "the throne of Saint Peter at Mexico City,"[24] the subject of a sermon pronounced by an archdeacon of the cathedral of Mexico City, could make the imperial city "a new Rome." The transfer of the capital of Christendom from Rome to Mexico would not only assure New Spain's spiritual preeminence over the Peninsula but had as a corollary the patronage of Guadalupe (with New Spain as mediator) over Spain herself. The creole Franciscan Fray Joaquín de Osuna expressed this idea in 1744 in his apologetical sermon, "The Celestial Iris of the Catholic Spains, the Apparition and the Patronage of Our Lady of Guadalupe."[25] As these few examples show (I could cite many others), the issue was nothing less than a total reversal of New Spain's dependent spiritual status in relation to Spain, a status going back to the "spiritual conquest" of Mexico by the mendicant orders in the sixteenth century. This aspect of the matter did not pass unnoticed, and the Dominican Juncosa, mentioned above, entitled his apologetical sermon on Our Lady of Pilar de Zaragoza "The Triumph of the Faith in Old and New Spain."[26] But by 1758 "Old Spain" had already virtually lost the game.

All arguments, whether derived from Scripture or not, were grist for the mill of the Mexican preachers as they strove to prove that Mary had chosen their country to be the stage where the last act of the history of Christendom as it moved toward its consummation should be played out. It was to flee the persecutions of Antichrist that the church would seek asylum at Tepeyac in the last times. The identification of the image of Guadalupe with the Woman of *Revelation* and the cryptic meaning of *Revelation* 12 furnish the key to this claim, which the Jesuit Carranza summed up as follows: "The image of Guadalupe will finally be the patroness of the universal Church, because it will be to the sanctuary of Guadalupe that the throne of Saint Peter will come in search of refuge in the last times. . . . Ave Maria."[27] Such opinions could persuade readers only if the "last times" seemed close. Although they may not have openly expressed this belief, I think it was in the hearts of creole religious who frequently referred to a Dominican of the previous century, Fray Tomás Maluenda.

In his book *On the Antichrist,* which appeared in Rome in 1604 and was dedicated to Pope Innocent X, Maluenda devoted considerable space to the spiritual problems posed by the discovery of the peoples of the New World.[28] In connection with the important question of the date of the coming of Antichrist, he affirmed that, in principle, God alone knew the answer. But Maluenda shared the common belief that this event could not take place until the Gospel had been preached throughout the world. Now, added Maluenda, this moment has not yet come (in 1604), for many islands and lands remained to be discovered, especially in the Indies; he cited specifically the vast regions situated to the north of New Spain, Florida and Virginia.

Half a century later, the expansion of the missionary enterprise from New Spain, which had resulted in the creation of the Jesuit and Franciscan missions of California, the Pimeria, and the Tarahumara, may have suggested to informed minds that the conditions for the coming of Antichrist would shortly be satisfied. Without this background of eschatological anxiety, the predicted translation of the church to Guadalupe would have had little meaning. In that mystical atmosphere the Jesuit Joaquín Rodríguez Calado, prefect of studies at the Colegio de San Pedro y San Pablo of Mexico City, could prophesy that there would arise at Tepeyac "the empire of the holy Church and the throne of Saint Peter, when that Church will be persecuted by Antichrist and compelled to leave the holy city of Rome."[29] The same eschatological perspective explains why one of the censors of "The Translation . . . ," carried away by his enthusiasm for Guadalupe, wrote: "Thou, my Queen and Lady, art our hope, *spes nostra,* and I might even call you my Goddess, O Immaculate Virgin."[30] Guadalupe, Mother of the Indians, Queen of the Mexicans, was truly the tutelary goddess (*diosa*) of the patriotic religious, although fear of falling into heresy placed some rein on the euhemeristic use of mementos of classical antiquity. The danger of a false step was equally great with respect to the Indian beliefs, as shown by contemporary efforts at Christian interpretation of primitive Mexican symbolism.

In fact, although the example of the cult of Our Lady of Guadalupe is most remarkable and therefore commands our principal attention, to divorce it from other comparable phenomena is to distort its significance. In addition to Guadalupe, which the Franciscan Fray José de Arlegui described as "The Sacred Palladium of the American World,"[31] Mexico claimed the protection of the apostle Saint Peter, hailed in a sermon by the Dominican Fray Antonio C. de Villegas as "The Stone of the Eagle of Mexico City. The Prince of the Apostles and Father of the Universal Church, My Lord Saint Peter."[32] For the rest, we know the use made in those same years of the presence of an eagle (boldly assimilated to the Aztec eagle) under the feet of the Woman in Revelation 12. The allegorical exegesis, with clear reference to Guadalupe, of the major symbol of the Aztec coat of arms, went hand in hand with audacious semantic readings which suggested such syllogisms as these: "And all this is found in Scripture: Peter asks to be allowed to join Christ on the waters: Christ is Mexico City: hence Peter asked to go to Mexico City."[33] If Scripture, according to the creole exegetes, attested to the election of Mexico City by the Virgin Mary and the preference of the apostle Peter for Anahuac, this did not exclude bold interpretations of the symbol of the cross and a joint allusion to the Holy Cross of Querétaro and the Maya Tree of Life, "The Cherubim Guardian of the Tree of Life, the Holy Cross of Querétaro."[34] Although the reference to the Tree of Life may have its origin in the symbolic exegesis which identifies the Tree of Paradise and the redeeming cross, the coincidence with ancient Indian beliefs does not seem a fortuitous one. The favor that the Mexican past enjoyed, especially as a result of the work of Don Carlos de Sigüenza y Góngora in the previous century, fully explains why the great figures of ancient Mexican mythology were added to the ranks of Hellenic heroes in order to increase opportunities for allegorical exegesis and euhemeristic comparison. We need not be surprised, therefore, by the title of a sermon which reads: "The Most Exact Replica of the Divine Hercules, and the Sacred Mars of the Church, the Glorious Archangel Saint Michael, at the Sacred Feet of Mary Our Lady in Her Image of Guadalupe, Which Miraculously Appeared for the Protection of Our New Mexican World."[35]

New Spain, more commonly called "Mexico" by the creole authors, thus had an armory filled to overflowing. Guadalupe appeared there surrounded by a chorus of other Marian images: The Virgen de Ocotlan, the Virgen de la Luz, the Virgen de San Juan de los Lagos, the Virgen de Macana, the Virgen de los Remedios, the Virgen del Carmen, the Virgen de los Dolores. Each was attached to a city, a convent, or a church of New Spain. Each of these local cults sought to justify itself by a miraculous tradition, whose foundations were as solid (or fragile) as the tradition of Guadalupe. All these pious traditions converged unknowingly toward the same great end: to purge Mexico of the ancient sin of paganism and idolatry.

The exegetic effort which I have briefly described was one aspect of the enterprise of spiritual emancipation which I do not hesitate to call "national." The great multitude validated the miraculous traditions by its pilgrimages: meanwhile the clerical elite scrutinized the prophetic books, the Apocalypse of Isaiah and the so-called Apocalypse of John, to discover the announcement of a supernatural destiny without peer: "No Nation Compares with Mexico," in the words of a popular song.[36] It remained to demonstrate this with historical and scriptural proofs, but since all were already persuaded (the inquisitors charged with watching over orthodoxy were as convinced as the rest), the task was not too difficult. We find a naive avowal of this complacence, the result of a collective illuminism, in the comment of a Carmelite censor: "If this is not supported by clear prophecies, one could at least deduce it from ambiguous prophecies."[37] Argumentation, even when presented in the form of syllogisms, was of secondary importance; rigorous logic was not necessary, for what was important in the last analysis depended on an act of faith, patriotic rather than religious faith.

Mexico City, The New Jerusalem

Guadalupe, once fought by the Franciscans, became the object of a growing popular cult and gained almost the unanimous support of the religious orders, so divided in other respects. Tepeyac was near Mexico City, and the inhabitants of the capital had favored the sanctuary as a place for promenades since the sixteenth century. If heaven had shown its grace to Mexico, that grace should manifest itself above all in Mexico City (we recall that it was in Mexico City that the flowery image of Mary had appeared on the *tilma*, or cloak, of the Indian Juan Diego). Local patriotism, in New as in Old Spain, had precedence over the still vague national spirit. To the degree that one can graph feelings, it seems that the aspiration to make Mexico City a new Rome played a decisive role. Other causes, which were not the result of choice but flowed from the city's power and its virtual monopoly of the printing press tended in the same direction. In particular, the Guadalupan fervor of the Jesuits, who made use at a strategic moment of the presses of the Colegio de San Ildefonso, and the fervor of Eguiara y Egurén, who established the printing press of the Bibliotheca Mexicana during those years, contributed appreciably to the spread of the Guadalupan apologetical tradition.

From the point of view of the Mexican national mystique, the choice by the Virgin Mary of the valley of Mexico as her residence, or rather "The Celestial Conception and the Mexican Birth of the Image of Guadalupe,"[38] was inseparable from Mexico City's imperial destiny. History, as conceived by Mexican religious of the mid-eighteenth century, nourished on Judeo-Christian prophecies, appeared as a terrestrial projection of the mysterious designs of providence, inscribed in cryptic form in the prophetic books of the Old Testament and also revealed by miracles. Miracles and prodigies must accompany the evangelization of the New World and the foundation of a new church in a world called "new" not so much for geographical as for eschatological reasons. The new church would be the church of Mary, certainly the Mother of God, but above all she who in the Revelation of John routed the dragon, symbol of Antichrist. And the new Rome of this new church must be Mexico City. With an impressive insistence, contemporary authors give Mexico City the name of "Imperial City" and usually compare it to Rome, for reasons that are now perfectly clear.

Comparison of Mexico City with ancient Troy at first glance appears less convincing, but here is the interpretation one censor placed upon it: "Minerva emigrated from Heaven to the city of Troy.... Mary wished the earth to celebrate this trophy and she descended from Heaven, apparently by means of a supernatural translation, to fortunate Mexico City, rival of ancient Troy."[39] This is the reasoning of a Mercedarian friar, then rector of the Colegio de San Raimundo Nonato, in Mexico City. The friar did not recall the siege and conquest of Troy to justify the comparison with Mexico City, but in the spiritual climate that I have attempted to capture men must have involuntarily remembered the siege of Tenochtitlan-Mexico by Cortés and the desperate resistance of Cuauhtemoc, last emperor of that "Mexican empire" whose memory was inseparable from the title "imperial" generously dispensed to the capital of New Spain by Charles V.

A halo of Greco-Roman and Mexican mythology, a Christian aureole, gave a radiant glow to the burgeoning capital of Mexico in the eyes of its creole apologists. They were intoxicated with what today we would call the "development" of their country, especially since they regarded its economic prosperity as a mark of divine favor. The flourishing state of the silver mines appeared to support the assurances of biblical exegesis concerning the glorious destiny of the Mexican nation. Like the people of Madrid a century and a half before, the people of Mexico City projected their megalomaniac dreams on their imperial capital. The empire over which it presided was the Indies; contemporary book titles and iconography alike confirm a bicephalic conception of the possessions of the Crown of Spain—the king is designated as king of the Spains and emperor of the Indies (a title which went back to Philip II). Except in this stereotype, however, the phrase "the Indies" was not used as frequently as "North America" or "Our America." Creole authors, it seems, deliberately avoided any allusion to Madrid which might cause the capital of Spain to suffer by comparison. Meanwhile, under the protective cover of devotion and especially of the Marian cult, the Mexican creoles could freely weave the most extravagant nationalist dreams during those thirty decisive years.

What were the objective material foundations of the Mexican patriotic visions? The discovery of new silver deposits at San Luis (called Potosí by comparison with the famous Potosí of South America) not only led to the rapid development of that city but had repercussions for the capital, Mexico City. On the spiritual level, the creoles reflected that the tardy revelation of these immense riches must have been providentially reserved for their time; this fact could be linked to the revival of missionary activity, the war against the English heretics, and the papal consecration of the patronage of Guadalupe. Simultaneously the generalization of certain amalgamation processes (treatises on this question were published during the period under study) permitted more systematic exploitation of the silver mines. The possession of a potentially inexhaustible source of precious metal at a time when mercantilist theories proclaimed it the prime form of wealth confirmed the creoles in the conviction that they were a new "chosen people." The very aspect of Mexico City changed. Great construction projects were undertaken, such as the building of the Casa de Moneda, begun in 1729 by the viceroy, the Marqués de Casafuerte, and completed in the year of his death, 1734; less than thirty years later it had to be enlarged to provide for the swelling influx of precious metal. The *Gaceta de México,* founded in imitation of that of Madrid, informs us that the construction of this single building alone had cost a considerable sum. A customshouse was built at the same time. The School of Mines played a large role in the life of the city; from time to time it figured among the subjects of poetic competitions. Any doubts concerning the connection in creole minds between Mexico's material wealth and its providential destiny must be dispelled when one reads the following: "The Mine of the Virgin, Hidden in Nazareth and Revealed on the Hill of Tepeyac, to Become the Universal Patroness of the Americans and Especially of the Miners; and, Because She Is a Gold Mine, of the Miners of Potosí. Panegyrical Oration. . . ,"[40] a sermon pronounced by a religious of the Visitation in 1757. The other great source of national wealth, the land, seemed comparatively exhausted, and the landowners offered novenas at Guadalupe in the hope of securing rain.

However, it was the burgeoning of Mexico City and other cities of New Spain that inspired Mexican self-admiration. When the Jesuit Carranza calls Mexico City "The Rome of the New World," we may be tempted to attribute his vision to patriotic enthusiasm; but the preacher defended himself against such a charge: "Let this not be regarded as a hyperbolic exaggeration." Another religious, a Mercedarian, affirmed: "Transported by love of country, I take delight in depicting Mexico City."[41] Yet the Baron von Humboldt, half a century later, saw Mexico City with the same eyes: "No city of the new continent, not even excepting those of the United States, can display such great and solid scientific establishments as the capital of Mexico. . . . What a number of beautiful edifices are to be seen at Mexico City! Nay, even in provincial towns like Guanajuato and Querétaro! These monuments, which frequently cost a million or a million and a half francs, would appear to advantage in the finest streets of Paris, Berlin, and Petersburg."[42] When the Spanish king decided in 1740 to found a brotherhood of Guadalupe at Madrid, with himself as protector, he acted not from devotion but rather, as Fray Servando Teresa de Mier later crudely wrote, "from love of hard cash [*pesos duros*]."[43] The hope of financial aid and legacies also may have influenced the attitude of the Holy See, which in previous decades had displayed an unfriendly attitude toward the Mexican Guadalupan tradition.

Be that as it may, we observe that the cult of Guadalupe, which was two centuries old in 1731, had to wait twenty-three years longer before obtaining canonical approval. Even that approval was given with reservations, as shown by the expression *fertur* (it is reported) in

regard to the miraculous tradition. The reversal of New Spain's traditional status of spiritual dependence on Spain took place precisely
during the years in which Spain relied ever more heavily on financial
assistance from the Mexican mineowners to carry on its European
wars, so that Old Spain appeared to have become a tributary of the
New. In the intellectual realm, the University of Mexico City and the
Jesuit colleges assured the creole elite of a formation which many
gachupines could well envy, if one can credit contemporary witnesses,
with due allowance for exaggeration. A tactless criticism of the
American intellect by the Spanish dean Martí provided the Mexican
canon Eguiara y Egurén with a pretext to request permission to establish a printing shop, import the needed equipment from Europe, and
publish a monument to the glory of creole writers, a Mexican national
Parnassus. We need not take the pretext too seriously; this generation
of creole apologists doubtless had need of camouflages and reassuring
pretexts but hardly of a goad or spur.

The creoles' enthusiasm for their country was so contagious that the
Milanese chevalier Lorenzo Boturini Benaducci undertook to rewrite
the history of New Spain, or of its Mexican antiquities. This effort
culminated in the publication in 1746 of the *Idea de una nueva Historia
general de la América Septentrional,* accompanied by a catalog of manuscripts and codices which he had collected. Boturini's project was
brusquely interrupted and his library confiscated by the Spanish authorities, ever jealous of any infringement on the royal prerogative in
ecclesiastical affairs, for he had formed the project of offering a
crown to the Virgin of Guadalupe, and to this end he began collecting
funds, appealing to the liberality of the pious. The attitude of Boturini, who decided to write a *Historia general* after he had assembled
numerous documents with whose aid he proposed to provide a historical foundation for the Guadalupan tradition, is suggestive. Eguiara y
Egurén also was a devotee of Guadalupe and an apologist for the
creole *patria* and for his countrymen. Certain remarks in his *Bibliotheca Mexicana* reveal a rancor directed not just at dean Martí but at
Spain herself. The creoles fought on all fronts to free themselves
from the tutelage of the *gachupines.*

Although it is always risky for a historian to make seductive infer-
ences, I may at least raise certain questions whose significance transcends the events in question. I have sketched with broad strokes a
picture of triumphant creole advance in the mid-eighteenth century. I
have suggested that it was based on a proud consciousness of New
Spain's wealth, of the urban burgeoning, of a real or supposed intellectual supremacy, and on the charismatic feeling of a chosen people.
But the spiritual combat waged by the Mexicans for their emancipation

took place within the Hispanic mode of thought and being; in this respect the principal battleground, the cult of the Virgin, is especially revealing. Since the ultimate foundations of Spain's domination over New Spain were of a transcendent, missionary character, only when New Spain in her turn became the springboard of a new missionary expansion could she free herself from Spanish tutelage. But that rupture implied a profound loyalty to Spanish ideals: the competition in the quest for the grace of Mary recalls the Spanish Middle Ages, when Our Lady of Covadonga, the Virgin of Pilar, and Our Lady of Guadalupe herself, the Virgin of Estremadura, competed for the fervor of the Spanish Christians.

How can we forget that the Guadalupe de las Villuercas (in the province of Cáceres), according to her earliest chronicler, appeared in order to "comfort the hearts of the Christians, in order that they might recover the strength that they had lost. Thus they regained their courage."[44] Her Mexican rival, Guadalupe of Tepeyac, played the same role among the Indian converts, decimated by great epidemics and excessive forced labor, and left adrift by the collapse of native society.

The feeling of eighteenth-century Mexicans that the world, like Scripture, was a tissue of signs that had to be deciphered, encouraged an anxious wait for the last times. In effect, a tragic ambiguity marked those decisive years. Continuity of office in the ecclesiastical realm contrasted with the unstable tenure of viceroys; but it was great seismic phenomena—comets, and above all, epidemics—that were interpreted as supernatural signs. Alegre speaks of the great "pests" of 1725 and 1736 in accents of terror; we recall that the patronage of Guadalupe was a consequence of the second of these plagues. The solar eclipses of 1752, followed six years later by the eruption of the volcano of Jorullo, the comet of 1742, the earthquake in Guatemala in 1751, caused great disquiet. The martyrdom of numerous missionaries in the northern provinces ravaged by Indian uprisings, the hagiography that kept alive the memory of such martyrs as the Franciscan Antonio Margil de Jesús and several Jesuit pioneers of the California missions, reminded men of the Revelation of Isaiah and that of John. Consequently, it was the prospect of the last days, more than the prosperous present, that fascinated the Mexican creoles. According to an inspired Jesuit, "The wisdom of God inserted the delicate weft of the highest secrets of the predestination of this New World into that divine fabric, the image of Tepeyac."[45] Carranza claimed that if Rome should return to paganism and the sacrifice of the mass should disappear from the world, the mass would continue to be celebrated at Tepeyac. The Mexicans were the new chosen people and Mexico City was not only the new Rome but the new Jerusalem. The creole Carranza based this conviction on exegesis of the Song of Songs and Revelation 12.

Mexican expansionist messianism of the eighteenth century, in a sense the work of a handful of men who had known each other on the benches of the Colegio de San Ildefonso and whom the mineowners supported with their economic power, had prophetic guarantees. Biblical exegesis and display of faith in dubious miraculous traditions, far from being only an obligatory style borrowed from the dominant nation, or a fashionable dress for national aspirations in search of their own language, were inseparable from those aspirations. Religious faith and national faith blended; the former served the latter as a metaphysical guarantee, the latter was the breath that inspired the former. The religion of the dominant nation could not truly strike root in Mexico until it had been assimilated, Mexicanized. If Mexico were to become in the approaching last days the *patria* of all the Christians of the world, refugees in Tepeyac, gathered in the folds of the starry mantle of Guadalupe, then the dependent Mexicans, threatened by English heretics, terrorized by scourges and by the elements, could regain courage. New Spain's preeminence over Old Spain in the key sector of metallic wealth in the eighteenth century, joined to the charismatic certitude based on a new epiphany (the "incarnation" of the Virgin Mary at Tepeyac), permitted the Mexicans to escape from the original stain of paganism and barbarism.

7   The Holy War
1767–1821

The Expulsion of the Jesuits (1767–70)

"The Reverend Jesuit Fathers throw themselves at Your Excellency's feet and beg him to grant them permission to commend themselves to Our Lady of Guadalupe and bid farewell to that divine Lady when they pass by her sanctuary."[1] This final prayer, addressed to the Marqués de Croix, viceroy of New Spain, by one of the last groups of Jesuits to take the road to exile, sets the tone of that historical moment. We recall the role played by the Jesuits in the development of the cult of Guadalupe and, later, in the recognition of the tradition by the Congregation of Rites. The triumphant advance of the eighteenth-century Mexican creoles merged with the apotheosis of the Society; this fact clearly emerges from devotional literature. We recall these eloquent titles of sermons and novenas: "Novena of the Triumphant Company of Jesus," or "Heaven Placed in Our Hands by the Hands of Ignatius and His Company."[2] Conditions following the expulsion of the Jesuits from New Spain were optimal for the appearance and development of a myth of the Jesuit Golden Age. This historical accident, the expulsion, had been preceded twenty years earlier by "signs"; in 1747 lightning had twice struck the chapel of Saint Ignatius Loyola, in the cathedral of Puebla, one of the centers of the Jesuit radiance and the theater of the first episode in the struggle of the Society against the secular bishops. The official lightning which struck the Jesuits of Mexico City on the morning of June 25, 1767, was all the more stupefying in its effects because it came out of a clear blue sky. Two years earlier the sovereign pontiff had confirmed the constitutions of the Society by the brief *Apostolicus pascendi;* the safety of the Society, installed in the most Catholic of monarchies, revered by a society as pious as that of the Mexican creoles in the eighteenth century, seemed assured. There were then nearly seven hundred Jesuits in New Spain, and many of them occupied eminent positions in society. Numerous documents testify that New Spain was struck with stupor. Despite the very great precautions that had been taken, the departure of the Jesuits was attended by emotional displays in the majority of cities and missions. The great distances, the slowness of travel, the wait for favorable winds before the ships that were to take the religious to Europe could get under sail, the crossing of the country by Jesuits (attached to the province of Mexico) who were repatriated from the Philippines, were responsible for the fact that more than three years after the arrival of the decree of expulsion in New Spain, groups of Jesuits, surrounded by soldiers, still were traversing the country.

The climate of those three years, decisive for the destiny of the Mexican nation, emerges from trial proceedings, travel diaries, and pamphlets. The situation provoked a wide variety of popular reactions. The most violent came from the Indians; at San Luis de la Paz, in Sonora, the Indians prevented "by main force the expulsion and departure of the Jesuits from the colegio that they had there under the name of mission."[3] It is a striking example of Jesuit influence in their missions. Such commotions were not rare in New Spain; similar episodes had taken place in mission territories since the sixteenth century. In general, Indian uprisings were frequent. What was to some degree special about this affair was the brutality of the repression and its swiftness. Less than a month after the rising, the sentences of the guilty parties were handed down: "As merited chastisement and a salutary warning to the others, I find that I must condemn and I do condemn to death Ana Maria Goatemala, an Indian widow; Julián Martínez Serrano; Vicente Ferral Rangel and Marcos Pérez de Leon, because it is said that he is the principal descendant of a cacique, to be shot by a firing squad as a traitor; and on the place of execution their heads will be separated from their bodies and placed on pikes where they shall remain until time consumes them."[4]

Those rotting heads that time consumed doubtless inspired the salutary fear that, the Visitador hoped, would prevent new convulsions. But they also prolonged the shock of the Jesuit expulsion; those Indian martyrs transformed what might have been an ephemeral episode into a decisive hour for the history of Mexico. To die for the Jesuits proved to have more exemplary value than to live according to Jesuit models. Comparable to the eviction of the Franciscans from their missions, the expulsion of the Jesuits could be regarded as a belated revenge of the Friars Minor, for to them were entrusted the majority of the former Jesuit missions. But there was no longer any hostility between Jesuits and Franciscans in New Spain.

A comparison of the Franciscan expulsion and that of the Jesuits from their respective provinces is illuminating chiefly because it brings out the differences between the two events. The abandonment of the Franciscan missions, begun in the last quarter of the sixteenth century, was an enterprise carried out by stages; it was not yet complete in the middle of the eighteenth century. The occasional riots to which the departure of the Franciscans or the arrival of the curates who were to replace them gave rise were local episodes, dispersed in space and in time. Moreover, the Friars Minor were not expelled from New Spain; they were sent to other mission areas or regrouped in convents. Their dispossession was not presented as a punishment or banishment. The progressive abandonment of the Franciscan missions had been preceded by an undeniable decline of missionary zeal among the mendicant orders in general. The expulsion of the Jesuits, on the contrary, in that second half of the eighteenth century which may rightly be called the "Jesuit age" of New Spain—as the splendor of the religious architecture of New Spain still attests—had the aspect of a sharp break. This aspect requires emphasis.

To begin with, its suddenness: from one day to the next a body of men who occupied a most important place in the life of New Spain and among all the social and ethnic groups that composed its population was torn away in a move so radical that none could have foreseen it. The Jesuits had achieved a moral leadership, an influence over the creole elite, that Indians, and the *castas,* comparable only to that of the Franciscan pioneers in the twenty years that followed the arrival of the Twelve in 1524. They were expelled at the peak of their power, after they had led the national-religious cause of Guadalupe to triumph, after they had checked the power of the viceroy over their missions, after they had defeated the secularizing bishops over the issue of beatification for Palafox. This last victory came shortly before the expulsion of the Society; it was, perhaps, the only portent of things to come for minds sensitive to subtle indications of a change in papal policy.

An essential feature of the expulsion was the simultaneous timing of the orders for expulsion; from one end to the other of the viceroyalty of New Spain and of the whole immense Spanish empire in America, Indians arose for the same reason; this fact was unprecedented. Even the rising led by Cuauhtemoc in the sixteenth century had only united the Aztecs of the valley of Mexico, whereas the Indians of the Jesuit missions belonged to ethnic groups widely separated from each other by distance and culture. One can speak here, for the first time, of a national movement, although it was not regarded as such either by its actors or by the repressive authority. This movement was national, above all, because it was the spontaneous reaction of all the social, regional, and ethnic groups of New Spain to a blow whose shock all felt keenly. For the first time, perhaps, the creoles, the *castas,* and the Indians made common cause from one end of the country to the other against a common enemy—an enemy who was no longer the anonymous *gachupín,* the traditional rival of the creole, but the king himself. A political power based on unity of faith had entered into open conflict with the men who appeared to be the interpreters of orthodoxy in New Spain, the Jesuits. In fact the Jesuits were the guardians of the faith of the Mexican people, whose aspirations they rightly interpreted when they became champions of the Marian cult, particularly of its Guadalupan expression. Thus the "station" made at the sanctuary of Guadalupe by groups of Jesuits on that way of the cross which was to lead them from from their country (first to Corsica, thence to Italy) had a national significance of capital importance. Mexicans of all races had communed under the aegis of the Society in a unanimous devotion to the Virgin of Tepeyac; henceforth Mexican Guadalupan Christianity had its martyrs and its memorial.

Great precautions had been taken to avoid all contact between the Jesuits and the rural population. In the cities, however, tension was great, as indicated by the journal of a Philippine Jesuit who crossed New Spain with his comrades from Acapulco to Veracruz. The date was February 1770; one might expect that by then the passions aroused by a measure decreed June 25, 1767, had subsided. But this is what the Jesuit writes: "Because of the roads, it was necessary to pass very close to Puebla, and for this reason they added as an escort a picket of mounted dragoons; and despite all their precautions, such as making us pass through very early in the morning and at a smart pace, there were people there who threw themselves on our carriages among the soldiers and tried at least to kiss our hands, at the risk of being crushed."[5] Next day, the Jesuits entered Veracruz "in Indian file, with soldiers in formation in front, in the rear and on the flanks."[6] Although the Mexican people, "the children of Guadalupe," were quite heterodox in their Catholic faith, they believed in it as firmly as the inquisitors; yet, they were subject to brutal religious persecution on the occasion of the Jesuit expulsion. One Jesuit, expelled from the California mission, left a moving account of the repression: "At the port of San Blas we found a number of Indians from San Luis Potosí and its environs, condemned for having revolted. They had taken to arms when they learned that their missionaries were being taken away. . . . One of us was summoned to hear the confession of one of these unfortunates: he found him so lacerated by lashes that all that one could see of him was blood and bones; yet they continued to lash him every day without pity."[7] The blood of the Indians and the menacing shadow of the dragoons, from north to south, from east to west, in New Spain, then sealed as if by a sacrament the union of all Mexicans. The work which the cult of Guadalupe had begun the martyrs of the Jesuit Guadalupan faith completed, and the result, a product of the time and the circumstances, was the Mexican fatherland itself.

The expulsion caused irremediable damage to loyalty to the Spanish monarchy. Doubt penetrated all minds; this admission of the bishop of Guadalajara, reported by the previous witness, is a good example: "We had hardly left Guadalajara when the bishop sent one of his canons to greet us in his name and to congratulate us—these are his own words—for enduring exile for the name of Jesus."[8] The rest of the journal gives a striking impression of the atmosphere in which the Jesuits left New Spain. The violent actions of the Indians and the *castas* who wished to prevent their departure found an echo in the efforts of the creoles to mitigate their sufferings. "In the small town of Xeres," reports the same Jesuit, "the nuns would not rest until they had obtained agreement that mass should be said the next day in each convent by one of us. The gentlemen of the town conducted us there in their carriages. The confessors of the different monasteries told us that the religious were practicing such great austerities to obtain the return of the Society from God, that some would have lost their health if they [the confessors] had not put a stop to it."[9] It may be objected that this testimony, like those which preceded it, is suspect because it derives from exiled Jesuits. No doubt these Jesuits wished to add a particularly edifying last chapter to the *Lettres édifiantes,* but they did not invent the facts. The summary judgments handed down against the instigators of the Indian uprisings, the creole pamphlets seized with notable lack of alacrity by the inquisitors, confirm that the Jesuit expulsion took place in the atmosphere that the Jesuits themselves described. The last piece of testimony cited shows the pro-Jesuit zeal of the nuns and the mortifications to which the faithful subjected themselves.

We must not forget that Jesuits had charge of the spiritual direction of numerous nunneries, and that since the sixteenth century they had been promoters of the Marian brotherhoods, which, like their colegios, were among the most effective instruments of Jesuit influence among laymen. Given the importance of the Marian brotherhoods in the life of New Spain, we may say that the expulsion of the Society eliminated one of the most vital institutions of urban and rural religious life, its true cell. Thus the Jesuit departure from the different towns and regions of New Spain was a cultural catastrophe, comparable in importance in New Spain's history to the effect that the departure for exile nine centuries before of the priest-king of Tula,

Quetzalcóatl, had in the history of ancient Mexico. Indeed, the stations of the cross of the Jesuits on their way to Veracruz more than once recall the stations of Quetzalcóatl, who performed miracles on the road and, before he disappeared amid the waves, promised to return in triumph. The cyclical scheme, implying the return of the Messiah in glory after the ordeal of death or exile, applies as well to Quetzalcóatl as to the Jesuits. Independence, won under the banner of Guadalupe which the Jesuits had been the first to raise high, amid cries of "Death to the *gachupines!*" (their persecutors) was to bring the triumphant return of the Society. Whether or not the multitude was aware of it, the similarity with the exile of Quetzalcóatl Topiltzin was striking. Like that exile, the Jesuit expulsion was accompanied by messianic and mystical developments and by supernatural signs.

The anonymous Jesuit of California left us another precious bit of testimony in this regard: "While the ship was being made ready to get under sail, April 4, about twenty minutes after six in the morning, an earthquake was felt which lasted about seven minutes. . . . In the public squares the people prostrated themselves on the ground, wailing and begging for divine mercy; many cried aloud that heaven clearly was beginning to punish the expulsion of the Jesuits."[10] It was in an apocalyptic atmosphere that these missionaries sailed from Veracruz aboard the *Santa Ana*, a rotten ship which allegedly could not have survived the crossing without the "protection from on high."[11] Some nuns who had recently been put under the spiritual direction of the Jesuits had "revelations" which announced the approaching restoration of the Society and the return of the exiles. The order forbidding the Jesuits to enter Mexico City while en route to their exile appears pathetic in the light of these facts. They had penetrated the depths of the collective consciousness, aureoled with the reputation of martyrs. The Jesuit myth, more or less confounded with that of the Virgin of Guadalupe, was to engender effects much more serious for the future of the Spanish domination than the riots which the authorities managed to prevent in the capital. From San Antonio in Texas to San Francisco, from the sanctuary of Tepeyac to the household altars which the modest Indian huts (*jacales*) still display to this day, the image of Guadalupe recalled the presence of the Jesuits and nourished the hope of their return.

Viewed in that light, the passionate polemic—with special reference to the Peruvian Jesuit Vizcardo, author of an *Open Letter to the Spaniards of America* (1791)[12]—about the role played by some former Jesuits in the independence movements of Spanish America to the close of the eighteenth and the beginning of the nineteenth centuries, loses much of its importance. On the ideological level, it is likely, as

Father Furlong has written in regard to Argentina, that the "populist" doctrine of the Jesuit Suárez prepared the soil for its penetration by the new democratic ideals disseminated by Rousseau and the ideologues of the French Revolution. But the "hidden mine" left by the Jesuits in the Indies after their expulsion, about which the bishop of Buenos Aires had a presentiment, was buried more deeply. In New Spain, especially, it owed its explosive power to the fact that it shook deep layers of the collective consciousness. The expulsion of the Jesuits was originally a historical accident that inserted itself into the religious consciousness on the level of the myth-creating faculty. The "revelations" of the *beatas* with regard to the return of the Jesuits were the belated resurgence, in this age of the Enlightenment, of the revelations of other nuns of the sixteenth century. We have seen with what pitiless severity the Inquisition repressed those religious. The Mexican Inquisition displayed an astounding passivity in the face of a proliferation of defamatory libels against the king, and toward the illuminist (and clearly heterodox) expressions of Mexican attachment to the Society. The confessors were equally indulgent with those of their penitents who accused themselves of desiring the death of a ruler as tyrannical as Charles III, plainly described as a heretic in placards posted on the walls of the cities of New Spain. Only after it received a severe reprimand from the monarch, did the tribunal resolve to prosecute priests who, not content with failure to denounce the potential regicides, encouraged them in the confessional box. We have come a long way from the confessor-seducers of the past; here political passion comes even with the collective consciousness. This great change was doubtless one of the most serious short-term consequences of the expulsion; in any case, it was one of its immediate effects.

By comparison with its decisive contribution to precipitation (in the chemical sense—in Spanish one would say, *ha venido a cuajar*) of the Mexican national consciousness, the other aspects of the Jesuit expulsion were of secondary importance. The secularization of the Society's real estate and personal property, to be sure, had an impact on the economic life of New Spain. Even that impact, however, seemed to have a religious aspect; when efforts were made to apply the official instruction directing the sale of the Society's livestock, they had to be abandoned on the local level, for the Indians regarded the cattle and horses of the Jesuit missions as sacred animals, protected by a taboo, and to put them up for sale would have provoked new uprisings. So sacred was all that pertained to the Jesuits, that the sacred person of the monarch suffered in consequence a corresponding irremediable diminution. The Spanish king had wished to consolidate his patronage over the church of the Indies and manifest his royal prerogative by expelling the Society; in succeeding years this measure was followed by others designed to make religious orders depending on the Patronato "keep to heel." But, through fatal political error, it caused a commotion that lighted the first spark of a holy war, a flame not to be extinguished until the achievement of Independence. Patron and protector of the official church, of the secular and regular clergy of New Spain, the king was neither the guide nor the preeminent head of the real Mexican church, that *Iglesia indiana* which ever since the sixteenth century had been the personal property of the friars. After long subterranean journeys, a new avatar of the *Iglesia indiana* of the Franciscan missionaries had arisen on the horizon of the Mexican consciousness; its emblem was the Virgin of Guadalupe, its sacerdotal body was composed above all of Jesuits. Their expulsion was the founding act, after two and a half centuries of evangelization, of a truly national church, which immediately and violently asserted its rights against the church of the colonizers. A combative church, from the first it was inspired by a great messianic aspiration that implied the return of the Jesuits.

The departure of the Jesuits from the mission territories often had disastrous consequences. The material absence of the spiritual support which they had given the Indians was felt the day after their departure, and many months frequently elapsed before the arrival of the Franciscan replacements. In places where secular clergy replaced the Jesuits, as a rule there followed the same spiritual shipwreck which had accompanied the replacement of the Franciscans by parish priests in the past. In the educational field, the university chairs vacated by Jesuits, who were receptive to the advanced European knowledge of their time, rarely were filled by teachers of comparable brilliance. In fine, the departure of the Jesuits created a spiritual and intellectual vacuum in different geographical regions and in many vital sectors of the life of the viceroyalty—a vacuum that could not be filled.

Into this vacuum rushed the Enlightenment with its train of heterodox ideas. The limited progress made by deism and even atheism, by revolutionary ideas that preached or at least accepted regicide in New Spain in the last quarter of the eighteenth century, would have been impossible without the spiritual disarray, the rancor against the monarchy, and the disorganization of the educational process, caused by the brutal Jesuit expulsion. Historians have amply discussed the causes of that event, but the question of its results forms a historical problem of much greater significance.[13]

In the preceding pages, I have called attention to the importance of the Jesuit contribution to the formation of a Mexican national consciousness. That brief survey of a very large topic would be incomplete without some mention of the role of the Jesuits in exile. I have alluded to those who took a direct part in the Wars of Independence. The *Letter to the American Spaniards* of the abbot Vizcardo, an ex-Jesuit from Peru, the activity of another ex-Jesuit of Tucuman, Father Diego León Villafañe, who returned to the Rio de la Plata and participated in the May Revolution in Argentina, deserve mention, at least. It is of interest that not a single Mexican Jesuit exile took an active part in the movement for Independence. In order to assess properly the contribution of the Jesuit refugees in Italy (most of them ultimately settled in Cesena) to the liberation of New Spain and the restoration of a largely mythical Mexican empire, we must forget revolutionary activity of every kind. In several masterful pages Father Batllori has disposed of pseudo-historical legends about a supposed Jesuit plot behind the American Wars of Independence. Obsession with the Jesuits, whether inspired by a denigrative or an apologetical spirit, has long been disastrous to history; I need not stop to refute it.

I prefer to cite a comment of Father Batllori's that makes a good point of departure. He observes that "these American Spaniards [*Españoles americanos*]—to use the terminology of Vizcardo, the most advanced thinker among them—were no longer pure Spaniards, but were not yet pure Americans; they represent a pre-national regionalist phase in which the nostalgia of the exiles played the role that historical romanticism was to play . . . in Europe."[14] A major thesis of the present work has been that from the middle of the sixteenth century the Mexican creoles were no longer completely Spaniards; they felt they were subjects of the Spanish king and descendants of Spaniards, to be sure, but maintained an attitude of opposition, indeed of rejection, toward the latter. The term "American Spaniards" appeared in the legal texts, but the spoken language (and often the written language as well) retained only the adjective "American" or that of "creole." At the close of the eighteenth century the Mexicans were not, and had not been for two centuries, "pure Spaniards" in any sense. Were they "pure Americans," then?

Francisco Javier Clavijero, in the dedication to the University of Mexico City of his *Historia antigua de México*,[15] dated 1780, at Bologna, betrays an existential anguish by his semantic uncertainty. His first words are: "A history of Mexico written by a Mexican," which seems to reveal a thoroughly conscious patriotic feeling and a pride in that feeling. In less than four pages he mentions his *patria* four times, and presents his work as "testimony of my most sincere love for my *patria*." The context leaves no room for doubt as to the identity of this country;

it is Mexico. He also writes, addressing himself to the professors of the University of Mexico City: "the history of our *patria*." Referring to the Mexican creoles, he writes "our compatriots." But we observe that Clavijero, having identified himself as a "Mexican," applies this term in the rest of the book only to the Indians of ancient Mexico. Here is an initial difficulty. Speaking of the sources for the history of ancient Mexico, he cites "the missionaries and other Spaniards of the past" on the one hand, and the Indians themselves on the other. Although he has described the creoles of the University of Mexico City as his "compatriots," in the prologue that follows he writes "my compatriots [*nacionales*]," in speaking of the Spaniards.[16]

The concept of "nation" in its classic sense, before the triumph of the national movements inaugurated by the French Revolution, belonged to the vocabulary of physical anthropology, an anthropology that was derived, like all knowledge, from Scripture. Originally we find the opposition between Israel and the "nations." This term was then almost synonymous with "tribes" in the language of modern anthropology. Clavijero called the Spaniards his compatriots (*nacionales*) because he was of Spanish stock. Thereby he distinguished them from his "compatriots," the creoles of New Spain, with whom he shared in common a *patria* (should this be understood in the peninsular sense of *patria chica?*), that is, a native land. "Nation" expressed the bonds of blood and *patria* territorial bonds. We also note that in the detailed account which he gives of the episodes of the Conquest Clavijero designates the Indians by the term "Mexicans" and the Spaniards by the name of "Spaniards," in the first case excluding the term "Indians," which he seems to reserve for the Indians of his own time, and in the second such terms as "our forebears" or "our fathers," which he applied to the Mexican creoles.

The founder of the *Real Congregación de Na. Sra. de Guadalupe de México,* of Madrid, had summed up the aims of this society in 1757 in the following terms: "The honor and glory of the nation; the benefit of the nationals and of those who have ties with the Indies, the advantage of the Americas, and the pride of knowing that they are as worthy as foreign nations."[17] Observe the value of the word "nation" and the application of the term "nationals" to the Mexicans; this use of neologisms ("nation" does not have here its ethnic sense of "peoples," derived from Scripture) is the more interesting for the history of Mexican national sentiment because it is opposed to "foreign nations," and in the first place to Spain.

If we compare this text with that of Francisco Javier Clavijero, which I have just analyzed, we get a clearer idea of the emergence of a Mexican national consciousness on the linguistic level and the approximate date of that phenomenon. We discover that each time we must push farther back in time the appearance of a conscious sentiment of national identity capable of explicitly asserting its primordial claim of dignity against the dominant Spanish nation. Amid these apparent indecisions, several facts stand out: Clavijero gives the name "Mexicans" to the Indians before their defeat, but also calls himself a "Mexican"; and he does not write "creoles" but "my compatriots."

Clavijero's history ends with the evocation of the siege of Tenochtitlan-Mexico and its destruction by the Spaniards, compared to the destruction of Jerusalem by the Romans. This image makes amply clear where the sympathies of the illustrious Jesuit exile lie; for the rest, he makes no effort to conceal them. "The king of Mexico, despite the grandiose promises of the Spanish general" (the circumlocution to designate Cortés reveals the repudiation of the Conquest by the creoles on the eve of Independence) "was a few days later ignominiously put to the torture." Clavijero sees in the abandoned state of the creoles as well as of "the vile African slaves and their descendants" a mournful example of divine justice and the instability of kingdoms.[18]

The noble title of "Mexican," then, Clavijero reserves for Indians of the past, masters of their own country, and for the modern creoles, who aspire to become its masters. The Spaniards in general are mentioned as mere foreigners; as for the castes, they are relegated to their servile condition. By refusing to integrate mulattoes and other mixed-bloods in his *patria*, Clavijero reveals his creole mentality (he is more backward in this respect than Sor Juana Inés de la Cruz, who antedated him by a century). The innovative aspects of his thought are the notable absence from his book of the expression "New Spain"—the only official title—and, above all, the ambivalence of the name "Mexican." It reveals a posture already evident in Sigüenza y Góngora, the determination to integrate the Mexican past in the creole *patria*, while excluding the contemporary Indian.

Clavijero was already a Mexican, highly conscious of being such. Should we censure him for being unaware that his country could only achieve true nationhood by integrating all its ethnic groups, when as late as a century after independence many intelligent Mexicans continued to think like eighteenth-century creoles? We may say that Clavijero's patriotism corresponded to "a phase of prenational regionalism," if by "nation" we mean a reality *sui generis,* characterized precisely by the integration of different ethnic communities, united by voluntary political bonds, by common interests, and by a common affective heritage.

It is one of those ironies of history, perhaps, that the Mexican Jesuit exiles in Italy, unconscious midwives of the Mexican "nation" (nation in the modern sense, this time), cut off from the daily reality of their *patria*, had no idea of the repercussions of their exile on the Mexican collective consciousness. These sons of the creole bourgeoisie whose expulsion had brought loss to almost every prominent Mexican family, rediscovered the biblical term "tribulation" in order to describe their exile and identified themselves half-consciously with the people of Israel, an analogy confirmed by comparison of Mexico-Tenochtitlan with ancient Jerusalem. (We have seen the creole preachers develop these themes.) To restore the Temple, to end their exile and first of all that spiritual exile that the colonial centuries constituted, was the profound, constant aspiration of the creole patriots. The erasure of the term "New Spain" from Clavijero's *History* is the prelude to its replacement with the word "Mexico," used by the liberators of the next generation to designate a *patria* whose masters they had at last—anew, they thought—become. Insofar as Clavijero's *History* tacitly completes the break of the link to Spain, he seems already to merit the name "Mexican," without any qualification.

Add to this the fact that Clavijero played a special role in the diffusion of Mexican culture in Europe. Let me explain my meaning. Father Batllori has commented disparagingly about the "provincial" character of the intellectual production of the American Jesuit exiles.[19] As concerns the Mexican Jesuits, to be sure, Clavijero and Andrés Cavo wrote histories of Mexico, Alegre a history of the Society of Jesus in New Spain, Rafael Landivar sang the *Rusticatio mexicana,* and Maneiro celebrated the illustrious men of Mexico. Add to this the fact that A. Diego Fuente and Clavijero published small works devoted to the glory of the Virgin of Guadalupe, and we may well conclude that the Jesuit writings breathe a regionalist spirit. But one may also ask whether any other spirit ever prevailed in the countries of the Hispanic world in the modern period, excepting only the transient interlude of the Enlightenment. On the other hand, it is certain (Father Batllori has done a notable study of this aspect for Italy) that the Mexican Jesuit exiles in Italy helped to rescue the past, the nature, the culture, and the intellect of their country from its "provincialism"—a term I prefer to use here instead of regionalism. The lucubrations of De Pauw, in particular, by provoking the detailed response of a Clavijero, aroused European curiosity about Mexico.

In that middle-class Germany in which the precocious genius of Goethe arose and where a passion for folklore, inspired by Herder, filled men's minds, a Schiller displayed enthusiasm for America. Thanks to the Jesuit nostalgia for their country, Mexico made a triumphant entry into Enlightenment Europe before she was admitted as an equal into the community of nations. It would be unjust to see in Clavijero only an offended provincial defending his *patria chica*. Using a prestigious tribune of contemporary Europe, the *Teutsche Merkur,* a journal published in Weimar, the Jesuit presented his distant fatherland to readers avidly interested in exotic subjects. The numbers for July, August, and October 1786 contained a series of articles by Clavijero in German translation, "Treatise on the Natural Conditions of the Kingdom of Mexico";[20] in the same number of the journal appeared a review of José de Acosta's *Historia natural y moral de las Indias* by Cornelius de Pauw. I should note that Mexico was then known in Europe almost exclusively through the *Historia de la Conquista de México* of Antonio Solís, which had been frequently reprinted, and Acosta's *Historia*. At that period no modern work by a writer in Spanish had yet appeared. The *History of America* (1777) by the Scot historian William Robertson came to fill this gap before the Academia de la Historia de España entrusted to Juan Bautista Muñoz the task of writing a great work, *Historia del Nuevo Mundo,* which he never brought to completion. Clavijero's work, devoted to ancient Mexico, and the histories of New Spain of the Jesuits Alegre and Cavo gave Europeans access to a whole corpus of encyclopedic knowledge about Mexico—a corpus which helped to slake the contemporary curiosity about exotic lands and peoples. It is fashionable to pay tribute to Alexander von Humboldt's incomparable *Essai politique sur le royaume de la Nouvelle-Espagne,* but little attention has been given to the fact that that young gentleman was only seventeen in 1786, and that were it not for the stir that arose in Enlightenment circles with regard to Mexico and that "Dispute of the New World" so ably studied by Antonello Gerbi, Humboldt may have never gotten the idea of visiting the New World to study its different regions. To be more explicit, let me recall Humboldt's discreet homage to Clavijero: "That empire, if we may believe Solís, extended from Panama as far as New California. But the learned studies of a Mexican historian, the Abbé Clavijero, have taught us. . . ."[21]

Without the presence in Italy of the Mexican Jesuits, and more especially of Clavijero, who, together with Cornelius de Pauw, was one of the protagonists in that great "Dispute of the New World," there would have been no polemics relating to America, or else they would not have had such enduring repercussions, reaching to Hegel and beyond. Thanks to the publications and the personal contacts of the Mexican Jesuit exiles in Italy, Mexico took its place among the nations as an autonomous geographic and cultural entity endowed with a prestigious past and the promise of a rich future. Insofar as European knowledge of Mexico's past and present (as seen by Clavijero, thirty years before Humboldt) became a component of the Enlightenment, Mexico entered universal history at the end of the eighteenth century. This was not a simple reentry; creole Mexico, breaking the cables that held it fast to its colonial provincialism, had nothing in common with the Mexico described by Cortés except a religious-national attachment to a brilliant past recreated by a nostalgic historiography. But the irruption, as sudden as the exile of the Jesuits, of Mexican antiquities into the world of the Enlightenment—that second, more critical European Renaissance—achieved the incorporation of creole values (through the creole vision of the past) into the new values, soon to triumph thanks to the nationalist movements. This original Mexican contribution, favored by the awakening of national consciousness in Europe, would have been lacking, or would have come too late, without the Jesuit exiles. Traveling in reverse the road taken by the first twelve Jesuits who had come from Spain in 1572 to found a colonial church supported by the Spanish government, the Jesuits expelled in 1767 founded the Mexican church in the hearts of men. From their Italian exile they diffused the message of that church to the Europe of the Enlightenment, that new religion which the French Revolution would soon transform into a religion of patriotism.

The Guerrilla Priests,
Hidalgo and Morelos (1810–15)

> What was the flag of that army?
> When he passed through Atotoniclo the parish priest Hidalgo took from the church a standard with the effigy of the Virgin of Guadalupe. He hung the cloth, cherished and revered by all Mexicans, on the staff of a lance and made it the flag of that strange and improvised army.
> What was the war cry of that army?
> "Long Live religion! Long Live Our Very Holy Mother of Guadalupe! Long Live America and down with the rotten government!"

In these words, in a history text for the use of students in the Mexican public schools, the writer Manuel Payno evoked the exploit of Hidalgo, parish priest of Dolores.[22] We note that he tells the story using a question-and-answer form, to be memorized like a civic catechism. The edition I used, that of 1883, was the seventh, but there must have been at least thirteen; we have to do with a stereotype that long ago entered the Mexican collective consciousness. The plaster-saint image of Hidalgo and the familiar slogans of the "Cry of Dolores" conceal a complex reality, that of the historical *moment,* the morning of September 16, 1810, when the cry of the revolutionary priest awoke a powerful echo in the popular consciousness. For almost three centuries Indian revolts, like seismic shocks and just as unpredictable, had shaken the different regions of New Spain; they were drowned in blood and a heavy calm returned for years or decades. The movement unleashed by the priest of Dolores differed from all previous ones in two ways: it ignited a train of gunpowder that ran throughout the viceroyalty and it lasted more than ten years, never subsiding until it had achieved its end, Independence. A contemporary Spanish *arbitrista* or "project-monger" wrote as follows concerning the progress of Hidalgo's rebellion: "Men of every condition came from everywhere to join him, soldiers, ecclesiastics, owners of *haciendas* and mines, in fine, all his countrymen, with very few exceptions . . . ; since the majority of the ecclesiastics and the people who know how to read and write and have influence over the masses are creoles, they did nothing to contain the people but rather incited them to disorder and rebellion; and if four ragamuffins cried out in a town with thousands of inhabitants: 'Long live Our Lady of Guadalupe and death to the *gachupines*,' the whole town rebelled."[23]

The atmosphere of the movement, then, was what Luis Villoro has defined as *el instantaneismo,* a revolutionary atmosphere of spontaneous actions. Hidalgo himself said to the judges of the tribunal of the Inquisition that he had acted "by instinct." Twenty years later another pioneer of Independence wrote of Hidalgo: "It is clear that this famous leader did no more than grasp a flag with the effigy of Guadalupe and run about from town to town with his men, without even making known the kind of government that he proposed to establish."[24] One might answer Lorenzo de Zavala that there is a time for every action; a revolution is not made with constitutional projects, and without the heroic initial leap of the parish priest of Dolores, the Constitution of Apatzingan would not have appeared two years later. Hidalgo had the makings of a revolutionary leader. Learning that he was about to be arrested, while he was deliberating with other conspirators about the tactics they should adopt, he made the "irrational" decision to precipitate the course of events. A confessor, he knew the souls of his parishioners; better still, he felt them. He knew that a political program was premature; what was needed was a flag and an enemy. What better symbol of popular aspirations could he have found than the Virgin of Guadalupe? What enemy was closer and weaker than the few thousand Spaniards who lived in New Spain? The doctrine that he proclaimed, therefore, was a simple one: "We know no other religion than the Catholic, Roman Apostolic Faith. . . . We will glady sacrifice our lives in its defense. . . . For the welfare of the kingdom it is necessary to wrest command and power from the hands of the Europeans. . . . Considering, therefore, the sacred fire that inflames us and the justice of our cause, take heart, sons of the fatherland, for the day of glory and happiness for America has arrived. . . . Arise, noble American hearts, from the profound abasement in which you have been buried. . . . Open your eyes: see how the Europeans seek to make creoles fight creoles."[25] The style of this proclamation struck home; Hidalgo raised the specter of fratricidal strife to dissuade creoles from joining the ranks of a counter-revolutionary army.

The ideological content and the revolutionary language used here by the former student of the Jesuit Colegio de Valladolid in Michoacán reveal a profound intellectual evolution in New Spain. The "sacred fire that inflames us," the "sons of the fatherland," the "day of glory," all textual borrowings from a verse of the "Marseillaise," announced that the insurrection that had begun was neither a peasant rising nor a pogrom (although it had those aspects) but the regional manifestation of a world revolutionary process that received a large impetus from the success of the French Revolution. In the microcosm of the rural parishes and Indian communities, however, the parish priest of Dolores appeared as the last Messiah. Loyalist pamphleteers, for their part, presented Hidalgo as the Demon, the Antichrist, and the "Napoleon of America." Whereas the revolutionary language was in process of change, rising to the level of a leader who knew French and had read the classics of the French Revolution, public consciousness still translated political facts into religious terms.

The repercussions of the "Cry of Dolores" (that first *Thunder Over Mexico*) are explained by all that had happened in New Spain since the expulsion of the Jesuits in 1767 and in Spain since the *dos de mayo* of 1808, when the people of Madrid rose up against the French troops. The complex political history of this troubled period reveals a relatively simple line of development and some critical moments. The emotion inspired by the expulsion of the Jesuits had not yet died down when other authoritarian measures of Charles III (less radical, to be sure) hit other religious orders. From 1770 to about 1778, the nuns of New Spain, in particular those of the convents of Puebla, refused to submit to a royal decree which enjoined them to return to a "community life." I have already described, in connection with Sor Juana Inés de la Cruz, the mode of life in seventeenth-century convents; it will be recalled that the nuns led a secular existence and were served by their personal maids. The Mexican convents thus resembled residential hotels in which each nun lived her own life. Many took in little girls whom they provided with an education. The proposed eviction of these children was a factor in the passionate resistance offered by the nuns; but the presence of children was certainly incompatible with a return to the rule of community life. The issue was the determination of the Crown, in the name of its royal prerogative, to impose a reform of the religious orders that would overthrow customs that had been established for two centuries. This was a revolution; the church bells rang a full peal; the bishop of Puebla resigned; the correspondence of the viceroy Bucareli with the *visitador* Gálvez is filled with episodes relating to this affair. Note that it came on the heels of the crisis caused by the expulsion of the Jesuits.

In a kingdom where the religious had occupied a dominant position since the coming of the first missionaries, such brutal attacks on the religious communities (by expulsion, suppression, or reform) inevitably shook Mexican society itself to its foundations. Like the expulsion of the Jesuits, the affair of "community life" was a political problem which revealed or revived tensions; the interventions of the ayuntamiento of Puebla and the audiencia of Mexico City leave no doubt on that score. These different measures, which were nothing more than a strict application of the prerogatives of the monarch by virtue of the royal patronage, were resented as tyrannical abuses of power because they infringed on the customary autonomy of the religious orders. That autonomy had been diminished in the preceding period by the expansion of the secular clergy under the leadership of elite bishops like Moya de Contreras and Palafox, but this struggle for control had been, in the last analysis, an internal question of the ecclesiastical estate. Charles II, an "enlightened despot" surrounded by Italian counselors and inspired by French philosophical ideas, although personally an irreproachable Catholic, came to be regarded as a heretic in New Spain as a result of the expulsion of the Society of Jesus. What the monarch and his counselors in Madrid had conceived as a restoration of royal authority over the regular clergy was resented in New Spain as a criminal attack (the new crime of lèse-religion) on the sacerdotal caste.

The consequences of the abandonment of the missions by the Jesuits and the "reclaustration" of the religious in the towns were in a sense as grave as the elimination of its priests had been for Mexican polytheism. Deprived of its arbiters of orthodoxy, the bearers of its faith, the friars, the Mexican people retreated to its parish life and its essential cults. The Virgin of Guadalupe, on whom converged the profoundest hopes of salvation, became even more the mother-goddess of the Mexicans. In the countryside, parish priests, less subject to governmental control, took over from the departed religious.

One must understand the immense role of the friars in New Spain's life to realize the extent of the revolution caused by unwise governmental measures.

At the same time that the religious, who had enjoyed an undisputed autonomy and preeminence since the first half of the sixteenth century, lost ground, the military class rose from obscurity as a result of the war with England. In 1758 the army of New Spain numbered only 3,000 men, the majority on the northern frontier, far from the "useful Mexico." In addition there were the militias, recruited from among the population (with the exception of Indians), of Mexico City and Puebla. In 1800 the regular army numbered more than 6,000 men, but the urban and coastal militias had grown even faster, rising from some 9,000 in 1766 to almost 40,000 in 1784. The numerical progress of the military class would have sufficed to make it a rival of the religious, but the "state of war" established in the viceroyalty in 1761, under Viceroy Cruillas, himself a military man, accentuated this evolution. The Seven Years' War, the capture of Havana by the English in 1762, which directly threatened the Gulf coast of Mexico and cut the maritime route from Veracruz to Cádiz (a vital link between New Spain and the metropolis), spurred the development of the army and a military spirit.

Gradually military parades came to share with religious processions the favor of the Mexican people. Whereas ecclesiastical privileges (*fueros*) were breached by new royal measures, the *fuero militar* was codified anew by a voluminous code in 1768. The military were made completely exempt from civil jurisdiction; this privilege was spiced with various advantages (including exemptions from taxes) which made the military equals of the religious in privileges. In 1784 the English War came to an end, ending as well the extraordinary taxes (*donativos*), but the prestige of the army did not cease to grow, especially after the arrival or rather return of the viceroy Bernardo de Gálvez, a young general covered with glory, in 1785. In 1796, Spain, allied with France, again declared war on England, reviving the threat of an English landing in the Indies. New Spain was burdened with extraordinary taxes, which continued to be levied until the coming of Independence. Viceroy Iturrigaray complained of the need to send money and troops to Havana to guard against a possible English attack. In 1807 the defeat of an English effort to seize Buenos Aires, reported in the *Diario de México,* caused a sensation in New Spain, enhancing the bellicose character of a new patriotism which joined religious fervor to hatred for heresy. The blessing of battalion flags and other religious ceremonies with which the military willingly surrounded their activities contributed, for the rest, to the transfer of the sacred ark (religion and the fatherland) from the hands of the declining religious caste to those of the military caste. The state of war, de jure or de facto, in which a generation of Mexicans had lived, ensured the preeminence of the military. Their legal immunity became a shield for abuse and tyranny even as the military class consolidated its dominant position.

While this profound revolution—the work of Charles III—was taking place in New Spain, Europe entered an unprecedented phase of revolutions inspired by nationalism and patriotism. The mother country did not escape these events; allied with revolutionary France and her imperial heir, Napoleon, Spain became a captive of France in 1808. The news of the rising of the people of Madrid on the historic second of May against the French unleashed a great movement of sympathy in New Spain. The declaration of war on Napoleonic France by Spain, August 3, was celebrated in numerous towns of New Spain. A sort of patriotic delirium made men believe that the French had been routed and that Ferdinand VII had returned to Spain; he became an idol, as the journals and prints of those years prove. Soon it became necessary to sing another tune, and Spain appeared in all her true weakness. The creoles were weary of paying taxes which were no longer exceptional; the sale of church properties through application of the Act of Consolidation of 1804, which had run into difficulties, did not produce enough to relieve the mother country. The accumulated rancor of the past forty years against a monarch regarded as tyrannical, the ancestral hatred of the *gachupín,* were stronger than a sentimental movement in favor of the mother country, victim of the new Antichrist. Communications with Spain were severed.

Since Spain now had no king (for there could be no question of recognizing Joseph Bonaparte), and the heir apparent was a prisoner in France, the juridical tie between Spain and New Spain was also cut. Neither being subject to the other, since both were subject to the king, who delegated his power to a viceroy, the latter lost his lawful status. The creoles were quick to see in this an opportunity to assume those powers which had been denied them since the deposition of Cortés and the establishment of the first audiencia. As soon as the mournful tidings from Spain became known in Mexico City, a religious by the name of Fray Melchor de Talamantes began to draft a constitution for an independent Mexico, vested with a congress which should have legislative power "and which should endow the realm of New Spain with that character of dignity, grandeur, and elevation needed to make it respectable among the civilized and independent nations of America and Europe."[26] The appeal to "the voice of the nation," represented by its notables, to fill the void left by the lapse of the viceroy and the audiencia, the biblical reference ("This voice, so respectable and so sovereign that it constrained God Himself to change the government of Israel and grant it the king it sought,"[27] sets the tone of these years, decisive for the Mexican national destiny. The borrowing from the ideology of the French Revolution of 1789—but with important omissions—and loyalty to the Christian humanism of Suárez (*vox populi, vox dei*) were to be the two faces of Hidalgo's ideology two years later. Hidalgo, like Fray Melchor, in principle wished to avoid the spilling of blood, but it had become inevitable.

Fray Melchor's project was inspired by resentment against a veritable coup d'etat perpetrated by a camarilla that included officials of the audiencia and Veracruz merchants, and that managed without striking a blow to seize the person of Viceroy Iturrigaray on September 15, 1810. The course of this conspiracy and its causes are described by Mier in his *Historia de la revolución de la Nueva Epaña*. Here I shall only note that the preventive "counterrevolution" of a handful of *gachupines* had destroyed all legality. Therefore Hidalgo could present his rising as a reestablishment of legality, the only possible legality in the absence of the viceroy named by the king: the national sovereignty. The situation created by the viceroy's imprisonment gave its full meaning to the phrase cited above, in Hidalgo's proclamation: "For the welfare of the kingdom it is necessary to wrest command and power from the hands of the Europeans." Spanish large-scale commerce, which had its center in Cádiz and its proxies in Veracruz, now had the upper hand in New Spain, a situation which promised new burdens for a country already in difficulties as a result of the authoritarian measures and financial exactions discussed above.

The war cry "Death to the *gachupines!*" was directed in the first place against the usurpers of power represented in the country by the Spanish merchants, but this does not exhaust its significance. "Death to the *gachupines!*" was the belated and therefore all the more irrepressible outburst of an old hatred, inherited from the conquistadores themselves, against Spanish *licenciados* eager to despoil the creoles as well as the Indians. A son of the creole bourgeoisie, educated at the Colegio de San Francisco Javier of Valladolid in Michoacán, with a doctorate from the University of Mexico City, a reader of Clavijero and French eighteenth-century authors (it seems he knew French well), Hidalgo became a village priest, first in Colima, later in the area of Guanajuato. With his knowledge and experience, Miguel Hidalgo y Costilla had to feel the aspirations of the creole bourgeoisie of the towns as well as those of the Indians of the countryside. The "Cry of Dolores" was uttered at the right moment; Hidalgo knew what he did when he brandished the banner of Guadalupe. It makes no sense to say, as did Lorenzo de Zavala in his *Ensayo histórico de las últimas revoluciones de México* (written in Paris in 1831), that "Hidalgo acted without a plan, system, or precise aim. 'Long live Our Lady of Guadalupe,' was his sole base of operations; the national flag on which her image was painted constituted his code and his institutions."[28] Hidalgo gave the Mexican people precisely what it needed in that hour of truth when he took into his hands its historic destiny: a flag that was also a symbol.

When he was rector of the Colegio de San Nicolas, in his town of Valladolid in Michoacán, he had a disciple, Jose María Morelos y Pavón, whom he made his lieutenant in 1810. Morelos was also priest of a rural parish, Carácuaro. But the two men were very different from each other. Morelos was born near Valladolid into a poor mestizo family, his father a carpenter, half-Indian, his mother a creole. Until 1790 he worked for his uncle as a cowhand. At the age of twenty-five he returned to Valladolid, where he studied just enough to be ordained a priest. After an interval of a year, he obtained the curacy of Carácuaro. In 1810, Morelos was forty-five years old; Hidalgo was fifty-seven. Hidalgo gave himself the title of "Protector of the Patria," which recalled the title "Protector of the Indians," worn by Las Casas and the first bishop of Michoacán, Vasco de Quiroga, who had tried to create there the utopia of Thomas More and whose memory the Indians revered under the name of *tata Vasco*. Morelos, in a gesture of pious humility toward a new divinity, called himself "Serf [*siervo*] of the Nation," an expression modeled on that of "serf of God," God's slave, applied to the religious.

The new gods who had just broken into the rich pantheon of the Mexican people were as intolerant as the church of the inquisitors, and as thirsty for blood as the war god of the Aztecs, Huitzilopochtli. Hidalgo, Morelos, and other curates like Matamoros, Belleza, Correa, Verduzco, or Dr. Cos, all members of the revolutionary general staff, presided over those great human sacrifices on the altars of the fatherland and the nation. Hidalgo, to be sure, constantly appealed for creole unity in order to avoid shedding blood. Morelos soon was transformed into a general who flew from victory to victory, whom the journals of Mexico called "the Lightning of the South." This man was, as it were, the emanation of his people; the inspired speech which he gave at the opening session of the Congress of Chilpancingo not only rose to the height of that great historical moment, it was also the best testimony to the climate of that first Mexican revolution:

This oppressed people, so like the people of Israel overwhelmed by Pharaoh, weary of suffering, has stretched its hands toward

Heaven and made its cry heard before the throne of the Eternal, and the Eternal, pitying its misfortunes, has opened His mouth and decreed the freedom of Anahuac before the court of his seraphim. The Spirit who animated the enormous amorphous mass of ancient Chaos, who infused life into it with a breath, and who created this marvelous world, that Spirit has now given an electric shock to our hearts, has caused the blindfold to fall from our eyes, and has changed the shameful apathy in which we lay into a terrible and warlike fury. It was in the village of Dolores that this voice sounded, a voice like unto thunder.[29]

Morelos, who possessed little culture, here spoke with true eloquence, a sacred eloquence that differed little from the baroque sermons of the eighteenth century into which he was born. In reality, the sacred ark of the Mexican *patria* had escaped from the grasp of the creole friars, the clerics of the university; it had passed, as once happened with the idols of ancient Anahuac, into stronger hands in a time of anarchy. The religion of the creole elite had given place to the faith of the people, a faith that had been elaborated in rural parishes and whose guardians were country curates; the most modest level of sacerdotal caste was now to play the role of keeper of the faith. The return of power to the people, the affirmation of national sovereignty as a consequence of the repudiation of the viceroy, were the secular expressions of this return of the sacred religious-patriotic patrimony to the nation itself. Morelos must have been confusedly aware of this fact, which he expressed with a biblical vocabulary and biblical images that were familiar to him and that constituted simultaneously the material and the style of his sermons. The transposition of Independence to the supernatural level by God's own hand is impressive. The use of the word "Anahuac"—"That Anahuac became free, by a decree of the Eternal"—reveals that Morelos was a spokesman for the creole utopia, the unconscious heir of Sigüenza y Góngora as well as of Clavijero and the conceptist preachers of the eighteenth century. In Morelos the romanticism of revolutionary action replaces nostalgia for the Indian past, but the reference to the chosen people of Israel, to Anahuac, and to that "marvelous world," which recalls the *Indian Spring,* leaves no doubt as to the continuity of creole illuminism. As Hidalgo had announced, the "day of glory" had arrived for . . . the "Indian democracy"?

The whole atmosphere of the epoch is in Morelos' resounding phrases. The divine breath which had organized chaos, has just changed the Mexican people into a furious lioness; a new Genesis is announced. But it is preceeded by "desolation and death";[30] it is thus that the Eternal must manifest himself before the millennium. The great voice of the curate of Dolores is the exact replica of that great voice which on the day of the Apocalypse will cause the earth to tremble. The first act of the liberation of Anahuac was conceived and defined by its principal actor as the *dies irae*, the Day of Wrath. In this inaugural address of a new era for Mexico, the mingling of the new and the old, of constitutional projects, eschatological hope, and modern science—that "electric shock" which kindles a revolution inspired by the Eternal—conveys very precisely the tone of the revolution of Independence. The final evocation of the spirits of the heroes, those slain fighting for their *patria*, founded the cult of great men on which the Mexican patriotic religion still rests and without which no political ideology can gain popular acceptance: "Spirits of the dead of Las Cruces, Aculco, Guanajuato, and Calderón, Zitácuaro, and Cuautla, joined with those of Hidalgo and Allende!" Morelos also invokes the Indian ancestors who were victims of *gachupín* barbarity: "Shades of Moctezuma, Cacahma, Cuauhtémoc, Xicotencatl, and Caltzontzin, come celebrate about this august assembly, in a sacred dance—that same *mitote* during which you were assailed by Alvarado's treacherous sword—the happy day on which your illustrious sons have assembled to avenge your sufferings and escape the claws of the Free-Masonic tyranny which was about to swallow them for ever!"[31]

Whatever Lorenzo de Zavala may say, Hidalgo certainly had ideas for a constitution which the licentiate Rayón expressed, with Hidalgo's consent, at least, in his *Elementos constitucionales*—ideas which Morelos incorporated in the Constitution of Apatzingan. The first article of the *Elementos* provided: "The Catholic religion will be the only one, excluding every other religion." Article 3: "Dogma will be defended by the vigilance of the Tribunal of the Faith."[32] We seem to be dealing with a religious rather than a political constitution, or at least with a political constitution whose primary concerns are the church and Catholic orthodoxy. Unity of faith, the foundation of New Spain, was to remain the base of a free Anahuac. The *Sentiments of the Nation,* published by Morelos in 1813, restate the same principles: Article 2: "The Catholic religion shall be the only one, to the exclusion of all other religions." Article 3: "All the ministers shall be subsidized with all the tithes and firstfruits, and in no other way, and the people shall pay no other fees save the offerings inspired by devotion." Article 4: "Dogma shall be defended by the hierarchy of the church, that is, by the pope, the bishops, and the curates."[33]

The first article proclaimed Independence, and only article 5 directed its attention to an essential political aspect, national sovereignty. A careful reading of articles 2 and 4 makes it clear that Independence signified above all for its promoters a strengthening of the position of the church in the country, the abolition of the tribunal of the Inquisition, whose role would be assumed by the secular clergy, and the suppression of prebends; in a sense, it was the last act in the dispossession of the regular orders by the secularizing bishops. It was, moreover, an act of revenge upon the canons of the cathedrals by the country curates. Finally, for the people it meant the abolition of ecclesiastical tithes. The Constitution of Apatzingan brought together and codified these different points; it made the electoral assemblies of the parishes the official cells of political life; it defined the citizen with the right to vote as follows: "He shall have reached the age of eigh-. teen, or at least shall be a married man, and shall have demonstrated his loyalty to our holy cause."[34] This sacred cause was indeed the cause of the people, taken up by curates who had issued from the people and had never broken their ties with them. By contrast with the missionary friars who had exercised a benevolent tutelage over their flocks, a protective mission, Morelos was on terms of equality with peons of haciendas and muleteers, having been one himself but a few years before. With Morelos, the Mexican church moves from paternalism to fraternity; this aspect of the revolution of Independence held the great promise for a democratic future.

Such upheavals, which threatened the authority of the ecclesiastical hierarchy as well as its prebends, inevitably provoked an immediate reaction on the part of the bishops. The first to excommunicate Hidalgo, and later Morelos, was the bishop-designate (he was only *designatus,* not yet consecrated, and Hidalgo used this as an argument to scorn his anathema) of Michoacán, Abad y Queipo, soon followed by the archbishop of Mexico City, Lizana y Beaumont. Abad y Queipo had a clear vision of the evils that afflicted New Spain; he was less lucid in regard to the remedies that the situation required. In 1814 he wrote the viceroy Calleja a letter proposing a policy of integration, the generalization of the *alternativa* between Spaniards and creoles, the nomination of meritorious creoles for the administrative posts in Spain, the grant of equal rights with European Spaniards to creoles and Indians. These suggestions came too late; they had been over-taken by events. More concrete were his requests for troops "to assure the pacification and preservation of the Americas."[35] At that date, three years had passed since the execution of Hidalgo; Morelos was captured and shot in his turn on December 22, 1815. In his last moments Morelos refused the assistance of a friar; it was the curate of San Cristóbal who received his last confession and blessed his temporary grave.

The records of the inquisitorial trial which led to this fatal and foreseeable outcome confirm that at this period political subversion was still regarded in New Spain as a product of heretical illuminism. Morelos was accused of having deserted "the pure and holy Christian flock" and joined "the impure and abominable horde of the heretics Hobbes, Helvetius, Voltaire, Luther, and other pestilential, deist, materialist, and atheist authors whom he must have read [*que seguramente ha leído*]"[36] In this pell-mell of contradictory accusations, lacking in proofs, we observe the style and stereotypes of the Mexican inquisitors of the last decades of the eighteenth century. They did not reproach Morelos as much for having had three children by different mothers (evidently conceived outside the sacrament of marriage), as for having sent his eldest son, aged thirteen, to study in the United States, regarded by the inquisitors as a heretical action. To the tenth accusation against him, that he persuaded the people "that the cause which he defended was the cause of religion, using his sacerdotal state as an argument in his favor," Morelos frankly replied "that he had often used his quality of priest and the credit which priests enjoyed with the people, to persuade them that this war had a religious character, for the Europeans sought to impose the government of the French, whom he regarded as heretics."[37]

Here we put our fingers on the vital contradiction of an insurrectionary movement that was inspired by the great principles of the French Revolution, in the first place the principle of national sovereignty, yet set itself the goal of defending Catholic orthodoxy. Morelos, also accused of having fostered the legend of a child with mystic powers who turned out to be his own son, defended himself against the charge (*asegura que él no tuvo parte en ese error*). What matters is not the strict truth of the charge, but the fact that a legend of the *muchacho a quien llaman el adivino*[38] ("the boy who is called 'the diviner'") had accompanied the second sortie of this "Don Quixote of Michoacán,"[39] whose first incarnation was the curate of Dolores. Clearly, we have not yet emerged from the religious atmosphere that had characterized New Spain since its origins, and that I depicted with broad strokes at the beginning of this book with the help of some samplings from the records of inquisitorial trials. This despite the agitation of some French patriots and republicans, and the more or less clandestine influx, for twenty years, of revolutionary publications and their diffusion in a variety of circles. Despite the appearance, in addition to the placards of yesteryear, of an authorized or clandestine press which served to spread the "new ideas" throughout the country, the great revolutionary ferment remained the religious passion, whose content was transformed in the course of those years while retaining its traditional processes.

When, in 1823, the government of Mexico, that Empire of Anahuac at last set free from its chains, decided to render solemn homage to the heroes of its liberation, it had a catafalque set up in the cathedral, where poems written for the occasion were displayed. The times badly needed a Sigüenza y Góngora, to judge by this elegiac ode:

> Tremble, tyrants; tremble again, impious men!
> For in the end Holy Providence
> remembers His own: be abashed
> by this catafalque which Honor has raised[40]

We observe the reassertion of holiness of the cause of Independence; "tyranny and impiety" are associated and defied together. One thinks of the legend that has Saint Josaphat's image cursing the enemies of the Society of Jesus, described as "impious." The homage of Mexican creole society to the dead heroes was thus in the tradition of funeral honors of New Spain; it preserved the creole charismatic spirit in the new political framework of independent Mexico. As in the case of the cult of Guadalupe, however, it is popular behavior which most clearly illuminates the cult of the newest Mexican tutelary gods. The Aztecs believed that warriors slain in battle went to the land of Tamoanchan, the paradise of Tlaloc. The new *teules* (the term designated both the gods and the spirits of forebears) of the new Anahuac were honored in the traditional manner. Carlos María de Bustamante found just the right tone with which to describe the "return of the ashes" in his *Diario histórico de México:*

> Look and write, said the Holy Spirit to Saint John, in Revelation; if I were a Puritan, I would think that the voice of my country resounded in my ear and told me the same thing.
>   Yesterday morning the venerable remains of Morelos arrived at Guadalupe; it may have been half past twelve when they arrived in the city and were displayed in front of the collegiate church. They were accompanied by three Indian musicians from different villages, who instead of canticles and funeral marches played joyous waltzes and sarabands.[41]

The basilica of Guadalupe, a place of pilgrimage for Mexicans both humble and illustrious since the 1620s at least, had become the temple of the national religion. The content of the faith had hardly changed; the Indian *areitos* and *mitotes* that Motolinia had described had been adapted to the taste of the day. But the waltzes and sarabands with which the Indians accompanied the remains of Morelos reflected a ritualism with regard to the *muertito* that had not changed since the days of Aztec polytheism. Even today the custom of the *velorio* (the funeral wake) reveals an attitude toward mourning that is very different from ours. The homage of the Indians, joined to the celestial music which, according to the chronicler, was to lull the liberator to sleep "in the region of peace," before the collegiate church of Guadalupe, was the first station of a hero who was to live forever in the popular consciousness. Morelos, like Cuauhtémoc, had become a "forebear of the country." All the efforts of the national consciousness tended toward effacing the "Middle Ages" of New Spain in order to achieve the rebirth of the Empire of Anahuac from its ashes. Hence the persistence with which there surged up, again and again, the myth of the phoenix bird in New Spain. By no accident, Bustamante did not write "Paradise" or "Glory" or even "eternal peace," but rather "in the region of peace," a phrase that evoked at least as well the ancient Tamoanchan and that prefigured "the most transparent region of the air"—that Anahuac assigned an ideal purity by one of the most authentic Mexican voices of our century, the voice of Alfonso Reyes.

The second stop of the funerary urns was the convent of Santo Domingo de México, where the heirs of the missionaries and the baroque preachers could in their turn, and in their own manner, pay posthumous homage to Morelos. That homage may have not been free from reservations, for the antipathy of the "Serf of the Nation" toward the friars was well known. Finally, the day after this September 16 anniversary (celebrated ever since as a national holiday) formations of the army conducted the remains of the heroes (*próceres*) from the convent of Santo Domingo to the cathedral. In a symbolic amalgam of the new national order, the procession in which military and ecclesiastics mingled, escorted by a squadron of grenadiers and by the national guard (*milicia nacional*), accompanied the dead heroes to the cathedral. Around the remains of Hidalgo, Morelos, and their comrades of the first hour, the chorus of the Mexican nation (hardly different from that which Sor Juana de la Cruz described in the seventeenth century in her *villancicos*) sang their praises in unison. The metamorphoses of faith and devotion were not to end there, but the discordant images of the dead heroes would not prove an obstacle to national unity, sanctified by the blood that had been shed. The intolerant concern of the founders of modern Mexico for Catholic orthodoxy undoubtedly reflected above all their fear of anarchy, a political anarchy flowing from a chaos of beliefs. With Morelos this idea was an obsession. Under a proclaimed unity of faith, the specific spiritual content of each of the different ethnic groups making up the Mexican nation continued to live on. The Mexican nation had achieved political maturity, had won its independence, but it was far from achieving a cultural integration, something which has not been completely realized to this day.

An Inspired Friar and a Providential General:
Mier against Iturbide (1821–23)

In no other part of the world are dead heroes so present and so active as in the lands of Middle America; that is why I have avoided separating the historical role of Hidalgo and Morelos from their posthumous destiny, which was, as it were, the emanation and accomplishment of that role. Recalling that both came out of Michoacán, once a rebel land on the marches of the Aztec empire, I see in this fact a clue to the truth about the independence of Mexico. Coming from the land of utopia par excellence, the bishopric of Vasco de Quiroga, they invoked the memory of King Caltzontzin, martyred by the Spanish conquerors. In that land crosses sprouted like the grass, the licentiate Matías de la Mota Padilla tells us in his *Historia de la conquista de la Nueva Galicia;* the tree of liberty, by virtue of this spontaneous generation of the Tarascan land, flourished there as luxuriantly as the miraculous cross of Tepic. The Spanish Conquest, led by the sanguinary Nuño de Guzmán, had been more cruel there than in the Aztec empire. Between the spirit of Vasco de Quiroga and the dreadful spirit of Nuño de Guzmán—those two aspects (*cara y cruz*, the face of salvation and the martyr's cross) of the European presence—the Indians of Michoacán had double reason to avenge the death of Caltzontin and achieve the long delayed utopia of their tutelary bishop.

These two high goals constantly appear in the speeches, proclamations, and constitutional projects of the first Revolution of Independence, begun in Valladolid de Michoacán. Hidalgo and Morelos were doubtless of Spanish stock, but blood counts less here than the spiritual inspiration. In this respect, both were sons of the Tarascan country. It was there that the first fighters of the war of liberation responded to their call. Humboldt wrote in Europe at the very time that the "Cry of Dolores" resounded through Mexico: "The whole southern part of the intendency of Michoacan is inhabited by Indians; in the villages the only white person to be found is the curate, who himself is often Indian or mulatto. The livings there are so poor that the Bishop of Michoacán has the great difficulty in finding clergy willing to settle in a country where one almost never hears Spanish spoken"[42] Hidalgo and Morelos, then, were elite curates in a land with a mission, their fatherland. The reconquest of Mexico started in what was perhaps the least hispanized region of New Spain, the region where the *leyenda negra*, the "Black Legend," was less of a legend than anywhere else. The decisive moments of the War of Independence took place in Michoacán; it was at Chilpancingo that Morelos summoned the first constitutional congress and proclaimed independence November 6, 1813; he suffered his first reverse because he tried to install his government at Valladolid. The fact deserves the more emphasis because his conqueror was a young officer, Agustín de Iturbide, who ten years later would enter Mexico City as a liberator.

As was the case in 1874 when Socorro Reyes rose up with the cry of *"Religión y fueros,"* and again in the twentieth century with the rebellion of the *cristeros,* the rising of Michoacán appears in its inception as the revolt of a rural region on the margins of national life against a remote central government. This fact does not exhaust the significance of the crusade against the *gachupines* unleashed by the curates of Michoacán, but it may explain why Hidalgo's appeals to desert, made with pathetic insistence to the loyalist troops, went unheard. This was the principal objective reason for the defeat of a war for liberation which seemed to have ended after Hidalgo and Morelos had been shot. The revolutionary wave had stopped at the gates of Mexico City, then had receded, as if Hidalgo had been intimidated by the sight of the imperial city. It was a fatal error, for Iturbide's victories over the insurgents and the skill of the new viceroy, Apodaca, soon dispersed the revolutionaries and broke their victorious élan. The congress had to flee as far as Apatzingan, and thenceforth led a nomadic life. On December 21, 1815, Morelos was executed as a traitor, and the defeat of the revolution seemed definitive. It would be an error, however, to classify this rising of the Indians of Michoacán, led by their curates, as just one more of the numerous Indian revolts which agitated New Spain periodically throughout its history.

The events which unfolded between 1810 and 1815 in New Spain coincided with one of the most troubled periods in the history of Spain. A series of political and juridical developments had a decisive influence on the course of Mexican events. The vacant Spanish throne weakened the power of the viceroys, the coup d'etat carried out by the Spaniards against the viceroy Iturrigaray destroyed an essential institution. Spain herself gave an example of armed revolt against the foreign occupier; if it required some stretching of the truth to proclaim the *gachupines* foreigners in Mexico, this could be done without difficulty. The cortes of Cádiz discussed the abolition of the tribunal of the Inquisition and decided upon it at the moment when the Mexican Inquisition handed Hidalgo over to the secular arm, and decreed freedom of the press just when revolutionary sheets were beginning to proliferate in Mexico: *The Centzontli, The American Awakening, The Mexican Eagle,* whose symbolic titles evoked the past even more than the future they announced. The confusion of new ideas and ancestral passions, the disarray of government, the cruelty of the repression, the audacity of a people which had just discovered its capacity to hold in check the regular army, the defeatism of the Spaniards, were the factors that converged toward a resumption of the War of Independence.

The great novelty was the appearance on the political scene of a personage who was to play a major role on the political stage down to the twentieth century, the *guerrillero*. Faithful to its own dynamic, which corresponds to certain socio-psychological and geographic conditions, an uprising, once launched, rebounds and continues on its course despite all efforts to stop it. In response to political fluctuations, endemic social banditry produces "caudillos" who, once victorious on the side of the dominant party, are transformed into liberating heroes, or, if defeated together with the weaker party, return to banditry if they manage to escape a violent death. Mexican *Costumbrista* writers of the nineteenth century have described this phenomenon, but it was a twentieth-century novelist, Mariano Azuela, who captured its reality in *Los de abajo*.

Just as the War of Independence appeared to be "finished," it received an unexpected boost from Spain. Francisco Xavier Mina, a guerrilla leader in the Spanish war of liberation against Napoleon's armies, was, like Hidalgo, a son of a strongly particularist province, remote from the capital; he was from Navarre. Repelled by the restoration of Ferdinand VII, who immediately began to act like a tyrant, Mina, having failed in an effort to foment revolution in Spain, fled to London. There he met creole emigrés from America, notably a Dominican from Monterrey who had gained considerable renown, Fray Servando Teresa de Mier. This alliance between a friar and a guerrillero resulted in the landing of a handful of men near Soto de Marina, on the Gulf coast of Mexico, in April 1817. Until October 27, when he was captured and shot at Venadito, Mina waged a brilliant military campaign, seized San Felipe, threatened León, and caused the government much anxiety, recreating the atmosphere of fear that had accompanied Morelos' victories some years back. The defeat of Mina did not deter one of Morelos' former lieutenants, Vicente Guerrero, from resuming the struggle in the south and achieving a series of victories in 1819.

Now there took place a dramatic coup which precipitated the success of the revolutionary armies; General Iturbide, sent by the viceroy to crush the rebellion of Guerrero as he had crushed that of Morelos, invited the enemy leader to a personal meeting at Acatempan. From this meeting issued the Plan of Iguala. The defection of Iturbide, who was now commander-in-chief of the armies of Independence, provoked panic in Mexico City. While this was going on, a new viceroy,

Juan O'Donoju, disembarked at Veracruz. Taken aback by the new situation, he agreed to meet Iturbide at Cordoba and signed a treaty in which he attempted to salvage what he could for Spain. O'Donoju was repudiated by the Spanish government, and for a decade Mexico was to live under the threat of a war of reconquest. However, the Army of the Three Guarantees (religion, union, and independence) entered Mexico City in triumph on September 27, 1821.

Mexico had finally achieved its independence as a result of the cumulative effect of the factors I have attempted to indicate, some linked to recent vicissitudes of Spanish history, others the fruit of a slow regional maturation. The atmosphere in which Mexico began its independent life has been felicitously recreated by Javier Ocampo in *Las ideas de un día (El pueblo mexicano ante la consumación de su Independencia)*. "The image of Iturbide appeared at that moment as the synthesis of the collective consciousness in its enthusiasm for Independence. His figure expressed, although very transiently, the charismatic dimension."[43] We have followed the trajectory of the charismatic sentiment and its metamorphoses in New Spain from the foundation of the first Franciscan mission in 1524. After Hidalgo, that charismatic sentiment was particularly present around Morelos, investing him with an aureole. But in the case of Iturbide, described in his turn as "Father of His Country," "Man of God," and, what is more interesting, "Star of the North," a new phenomenon emerges. This "polestar," who recalls the Virgin of Guadalupe (Mexico City's polestar), for the first time in the history of what had been New Spain was a general. To be sure, Hidalgo had called himself "captain general," then "generalissimo," and Morelos had been a great soldier, but both were incontrovertibly priests. Iturbide, on the contrary, had adopted the military career at sixteen and had never left it. He was called the "new Joshua"; Mendieta had once given the same name to Cortés.

The road to the Mexican promised land, had been a hard, bitterly disputed one. Instead of the "happiness" announced by Hidalgo, the Mexican people fell into the anarchy that Morelos had feared. The tribunal of the Inquisition had banned Milton's *Paradise Lost,* but the Mexican "Western Paradise" also fell into ruin. The secular struggle of a government whose regalism had stiffened under Charles III and of the ecclesiastical hierarchy against the religious orders had sapped the socio-spiritual foundations of New Spain. The friars had struck their tents or had been driven into exile, like the Jesuits; they had left behind them, in the hands of novices, an infernal machine, the utopian aspiration and the charismatic certainty of the Mexican people. That machine rained fire in all directions as a result of a conjunction of political events that generated fear and disarray, at a moment when the liberal policies adopted by Spain had brought down the last barriers of political and religious orthodoxy. The figure of the missionary friar had dominated New Spain's hagiography since its beginnings; the creole charismatic sentiment had been developed in the Franciscan and Augustinian convents and diffused from the pulpit by the preachers, often Jesuits. Now, at the beginning of the nineteenth century, when light (so different from the Enlightenment) came from the curates of Indian parishes in Michoacan, creole charisma was drowned in a flood of Indian cults, magnificently represented by the standard of Guadalupe.

In today's revolutionary language, we would say that supernatural inspiration henceforth would "come from the base" instead of remaining the privilege of the clergy. It was in this realm that there unfolded a democratic revolution that historians have hitherto failed to perceive. Rather than speak of a complete revolution, one is tempted to call it a "new equilibrium," for the beliefs, the local cults, and the pilgrimages had been vital expressions of popular faith in New Spain since the first half of the seventeenth century. What most profoundly affected the Mexican collective mentality during the years of the War for Independence and down to the government of the Reforma was the effacement of the friar and the emergence of the military man. As a result of the Wars of Independence (coming after or leading to a crisis of ecclesiastical and university *fueros,* or immunities), appearing at the end of almost a half century of a "state of war," the figures of the military officer or his antithesis, the *guerrillero,* polarized the nation about themselves.

Iturbide, who had destroyed the forces of the curate Morelos, who had also come out of Michoacán, "like the eagle who should strike down the Spanish lion with his wings," therefore appeared to be "the man sent by God" and "the father of his country"; the political result was his coronation. Elected, under popular pressure, Emperor of Anahuac, with the title of Agustín I, he was thought to be reviving the Aztec empire (the Aztecs were bitter enemies of the Tarascans, but that did not matter). Iturbide himself was of Basque origin, but we know how from the time of Sigüenza y Góngora the irreconcilable was reconciled for the greater glory of Mexico. The day of Independence was, as Javier Ocampo has well observed, "the impossible become deed"; if the Mexicans remained united (the obsession with unity, expressed in politics by the quarrel between centralists and federalists, was to dominate the history of Mexico after Independence), Mexico City could become "the capital of the globe."[44] A relative secularization of the religious charisma of the eighteenth and nineteenth centuries, to which I have called attention above, took place under the shock of the ideology of the Enlightenment, which gave its language to the political revolution.

From the end of the eighteenth century, the demographic development of Mexico City, the growth of consumption, and the like, became a source of concern for Spaniards, worried lest the capital of New Spain should be eclipsing Madrid. After the occupation of Madrid by Napoleon's troops, Mexico City alone bore aloft the torch of what was not yet called *Hispanidad,* but which nevertheless had a rich affective content. When a deputy of the cortés of Cadiz exclaimed in that assembly: "Nature has so united the Europeans and the creoles that even if she wishes, she could not separate them,"[45] one might conclude that events had handed him a stinging refutation, but on a certain interior level he was entirely right. In 1828, and again in 1833, expulsion decrees struck at the Spaniards who still lived in Mexico, thus nullifying in fact one of the "three guarantees," that of union, but the competition for grace between Guadalupe and the Virgin of Pilar, between Mexico City and Madrid, which was a secular expression of the rivalry over leadership, not of Hispanic lands alone, but of the world—the fratricidal struggle transposed to the level of charismatic dream—long maintained the spiritual bonds between the former New Spain and Old Spain in decline.

Probably no other work expresses with a richness comparable to that of Fray Servando Teresa de Mier the vital ambiguity of this historical situation of simultaneous rupture and loyalty between Spain and her American projection, newly independent Mexico. In a sense this Dominican was the last of those creole friars who forged the American *patria* in the course of the colonial centuries. Born in Monterrey, capital of Nuevo Leon, he belonged to a noble family which included in its ranks a governor of that province and a president of the tribunal of the Inquisition; on his mother's side he claimed to descend from Moctezuma. But his main interest was in defending the privileges of the creole nobility, shunted away from honors and jobs. In his *Historia de la revolución de la Nueva España,* the reasons he advances to justify the independence of New Spain merge with the "defense and explanation" of the Mexican aristocracy. The straightforward claims of the creole apologists of previous decades became passionate polemics as rephrased by Fray Servando, who wrote as an exile in London, after having fled from Spanish prisons.

In the first place, Fray Servando disputed the validity of the historical-providential foundations of Spain's claims to America. "We, the creoles, declare that the religion now existing in America was not brought by you Spaniards, but by us through our forebears."[46] He attacks the *alternativa* in the religious orders, showing that the expenses of the church in New Spain were borne entirely by the creoles. Writing at the dawn of the nineteenth century, his pen still expresses the rancor of the conquistadors against the monarchy and that of creole friars denied prelateships and the richest livings. Because he had been persecuted by Archbishop Haro y Peralta and the tribunal of the Inquisition in Mexico as a result of a sermon pronounced in 1794 that was regarded as subversive, in the course of his tribulations in the Peninsula he contracted a sort of persecution mania which Antonello Gerbi compares to that of Jean Jacques Rousseau. Mier considered himself a victim of the distrust felt by the *gachupines* for all creoles endowed with talent. But this state of affairs, closely resembling the phenomenon of racial discrimination (although one cannot properly speak of "race" in this connection) did not lead him to assert the principle of equality or propose the abolition of slavery and the system of *castas*. In these matters he shared creole prejudices.

What Mier demanded, above all, was the strict application of a body of ancient laws and measures which in their totality formed, according to him, the true "American constitution" within the framework of the Spanish monarchy. The juridical tinge of his arguments revealed the specialist in canon law that he remained throughout his stormy life. New Spain had never been free from the influence and the manifestations of Spanish juridical thought. Fray Servando represents the extreme of what might be called Mexican revolutionary "legalism"; I have called attention to its importance in the thought of Hidalgo and the licentiate Rayón. The creoles, in principle, did not reject allegiance to Ferdinand VII, but proposed to install a caretaking regime during his absence and, taking advantage of that absence, to strengthen their privileges of a ruling caste. Morelos, the first champion of popular sovereignty, in its broadest democratic sense, had to bring pressure on Rayón to erase the name of Ferdinand from the first Mexican constitution.

Mier, by contrast, distrusted the principle of national sovereignty. "Popular sovereignty means nothing more than this: from the people emanates the authority which the people must obey, for the people as a whole cannot rule." When he wrote the following lines his mind was on the events of the French Revolution, some of which he had witnessed. "As for the principle of equality, it cannot in a strict sense exist among men, save in the measure that they are protected by just laws from which none is exempt. . . . The French have deduced that they must cut each other's throats in order to be equal in the grave, the only place where we are all equal."[47] In fine, the man who was persecuted uninterruptedly from 1794 on, first by the Inquisition and finally by Iturbide, for his nonconformist spirit and his revolt against the political and spiritual authorities, taught his countrymen, at the height of Morelos' rebellion, counsels of moderation: "The peoples have never been ruled save by customs, prescriptions, and laws. That is why I have been at such great pains to make ours known. Our laws make us independent of Spain and by virtue of those laws we are justified in becoming completely independent; thus other nations will respect our separation from Spain as in conformity with the law of nations, but all the Americans will remain united. Do not make new laws, much less innovations in matter of religion."[48]

The obsession with civil war, or, to call it by its right name, "fear of revolution," made Mier the spokesman at that date for a strong current of creole thought, that current which was to impose the first of Iturbide's "Three Guarantees,"—"union" with Spaniards but independence of Spain (that Spain of which Mier could not speak harshly enough in his *Memoirs*). He could strike off trenchant phrases to express the traditional creole complaints: "Spain lives off America the way Rome lives off papal bulls," and again: "However, there is a very great difference between the people of each kingdom or province of Spain; . . . they have nothing in common save their brutality, their pride, their ignorance, and their superstitions. As concerns this last point, I speak of the multitude, which includes the friars and the soldiers. As for the others, they are in the same state as the rest of Europe, dominated by deism, and even by atheism."[49]

Clearly, Fray Servando's sympathies are with the defenders of social order and religious orthodoxy; largely because of him, the revolution of Independence can be viewed as a "counterrevolution." It is true that Mier played only secondary roles in the revolution, but this did not keep him from being present everywhere. Exiled to a convent in the Montaña de Santander by the Mexican Inquisition, twenty years before the outbreak of the Wars of Independence, he was the only Mexican who knew Spain and described it during the years which preceded the political separation. In Italy he knew the exiled Jesuits and followed the course of the dispute which confronted Clavijero with de Pauw and Buffon. In the course of his stormy career he met Clavijero, the abbé Gregoire, and Alexander von Humboldt (whom he tried to win over to his ideas about an early apostolic evangelization of America), and he obtained from the Academia de la Historia de España an opinion on the subject of the tradition of Guadalupe. At the time of the cortés de Cadiz he engaged in a polemic with the *consulado* or merchant guild of Mexico City, which sought to restrict the American parliamentary delegation. Made a military chaplain in the Spanish armies which fought against Napoleon, he was taken prisoner by the French. Escaping to London, he moved in the conspiratorial circles from which emerged Vizcardo and Miranda. He probably instigated the Mina expedition to Mexico but played a very minor military role in that affair; imprisoned a second time by the Inquisition, he was released by the coming of Independence.

At the time of the election of the first Mexican constituent congress, after the entrance of the Army of the Three Guarantees into Mexico City, his countrymen of Monterrey, who had forgotten him during his years of exile, were happy to find in their midst a genuine revolutionary to represent them, and elected him deputy. His first speech in the congress developed his familiar arguments in favor of a revision of the Mexican tradition of Guadalupe. In sum, they consisted in the suggestion that the miraculous cloth had been left as a relic for the ancient Mexicans by the apostle Saint Thomas, the first missionary in Anahuac, known in native traditions by the name of Quetzalcóatl. A speech of this kind may seem untimely in a revolutionary congress, but we must not lose sight of the national emblem, the banner of Guadalupe, which had led the "Americans" to victory. As the deputy from Monterrey recalled, it was a question of purging Mexico of an original stain: "The question involves nothing less than knowing whether the greatest single portion of mankind was unworthy of a compassionate look from Jesus Christ and his Mother until six thousand years after the death of the Redeemer, or if in fact it received that grace at the same time as the other continents."[50] In the millenarian atmosphere in which the Wars of Independence unfolded, the assertion of a grace shared by the Mexicans with other peoples from apostolic times represented a necessary condition for the recognition of a new chosen people with planetary ambitions. Despite numerous contradictions, some only apparent, others real, the political views and the religious thought of Mier were coherent. Both looked to the past with the aim of founding there a glorious present which in essence would be a restoration of a golden age, both legalist and charismatic. The dual influence of millenarianism, with which he had flirted in Europe, and of the Indian messianic cycle, which promised the return in glory of Quetzalcóatl, seems unconsciously to have dominated his mind.

The terrible impression left on his memory by the excesses of the Terror in France made him fear a leap into constitutional and religious novelty, above all. That is why he sought support in the laws of the Indies, in Scripture, and in the Mexican hieroglyphical and oral tradition in order to found a new political order on old principles. To preserve the quasi-sacred union with the Spanish Crown and unity of faith were in his eyes the means of guaranteeing respect for the laws and avoiding anarchy. Fray Servando had no wish to undermine a social order which would assure his circle (the creole nobility) preeminence just as soon as the *fueros* (the traditional privileges) were properly implemented. His position coincided with that of many Mexicans, including some very prominent men, at the time of Independence. José Joaquín Fernández de Lizardi, the *Pensador Mexicano,* had protested against the suspension of ecclesiastical privilege at the moment of the outbreak of the Hidalgo revolt; this protest caused his imprisonment. Still more significant are the borrowings (it makes no sense to speak of plagiarism at a time when this idea had little meaning) that Simón Bolívar made from Fray Servando, as André Saint-Lu has shown. In the famous "prophetic letter" of the Liberator, the juridical argumentation relative to the Laws of the Indies is copied entirely, sometimes textually, from Mier's *Historia de la revolución de Nueva España,* which had appeared two years earlier; the borrowing includes Mier's eulogy of Las Casas which ends the work of this "last Dominican of New Spain"—something Fray Servando really was.

The defense Mier made of his illustrious forerunner poses certain difficulties when he describes Las Casas as "a heavenly man, who struggled so hard for the freedom of the ancient Americans against the fury of the Conquest, our indefatigable advocate, our true Apostle . . . , the tutelary genius of the Americas."[51] Sometimes Mier demands the application of the laws of the Indies as due to his ancestors the conquistadors, sometimes he regards himself as an heir of the "ancient Americans," the Indians, in order to protest against Spanish barbarity—forgetting that the barbarians were those same conquistadors, Las Casas' enemies. Did he perceive the contradiction? The hypothesis of a cynical bad faith is not convincing. In reality, the historiography of the Indies, which had been a closed preserve for three centuries, and whose providentialist orientation had guaranteed the legitimacy of Spanish predominance, had to be revised in the hour of Independence. A weapon used by the monarchy to justify its domination must become a weapon used by Mexican patriots to promote national liberation. Las Casas, who had supplied the original material for the "Black Legend" opposed to the "providentialist legend," had to emerge retrospectively as the apostle and precursor of American liberation.

The trilogy, "Guadalupe—Quetzalcóatl—Las Casas," disembarrassed the cause of Mexican Independence of what could have been a source of difficulty for a "revolution" whose initial war cry had been "Long Live Religion!" and whose constitution had just acknowledged the holy Roman, Apostolic, Catholic religion as its first principle. A modern reader may be more surprised to find Bolívar echoing the ideas of Fray Servando relative to an apostolic evangelization of

America by Quetzalcóatl. To me it suggests at least that this son of Monterrey was not the "poor and incoherent" intellect that Antonello Gerbi sees in him; I find juster, in the last analysis, the eulogy that Mier's talented countryman, Alfonso Reyes, bestowed upon him when he called Mier "the forebear of his country." Deputy Mier, impressed perhaps by the results of Bonapartism, brilliantly fought the nascent Caesarism represented by Iturbide, whom his partisans then described as "the father of his country." In a letter to a friend, Fray Servando recalled with a bit of vainglory the posture which led to his being imprisoned a second time: "Iturbide himself could not bend me, even though he made a thousand promises of favors to me and my family, and the day I entered Congress I spoke as if I had a personal guard of fifty thousand men at my back."[52] One of the last victims of the Inquisition, one of the first victims of Mexican military *caudillismo,* a great adapter of pious traditions and the national historiography who furnished constitutionalist ideology to a movement with a vital need to reconcile tradition and innovation, an inspirer of Simón Bolívar, Fray Servando well deserves his place in the pantheon of the "ancestors of the country."

Part 2

Quetzalcóatl,
or the
Phoenix Bird

8 The First Franciscans

Fray Toribio de Motolinia

One of the first twelve Franciscans who arrived in Mexico in 1524 was Toribio de Paredes, from the Spanish town of Benavente. Seeing his threadbare garments, the Indians called him *motolinia* ("poor man"); he resolved to adopt this name and signed it to his writings. Active as a missionary in Mexico and Yucatan, he was guardian at different periods of the convent of Texcoco and for a long time of the convent of Tlaxcala. He took part in the founding of Puebla de los Angeles, near Tlaxcala, and presided over the first mass celebrated in Puebla, in 1530. He founded the convent of Atlixco and was the seventh provincial of his order in New Spain. He won a reputation for charity among both Indians and Spaniards. A past master of the Nahuatl language, he also knew other Indian languages.

His prolonged sojourn in the Tlaxcala-Puebla-Cholula area enabled him to gather at the source, in the holy city of Quetzalcóatl, the information which he left about that divinity and his cult as it was celebrated at the arrival of the Twelve. In Tlaxcala he could also learn about Quetzalcóatl's mythical double, Camaxtli, who was worshipped in that city. Motolinia's most important work is his *Memoriales,* published by the son of J. García Icazbalceta in 1903; Robert Ricard has studied Motolinia's successive revisions and rearrangements of the chapters of this work. In 1541 Motolinia addressed to the Conde de Benavente the dedicatory epistle of his *Historia de los indios de la Nueva España.* He may therefore be regarded as the first writer of a history of the Indians of Mexico. Only Father Andrés de Olmos (another of the Twelve) could dispute Motolinia's priority, but none of his works can be identified with certainty. Sahagún, who came to Mexico shortly after Motolinia, wrote his great work some thirty years later than Fray Toribio. José Fernando Ramírez wrote a brief life of Motolinia; although time has partly outdated his book, it can still be consulted with profit. Motolinia, last of the Twelve, died in 1568.

By contrast with Sahagún's *Historia,* we possess no rough drafts of

Motolinia's work, and he provides no information about his research methods or his native informants. Motolinia was guardian of the convent of Tlaxcala about 1536, when he was writing his *Historia,* and naturally assigned a prominent place to Quetzalcóatl, an important regional divinity. In chapter 24 of the *Memoriales,* Motolinia informs us that he lived six years in the Tlaxcala area and that the principal god of Tlaxcala, Huexotzinco, and Cholula was known by three names. "In Tlaxcala and Huexotzinco he was chiefly called Camaxtli, but was also called Quetzalcóatl, and that name was much used in Cholula; they also called him Mixcoatl."[1] The identity of Camaxtli with Quetzalcóatl is generally recognized, but the identification with Mixcoatl is perplexing. Perhaps the Franciscan suffered a lapse of memory, for he later writes: "To tell the truth, I do not remember many ceremonies and cruelties very well."[2] I believe that Motolinia, who claimed to have baptized 400,000 Indians and to have confessed a great number of natives, reflects (perhaps more than Sahagún, whose informants were elders or priests of the old religion) the common opinion, the popular cult rather than the esoteric truth. If this interpretation is correct, it would tend to confirm my view that the Quetzalcóatl myth underwent profound changes in the period immediately before the Spanish Conquest. Motolinia agrees with Sahagún and all the chroniclers about the character of the holy city of Cholula. "They held this Chololla to be a great sanctuary, a new Rome, and there were many temples consecrated to the Demon."[3] We also learn (most of chapter 24 is devoted to the subject) that ritual human sacrifices were offered in honor of Quetzalcóatl. This fact proves the Aztecization of the cult of Quetzalcóatl, for the most important legends depict him as an irreconcilable foe of human sacrifice. Motolinia witnessed the last Indian avatar of Quetzalcóatl.

But it is the traditional Quetzalcóatl, he of the *Leyenda de los Soles,* of whom Motolinia tells in the prefatory epistle that introduces the *Memoriales.* "That same old man Itzamixcoatlh . . . had another wife called Chimalmatlh, by whom he had a son called Quetzalcòatlh. He became a chaste and temperate man. He began the practice of penance by fasting and discipline, and it is said that he preached the natural law. . . . The Indians of New Spain regarded this Quetzalcóatlh as one of their principal gods; they called him the God of Air, and built temples to him on all sides."[4] This description, which associates Quetzalcóatl with natural law, seems to imply a forerunner of Christianity; the same idea is suggested by this remark: "It is said that Quetzalcóatlh began the sacrifice of scarifying the ears and tongue, not, it is claimed, to serve the Demon, but to perform penance for the sins of evil speech and hearing; the Demon later turned these sacrifices to the use of his cult and service."[5] This notion of an ascetic whose preaching conformed to natural morality, of a pure cult led astray and perverted by the demon, may have prepared the ground for the seventeenth-century legend of Quetzalcóatl-Saint Thomas.

In chapter 29 of the *Memoriales,* Motolinia describes the great feast held every four years for Quetzalcóatl in Cholula; it lasted eighty days and was marked by fasting on the part of the priests. On this occasion the god's statue was ritually decorated "with his special insignia; he was adorned with precious stones and gold jewels and they offered him many pheasants and rabbits and much paper and many strings of ears of maize." Motolinia adds that "very few performed sacrifices during this festival."[6] In chapter 24, describing the festival of Camaxtli at Tlaxcala, Motolinia reports that "it was said that this Quetzalcóatl was the son of Camaxtli."[7] We also learn that the Tlaxcalans wore Quetzalcóatl's dress in order to "sacrifice to the demon"; these clothes and insignia were brought from Cholula for the occasion; the same was done at Cholula with the insignia of Camaxtli. Clearly, the link between the two divinities was extremely close.

Speaking of the calendar, Motolinia turns to discuss the star Lucifer, or Hesperus, and observes that "Spain at one time was called Hesperia" after this star's name.[8] The ancient Mexicans "adored this star more than any other save the sun, and performed more ritual sacrifices for it than for any other creature, celestial or terrestrial."[9] Motolinia recalled that the Mexican astronomers had a very precise knowledge of the revolutions of this planet, Venus, and concluded: "The final reason why their calendar was based on this star, which they greatly revered and honored with sacrifices, was because these misguided people believed that when one of their principal gods, called Topiltzin or Quetzalcóatl, died and left this world, he was metamorphosed into that radiant star."[10] This comment suggests the importance of Quetzalcóatl in his aspect of Tlauizcalpantecuhtli and his role in the calendar, but it confuses the historical Topiltzin of Tula with the original Quetzalcóatl. In fact, only after his death did Topiltzin become a god. Motolinia also notes that the dead were called *teotl fulano* (such-and-such a blessed one); the word *teotl* or *teul* thus meant "spirit" or "blessed one" as well as "god."

Motolinia also helps to explain the claim of the sovereigns (*tlatoani*) of Tenochtitlan that they descended from Quetzalcóatl. In the *Historia de los indios* he relates that "an Indian named Chichimecatl tied a ribbon or leather strap to Quetzalcóatl's arm near the shoulder, and for this feat he was thenceforth called Acolhuatl. It is said that from this man descend the Colhua, Moteuczoma's (sic) predecessors, the lords of Mexico and Colhuacan."[11] Whatever we may think of this

ingenious explanation, it clearly points to the degradation of the Quetzalcóatl myth in the political and juridical interests of a dynasty. For
the rest, the *Historia* duplicates the *Memoriales,* which seems to be a
sort of rough draft or sketch of the *Historia,* almost word for word. We
note that in the *Historia,* Motolinia describes the principal temples of
Mexico and devotes a paragraph to the *teocalli* of Cholula (the great
temple of Quetzalcóatl), which is here for the first time compared to
the tower of Babel. The unrestrained ambition of the Cholulans, like
that of Babel, had been punished by a scourge from heaven.

In fine, it seems that the different, disconnected aspects of Quetzalcóatl presented by Motolinia chiefly reflect the popular ritual and
beliefs of Tlaxcala and Cholula but also derive from important written sources. We find here Quetzalcóatl's metamorphosis into the
Morning Star, which Motolinia apparently encountered in Nicaragua
and is also reported by later authors.[12] Motolinia's confusion of the
different Quetzalcóatls was not due, I believe, to a lack of information
but to the degenerate state of these different beliefs by the end of the
Aztec period. Motolinia has left us a precise description of the Quetzalcóatl myths as they were presented in Mexican annals and sacred
books at the time of the Spanish Conquest.

Fray Bernardino de Sahagún

The most illustrious early historian of Mexico was also a Franciscan
and devoted a part of his life to the Colegio de Santiago Tlatelolco,
established for the education of young Indians. He composed the
Historia General de las cosas de la Nueva España, also known as the
Calepino, between 1558 and 1569. This work, a kind of encyclopedia
of ancient Mexico, is later than the writings of Olmos and Motolinia,
but Sahagún's research methods, which he described, give his testimony a special value. I cannot give a detailed account of those
methods; they mark him as a true forerunner of modern ethnology.
He was able to separate the missionary that he remained to the last
from the indigenist that he had become. His avowed purpose was to
arm Spanish priests with knowledge of Indian beliefs and superstitions in order to help them extirpate idolatry. In fact, Sahagún had
the curiosity of an ethnologist, and his love for Indian culture shines
through his writings. The Franciscan was as anxious to preserve the
essence of the native culture—its crafts, whose masterpieces he had
seen, its folklore (insofar as it could be divorced from the old religious
beliefs), and above all its language, which he spoke and transcribed in
alphabetic script—as he was to extirpate paganism.

Since Quetzalcóatl and his cult were one of the most important aspects of the old pagan beliefs of Mexico,[13] Sahagún naturally wrote about this divinity and his legend more than once. He dealt with Quetzalcóatl in particular detail in book 3 of the *Historia,* entitled "Of the Origin of the Gods"; chapters 3–14 are devoted entirely to him. Here Quetzalcóatl appears under the aspect of the high priest of Tula, who probably came from the Gulf coast. His pontificate coincided with the temporal reign of Huemac and especially with the Golden Age, described by Sahagún at length: "Moreover, this Quetzalcóatl possessed all the riches of this world, gold, silver, and green stones, . . . and the vassals of this Quetzalcóatl were very rich."[14] Here Quetzalcóatl appears in the likeness of the Scandinavian Njordr and the "good jinni" of the American Indian mythologies. Quetzalcóatl also appears here, briefly, as the initiator of mortification. Then comes a long account of the persecution which he suffered at the hands of the sorcerers (*nigrománticos*) and his exile, with the miracles which accompanied it. Quetzalcóatl constructs his subterranean house, called *Mictlanalco.* Tlapallan, the goal of his flight, is named but not otherwise described; there is no mention here of his metamorphosis into the Morning Star. However, Sahagún had collected the tradition of a wondrous navigation: "Arriving at the sea shore, he constructed a raft of serpents, called *coatlapechtli;* he boarded the raft, sat down as if in a canoe, and set off across the sea; it is not known how he arrived at the place called Tlapallan."[15] This version strengthens my conviction that Quetzalcóatl was a sea god, who came from the coastal region; association of a god of the winds with the sea god is a natural one.

In chapter 5 of book 7, Sahagún presents Quetzalcóatl as the god of the four winds, blowing from the four cardinal points and imbued with their respective moral and metaphysical qualities. In book 4, apropos of the calendar, he devotes chapter 8 to *Ce acatl,* the sign of Quetzalcóatl, "the day on which the nobles made many sacrifices and offerings in honor of this god."[16] This statement confirms that on the eve of the Spanish Conquest Quetzalcóatl had become the god of the ruling class and the "Toltec" guarantee of the Aztec dynasty; Sahagún adds that all who spoke Nahuatl well were descended from Toltecs who could not follow Quetzalcóatl into exile. Even more interesting is the distinction that Sahagún makes between the historical Quetzalcóatl, high priest of Tula, and the god Quetzalcóatl, when describing the monotheistic character of his cult: "They adored one lord only whom they believed to be God; they called him Quetzalcóatl and his priest bore the same name and was also called Quetzalcóatl. . . . This priest told them over and over that there was but one god and lord whose name was Quetzalcóatl."[17] Here is one reason why other Spanish religious, anticipating some modern historians, saw in Quetzalcóatl an apostle of Christ or an Irish missionary. Sahagún also presents the first Quetzalcóatl as a divinity with a long face and a beard; these features contributed to the belief that he was a Spaniard.

In chapter 5 of book 1, however, Sahagún puts himself on record against future efforts to assimilate Quetzalcóatl into the Christian tradition. "Although this Quetzalcóatl was a man," he writes, "they [the Indians] held him to be a god."[18] Farther on he says: "This Quetzalcóatl, who was a mortal and perishable man, they called a god. Although he had some appearance of virtue, judging by what they say, he was nevertheless a great sorcerer, a friend of demons . . . and deserved to be assigned to the flames of Hell. . . . When your ancestors said that this Quetzalcóatl went to Tlapallan and would return, that you must await his return, they lied, for we know that he is dead, that his body was reduced to dust and that Our Lord God hurled his soul into Hell where he suffers eternal torment."[19] This expresses the policy of "rupture" of the first generation of Spanish missionaries in the New World. Sahagún's assimilation of pagan divinities, even those who have "some appearance of virtue," to demons is of special interest. The first missionaries were anxious to prevent the use of a messianic movement inspired by prophecies of the return of Quetzalcóatl. Sahagún and his comrades were clairvoyant, for several Indian risings of later date were inspired by Quetzalcóatl's old promise to come and liberate his people. Openly rejecting the hypothesis of an ancient evangelization, Sahagún wrote: "I have always held that the Gospel had never before been preached to them, for I never found anything that suggested the Catholic faith, but just the opposite; I found so much idolatry that I refused to believe that the Gospel had been preached to them at any time."[20] Sahagún thus beforehand assigned to the category of fantasy the identification of Quetzalcóatl with the apostle Saint Thomas, a thesis that would find general acceptance some forty years later. The Franciscan's posture may be compared to his order's hostile attitude to the cult which later developed about the alleged miraculous image of the Virgin of Guadalupe, near Mexico City. Sahagún's cautious and skeptical attitude toward syncretic phenomena or prodigies without adequate proofs was characteristic of the first generation of Franciscan missionaries. Yet, farther on, Sahagún contradicts himself. Discouraged by the failure of conversion—a failure which his fatigue doubtless exaggerated—Sahagún wrote: "It seems to me quite possible that they were evangelized at some time in the past, and that after the death of their preachers they completely lost the faith that had been taught them. . . . What inclines me toward this conjecture is the great difficulty I have had in planting the faith among these peoples during the forty years I have preached in these regions of Mexico. . . . Consequently I am sure that if they were left to themselves, in less than fifty years after their conversion, every trace of the preaching that had been done among them would disappear."[21] In moments of discouragement, therefore, Sahagún did not totally exclude an early evangelization of Mexico, but he never suggested that Quetzalcóatl may have been a missionary. On the contrary, he took him for a sorcerer (*nigromántico*).

Because of its wealth of detail, its sober transcription of native testimony, oral and written, and the clear separation of the information which he collected and carefully cross-checked from his opinions as a missionary, Sahagún's *Historia* may be considered the most faithful version of native beliefs at the moment of the Conquest, the most accurate reflection of the ancient Mexican mythology. It is encouraging to find that a reading of Sahagún leads to the same conclusions with regard to the pre-Hispanic Quetzalcóatl as do the most recent works on Mexican archaeology, history, and mythology.

The Histoyre du Méchique

Eduard de Jonghe first published this document in 1905. It is a French translation or adaptation, attributed to André Thevet, of a writing by a Spanish Franciscan, a contemporary of Motolinia, also a missionary in Mexico, Father Andrés de Olmos. It appears to be a fragment of a larger work, the lost *Memoriales* of Father Olmos. Father Olmos employed the methods of what retrospectively might be called the Franciscan school of Mexico. The last part, the only one which can be attributed to Olmos, according to Father Garibay, and which comprises the tenth and last incomplete chapter of the text published by Jonghe, is entitled: "Of an Idol Named Quetzalcóatl, of His Origin and the Time of His Rule." Garibay assigned it to Olmos because it reveals an effort at synthesis of different native sources. Olmos was another Sahagún; his work has been lost, but chapter 10 of the *Histoyre du Méchique* must be a good example of his method. Although truncated, chapter 10 has the interest of a synthesis and offers information not found in any other source; its authenticity is beyond suspicion.

According to this document, Quetzalcóatl was a son (not the only son) of Comachtli (Camaxtli) and Chilmalma, which confirms the Tlaxcalan legends collected by Motolinia. His brothers several times tried to kill him, but finally it was he who killed them to avenge the death of his father. His vassals, "who loved him very much, looked for him in order to honor him,"[22] and, after rejoicing over the victory, "they went to the land of Mexico, and he remained some days in a village called Tulacingo, and then went to Tula, where men did not yet know how to make sacrifices, and because he brought them this custom of sacrifice they held him to be a god."[23] The whole first part of this legend is known only through the *Histoyre du Méchique*. We seem to hear in this legend an echo of cosmogonic struggles between Quetzalcóatl, Tezcatlipoca, and the other gods born to the primordial couple, the dual principle Ometeotl. Other legends relate that Quetzalcóatl killed the sun with arrows; this must be a symbolic account of the struggle between the gods. Then follows an account of the migration of the Toltecs from Tulancingo to Tula; the length of their stay is given as "several days," which perhaps should be understood as "several years." Farther on, the author writes that the reign of Quetzalcóatl in Tula lasted one hundred and sixty years; this may refer to three successive eras of fifty-two years each (the Mexican "century"), that is, one hundred and fifty-six years.

Chapter 11 is entitled "Of the Coming of Tezcatlipuca to Tula and How He Made Quetzalcóatl Flee." Here the familiar tradition of the ruses employed by Tezcatlipoca to defeat Quetzalcóatl appears, but in a special form. The *Histoyre* clearly expresses the idea that the pagan divinities of the ancient Mexicans were devils. "Devils being former angels, and some angels being greater than others, so it is with devils." This analogy, implied throughout the writings of the missionaries, had certain consequences: "Now, this Quetzalcóatl was not as great as Tezcatlipoca and therefore feared him."[24] The tricks played by Tezcatlipoca are grosser than in other versions and culminate in the brutal destruction of the effigy of Quetzalcóatl, who flees with some of his servants. He is pursued by Tezcatlipoca and his followers; this agrees with other known versions of the legend.

A unique feature of the *Histoyre du Méchique* is its account of the "stations" of Quetzalcóatl on his way to exile and their duration. First he stops for "some time" at Tenayuca and then proceeds to Culhuacan, "where he remained a long time, it is not known how long."[25] Then he crosses the sierra and goes to Quauhquechula (near Huexotzinco) where he "erected a temple and an altar for himself, and was adored as god, and none was there but he, and he remained there two hundred and ninety years."[26] We have here again an event of mythical duration. Quetzalcóatl then departs for Cholula (after entrusting his power to a lord named Matlacxochitl), where he remains one hundred and sixty years; according to the *Histoyre*, he built there the famous temple whose vestiges remained, the work of giants of whom nothing more was known. Is this a record of Toltec migrations across Mexico, as some writers suggest? From Cholula Quetzalcóatl goes to Cempoala and remains there two hundred and sixty years, but Tezcatlipoca's persecution finally causes him to flee into a desert where he commits suicide. Is this a symbolic account of the advance of Chichimec invaders (the Aztecs?) or of bloody cults which demanded human sacrifices? In any case, the indications of place and duration (although symbolic) are valuable. The denouement, agreeing with that of other traditions, is the holocaust of Quetzalcóatl; incinerated by his companions, he is metamorphosed into the planet Hesper or Vesper (Venus). The author of this chapter knew the familiar variant: "Others say that when he `was about to die he went to another place. . . ."[27] The manuscript breaks off at this point, but we may guess that it went on to tell of that mythical Tlillan Tlapallan from which Quetzalcóatl, prophesying the eventual restoration of his kingdom like a true Messiah, sailed eastward on a raft of coiled serpents.

The absence of one aspect, that of Quetzalcóatl as Ehécatl, is interesting. It is implied in his cult at Cholula, but if the author had considered it essential, he would have mentioned it. The hero of the *Histoyre du Méchique* is a Quetzalcóatl who most closely resembles the more or less mythical chief of one of the Chichimec tribes of ancient Mexico. Of the different versions that have been preserved of the Quetzalcóatl legend, it best unites the historic Quetzalcóatl and the divine Quetzalcóatl. The legend is rooted in geography and chronology. The story of Quetzalcóatl's flight makes it possible to link the Quetzalcóatl of Cholula to that of Tula, and the legend to the Toltec migrations. The metamorphosis into Venus forms a link to the Mexican calendar. The *Histoyre du Méchique* is the only text that takes account of all aspects of Quetzalcóatl (with the exception of Ehécatl), tying them together into a coherent historic-mythical whole. Chapters 10 and 11 of the *Histoyre* shed light on the *Leyenda de los Soles* and the *Anales de Cuauhtitlan,* esoteric single-level expositions of the Quetzalcóatl complex, a complex that is both historical and mythological.

The *Histoyre du Méchique* presents Quetzalcóatl as the initiator of penance whom the Indians therefore adored as a god. Here is the textual basis of future hypotheses which tended to assimilate him, first, to a Spanish Christian missionary, then, more daringly, to the apostle Saint Thomas, and still later to an Irish monk or a Buddhist priest. In any case, the *Histoyre du Méchique* leaves not the slightest doubt that Quetzalcóatl, son of a god and a goddess, had a human career. Imagine the power of suggestion that this man-god, who came to restore piety among men, must have exercised on the minds of sixteenth-century Spanish missionaries. But the Franciscans courageously rejected the temptation of easy analogies which could have served their cause, among both Indians and Spaniards. Father Olmos—if he was the author of these chapters—was content to establish a logical link between the different Indian versions of the Quetzalcóatl legend. Thevet, who joined together pieces of Spanish chronicles, preserved the sober spirit of the native legends transcribed by the Franciscans. For these reasons, although the *Histoyre du Méchique* is less complete and detailed than Sahagún's testimony, I consider it the purest source (I am not comparing it, naturally, with the Nahuatl *cantares* or songs) of the Quetzalcóatl legend. Later historians, working with much the same data, created the creole Quetzalcóatl whose origins I now propose to study.

9   The Genesis of the Creole Myth

The Indian Prophecies and the Portents of the Conquest

The Indians generally believed that Quetzalcóatl would return from exile and restore his kingdom, which they identified with the Golden Age. The efforts of the Catholic missionaries to discourage this messianic hope indirectly testify to its vitality: "When your ancestors said that this Quetzalcóatl went to Tlapallan and would return, that you must await his return, they lied, for we know that he is dead."[1] The glorious return of messiahs is commonly announced by prophecies. We recall the return of the Heraclides in Hellenic antiquity; even more striking is the resemblance of the Quetzalcóatl myth to the contemporary myth of the return of King Sebastian of Portugal. If a myth of this kind, which challenged Christian doctrine, could arise in Portugal, in principle a Catholic country, it is not surprising that a similar myth developed in Aztec Mexico. Was this Quetzalcóatl whose return was awaited a man or a god? The question seems pointless, for, according to Motolinia, the word *teotl* designated the dead who were admitted to the paradise of Tlaloc. The chronology of the prophecy was very precise; the hero would return in the year of his calendrical sign, One Reed. Now, the sign of the year 1519 in which Cortés landed in Mexico was One Reed. Consequently there was a first highly syncretic colonial avatar, Quetzalcóatl-Cortés. The belief that Juan de Grijalva, first, and Hernán Cortés, later, was Quetzalcóatl of Tula, coming to regain his throne and oust the Aztec *tlatoani* or rulers (who seem to have regarded themselves as his regents), evidently was very strong among the Aztecs.

This belief was short-lived. If Moctezuma ordered the sacred ornaments of Quetzalcóatl brought to Cortés—perhaps in order to verify his identity—his illusion was quickly dispelled. Bernal Díaz, the most reliable contemporary witness, says only that when the conquistadors arrived in Tenochtitlan, Moctezuma declared: "It must be that we [the Spaniards] were the men of whom their ancestors had said, a long time ago, that 'men coming from the direction of the rising sun

149

would come to reign over these lands,' that we must be those men."[2] Laughing as he spoke, the Aztec sovereign declared that he had never taken the strangers for gods who hurled lightning, but for men of flesh and bone like himself. Indian confusion of the Spaniards with the comrades of Quetzalcóatl soon disappeared. In Cortés' own letters we read a version of a speech by Moctezuma that sounds as if it had been written by a classic Latin historian; it is too polished, too perfect. Moctezuma is supposed to have said to an assembly of his lords: "Quetzalcóatl departed, saying that he would return, or send such a force that they would be compelled to submit. You also know that we have always expected him. According to what this captain has told of the king and lord who sent him here, and according to the direction whence he says he comes, I hold it to be certain, and you must also hold it thus, that this king is the lord we have been expecting, especially as the captain says that they had information about us. Since our predecessors failed to act justly toward their sovereign lord, let us do so, and let us give thanks to our gods because that which our ancestors so long expected has come to pass in our time."[3] That long-awaited event was the return of the Golden Age. But the massacre of Cholula, the holy city of Quetzalcóatl, together with other indications, must have dispelled that terrible misunderstanding.

Is Cortés' text a summary version for the use of Charles V of Doña Marina's paraphrase translation of Moctezuma's words? Is it a pure invention of the Conqueror? Cortés' report was the most important source used by many later historians, notably Gómara, who in turn became the principal source of the majority of historians of the next century. Moctezuma took Cortés and the Spaniards for descendants of the Toltecs who had accompanied Quetzalcóatl from Tula in his exile—descendants who came to accomplish the prophecy by regaining by force the kingdom of their forebears. Thus reduced to human proportions, the historiographic legend of Quetzalcóatl-Cortés loses much of its marvelous character. In book 12 of his *Historia General* Sahagún gives a Nahuatl account of the arrival of the Spaniards in Mexico. This account supports the idea that Moctezuma took Cortés for Quetzalcóatl, at least before he saw him and his works: "It was as if he thought that the newcomer was our prince Quetzalcóatl."[4] But this is an Indian post-Conquest account; one suspects a design to save the honor of Moctezuma and the Mexicans, or to reknit the broken thread of Mexican history. If the Spaniards had come to accomplish the prophecy of the high priest of Tula, then the cyclical history of ancient Mexico had simply entered a new "sun" (a new era of Quetzalcóatl). Quetzalcóatl, it was known, had departed toward the East from the Gulf coast; and the Spaniards, coming from the East, had landed on the same coast in the year of the calendrical sign One Reed, symbol of Quetzalcóatl.

The prophecy of Quetzalcóatl was a specific Mexican instance of a belief common to the majority of the Indian peoples, the belief that men from the East would come to dominate them. Alvar Núñez Cabeza de Vaca heard of it during his trek across the Southwest; Gómara cites it for Española; the Chibchas, the Tupi of Brazil, the Guarani of Paraguay, had similar beliefs. In different regions of the New World the Spaniards were taken for "Children of the Sun." What interests us is the mutation this belief underwent. Regarded by the conquistadors as merely a political device for conquest of the continent, the prophecy soon became a subject of reflection for the missionaries and presently became a two-edged sword whose effects we shall observe.

The prophecy attributed to Quetzalcóatl was the principal reason, perhaps, for his later identification with a missionary. But a political leader departing for exile would naturally promise to return in force to regain the power he had temporarily lost. Quetzalcóatl's prophecy, which made him appear to the Indians as a prophet of the Spanish conquest, mediator between the past and the present, also provided the Spaniards with proof of their providential role. Man, hero, god, or necromancer (shaman), this personage soothed the consciences of both Indians and Spaniards. To the Indians he was the sole metaphysical compensation for the cataclysm of the Conquest; for the Spaniards he was God's seal upon an incredible adventure, a precious key to the understanding of an otherwise inscrutable history.

Quetzalcóatl alone could span the historical and cultural chasm separating the New World from the Old. Thanks to Quetzalcóatl's prophecy, Indians and Spaniards found that they shared the same history. The process of creating a collective god-hero reaches its logical conclusion in the title of a chapter of the *Historia de las Indias* of the Dominican Durán: "Of the Idol Called Quetzalcóatl... Who Was the Father of the Toltecs, and of the Spaniards Because He Announced Their Coming."[5] The legend threw a bridge over the gulf of metahistory and the juridical fault of the Conquest. Just as Aztec sovereigns had justified their rule by a supposed relationship with the ancient Toltecs, so the Spaniards could claim Mexico by virtue of Quetzalcóatl's prophecy. Neither Mexicans nor Spaniards, it seems, questioned that Quetzalcóatl had announced the coming of the Spaniards. Sahagún varies the account slightly: "They thought Grijalva was the god Quetzalcóatl returning."[6] The commentator of the Codex Vaticanus 37–38 thought the supposed prodigy was the result of chance and a trick of the Devil who wanted to preserve his credit among the Indians by making it appear that he had foreseen the invasion: "He told them this so that if some people conquered them he would preserve his credit by claiming to have foretold the event."[7]

A ruse of the Evil One could explain Quetzalcóatl's prophecy—a prophecy that played into Spanish hands, especially in view of the striking coincidence of dates. But it was not the only possible explanation. Fray Bartolomé de Las Casas devotes a chapter of his *Historia de las Indias* to the following theme: "How Divine Providence Never Permits Important Events for the Good of the World, or for Its Chastisement, to Take Place Before they Had First Been Announced and Predicted by the Saints, or Even by Infidels or Evil Persons, and on Occasion by Demons."[8] Las Casas drew his examples from pagan writers of antiquity and especially from Seneca, who was supposed to have prophesied the discovery of the New World in his tragedy *Medea;* that was not the important proof, however, but the authority of Saint Augustine, invoked by Las Casas in support of his explanation. Las Casas concluded that a merciful God had announced the coming of the Spanish missionaries to the misguided pagans through the lips of a demon, Quetzalcóatl. This explanation, if valid, made the portents which preceded the arrival of the Spaniards comparable to those which announced the coming of Christ. Sahagún devoted the first chapter of his book 12, "Wherein is Told of the Conquest of Mexico," to this theme.[9] He enumerates eight omens, including lightning, storm, monsters, and comets—the whole contemporary gamut of prodigious events.

But the Franciscan did not say that God had produced these omens. Nowhere does Sahagún claim that Quetzalcóatl had foretold the arrival of the Spaniards; he simply says that the prophecy of Quetzalcóatl's return made the Mexicans think the Spaniards were Quetzalcóatl's comrades. Las Casas also reports the prophecy, enriching it in the process, writing: "When they first saw the Christians they called them 'gods, sons, and brothers of Quetzalcóatl,' but later, having seen their works, they ceased to consider them celestial beings."[10] Certainly the Mexicans soon lost their illusions, as shown by their resistance— Cuauhtemoc's revolt—and, much later, by the Zapotec revolt of 1550. "The reason they gave for the rising," writes the commentator of the Codex Vaticanus 37–38, "was that their god, who would redeem them, had returned."[11] Thus the messianic movement linked to Quetzalcóatl survived the Conquest and a conversion which made little or no change in the Indian mentality. Certainly a sense of history, inherited by the Spaniards from the Judaic prophetic tradition, by the Indians from their ancestral polytheism, gave Quetzalcóatl's prophecy an importance that mere calendrical coincidence could not have conferred upon it. By a kind of tacit accord, Spaniards and Indians turned to the Quetzalcóatl legend to extricate them from a situation that their religious conscience found intolerable, the situation of living a moment of history—henceforth to be their common history—not foreseen by their respective prophets. What Cortés viewed as a clever ruse (taking advantage of an Aztec religious tradition for political ends) became for missionaries and theologians the happy solution to an exegetic difficulty.

The Cruciform Signs and the Ritual Analogies

Independently (at least at first) of the prophecy which was supposed to have announced their coming to the New World, the conquistadors, followed by the missionaries, found in the temples, sacred images, and codices of the ancient Mexicans signs which they believed must be of Christian or Judaic origin. The most impressive of these finds were the crosses. Bernal Díaz, who first reported such a discovery, relates what he saw in Campeche during the Grijalva expedition: "There were many painted idols and bas-reliefs of serpents on the walls . . . and we saw there a kind of cross, painted on the Indian statues; this astonished us, for we had never seen such a thing before."[12] Bernal Díaz's chief reaction was surprise. But a century later the Franciscan López Cogolludo, citing Bernal Díaz, added: "In the kingdom of Yucatan was found a basis for this theory [of a previous evangelization of the Indies by the Apostles] that gave the old authors much to think about. When the Spaniards entered that land they found crosses there, in particular a stone cross with an image of Christ the Redeemer in relief (it is now in our convent in Mérida), and the Indians venerated it."[13]

Crosses with religious significance were numerous in ancient Mexico. One of the best known, that of Palenque, presents the Maya Tree of Life in stylized form. The cross that Quetzalcóatl bore on his head, like that other cross of the *Codex Fejervary Meyer* on which is drawn a bearded personage, was the symbol of the four directions of space, of the cardinal points, as befitted the god of wind, Quetzalcóatl-Ehécatl. But the complicated religious symbolism of the ancient Mexicans was incomprehensible to the first Spaniards; or rather they could understand it only in terms of analogy. Bearers of a strong Judeo-Christian tradition, they focused attention on a symbol, the cross, that had significance for them, but they exaggerated its importance and gave it an erroneous interpretation. Coming from a closed, exclusive spiritual world, they could not conceive that a cross could have an origin or meaning other than that of the Christian cross.

Thus they combined and reduced the crosses of ancient Mexico, which differed greatly from each other, to their own cruciform pattern and interpreted them as signs of a previous evangelization. In reality, the cross on Quetzalcóatl's mantle, a Saint Andrew's cross, symbolized the dual principle which had created both gods and men. At the foot of the temple of Ehécatl, at Calixtlahuaca, is a funerary monument whose design also is cruciform. Thus a kind of law of frequency began to operate that associated Quetzalcóatl and the cross in Spanish minds.

Searchers for a providential explanation and a prophetic announcement of the Spanish conquest could not overlook this phenomenon. The prophecy attributed to Quetzalcóatl and the symbol of the cross associated with him together constituted a mystery. Again, the hero was a star, recalling the star of David. The numerous representations of Quetzalcóatl showed him wearing a conical bonnet which resembled the papal tiara and carrying a curved stick shaped like a bishop's crosier, although smaller. Was he not called "Pope" Quetzalcóatl? These formal resemblances greatly intrigued the missionaries. There was even a physical trait—the beard which almost all the Quetzalcóatls displayed—that appeared to make him an European, or at least a foreigner among the beardless Indians. Sahagún himself, despite his great caution, wrote: "I have also heard say that at Champoton, or in Campeche, the first religious who went there to preach to the Indians found many things that alluded to the Catholic faith and the Gospel. If there was an apostolic preaching of the Gospel in those two regions, doubtless it also happened in this region of Mexico and the neighboring provinces and even throughout New Spain." He also called attention to things that seemed to strengthen the presumption of a previous evangelization: "In 1570 or thereabouts two religious worthy of credit assured me that they saw in Oaxaca, which is about sixty leagues to the east of this city, some very old paintings on deer skins which contained many references to the preaching of the Gospel; one painting showed three women wearing Indian dress and hairdress and seated in the manner of Indian women. Two were on either side of the third, who was shown in the foreground and had a wooden cross attached to the plait of her hair. On the ground before them was a naked man whose hands and legs were extended on a cross, with his ankles and wrists tied to the cross by ropes. It seems to me that this refers to Our Lady and her two sisters and to Our Lord, whom the Indians must have known as a result of an ancient conversion."[14] Here is a very exact and troubling report, by a supreme authority; unfortunately, Sahagún's testimony is second-hand; he himself did not see the codex which he describes so precisely. Note that Sahagún does not claim any relation between Quetzalcóatl's prophecy and the preevangelization of Mexico. He views Quetzalcóatl as a great native sorcerer, not as a precursor of the missionaries.

Nevertheless, the multitude of signs of a pristine evangelization inevitably inspired a search for an Apostle among the heroes of ancient Mexico. Quetzalcóatl was an eminently suitable candidate. A chaste, ascetic foe of human sacrifice, he had initiated the practice of mortification, promoted belief in one god who created all things, and prophesied the Conquest. Cast down and persecuted, he had ended his existence by ascending to heaven and promising the future restoration of his benign rule. The many traits that Quetzalcóatl shared with Jesus were bound to provoke passionate disputes. According to certain versions of the legend, the hero was born of a virgin, having been miraculously begotten by a ball of down whose light and airy character could well symbolize the Holy Spirit. The ritual of the ancient Mexicans included circumcision, oral confession, fasting, the tonsure, and the like—customs that Catholic missionaries thought could only derive from the Judeo-Christian tradition. It was the same with the belief in the Deluge, and the "tower of Babel"—which the ancient Mexicans had tried to build precisely at Cholula, Quetzalcóatl's holy city. The commentator of the *Codex telleriano remensis* writes concerning this: "In the year One Reed they celebrated the other great festival at Cholula, the festival of Quetzalcóatl, the first *papa* or high priest, who was saved from the Deluge."[15] Regarded from this angle, Quetzalcóatl became a new Moses. It was a temptation for the missionaries to try to prove that this Indian messiah was the promise of the Light, of the Messiah Jesus Christ whose Word and Truth the Spaniards had brought. But there was more. In his aspect of Tlauizcalpantecuhtli, god of the dawn, created before the sun according to the commentator of the Codex Vaticanus 37–38, Quetzalcóatl supplied proof of "the great knowledge they have of Genesis, for (despite the Demon's efforts to mix it with many errors) their lying fable so conforms to Catholic Truth that one might well think they had knowledge of the Book of Genesis."[16] Such a multitude of signs clustered about Quetzalcóatl's figure that he inevitably became the center of hypotheses relative to a previous evangelization.

A knowledge of Judeo-Christian ideas (or very similar notions) by the Mexicans before the arrival of the Spanish missionaries thus appeared certain, but there were two possible and opposed interpretations of this fact. One might be called "Augustinian" and was represented by Las Casas, who saw in that knowledge the designs of a merciful God who wished to prepare the Indians to receive the Light (if not actually enlighten them) by means of the formal analogies between their ancient beliefs and the new faith. The name of the sacred book of the Maya, *Chilam Balam,* was boldly compared with the name of the magus Balaam who had predicted the coming of the Messiah. Since the figurative meaning of the name Quetzalcóatl was "precious twin," it appeared to be a synonym of the Greek *Thome,* which also meant "twin," whence the translation of Quetzalcóatl by *Santo Thome* or *Thomas.* With philology buttressing ritual, beliefs, and the pictorial representations in the old Mexican polytheistic religion, Quetzalcóatl soon presented all the traits of an apostle of Christ or a Spanish missionary; consequently he became the most important and interesting personage of ancient Mexico in Spanish eyes and particularly in the eyes of the missionaries.

In the last analysis this interest reflected the spontaneous ethnocentrism of the Spaniards, unconsciously driven to seek familiar landmarks in the wilderness of New World religious phenomena. For the rest, the very notion of confronting something radically new was abhorrent from the point of view of revealed truth. That is why a hermeneutics of allegorical inspiration discovered in Old Testament prophets the cryptic meaning of passages which seemed to foretell the voyage of Columbus to the New World, which therefore became Spain's property forever and ever, because it had been so *written.* We would be wrong and malicious to see dishonesty or naiveté in this position. Given the a priori rejection of novelty—which would have implied an intolerable gap in the totality of revealed truth claimed for Scripture—it remained only to search in the Prophets, on the one hand, and in America, on the other, for signs linking the New World to revelation. Quetzalcóatl appeared to combine in himself a number of luminous signs. There was only one problem. What if, as Sahagún thought, Quetzalcóatl had been a minister of the native religion, a sorcerer; what if the analogies with Christianity were all a devilish parody? Some, conceding this, nevertheless concluded that God had utilized this diabolic aberration as a kind of preparation for or initiation in the true faith.

The idea which soon won out over all others was that Quetzalcóatl was the apostle Saint Thomas, and that all the analogies of belief and ritual between ancient Mexico and Christianity resulted from a very ancient evangelization of America, with a later degradation of Christian doctrine. This idea was not a mental aberration; it was based on the *Acta Thomae* (since recognized as apocryphal), which declared that the Apostle had evangelized the Indies *supra Gangem* (beyond the Ganges). The rediscovery by the Franciscan and Dominican missionaries of "the Christians of Saint Thomas" in the region of Mylapore in East India gave support to this hypothesis. The initial geographical confusion which caused America to be baptized with the name "West Indies" tended to strengthen the "Thomist" hypothesis. Another argument, essentially theological, also exerted considerable weight. The Indians seemed innumerable and the New World immense; how could Christ have forgotten a portion of mankind, then believed to be the largest portion of all and to occupy the greatest part of the world, in the distribution of mankind he made among his apostles: *Ite et docete omni creaturae* ("Go and preach to all men")? Quetzalcóatl alone was well enough known and sufficiently enigmatic to provide a solution to these perplexing questions. Only this perspective of a metaphysical riddle that had to be resolved will enable us to understand the creole avatar of the ancient Mexican god-hero Quetzalcóatl, who, to our modern way of thinking, bears not the slightest resemblance to an apostle of Christ. Quetzalcóatl was a partial reply to a multiform spiritual problem, the American problem of the sixteenth and seventeenth centuries.

The Defenders of an Apostolic Evangelization of Mexico

Fray Diego Durán

The Dominican Durán was almost contemporary with the first missionaries and exactly contemporary with Sahagún; he too knew well the last survivors of the prehispanic Aztec world. This fact lends a special interest to his image of Quetzalcóatl, compared with those we found in Motolinia, Sahagún, and the author of the *Histoyre du Méchique*. Reading Durán, one gets the impression that years, even decades, separate him from the pioneer missionaries. Unlike them, he does not set himself the task of writing the history of the ancient Mexicans and their beliefs; he is intent on *interpreting* it as the history of his adopted country. By no accident, it is precisely in Durán that we encounter the first great literary mutation of the figure of Quetzalcóatl.

Durán presents his vision of Quetzalcóatl in chapter 69 of his *Historia de las Indias de Nueva España*. We should note that this vision of the hero forms part of a larger plan, a defense of ancient Mexico. At the very outset of the work the author announces his design: "My wish has been to make it [ancient Mexico] live again, to rescue it from the death and oblivion in which it lay, in order to disabuse newcomers and foreigners of the evil and false opinion that makes them condemn the supposed barbarism of the Mexicans."[17] In the last paragraphs of chapter 78, which immediately precedes the chapter devoted to Quetzalcóatl, Durán deplores the destruction of the ancient codices: "They who with a fine zeal (but very little common sense) on their arrival burned and destroyed all the Indian paintings and antiquities committed a grave error; for they left us with so little information about their beliefs that the Indians can give themselves up to idolatrous practices before our very eyes, yet we see nothing."[18] Father Durán, a missionary friar, thus has the same objective as Sahagún. But whereas Sahagún applies undeviatingly the doctrine of *tabula rasa,* showing no mercy to any doctrine of the ancient Mexicans, Durán takes the first step toward acceptance of the hypothesis of preevangelization. The very title of chapter 79 announces an interpretation: "Of the Probable Identity of a Great Man Who Lived in This Country, Named Topiltzin and Also Called Pope, Whom the Mexicans Called Huemac and Who Lived in Tula."[19] Observe that the name Quetzalcóatl does not figure in this title and does not appear in the chapter. Durán is speaking here of "Pope Topiltzin"; that is, the historical Quetzalcóatl, high priest of Tula, the man and not the god; consequently there is no allusion to his metamorphosis into the Morning Star. Only much later in his book does Durán treat "Of the Idol Called Quetzalcóatl, God of the Cholulans."[20] Although this idol is described as "father of the Toltecs, and of the Spaniards because he announced their coming," he is nowhere linked to "Pope Topiltzin."[21] Durán thus divorces the god of the Cholulans, Quetzalcóatl-Ehécatl, from the historic Quetzalcóatl. Moreover, he confuses his "Pope Topiltzin" with Huemac of Tlaxcala. Concerning "Pope Topiltzin" Durán writes: "He was a very venerable and religious person whom the Indians greatly revered; they honored him and felt as much reverence for him as if he were a saint."[22]

Durán had uttered a key word, one that had a great future: "Pope Topiltzin" was a *saint.* Durán's description of Topiltzin's conduct and the history of his life conformed to his presumed saintly character. Durán was not content with formal analogies. For him the word *Papa* had no etymological link to the Romance languages of the Old World; it signified "the man with long hair," that is, a priest, for the priests of ancient Mexico let their hair grow long. The analogies are more subtly suggested: "He was always retired in his cell, engaged in prayer. ... He was a very abstemious man and fasted continually.... He lived chastely and practiced much penance; he had the custom of building altars and oratories everywhere, of placing pious images on walls and altars, of kneeling before them to pray, and of preaching."[23] He also taught his disciples to pray and preach.

The use of a Christian vocabulary to depict Topiltzin's piety ("cell," "pray," "penance," "oratory"), and the mention of traits such as "abstemious," "given to fasting," "genuflection,"[24] had to impress Durán's contemporary readers. Add his statement that "the exploits and prodigies of Topiltzin" had "the appeareance of miracles," and the picture of a Christian Topiltzin takes very clear shape.

Durán based his argument for the identity of "Pope Topiltzin of Tula with an apostle of Christ on theological reasons and on alleged facts. He protested his orthodoxy: "I subject myself in all things to the correction of the Holy Catholic Church. Although I adhere to the Holy Gospel of Saint Mark, who states that God sent the Holy Apostles to all parts of the world to preach the gospel to his creatures, promising eternal life to all baptized believers, I dare not dare affirm that Topiltzin was one of the blessed apostles. Nevertheless . . . , since the natives were also God's creatures, rational and capable of salvation, He cannot have left them without a preacher of the Gospel. If this is true, that preacher was Topiltzin, who came to this land. According to the story, he was a sculptor who carved admirable images in stone. We read that the glorious apostle Saint Thomas was a master craftsman in the same art. We also know that this apostle was a preacher to the Indians."[25]

Durán thus laid the foundations for the identification of Topiltzin with the apostle Saint Thomas. This fact alone invalidates the hypothesis that reduces Durán's role to one of simple translator of an Indian chronicle called *Cronica X,* for want of a better name. To be sure, Durán, like the Franciscans whom we have already studied, had codices before him when he wrote and had knowledgeable natives gloss these codices. Possibly one of these codices, no longer extant, was his principal source. But Durán's vision of Topiltzin proves that the Dominican freely elaborated the material in Indian chronicles. Later writers would complete his portrait of an apostolic Quetzalcóatl. Another Dominican, Las Casas, described him as follows: "He was a white man, tall, with a great forehead and large eyes, long brown hair, and a long full beard."[26]

The interest of Durán's Topiltzin consists in the fact that it reveals the chain of ideas leading to the identification of Topiltzin of Tula with the apostle Saint Thomas. A number of traits attributed to Topiltzin by legend, and his "miraculous reputation," inspire the suspicion that he was a Christian missionary.[27] Acceptance—after controversies in which Las Casas, Sepúlveda, and Vitoria played the main roles—that the Indians were God's creatures, endowed with reason and capable of salvation, together with a reading of the Gospel of Mark and the Acts of Thomas, led to the conclusion that the Indies had been evangelized by an apostle, more precisely by Saint Thomas. A series of coincidences reinforced the analogies between the apostle and Topiltzin: Topiltzin had sculptured in stone, so had Thomas, and so on. These resemblances might have gone unnoticed, however, were it not for the theological need to find traces in the New World of an early apostolic evangelization.

In Durán's work Topiltzin's prophecy acquires a very specific character; the description of the strangers to come from the East sounds like a naive depiction of Spaniards, and the prophecy is given a new meaning that smacks of the Christian ethic: "God would send them this punishment for their mistreatment of him [Topiltzin] and the affront of driving him away."[28] Topiltzin now speaks like Saint Thomas—or rather as a sixteenth-century Spanish religious might imagine the apostle to have spoken. There was, of course, a whole party that justified the crimes of the Spanish conquest by proclaiming they were divine punishment of the Indians for their stubborn incredulity and their vices. Durán may have invented the remarks he assigned to Topiltzin, perhaps because he thought they fitted the character of the personage he conceived him to be, namely, Saint Thomas. In so doing, Father Durán, like all his contemporaries, only followed the example of prestigious Roman historians like Sallust and Livy. But it is also possible, though less probable, that the Dominican obtained this version from the lips of a native informant. Now, Durán, like all the Spanish missionaries, knew how fragile such accounts were and distrusted them, for a few lines later he writes: "When I questioned another old Indian about Quetzalcóatl's exile, he began to tell me the content of chapter 14 of Exodus. . . . Seeing that he had gone to the same source as I, and knowing where it would lead, I did not bother to ask him other questions."[29] If an old Indian recited Exodus in telling the story of Quetzalcóatl's flight, one can imagine what the accounts of young acculturated Indians must have been like.

In any case, even before Durán, the image of Quetzalcóatl must have been strongly syncretic. Durán reports: "An old Indian also told me that when Papa Topiltzin passed through Ocuituco, he left them a large book, and the Indians swore to me that six years before they had burned it because they could not understand the writing. . . . I was very sorry to hear this, for this book could have shed light on our suspicion that it might have been the Holy Gospel in Hebrew."[30] A simpler explanation might be that this old Indian did not know how to read the ideographic writing of the codices or that the book was a Mixtec, Maya, or even Toltec codex, incomprehensible in Zapotec country. Note the progression of ideas here: with revealed truth (the Gospel of Mark and the Acts of Thomas), as his point of departure, Durán proceeds to search, not for factual *proofs,* but for material *signs* of a past known through revelation. Sensing what the missionaries wanted them to say, the Indian anticipated their wishes; when this desire to please was too obvious (as in the case of Exodus, cited above) it fooled no one. But who could unscramble the subtle deformations of the Quetzalcóatl legend that by way of successive touches and retouches led to a confusion between the Mexican god-hero and the current conception of an apostle of Christ? The Indians had an obvious interest in persuading themselves of the identity; it proved that their past was not enveloped in darkness, that their present was not a leap into nothingness. The word of Christ was infinitely closer to them if it had been proclaimed by the lips of Quetzalcóatl. The pro-Indian missionaries found in this Christian tradition of the New World a sign of God's grace to the Indies and their peoples and, consequently, as new metaphysical ammunition against the slave-hunters and executioners of the Conquest, against the defenders of colonization by fire and sword. The first creoles saw in the apostolic evangelization a sign that the Lord had not rejected or forgotten their *patria*.[31]

Fray Diego Durán was not a creole, but he was very likely a *converso*, a descendant of converted Jews. In the hotly debated problem of the origin of the Indians he was one of those who thought "that they [the Indians] are by nature Jews and Hebrews"; he added, "I want no other proof than Holy Scripture, which clearly confirms the truth of this opinion."[32] It is risky to try to penetrate the hidden motives of a sixteenth-century Spanish religious. If Durán was in fact a *converso*, he may have felt a call to lead the "hidden Jews" of whom the Prophets spoke to Christianity, this being a prelude to the coming of the Kingdom. If this was in fact his motive the Dominican reveals the powerful impact of millenarian thought, whose influence was not limited to the Franciscans.

Durán passionately proclaimed his love for his Mexican *patria:* "In government, polity, obedience, reverence, grandeur and authority, courage and strength, in will to distinguish itself in all things so that its memory may endure forever, I find no people superior to the Mexican."[33] These were qualities to which contemporary Spanish readers were especially responsive. The ancient Mexicans had in common with the conquerors the heroic ethic, a thirst for glory, fame, and honor. This passage shows that the identification of Quetzalcóatl with Saint Thomas formed part of a general effort to overcome the radical novelty of the New World and the customs of its peoples. The Indians must be attached to the only possible world, the Judeo-Christian world, by prophecies, by beliefs, by a system of values. Quetzalcóatl was a trump card in the game the missionaries played against the conquistadors. In the relations of the latter, the Indians appear above all as cannibalistic pagans; the religious defend them with the spiritual arms of the epoch.

Juan de Tovar

There exist a closely related group of texts: the *Historia de las Indias* of Fray Diego Durán, the *Historia* of Juan de Tovar, the *Historia natural y*

moral (at least book 7, dealing with Mexico) of José de Acosta, and the
Crónica mexicana of Hernando Tezozomoc. Two letters, one from
Father Acosta to Father Tovar, the other Tovar's reply, help to clarify
the relationship between these works.[34] The manuscript of Tovar's
Historia (called *Tovar de Phillipps*), probably an autograph of Tovar,
appears to be a summary of an earlier lost *Historia* by him. Tovar sent
this summary to Acosta, who made marginal notes in it with his own
hand. By Tovar's own admission, he had used a history by a Dominican, who could have been no other than Diego Durán. Thus the links
between these works form the following chain:

Durán = Tovar I = Tovar II = Acosta

The Mexican scholar José F. Ramírez discovered in the convent of
San Francisco de Mexico a document called ever since the *Codex
Ramírez*. Adolph Bandelier established that the *Phillipps manuscript*
and the *Codex Ramírez* were by the same author. The undisputed
identity of the *Phillipps manuscript* with the *Codex Ramírez*, the former
being a copy of the latter, with only slight variations; and the identification of these two manuscripts with another *History* by Tovar, written in 1586 or 1587, suggest the following connections:

Durán = Tovar de Phillipps = Tovar Ramírez = Acosta = Tezozomoc

Geoɤge Kubler and Charles Gibson studied the various hypotheses
and concluded that Durán's *Historia* was the mother work. Meanwhile
Robert·H. Barlow had offered an "indigenist hypothesis," suggesting
that a *Crónica X*, now lost, was the common native source of Durán
and Tezozomoc. It is doubtful whether *Crónica X*, if such a work
existed, will ever be discovered and identified. The problem reduces
itself to the relations between Durán and Tovar, the question being
whether the latter summarized the former or whether both men (and
Tezozomoc) utilized a common source, the *Crónica X*. Viewing the
problem from the special angle of Quetzalcóatl, I shall try to shed
some light upon it.

In the absence of the hypothetical *Crónica X*, I begin by studying the
image of Quetzalcóatl in the Tovar manuscript, but with the premise
that Durán's *Historia* is the richest and earliest of the works under
discussion, and probably the principal source of the Tovar manuscript
and the *Codex Ramírez*.

Tovar assigns Quetzalcóatl's prophecy to the time of the Spanish
conquest and not to the moment when the historical Quetzalcóatl
departed into exile. He writes: "At that time the idol Quetzalcóatl, god
of the Cholulans, announced that strangers were coming to possess
themselves of these realms." The expression "at that time" refers to
the period when "ships bearing strange men appeared in the harbors,"[35] an allusion to the arrival of Grijalva in 1518, or Cortés in

1519. By changing the time of the prophecy, Tovar made perfectly clear that it announced the coming of the Spaniards. Among the omens which preceded the Conquest, Tovar relates the story of the peasant who was transported by an eagle to a cave and summoned by God's voice to burn Moctezuma's thigh for "the time has come when he must pay for all the offenses he has done to God."[36] This presents in slightly altered form Durán's idea of the Conquest as a scourge sent by God to punish the Indians for their paganism and vices. This notion, which was very early used to justify the atrocities of the Conquest, must be considered a Spanish creation; certainly it had nothing to do with the native prophecies.

The spies sent by Moctezuma "said that doubtless their great emperor Quetzalcóatl had arrived, for he had said that he would return at a certain time and that we must go to receive him."[37] This recalls the only Indian prophecy documented by the best sources, the prophecy of Quetzalcóatl-Topiltzin departing for exile. The other prophecy, that of the idol of the Cholulans, contemporary with the Conquest, probably had its origin in the confusion engendered by the name of Quetzalcóatl. By including that prophecy among the various omens described by other chronicles, Tovar linked the Quetzalcóatl of the ancient Mexicans more closely to the Spaniards. Tovar went on to say: "For a better understanding of this, it must be remembered that long ago there lived in this country a man who, according to tradition, was a great saint and came to this land to announce the Holy Gospel."[38] Tovar was careful to add the qualifying phrase "according to tradition"; one wishes that he had been more specific. If, as there is reason to believe, his source was Durán's *Historia*, that account is even more cautious than Tovar's, for Durán wrote: "This Topiltzin was a very venerable and religious person . . . and the Indians honored him and revered him as if he were a saint."[39] Tovar, summarizing Durán's text, took his conditional statement for a statement of fact, affirming that Topiltzin was "a very holy man," but immediately hedged, adding, "many persons affirm that he was one of the saints."[40] Tovar obviously wanted to add weight to his testimony by the reference to "many persons" but fails to give their names. If they were native informants, we know how suspect their testimony was; if (as was almost certainly the case) these numerous witnesses were Durán alone, we must deplore Tovar's vague turn of phrase. Tovar appears to be paraphrasing Durán, but in order to heighten the impression that Topiltzin was a missionary he adds details that have little in common with the Indian conception of Quetzalcóatl as it emerges from the most authentic sources. Thus Tovar alludes to a "very ancient tanned skin on which were shown in Mexican hieroglyphs all the mysteries of our faith, though mixed with many errors." He adds that "the persons most convinced of this [that Quetzalcóatl was a Christian missionary] are those who found a tanned skin in a village on the Gulf coast."[41] The Jesuit's credulous attitude contrasts sharply with that of Sahagún who, confronted with similar testimony, expressed surprise that he had not discovered such a thing in central Mexico.

Enumerating the hero's different names, Tovar writes: "The first was Topiltzin," which suggests that, like Durán, he identified Quetzalcóatl with the historical Quetzalcóatl Ce Acatl Topiltzin of Tula. Coming to the third name, Tovar noted that it was "pope," "and some of his paintings show him wearing a tiara with three crowns, like that of our Very Holy Father, the sovereign pontiff."[42] Tovar did not draw any conclusion from these two facts, leaving it to the reader to make the connection between the name of "pope" given to Topiltzin and the "tiara" which he wears in the Indian codices. These external signs of Christianity reinforce the impression produced by the hero's asceticism, piety, love of virtue, and miracles. Tovar does not mention that the ancient Mexican priests were called *papa* because they wore their hair long. Omission of this detail, mention of which would have sufficed to destroy Tovar's "Christian" assumptions, must have been intentional on the part of Tovar, who had an expert knowledge of the Indians and the Nahuatl language. Durán's explanation of the etymology of the word *papa* clearly proves that in the evolution of the myth which identified Quetzalcóatl with the apostle Saint Thomas he represents an earlier stage of the legend. This fact by itself does not prove that Durán was the source of Tovar's work; but, added to the facts I have indicated above, it reveals a general design on Tovar's part to strengthen the presumption of an evangelization of Mexico by Saint Thomas. By a series of revisions of details of Durán's testimony, sometimes omitting, sometimes adding material, by his use of different words, Tovar seeks to present Quetzalcóatl as an apostle of Christ. My analysis of the figure of Quetzalcóatl Topiltzin in Durán and Tovar makes it most unlikely that Tovar was the source of Durán. I may add that, contrary to the conjectures of Ramírez and Chavero, the vision of Topiltzin in Durán and Tovar owes very little to an anonymous Indian author, nor, for that matter, does it owe much to Sahagún or Motolinia. The same is not true of the idol Quetzalcóatl, god of the Cholulans, the subject of chapter 4 of the *Codex Ramírez*. He is described in language very similar to that of Sahagún and is not linked at all to the historical Quetzalcóatl, called also "Pope Topiltzin." This separation of the various aspects of the Mexican divinity in part of the missionary literature show that the effort of the religious to synthesize the Indian pictographic and other sources reflected a general vision of the Indian world and its beliefs, a vision profoundly different from that of the pre-Conquest Indians. Durán and Tovar render certain aspects of the ancient religion more faithfully, but the student must learn to recognize and distinguish these faithful renderings from invented material; the treatment of Quetzalcóatl, idol of the Cholulans, is a case in point. We see Father Durán even presenting Quetzalcóatl as a persecutor of Topiltzin, including him among the necromancers: Tezcatlipoca, Ilhuimecatl, and Quetzalcóatl. This is a far cry from Motolinia, Sahagún, and the Nahuatl literature.

The Commentators of the Rheims and Vatican Codices

Although the written sources discussed above are the most important, they are fortunately supplemented and completed by pictographic codices. It seems that the Jesuit José de Acosta, had already referred in his *Historia natural* to the Codex Vaticanus A, Mexican manuscript nos. 37–38 of the Vatican Library, called Codex Ríos. This confirms that the document has been in the Vatican Library since the end of the sixteenth century. The Italian commentary which accompanies the codex seems to be a clumsy translation of an oral commentary by a Spanish Dominican. A Father Pedro de los Ríos appears to have been attached to the Dominican mission of Oaxaca until about 1566. It is uncertain whether he reproduced a Mexican codex or merely glossed its meaning. Acosta informs us that a Jesuit explained the meaning of the codex to His Holiness's librarian, who could not make head or tail of it.[43] This Jesuit, probably Italian, must have translated Father Ríos' Spanish commentary.

There exists a replica of the Codex Vaticanus 37–38; it is a Mexican codex from the collection of the Bishop of Rheims, Le Tellier, and for this reason it is called *Codex Telleriano remensis*. The execution of the drawings of the *Telleriano remensis* is more finished and delicate than that of the Vaticanus 37–38, which could easily pass for an imperfect copy of the other, perhaps made by Father Ríos or in any case by a Spaniard ignorant of the symbolic or hieroglyphic significance of certain details. Moreover, the *Telleriano remensis* is accompanied by a Spanish manuscript commentary which only partially corresponds to the Italian commentary of the Vaticanus 37–38.

In the Spanish commentary of the codex *Telleriano remensis*, Quetzalcóatl appears several times, first as one of the signs of the second *Tercena* or thirteen-day cycle of the *tonalamatl* or sacred calendar. The rather rambling commentary recalls the principal traits of the god-hero: "He was born of the virgin named Chimalma. . . . He was saved from the Deluge. . . . He seems to have performed penance. . . . They say this Quetzalcóatl was the creator of the world, and they call him the Lord of the Wind, for when Tonacatecuhtli thought it convenient he engendered this Quetzalcóatl with his breath. They build churches for Quetzalcóatl that are entirely round, without any angles. . . . The Indians say that he created the first man. . . . Long after the Deluge, they practiced penance, but without human sacrifices."[44] We also learn that Quetzalcóatl's twin, Xolotl, was saved from the Deluge. The association of Quetzalcóatl with the Deluge appears particularly clear in the *Telleriano remensis;* it may have been a vehicle for assimilating ancient beliefs about Quetzalcóatl into the Judeo-Christian tradition. The commentator also recalls that he was born of a virgin and engendered by the "breath" or "spirit" of a god, indeed of the "Lord of Gods," Tonacatecuhtli. Mention of Quetzalcóatl's practice of penance recalls the mortifications practiced by Christian ascetics. This group of traits, directly linking Quetzalcóatl to Christianity, does not appear in the traditions most closely conforming to the Indian sources.

In the commentary on the third *tercena* of the ritual calendar, it is written that "Topiltzin Quetzalcóatl was born on the day Seven Reed and on that day a great festival was held at Cholula . . . and a great festival was also held the day One Reed when he departed for exile or died."[45] This is an interesting passage; it shows that the commentator of the codex *Telleriano remensis* (unlike Durán) identified Topiltzin with Quetzalcóatl and with the great god of Cholula (the Camaxtli of the Tlaxcalans). The indecisiveness of the phrase "departed for exile or died" reflects the cleavage in the Quetzalcóatl traditions to which I called attention above. In his commentary on the ninth *tercena,* the author writes: "This light or star was created before the Sun, and this Tlauizcalpantecuhtli or the star Venus is Quetzalcóatl—he took that name when he departed or disappeared."[46] This account evokes Genesis and also recalls the star in the East which announced the coming of the Messiah. The commentary on the fourth *tercena* informs us that "they fasted the last four days in honor of Quetzalcóatl of Tula, who borrowed his name from the first Quetzalcóatl, who is now called One Reed and is the star Venus."[47] The writer, commenting on the fifth *tercena,* adds: "On this day, One Reed, they celebrated at Cholula the other great festival of Quetzalcóatl, the first pope or priest. . . . He was saved from the Deluge."[48] Here a clear distinction is made between the original god Quetzalcóatl and the Quetzalcóatl Ce Acatl of Tula, who appears as "first pope or priest" of the former; this second Quetzalcóatl, who was saved from the Deluge, is obviously the initiator of penance. Thus the codex *Telleriano remensis* reveals the different faces of Quetzalcóatl in the Mexican traditions, by means of a summary (and consequently a trifle incoherent) account of the principal Indian traditions. A special role is assigned to the Deluge, which here appears to be of Christian origin, not because the Deluge is absent from the Mexican traditions but because it is not traditionally associated with the Quetzalcóatl myth. If I am correct in dating the codex *Telleriano remensis* as earlier than the Vaticanus 37–38, which was probably copied from a Mexican original (perhaps the *Telleriano remensis* itself) some time after 1555, we must regard the commentator of the *Telleriano remensis* as one of the first historians of Mexico, at least as early as Durán and earlier than Tovar. The anonymous author seems well informed on the subject of Quetzalcóatl in the different native traditions and is much more cautious than Durán and Tovar about establishing analogies between the Quetzalcóatl myth and the biblical traditions. He seems determined not to be led astray by misleading similarities. Was he prudent from fear of the Inquisition or was he an adherent of the *tabula rasa* school?

The Italian Jesuit commentator of the codex Vaticanus 37–38, who probably transcribed the oral commentary of the Dominican Fray Pedro, lacks the concise style of the codex *Telleriano remensis*. Although his text is more elaborate, it is poorer in content and neglects important aspects of the native traditions. On the other hand, it freely develops the Judeo-Christian analogies. We seem to have here a case resembling the Durán-Tovar connection; a Jesuit, inspired by a Dominican, goes much farther than his teacher in the way of accommodating pagan beliefs to biblical tradition. (The seventeenth-century dispute over Chinese rites was but the acute phase of a divergence that goes back to the beginnings of missionary activity.) In arguing against the uncompromising rigor of other missionaries (the Franciscans in particular), the Jesuits had a good argument; they could point to the pagan survivals in Christianity. Like his coreligionist Father Durán, Father Ríos (who may also have been a *converso,* as his name suggests) thought that "these people descend from the Hebrews," adding "one of the arguments that persuade me is that they have such great knowledge of Genesis."[49] This knowledge of Genesis is closely linked to Quetzalcóatl, for Father Ríos refers to the belief that Tlauizcalpantecuhtli, divinity of the dawn, had been created before the sun. "How they [the Indians] came to this country is not known." The implicit diffusionism of this line of thought, expressed by a European at the end of the sixteenth century, should occasion no surprise.

To argue, on the basis of such analogies, that the ancient Mexicans were the famous "hidden Jews" of the prophetic tradition amounted

to assigning a Judaic origin to Quetzalcóatl. Since Hebrew piety was
well known, the hero-priest Quetzalcóatl naturally appeared as "the
first to invoke the gods and celebrate their sacrifices, and the first to
perform penance in order to appease the gods."[50] Quetzalcóatl, the
first builder of temples, presents all the characteristics of a Hebraic
hero; more, he is a new Moses who mysteriously crossed the sea, for
the word Tlapallan "means the same thing as 'Red Sea.'" The messianic character of Quetzalcóatl did not escape the commentator, who
recalled the Zapotec rising of 1550: "For their god had come, who
would redeem them." Yet, despite all these analogies, contradicting
his own thesis of the Hebraic origin of the Indians, the author writes
about the prophecies of the return of Quetzalcóatl: "One must not
infer from this that the demon, who invented all this business, could
foretell the future."[51] It was a simple trick of Satan designed to preserve his credit among the Indians; the devil could easily foresee that
some day or other an invasion must come.

Referring, in the commentary on figure 14, to the origin of Quetzalcóatl, born of a virgin and a divine spirit, that of Citlaltonalli,
Father Ríos, (or his interpreter) objects to the attribution to this demon, Quetzalcóatl, of the providential role of Jesus. "It was He who
found the world corrupted and reformed it by performing penance
and dying on the cross for our sins, and not this miserable Quetzalcóatl, to whom these unhappy beings assign Christ's works."[52] Here
the Franciscan theme of the devil's parody of Christianity reappears. I
do not know whether to attribute it to the Dominican Ríos or to his
interpreter, the anonymous Jesuit. Whoever it was, he apparently felt
that the pictorial Christianization of the Quetzalcóatls of the codex
Vaticanus 37–38 no longer held any dangers for orthodoxy. The author of the drawings in this codex, simplifying those of *Telleriano
remensis,* replaced the creator-god or dual principle of the ancient
Mexicans with Christian crosses on the mantle of a Quetzalcóatl walking on the waters of Tlapallan, "the Red Sea." I need not stress the
suggestive value of these coincidences for one who wished to show
that Quetzalcóatl belonged to the Judaic tradition. The commentary
on codex Vaticanus 37–38 is interesting because its portrait of Quetzalcóatl accents the resemblances to Jesus and to Judeo-Christian beliefs in general, while offsetting these analogies by its affirmation of a
devilish parody. In short, the origin of the efforts to assimilate Quetzalcóatl to a figure of the biblical tradition seems to be Durán's *Historia,* chronologically the first work to deviate from the early Franciscan histories (Sahagún, Olmos, Motolinia) and from the Dominican
school as well (here represented by Father Pedro de los Ríos).

An Official Censor, The Jesuit José de Acosta

The two letters (one from Father Tovar, the other from Father Acosta) published by J. García Icazbalceta and reproduced by George Kubler and Charles Gibson in their study of the Tovar manuscript prove that Father Tovar's *Historia* (*Tovar Manuscript–Codex Ramírez*) was almost the only source used by Acosta in writing the part of his *Historia natural y moral de las Indias* that dealt with Mexico. The famous Jesuit had a long direct knowledge of Peru, but in Mexican matters he had to be content with information secured at second hand. His letter to Father Tovar shows how painstakingly he examined this material. It is interesting to see how a mind like Acosta's received Tovar's suggestions about Quetzalcóatl.

With respect to the general problem of the providential character of the discovery and the evangelization of the New World, Acosta shared the opinion of all his contemporaries. Like them, he thought that the Prophets must have announced such an important event: "It seems reasonable to assume that the Holy Scriptures mention a matter of such importance. Isaiah says: 'Woe unto the ships that go beyond Ethiopia.' Learned authors whom I trust relate this whole chapter to the Indies."[53] The vagueness of the prophecies and of ancient geography, even of the geography of the late sixteenth century, with regard to Asia and America, explains the obvious fragility of this interpretation. Moreover, Acosta takes shelter behind "learned authors" whom he does not name and for whose views he does not seem to feel any enthusiasm. Commenting on Isaiah on his own, the Jesuit continued: "The very important affirmation of the Lord, according to which the Gospel will be preached throughout the world, and then will come the end of the world, makes plain that as long as the world endures there will yet be peoples to whom Christ has not been announced."[54] This interpretation of the *Ite et docete omnes gentes* of the Vulgate (Matt. 24:14) makes plain Acosta's dissent from the millenarian current of the Franciscan pioneers of New Spain. Acosta's reading of Christ's message did away with the need for an early evangelization of the Indians and the need to identify Quetzalcóatl with an apostle of Christ.

Accordingly we find in Acosta a vision of Quetzalcóatl profoundly different from that presented by the Tovar manuscript which he had read and annotated. "At Cholula they adored Quetzalcóatl because, like another Mammon, or a rival of Pluto, he made wealthy those who loved him. . . . The Indians called him Quetzalcóatl, that is, a serpent with brilliant plumes, an image of the demon of greed,"[55] wrote

Acosta. This image of Quetzalcóatl, which conforms to widespread Indian belief in a "good jinni," seems more correct than that of Tovar. Where did Acosta obtain this information? Perhaps from the Franciscans, more likely by word of mouth from other Mexican Jesuits. The reference to Mammon is particularly striking; if "one cannot serve God and Mammon," the Quetzalcóatl of Acosta is the exact opposite of that of Tovar, Acosta's principal informant. An apostle to Tovar, Quetzalcóatl embodies idolatry, diabolism, for Acosta. Acosta does not deny the prophecy of Quetzalcóatl ("The idol of the Cholulans, named Quetzalcóatl, announced that strangers would take possession of these realms"), but explains it in a different manner. Instead of attributing the prophecy to a missionary, Acosta likens it to that of Netzahualcóyotl, king of Texcoco. Netzahualcóyotl "who was a great magician and had a pact with the devil, paid a visit to Moctezuma at an untimely hour and assured him that his gods had told him that disasters and great ordeals threatened his person and his kingdom. Many sorcerers and enchanters came to tell him the same thing."[56] The inevitable conclusion followed: "God wished to make the demons give unwilling witness to the coming of the true Law, of the power of Christ and the triumph of His cross, as the portents and prophecies, the signs and the prodigies, clearly prove."[57] Acosta made special mention of the supernatural voice which a peasant heard in his field and which assigned him the mission of "awaking Moctezuma from his sleep"; this voice had said, among other things: "the time has come for him to pay for all the offenses that he has done to God."[58] We have seen this phrase, in a different context, in Tovar, where it served admirably to complete the image of an apostolic Quetzalcóatl.

Acosta, consistent with himself, explains the prodigy in this way: "It is possible that the peasant's story was the recollection of an imaginary vision. We may suppose that God gave this warning to the peasant (although an infidel) through the agency of a good angel or even permitted it to be given by an evil angel, for the chastisement of the king. For we read in divine Scripture that such visions were given to infidels and to sinners, such as Nebuchadnezzar, Balaam, and the pythoness of Saul."[59]

Acosta reveals here his discreet and cautious character. By contrast with the fiery Tovar, Acosta, *visitador* of the Society of Jesus in the Indies, a diplomat, would not take a firm stand on such a controversial question. He knew the fears of the Inquisition in such matters, and its powerful weapons. But it is interesting to see where his preferences lie. They are based on scriptural authority. The early historians of America explained the native prophecies by reference to scriptural precedents. Acosta, taking a position that held no political dangers for

Spain and that was theologically Augustinian, would long represent a certain orthodox posture on the problem of apostolic evangelization of the New World. No doubt he had been officially entrusted with the task of purifying the historiography of the Indies. In 1571 a royal order had defined the tasks of the royal cosmographer and historiographer of the Indies: he was to write a general and natural history of the Indies.[60] This corresponds almost word for word to the title of the *Historia natural y moral de las Indias* (1590) of José de Acosta. Acosta's position represents a retreat from the stance of that other Augustinian, Las Casas, who regarded the belated revelation of the Truth to the Indians as a striking manifestation of God's grace. God had wished "that His grace be the more abounding, because it was less deserved."[61] But Las Casas, who may have read Sahagún, considered Quetzalcóatl a virtuous man after the manner of the philosophers of classical antiquity: "These Indian peoples were superior to the Greeks and Romans in this respect, that they did not choose for their gods depraved, criminal, or infamous men, but rather virtuous men (in the measure that virtue can be found among peoples deprived of the knowledge of the True God, which may only be attained by faith). Such a man was he . . . whom they called Quetzalcóatl."[62]

Acosta thus offers the most unfavorable image of Quetzalcóatl since Sahagún. He returns to the *tabula rasa* doctrine of the first missionaries and effectively undermines the hypothesis of a Quetzalcóatl-Saint Thomas that Tovar had advanced. Acosta proposed an explanation of the Indian prophecies that was theologically acceptable and that made vain and dangerous the hypothesis of an early apostolic evangelization. Not even Las Casas, apologist par excellence for the Indians, claimed any more for Quetzalcóatl than had Motolinia; he was content to describe him as a virtuous man from the viewpoint of natural morality and by comparison with the gods of classical antiquity. Durán's hypothesis, accepted by Tovar, of a "Pope Topiltzin," Christian missionary, was the first creation of the creole intellect vis-à-vis the scornful *gachupines*.

A Demoniac Image of Quetzalcóatl in Juan de Torquemada

The *Monarquía Indiana* of Fray Juan de Torquemada, provincial of the Friars Minor in New Spain, belongs to the early Franciscan tradition. The *Veinte y un libros rituales de la Monarquía Indiana* were composed during the first years of the seventeenth century, several decades after Durán's *Historia*, the *Tovar Manuscript*, and Acosta's *Historia*, which derives from Durán and Tovar, but deviates from them on some important points. Now, the *Monarquía Indiana* presents a picture of Quetzalcóatl that has nothing in common with that of Durán and Tovar. More fluent than his Franciscan predecessors, whose writings he knew directly or through Mendieta, Torquemada had literary pretensions and, being closer to the written Indian sources, elaborated more amply the new facts at his disposal.

Torquemada considered Quetzalcóatl a demon, adored by the Cholulans, and as thirsty for Indian blood as the other divinities of ancient Mexico, whereas Torquemada's predecessors had absolved Quetzalcóatl of this fault.[63] Torquemada defined his position with respect to the problem of the two Quetzalcóatls as follows: "We do not know whence came this people . . . ; they brought with them a personage of very high rank who governed them and whom they called Quetzalcóhuatl (later the Cholulans adored him as a god)."[64] Torquemada thus regards the god Quetzalcóatl as the ancient divinized chief of an unknown people who landed in Mexico in the region of Pánuco, tried to establish themselves at Tula, and then dispersed because of difficulties with the city's old occupants; more especially, some established themselves at Cholula. Cholula "was the principal hearth of the superstitious religion of this New Spain."[65] For Torquemada, no doubts remained; Quetzalcóatl had been the supreme divinity of a pagan religion: "When they swore an oath they said 'By Our Lord,' meaning thereby Quetzalcóatl and no other god."[66] Torquemada explains the fall and flight of the historic Quetzalcóatl of Tula as follows: "The reason why this Quetzalcóhuatl allowed himself to be so easily persuaded by Titlacahua was his profound desire to become immortal."[67] Torquemada views Quetzalcóatl in the same light as Sahagún did; he was a "great magician and necromancer."[68] Torquemada recalled how Franciscan pioneers had planted the cross on the great temple of Quetzalcóatl at Cholula and built there a chapel consecrated to Our Lady de los Remedios. The only aspect of the old Indian belief in Quetzalcóatl that found favor in Torquemada's eyes was the ritual exhortation addressed to the children consecrated to Quetzalcóatl and sent to the *calmecac:* "You must know that the invisible god, creator of all things, called Quetzalcóatl, created you, and that you have come into the world by his will." There follow counsels of abstinence and penitence which inspire this reflection in Torquemada: "I do not know how these Indians came to profess this doctrine, which is in the very language of Saint Paul (*Ad Ephes.*, *Parénèse*, 6)." He continues: "In truth, I do not know what more Christians could say than was said by these misguided people; and I believe that their speeches should be carefully preserved, for it does not matter that they come from gentiles, since their tenor is Catholic; as Saint Augustine said: "Whatever is good in the sayings of the gentiles we should take and apply to the matters of our Faith.' "[69]

Here is a new attitude on the part of the Franciscans, an attitude more receptive to the ancient Mexican values and civilization. To view the Aztecs like the ancient Greeks represented a bold forward step, although Torquemada largely offsets this concession by rejecting all the pagan beliefs. The Franciscan's posture remains profoundly different from that of Duran and Tovar. For the latter, the numerous analogies between Quetzalcóatl's conduct, aspect, and speeches and those of an apostle of Christ compel the conclusion that he was a Christian missionary or apostle. Torquemada does not even entertain that hypothesis.

For the Franciscan, as for his predecessors, the problem of Quetzalcóatl is linked to that of the origin of the Indians: "Some claim that they were Romans or Carthaginians. . . . Others say that they were Irish. In this matter, on pain of going astray, we must leave the matter to God."[70] Note that Torquemada does not even suggest the possibility of a Judaic origin for the Indians (by contrast with Durán and the commentator of the Codex Vaticanus 37–38, both of whom adhere to that hypothesis). Torquemada refuses to take a position on such a doubtful problem. However, he gives support to the thesis that Quetzalcóatl was a white man: "It is held certain that he was a very fine looking man, white, blond, and bearded, and of very good character."[71] The physical description depicts a Scandinavian or a German; (it could fit Cortés' lieutenant, the conquistador Pedro de Alvarado, whom the Mexican Indians called Tonatiuh, the name of their solar god). This description differs partly from another that Torquemada gives of the high priest of Tula. "It is said that he was a tall white man, with a large forehead and large eyes, long brown hair, and a great full beard."[72] The personage described here could more easily pass for a Mediterranean type. However, Torquemada reports the traditional physical descriptions of Quetzalcóatl without drawing any inference as to his possible origin. This restraint may reflect Torquemada's insistence on the writing of truthful history, a subject which he discusses at length in the prologue to book 1.

Torquemada's most original contribution was his interpretation of the prophecy of Quetzalcóatl's return and its role in facilitating the Spanish conquest. "It was folly on the Indians' part . . . to believe that this enchanter had gone to join the Sun, and would later return to reclaim the temporal power which he had abandoned. I believe that the devil invented this lie and performed this trickery to lead these people astray. God permitted it, not so that these misguided beings should persevere in their error, but in order that the Indians might be partly prepared to receive His Word . . . when the Christians arrived in these parts with His Holy Gospel, and if the devil had understood the matter well, he would have known that this Quetzalcóatl, whom he falsely gave out to be the king and god of these peoples, was not the true God, king and lord of all creation."[73]

Here Torquemada propounds a subtle providentialism which complements the theory that the devil had parodied the Christian ritual in order to lead the Indians astray. We know that a providential atmosphere pervaded the discovery and conquest of America. Coming after Columbus, another providential man, Cortés, was depicted as having been chosen by God to accomplish a mission that was more eschatological than military and political. In Torquemada the designs of God flow in the predestined mold of pagan prophecies and diabolical beliefs. Aware of or foreseeing the messianic significance of the Quetzalcóatl myth, Torquemada transformed the prophecy of his return into a providential announcement of the Word of the true Messiah. This is not a case of identity, but rather of a mysterious coincidence between Quetzalcóatl and Jesus. This conception forms part of a larger theory which taught that the belief in the Deluge, the rite of confession, the sacrament of baptism, penance, and other features of certain Indian religions were so many spiritual "teething rings" given to the Indians in conformity with a divine plan of preparing them for Christianity. The Inca Garcilaso de la Vega, citing the precendent of the Roman Empire as interpreted by Saint Augustine, applied and developed this same thesis in reference to Inca religious beliefs.

Torquemada, it may be said, contributed a new interpretation of the formal analogies between Christianity and the ancient Indian religions, especially with respect to Quetzalcóatl. Durán and Tovar, impressed by the number and quality of their similarities, refused to reduce them to simple accidental resemblances. This was a natural attitude on the part of Europeans and especially European religious of the sixteenth century, who saw the hidden hand of providence behind all apparent coincidences, a fortiori behind the American realities, regarded as revelations. The theological reasons I have mentioned (apostolic preaching *in omnibus partibus*) had convinced them that these analogies were traces of an apostle of Christ, Saint Thomas, the apostle of the Indies. Torquemada, more stongly influenced than the Dominicans and the Jesuits by his Franciscan predecessors, could not out of hand reject their doctrine of the devil's parody. His optimism found a compromise solution in the notion of a providential use of the Evil One's diabolical designs. Had not a pagan prophecy, that of Balaam, involuntarily announced the coming of Christianity and the universal King?[74] More than once in history the meaning of obscure pagan prophecies had not been revealed until the passage of many years. In Europe, for example, Virgil had announced the coming of the Messiah in terms that were inscrutable to his contemporaries.

Seneca had also announced the providential voyage of Columbus in a mysterious language. For Torquemada, Quetzalcóatl had played a similar historical role. Torquemada's classic culture, his taste for figures and images, impelled him to project upon the pagan past of ancient Mexico the providential, prophetic vision which inspired all the histories of the Conquest of his time.

But Torquemada's providentialism influenced his treatment of only one aspect of Quetzalcóatl: the prophecy of his return. For the rest, Torquemada's demoniac conception of the Mexican god resembles that of Sahagún. Torquemada wrote: "They said of Quetzalcóatl that he was very humane and merciful. This lie was unquestionably believed in those times."[75] Torquemada thus disputes even Quetzalcóatl's moral virtue, which Motolinía had compared with natural morality. Was Torquemada obeying orders from above? All that favored the assimilation, survival, or resurgence of native beliefs—and thereby might awake ideas of independence—had been proscribed, as witness the confiscation of Sahagún's manuscripts and the oblivion that engulfed Mendieta's manuscripts, Torquemada's principal source. Torquemada's assimilation of Quetzalcóatl to a demon is complete. Nor does he doubt that it was a supernatural being whose voice summoned the *macehuales* of Tzatzitepec, near Tula: "Clearly this could not have been a human voice, but must have been a devilish trick and invention," adding, "this can be held for certain."[76] Torquemada also mentions a sign—the supposed footprints of Saint Thomas—found in many places in the New World. For Torquemada, however, these were prints left by Quetzalcóatl's hands on a rock near Tlalnepantla (close to Mexico City) "whose traces are still visible."[77] The author does not say if it was a devilish prodigy, but that may be inferred from the above.

Belief in the influence of the stars on men's lives was as widespread in sixteenth-century Europe as it was among the ancient Mexicans. "The soul of this Quetzalcóatl was metamorphosed into a star . . . and this comet or this star has appeared various times, and its appearance has been followed by epidemics among the Indians, and other calamities."[78] Here ancient Mexican paganism and European paganism seem to join hands. Whereas Quetzalcóatl-Topiltzin was simply a wicked demon, Tlauizcalpantecuhtli is a comet that portends plagues. Note that in Torquemada's account Quetzalcóatl never appears as a "myth." Indeed, the very idea of myth which is so familiar to us was completely foreign to sixteenth-century men. There was the true faith, which obviously had nothing to do with myth, but was adherence to the truth, or rather the grace of truth. Opposed to the truth was nonentity, falsehood, absolute evil, the Devil. The pagan gods were not creations of human imagination but inventions of the Devil and his lieutenants, that is, of demons. To say that Quetzalcóatl was a demon was not to deny his reality but, on the contrary, fully to affirm it; Quetzalcóatl was a messenger of the forces of darkness. Such was the Franciscan conception of Quetzalcóatl, or at least that of Sahagún and Torquemada. This is the very opposite of the "apostolic" conception of Durán and Tovar. It was the latter, however, which prevailed and underwent a notable development down to the end of the eighteenth century.

Saint Thomas-Quetzalcóatl, Apostle of Mexico

Saint Thomas in East India, According to Marco Polo

The belief in a pristine evangelization of the New World by the apostle Saint Thomas resulted from the collation of a series of biblical texts and new facts with ancient beliefs. According to the *Acta Thomae*, this apostle had preached the Gospel beyond the Ganges (*supra Gangem*), that is, in India. The Franciscans, who were the first to send missionaries to the coast of Malabar, found there Nestorians whom they called "Christians of Saint Thomas," that is, Saint Thomas of Mylapore. A Spaniard, Fray Antonio Caballero de Santa María, wrote: "Tradition affirms that Saint Thomas journeyed in China, and then retired to India."[1] Another Franciscan, "Padre custodio Fray Martín Ignacio," a missionary in China, wrote in his *Itinerario:* "There are proofs certain that at one time they had direct knowledge of the Evangelical Law. . . , thanks to the preaching of the blessed apostle Saint Thomas, who passed through this kingdom when he went to India, and thence to the city of Salamine (which in their language is called Malipur), where he suffered martyrdom for the name and faith of Christ; they say he is still remembered in that kingdom by ancestral Tradition."[2] In his *Viaggio dell' Indie*, Father Giovanni Battista Lucarelli of Pisauro reports the conversion to Roman Catholicism of "Mar Simeone, a Chaldean bishop," in these terms: "The glorious apostle Saint Thomas, my special advocate, obtained this favor at the price of his own blood, imitating the only son of God by founding the Church of this India on the sacrifice of his life."[3] For his part, Father Giovanni de Marignolli writes in his *Relatio:* "The third province of India is called Malabar, and there is found the church of Saint Thomas, which the apostle built with his own hands." The apostle is supposed to have thrown a log into the sea and said to it: "Go and await us in the port of the city of Mylapore."[4] Despite the efforts of 10,000 men, the city's ruler could not get the log ashore without the miraculous assistance of Saint Thomas.

The Jesuits corroborated the Franciscan discoveries, and the name of Saint Francis Xavier is attached to the belief of Saint Thomas of Mylapore. The great centralization of the Society of Jesus may have been an important cause of the discovery of traces of Saint Thomas in Brazil and Paraguay. But whereas the signs of Christianity at Mylapore have withstood the probing of modern science, the same is not true of the supposed traces of Saint Thomas of America. Saint Thomas of the East was not Saint Thomas the Major but a later missionary. The symbols the the Franciscans, followed by the Jesuits, interpreted as Christian symbols were really such—at least some of them were. To understand the importance of the hypothesis of an early evangelization of the "Indies" by the apostle Saint Thomas, we must comprehend the spiritual climate of the period of great discoveries and the missionary upsurge that followed. To begin with, we must remember that the belief in an evangelization of the East by the apostle Saint Thomas was a tradition inherited from previous centuries. Marco Polo had brought back a little earth from the place where, according to tradition, the apostle had suffered martyrdom: "The body of Saint Thomas the apostle is buried in the province of Malabar, in a little town[5] . . . and I must tell you that all year long other miracles occur there, especially the healing of Christians who are crippled or injured."[6] The great popularity of Marco Polo's *Description of the World,* from the last years of the thirteenth century to the seventeenth, first in a Latin version, then in the Italian version of Ramusio's *Navigazione e viaggi* (1559), helped to diffuse widely the tradition of Saint Thomas of Mylapore. The Italian Franciscan Fra Giovanni de Monte Corvino had visited the sepulcher of Saint Thomas at Mylapore, no doubt in the same year as Marco Polo, in 1292 or 1293.

To this tradition, buttressed by the accounts of Marco Polo and the Franciscan missionaries, were added scriptural "proofs" of the evangelization of the East by the apostle Saint Thomas. Now, a part of the Acts of the Apostles was later recognized to be apocryphal; the *Acta Tomae* seem to have been the later work of Saint Gregory. But in the sixteenth century Catholic doctors did not question the authenticity of the *De miraculis beati Thomae.* According to the text, the apostle had been assigned the regions "beyond the Ganges." Ptolemy's geography, which was still, broadly speaking, the geography of Christopher Columbus and the majority of his contemporaries, and even of seventeenth-century Europeans, made it impossible to give more precise contours to "India." Africa south of the Maghreb was called Ethiopia to the east, Guinea to the west. Asia, beyond the empire of the Grand Turk, was India. It was very difficult to define the boundaries of India, Cathay (China), and Cipango (Japan). Even after the voyages of Columbus, of the fortunate Florentine Amerigo Vespucci, and of the Spanish navigators had made known the Antilles and the east coast of the New World, and the existence of a vast continent had little by little been revealed, men continued for about a century longer to believe that this continent was an extension of Asia. Only later did they become aware of the immensity of the Pacific ocean. Accordingly, there seemed to be no insurmountable geographical obstacle to a more or less complete fusion of eastern India with the western Indies, called simply "the Indies." Consequently, the tradition of Saint Thomas of the East seemed applicable to the West.

Indeed, the idea of pristine evangelization of the Indians by the apostle was a reassuring thought. Jesus had sent his apostle throughout the world, and Saint Paul had confirmed this universal evangelization of apostolic times: "Their sound has gone throughout the earth and their words to the ends of the world."[7] Revealed truth would not permit the newly discovered Indies to be excluded from a grace dispensed to all men—unless the Indians were also excluded from mankind. In effect, some Spanish *encomenderos* sought to reduce the Indians to the level of "beasts" so that they could exploit them beyond measure. Catholic missionaries, theologians, and jurists were resolved to bring the Indians into the bosom of the Catholic church by preaching, but they must first be included in the history of mankind, which was one with the history of Christendom marching toward its preordained goal.

We have seen that the ideas of Joachim of Floris, which were very influential at the beginning of the sixteenth century, a century racked by spiritual fever, postponed the end of the world until the conversion of the last gentiles. The early successes of conversion in the New World, the great number of the converts and their enthusiasm, made the accomplishment of the prophecy seem imminent. Acceptance of an original evangelization of America by Saint Thomas inevitably tended to reduce the millenarian fever. The campaign against all forms of prophetism and illuminism which followed the decline of Erasmianism and evangelism in Europe—a campaign that coincided with the movement somewhat crudely called the "Counter-Reformation"—benefitted from the idea of an apostolic evangelization of the Indies. The leading role played by the Jesuits in the Counter-Reformation may explain why they were among the first to discover traces of Saint Thomas in the Indies. In addition to the cruciform signs found in the symbolism of ancient Mexico and elsewhere, such mythological coincidences as the belief in the Deluge, and such ritual customs as fasting, the problems which the missionaries encountered in working with the Indian converts soon provided a new reason for believing in the missionary work of Saint

Thomas. In the partition of the world among the apostles, doubting Thomas had received the Indies; that is, he had been assigned the most ungrateful task of all: "Send me where you will, O Lord, but not among the Indians."[8] Thus the Indies entered history as early as apostolic times, and not sixteen centuries later, a delay which would have been incompatible with the doctrine of grace dispensed to all mankind. Rational theology and Scripture aided each other in the effort to establish that Saint Thomas the Major had brought the Word to the Indians before the Spanish Franciscans. It only remained to find traces *in situ* of the apostle's passage, but at a time when revelation was more important than discovery the latter was a secondary aspect of the probative effort.

The goodwill of the Indians, their enthusiasm as converts and their veneration for the missionaries facilitated discovery of vestiges of the original evangelization. The first discoverers of Saint Thomas's traces were the Augustinians of Peru, but it was Jesuit writings, quoted by various historians of the New World in the sixteenth and seventeenth centuries, which above all bore witness to the presence of such traces. The following passage from a letter written by Father Manuel da Nobrega, April 15, 1549, from Bahia, may be called his certified report of the presence of Saint Thomas in America: "A person worthy of faith also told me that the roots [manioc] from which the bread of this country is made were a gift of Saint Thomas, for previously the Indians had no kind of bread at all. This is known through an oral tradition that is preserved among them *quia patres eorum nuntiaverunt eis* [because their parents informed them of it]. Not far from here are traces of footprints on a rock, and everyone says that these are Saint Thomas' footprints."[9]

The Road of Saint Thomas in the Indies

These footprints on a rock, showed by the Tupinamba of Brazil to Father Nobrega, evoke memories of the founder of the Society of Jesus, Saint Ignatius Loyola. Father Gonçalves de Camara, his biographer, reports that when Ignatius made a pilgrimage to the holy places he wished to return to the Mount of Olives before departing, because "there is a stone from which Our Lord ascended into Heaven, which still bears the visible imprints of his feet, and this is what Ignatius wished to see again." Bribing the Turks with some trifling presents, Ignatius obtained permission to examine the stone in order to verify "on which side was the right foot and on which side the left foot."[10] Like the founder of the company, Father Nobrega wanted to get to the bottom of the matter: "Since we shall have to journey about, we shall go to see them [the footprints]";[11] and the next August "I went to see them to be absolutely certain and saw with my own eyes four footprints, very distinct, with the toes well marked"[12] Since the Jesuit had confirmed the existence of the footprints, their apostolic origin could no longer be questioned. This hermeneutics, which we may find startling, is based on the revelation of the passage of Saint Thomas to the New World. The analogy of the apostles' traces with those of Jesus on the Mount of Olives reinforced their probative value. Three years later we find other Jesuits on a pilgrimage to the site of the footprints of Saint Thomas. The Indians accompanied them, crossing themselves as they went. On arrival at the site, the Jesuits were hospitably received by the chief of the neighboring village: "In this village we danced and sang in their fashion, singing hymns in their language, and the wife of the principal lord got up and danced with us. . . . From there we went in the direction of the footprints, singing Christian hymns, and the gentiles of the village accompanied us. At the site of the footprints we sang a hymn to the Holy Spirit."[13]

This remarkable testimony invites reflection about the origin of the legend of Saint Thomas in America. Who were the dupes in this affair, the Tupinamba or the Portuguese? Father Nobrega offers an interesting detail; the Tupinamba called Thomas *Zumé*, which was the name given by this people to all prophets, sorcerers, shamans, called *Pay* (was *Pay Zumé* or *Zomi* a local prophet?). It was certainly a widely held belief among the Tupinamba tribes, for the Tupinamba chief of Marañón, Iappy Ouassou, told the French Capuchins in 1612: "The prophets (*pay*) seeing that the people of our nation would not believe them, flew off to heaven, leaving the marks of their bodies and feet, as well as crosses, imprinted on the rock which is near Potyion."[14] What was the origin of the legend? The fact that when Claude D'Abbeville wrote this account the Portuguese had maintained close relations with the Indians for half a century suggests that Indian mythology may have been influenced by Christian messianism. About the same time, an Indian prophet seems to have borrowed some traits from Jesus.[15] The close resemblance of the Saint Thomas of the Tupinamba to the "good Jinni" of American mythology arouses suspicion. This myth is found throughout the American continent; its permanent elements are the prodigious prints and the wearing of the beard, the prophet's attributes are those of the benign Indian hero. Called *Pay Zumé* in Brazil and in Paraguay, Viracocha in Peru, Bochica in Ecuador, the benevolent hero identified with Saint Thomas is also found under other names among the Aymará, Chibcha, Tupi, and Guarani, and among the Mapuche of Chile. The glorious martyr Nicolas Mascardi learned "that in the Valley of the Jaurua, in the pampas, there was a peak which Saint Thomas or Saint Barnabas had ascended to preach; on a stone they left traces of their feet and their staffs; what is more, there were letters engraved on the rock by the apostles' hands, letters which Father Mascardi split off from the rock and sent to Rome for inspection."[16] The incident shows how exigent were the Jesuits in the matter of proofs; Father Mascardi's action, in the sixteenth century, in sending a stone from Chile to Rome, in order to verify its authenticity, is worthy of a modern scholar. I have explained why no doubts clouded the belief in the prints. Repetition of the signs and attributes of the beneficial hero in different regions of America seemed to confirm that everywhere they referred to the same personage, whose journey across the continent they documented.

The preamble of the celebrated work of Fray Gregorio García, *Orígen de los Indios del Nuevo Mundo, e Indias Occidentales,* reveals the importance of the alleged Saint Thomas of America. The Dominican, we recall, wrote: "Three questions above all others, have claimed my attention. . . . The third question is whether the Gospel was preached in these regions in the time of the Apostles."[17] The "Indies" posed before the Europeans of the sixteenth and seventeenth centuries a historical (principally dynastic) problem, an anthropological problem (the origin of the peopling of America), and a theological problem, that of the apostolic evangelization of the Indians. It involved nothing less than the doctrine of grace and the Christian conception of history. It was the options with respect to these theological problems, and not the authenticity of the alleged vestiges of primitive Christianity discovered in the Indies, that divided the partisans and adversaries of Saint Thomas of America.

Proof that the idea of an apostolic evangelization of the New World had been formulated even before the hypothesis of Saint Thomas-Quetzalcóatl appears in the fact that there had been speculation of much the same kind about other apostles: Saint Barnabas in southern Chile by Father Mascardi, Saint Matthew in Nayarit by Fray Francisco de Burgoa, and again Saint Matthew in Brazil by the Calvinist Jean de Léry of Geneva, who wrote: "I do not approve the fabulous books which, going beyond what the Word of God says on the subject, tell of the voyages and peregrinations of the Apostles. However, Nicephorus, recounting the history of Saint Matthew, says expressly that he preached the Gospel in the land of the Cannibals who eat men, people not very different from our American Brazilians." How fragile was this proof, how much more decisive the belief in a universal apostolic evangelization, becomes clear from Léry's next words: "But I much prefer to base myself on a passage of Saint Paul, taken from Psalm 19, namely: 'Their sound has gone throughout the earth, and their words to the ends of the world,' a passage which certain sound commentators apply to the Apostles. . . . But I will affirm nothing more than this with regard to the apostolic times."[18]

Lery's cautious attitude contrasts with the decisiveness of a Spanish Augustinian of Peru, Fray Antonio de la Calancha (writing a half-century later than the Genevan): "They [the Europeans] who will not admit that one of the Apostles preached the Gospel in the New World offend the natural, divine, and positive laws and diminish God's mercy and justice; they offend the natural law, because they wish for those countries the misfortune of not having been evangelized by an apostle, something the Europeans would not accept for themselves."[19] The year is 1639, fifteen years after Fray Gregorio García had critically examined all the hypotheses relative to the preaching of the Gospel in the New World during the lifetime of the apostles.[20] Calancha's emotional tone sharply contrasts with Gregorio García's serene attitude; differences in temperament were not the cause of this contrast, or not the main cause, at any rate.

The focus of the dispute had shifted; it was no longer a question of two opposed hermeneutics, or, if that question was raised, it was not the real issue. What angers the creole friar Calancha is that the Europeans wanted for the Indies what they would not accept for themselves.[21] Belief in the apostolic evangelization of the New World is now not so much a theological question as a question of national pride. For Calancha Saint Thomas of America has become a war-horse in the creole crusade in favor of their dignity and equality with the Europeans. In this same period there took place the flowering of the Marian cult, while miracles attributed to the Virgin (already recorded by the Inca Garcilaso de la Vega) multiplied in the New World and appeared in creole eyes to be a clear sign of heaven's gift of grace to them and their American *patria*. It would all have been very innocuous if this rising creole self-esteem had not been intimately associated with feelings of rancor against the Spaniards. The attachment of the *gachupines* (called *chapetones* in Peru) to the Virgin of Pilar, whose miracles the creoles relegated to a secondary level, had as its corollary an incredulous attitude toward the American apparitions. The creoles naturally found a parallel between the Virgin of Guadalupe and the Virgin of Montserrat in Catalonia. A competition arose between Saint Thomas, apostle of the Indies, and Saint James, apostle of Spain. The Saint James of the conquistadors, supernatural ally of the Conquest, became the god of thunder of the Indians of Peru; but the creoles preferred Saint Thomas, who redeemed their American *patria* from the stigma of having lain in darkness for sixteen centuries, isolated from revelation.

Despite his patriotic creole passion, Calancha gave an excellent exposition of the problem of Saint Thomas of America. The Augustinians cited Saint Thomas Aquinas, "in his *prima secundae quaestio 106,
art. 4*, as well as other exegetes."²² The problem was whether the
wording of the Vulgate ("The Gospel will be preached throughout the
earth. . . . and then will come the end of the ages") referred to the
Apocalypse or to the destruction of Jerusalem. Calancha invoked the
authority of Saint John Chrysostom, Saint Mark, and Saint Jerome,
among others, in favor of the second interpretation. If the universal
evangelization was accomplished before the destruction of Jerusalem,
the Indies had been evangelized in the time of the Apostles. This
interpretation, which may be called literal (it considers the historical
Jerusalem and not, symbolically, the terrestrial Jerusalem), in effect
annihilated the millenarian hopes of the first missionaries of the New
World. A geographical and statistical argument employed by
Calancha to buttress his thesis suggests the spiritual commotion
produced by the discovery of the New World. "Since the apostles were
twelve in number, how can they [the Europeans] argue that God sent
all twelve to the smallest part of the world [Europe], and did not send
at least one to a much larger part [America]?"²³ Here is an early
effort—Gómara had pioneered in this line of thought—to view the
world, with America as one of its parts, as a whole and to question the
validity of Eurocentrism, which had become a dogma.

In the last analysis, the debate revolved about the question whether
the people of Israel would be the chosen people until the end of time.
This was generally denied, but while the Portuguese, through the
mouth of the Jesuit Antonio Vieira, professed to be the new chosen
people by virtue of a new covenant, the Spanish imperial doctrine
(One monarch, one empire, and one sword) claimed that Spain was
charged with a providential mission. About the same time appeared in
Amsterdam the famous book of Menasseh Ben Israel, a Jewish
theologian and philosopher, bearing the significant title, *Origin of the
Americans, or, the Hope of Israel*.²⁴ According to the Jewish philosopher,
certain tribes of Tierra Firme (Venezuela) were the *Judaei clausi*, the
hidden Jews descended from the lost tribes of Israel after the great
diaspora; their discovery and early return to the promised land in the
reign of Messiah, son of David, as a result of the discovery of the New
World, would accomplish the Judaic prophecies. Given this spiritual
climate, in which America's geographical novelty inspired the wildest
dreams, we should not be surprised that the creoles in their turn
caught the illuminist fever and claimed for themselves and their *patria*
the honor of being the new chosen people.

Since the traces of the apostle Saint Thomas were so many signs given by God to the American creoles, Calancha had no difficulty in finding them in Brazil ("where the traces begin"), in Paraguay, and in Peru. Despite his certainty, Calancha felt an uneasy need to pile up authorities in favor of his thesis, assuring his readers "that I have consulted all the books that treat of this question, some by persons who lived in this country and by order of the viceroys wrote reports which were later published, others by authors who got their information at second hand, and still others by living persons who have seen these things with their own eyes."[25] The identification of Saint Thomas as the apostolic missionary of the New World was based on an apocryphal text, the *Acta Thomae*. But the identity of the apostle was basically unimportant; men sought the traces of an "apostle type," so to speak. The European vision of an apostle was that of a Semite with long thick hair and beard, dressed in a long white tunic, and holding an apostolic staff in his hand. The apostle typically conducted himself like a Spanish missionary of the sixteenth century, but—this was a specific feature—he proved the truth of the religion he preached by prodigies and miracles. As might be expected, the principal Christian symbols, crosses in particular, were associated with his traces.

Instead of being surprised that American Indian "good jinnis," providers of edible plants, born of virgins under supernatural circumstances, capable of walking on water and of disappearing without leaving a trace, should have passed for apostles of Christ, we should admire the caution of the missionaries, who refused to see apostles everywhere. Consider the pull exerted on the Indian mind (traditionally receptive to all messianic currents) by the Christian religion, and their desire to anticipate the wishes of the missionaries and link their ancestral beliefs to the new faith. The remoteness in time of the supposed evangelization, and the devil's tricks, perverting the original Christianity of the Indies, made it seem natural that this Christianity should have become almost unrecognizable. The legends soon surrounding the personalities of certain Spanish missionaries among the Indians suggest that if an inquiry had been made half a century later they would have receded so far back into the Indian mythical past that they too could have been taken for apostles. As concerns the doctrine they taught, by the admission of Father Sahagún, it too would have become unrecognizable. The Indians' receptive attitude with regard to every new revelation had for its obverse a tendency to forget rapidly. Thus the Indian "good jinnis" tended little by little to lose their traditional attributes of benevolent divinities on the terrestrial plane, becoming prophets always in attitudes of prayer, living the life of hermits, while their clothing more and more resembled the sixteenth-century Spanish conception of the apostles.

Since an evangelization of the Indies by Saint Thomas was certain, being a revelation, the only problem was to identify the true traces and tradition of Saint Thomas. To distinguish the true Saint Thomas from false apostles was all the more difficult a task because the Indians (like the Spaniards) felt a burning need to explain the cataclysm through which they had just passed. It was as crucial for them to root their new condition of Christian neophytes in the tradition they had inherited from their forebears as it was for Europeans to find in the Bible a prophesy of the discovery of the New World. Thus, despite the reciprocal incomprehension of the two worlds that confronted each other, their respective spiritual aspirations impelled them to bridge the gulf opened up by the Conquest, a metaphysical gulf which threatened to swallow both. The Indians had just suffered a total military and political defeat; their idols had been routed, their priests persecuted, they faced a void. They could only recover their full human condition by conversion to the faith of the conquerors, but they could more easily internalize that faith if some sign in their past linked them to the new religion; that sign was the pristine evangelization by Saint Thomas. As for the Spaniards, their world system, founded on revelation, and their very religion would collapse if the Bible had lied or simply omitted mention of America; ignorance, forgetfulness, and injustice on the part of God were all equally untenable. If there existed a positive truth independent of revealed truth, all European thought, from Saint Augustine to Suárez, must go out the window.

Thus the hypothesis of an apostolic evangelization simultaneously saved the Indians, by inserting the Conquest within the cyclical movement of their history, and the Spaniards, who regarded their religion as their ultimate guarantee. The mestizos, mixed-bloods born of the union of the victorious Spaniards and Indian women, inherited this double aspiration. In the case of the creoles—spiritual mestizos— this unrest of the Indians and Spaniards became even more internalized. To link Indian historical tradition and beliefs with the Bible was a vital problem for the American creoles; Saint Thomas, missionary to the Indies, was the unexpected way out of the impasse. Among the various Indian divinities identified with Saint Thomas, the most representative of Indian spirituality in its most evolved forms was the Mexican god-hero Ce Acatl Quetzalcóatl-Topiltzin, called also Ehécatl, and identified with the Morning Star, Tlauizcalpantecuhtli. Quetzalcóatl-Saint Thomas is thus the most outstanding example of syncretism between the cosmological myths of ancient America and Christianity, the extreme point of contact reached by the two worlds in their advance toward each other. Saint Thomas of America was also one of the roots of the American consciousness, a consciousness that even now remains charged with charismatic certainty and messianic hope.

The Plumed Serpent, New "Phoenix of the West"

I have made a detour through the Peruvian Saint Thomas of Calancha, a specifically South American variant of the apostle, because he represents an intermediate stage between the Quetzalcóatl-Saint Thomas of Tovar and that of Sigüenza y Góngora. A reading of Calancha makes perfectly clear that for the creoles the Indian tradition was not important in itself; what mattered was its utilization by the creole intellect for its own ends. Ever since Tovar's time the danger of such assimilations had been sensed by the Spanish Crown, which ordered the seizure of Sahagún's manuscripts and forbade "any person to write about anything related to the superstitions and way of life which these Indians had."[26] The "political" future of Quetzalcóatl would prove how well founded were Spanish fears. Quetzalcóatl-Saint Thomas was to become a most effective instrument used by the creoles to pry New Spain loose from Old Spain while forging a link with the glorious past of Anahuac. But that purpose does not yet appear in the work of that universal man Sigüenza y Góngora, mathematician and historian, an ex-Jesuit banished from the Pueblo convent and the best writer of colonial Mexico after Sor Juana Inés de la Cruz.

The collection of writings relative to Quetzalcóatl and variously attributed to Sigüenza y Góngora and the Jesuit Manuel Duarte (I shall presently discuss this problem, which has little importance here), scanty fragments whose only connection is their reference to the apostolic evangelization of America, appears to constitute the first complete "dossier" on the subject. About 1675 the Mexican scholar Sigüenza y Góngora became interested in composing a synthesis of the ideas circulating on the subject of the preaching of Saint Thomas in the New World. The collection of texts, long lost and then rediscovered by Ramírez, is in the hand of Father Manuel Duarte. The Portuguese Jesuit must have given his manuscript to Don Carlos, as he himself indicates: "I wrote these things down in a manuscript which I left with the *bachiller* Sigüenza."[27] And again: "In 1680, when I returned to the Phillipines, I left this manuscript, together with a manuscript notebook of more than fifty-two sheets, containing information relative to the preaching of the apostle Saint Thomas in New Spain, with the *bachiller* Don Carlos de Sigüenza y Góngora, professor of mathematics."[28] Ramírez based his attribution of the manuscript on these statements. But Sigüenza y Góngora had referred, in the prologue to his book *Parayso Occidental*, to something he had written to prove the preaching of Saint Thomas, a writing which he wished to see published before his death. Discussing the various points of view expressed on this problem, the American scholar Irving Leonard calls attention to a passage in the *Catálogo* of Boturini: "Moreover, I have historical notes on the preaching of the glorious apostle Saint Thomas in America. They are contained in thirty-four sheets of China paper which, I suppose, were used by Don Carlos de Sigüenza y Góngora in writing a work on the same subject, entitled *Phoenix of the West*, which I have not been able to obtain because it was never published."[29] These facts persuade me of the identity of the texts rediscovered by Ramírez and published by Nicolás León and those which Boturini possessed; the reference to "China paper" is another indication that the manuscript referred to by Boturini was that of the Jesuit from the Philippines, Manuel Duarte. The internal evidence in favor of assigning the manuscript to Duarte is even stronger:

1. Duarte explicitly names himself as the author.

2. He speaks on several occasions of "The Fathers of Our Company."

3. The treatise which Sigüenza y Góngora claimed to have written was a complete essay, not a simple collection of independent documents.

The last reason is especially convincing to one who knows how the historians of that period worked. The process is illustrated by Motolinia, Acosta, and others. Duarte copied from previous historians all that related to the preaching of Saint Thomas and that constituted an argument in favor of this preaching. He translated into Castilian a native history, that is, the Nahuatl commentary on a codex, prepared either by an Indian student of the missionaries or by a friar expert in Nahuatl. Duarte turned over these texts, together with his evaluations, to Don Carlos, who used them in writing his synthesis. This was the method used by the majority of historians of Mexican antiquities in the sixteenth centuries. The future may reveal whether the essay written by Sigüenza y Góngora was destroyed or has only been lost for more than three centuries. In my opinion, the fragments published under the title of *Pluma rica, nuevo Fénix de Occidente* are materials collected by Manuel Duarte and turned over by him to Don Carlos, who utilized them to write an essay that disappeared long ago. The *disertación*—this word alone excludes any possible identity with the fragments that we possess—of Sigüenza y Góngora is cited by Sebastian de Guzmán, by Vetancurt, and by Boturini; we know the work only through these allusions, and the old authors who mention it had not themselves seen it.

From the point of view of the history of ideas in New Spain, it really matters little who was the author of the *Fénix de Occidente*, once we know its date. The only candidates for its authorship are Duarte and Sigüenza y Góngora. Duarte was a Jesuit; Sigüenza y Góngora, expelled as a youth from the convent of the Society in Puebla, passed the last years of his life in trying to reenter the Society of Jesus. Both of the possible authors thus represent the Mexican Jesuit mentality. It appears that by 1675 the hypothesis of an apostolic evangelization had matured sufficiently to justify a systematic review of the question. Hitherto the champions of the evangelization of the New World by Saint Thomas, headed by the Augustinian Calancha, had advanced the hypothesis only in the context of a general history of the Indian past, the Conquest, and the missionary movement. In Duarte's manuscripts, the evangelization of the New World by Saint Thomas became for the first time the exclusive object of a special inquiry. This fact itself indicates the importance assigned to the problem, which went to the very heart of the spiritual disquiet of the New World, and therefore inspired a general challenge to the previous historiography of the Indies, "because the few authors who have written about the events of the Indies did not know them." Herrera, the official royal chronicler, is often quoted, but is also taken to task. Duarte opposes to "the pure and true history" the history written by Spaniards who were ignorant of the subject. The native authors "knew their history well and wrote the history of events, at first using their figures and hieroglyphs; later, when they learned to write in our script, some scholarly minds among them wrote history. These histories I have in my possession, and I am filled with jealous admiration of the language and style in which they are written, so that I wish I could translate them into Castilian with the elegance and grace they have in their Mexican language."[30]

The last quarter of the seventeenth century sees the posthumous revenge of Sahagún, invoked by Duarte in the same passage as the great precursor who "knew all the secrets." Creole distrust for the official Spanish history goes hand in hand with exaltation of the native histories and of the Indian past. Amid the jumble of borrowings from the Brazilian Jesuits (Nóbrega and Vasconcelos), from Calancha, Torquemada, Las Casas, and Solórzano Pereira, we can discern the broad lines of what the *disertación* of Sigüenza y Góngora must have been. To begin with the failure of the apostles to evangelize the Indies would have been incompatible with the commandment *"docete omni creaturae"* in the Gospels. The Indies represented a third of mankind; it was theologically impossible, therefore, that they should not have been evangelized by an apostle of Christ. Now, we know the lives of the Apostles. The only one who could have evangelized the Indies, from what we know of his life, was the doubting Saint Thomas. Spaniards who refused the gift of grace to the Indians were the very persons interested in consigning them to perdition. Granted that the evangelization by Saint Thomas was an integral part of revelation, what material signs have we of Saint Thomas' passage to the New World? The indelible traces of his feet, the miraculous springs and the crosses found here and there from Bahia in Brazil to Guatulco, were convincing signs. The totality of Indian rites that vaguely evoked Christianity: confession, fasting, circumcision; the belief in one creator God, in a virgin miraculously made mother, in the universal Deluge; bold interpretations of the cruciform symbols of the temples and the codices; daring philological analogies; the discovery of tonsured Indians—all these things were claimed to be vestiges of a Christianity degraded over a long period of time.

A personage found everywhere in America, called Zumé in Paraguay and Brazil, Viracocha in Peru, Bochica in Colombia, Quetzalcóatl in Mexico, Cuculcan among the Maya, collected about himself the maximum number of Christian analogies. His history, his appearance, as told by the native traditions, facilitated his identification with an apostle of Christ; his remoteness in time helped to dissipate lingering doubts: he must really be the apostle Saint Thomas. This "demonstration" drew on convergent presumptions borrowed from chroniclers, and on symbolic interpretations of Scripture and the Mexican codices. The suggested analogies simply reflect the common background of all the great religions; the translations from Greek into Tupi fall before the most superficial linguistic examination. If we discard this rudimentary scholarly apparatus, what remains is a mode of reasoning that has been obsolete since the Enlightenment. Duarte's whole argumentation rests on an interpretation of revelation; his only task is to find its manifestations. There is no submission of *proofs* in the modern sense, but a summary of the *signs* of the passage of Saint Thomas through America.

Duarte is as selective in his choice of authors as of the native pictures and beliefs: he cites only those passages of Las Casas and Torquemada which are favorable to an early evangelization. He ignores or passes over in silence the doubts of Sahagún. A spirit of sympathy with the Indian world—the heritage of Sahagún and Las Casas—pervades Duarte's work. Acceptance of the thesis of Saint Thomas of America becomes for Duarte the touchstone of a writer's willingness to do justice to the Indian past, and hence to America and its modern children, the creoles. The evangelization of Saint Thomas, sign of God's grace, is the form that the creole claim of spiritual equality with Spain, of dignity vis-à-vis the Old World, assumes at this date (1675).

Becerra Tanco underlined this link between the Indian past and the American colonial present when he linked Saint Thomas Quetzalcóatl with the miraculous virgin of Guadalupe. "In order that you may see that he was in New Spain, read the apparition of the Virgin of Guadalupe, printed in Mexico in 1675, Chap. *Verbe divin*, fol. 76. There you will see that Saint Thomas was in Tula, as is clearly shown by the *bachiller* Becerra, professor of the Mexican language, who read about it in the Indian histories which tell of the prodigious works and the doctrine taught by this Ketzalcóhuatl."[31] The grace continually dispensed to America and its people since apostolic times, and the recalling of it, which facilitated the work of conversion by making the Indians feel that this was no break with their past but the accomplishment of their supernatural destiny, was the indispensable spiritual base for creole assertions of their dignity in the seventeenth century.

The most remarkable aspect of the matter is the manner in which the creole descendants of Spaniards exalted and took over as their own patrimony the Indian past recorded in Nahuatl sources. The sentiment of the American *patria*, we have seen, arose in part as a reaction to the scorn heaped by Europeans upon both Indians and creoles. Since the creoles were, after all, America's favorite children, they appropriated for themselves America's pre-Columbian history, telluric predestination prevailing over ties of blood. In the last analysis, the question was whether the peoples of America had shared the human condition and its supernatural adventure since the beginning of the Christian era or if America had been for sixteen centuries a spiritual no-man's-land. The second hypothesis, based on an interpretation of Christendom as an adventure unfolding in time, played into the hands of those who identified the "Indies" with a Babylon that merited the scourges of God. On the other hand, to set a time limit of thirty years for the accomplishment of Jesus' missionary injunction stripped the crimes of the Conquest of all possible justification and conferred on Spain's American dependencies and their populations, ancient and present, a dignity equal to Spain's. Duarte, who had read carefully the *Apologética Historia* of Las Casas, recalled all the superstitions of the Greeks, the Romans, and the Iberians; he regarded them, like the Indian superstitions, as crude approximations of the true faith. The meaning of the evidence gathered by Duarte for Sigüenza y Góngora, then, was that it abolished the break with the American past that the Conquest represented and thereby endowed America with a spiritual status (and consequently a juridical and political status) that put her on a footing of equality with the tutelary power, Spain. The skillful use of biblical prophecies, Mexican codices, and missionary accounts makes Duarte's collection a true dossier in support of America's application for admission into a "spiritual society of nations," a society none the less real because it lacked juridical status. In order to join the community of nations, the American lands must show their apostolic "patent" proving they were "old Christians"; they must prove they had been part of Christendom from its beginnings. Between the categories of Christians (Catholics) and Moslems there was only an inferior and dependent status, that of newly Christianized barbarians. From the status of spiritual dependence inevitably flowed political and administrative subjection. If the American *patria* was to take root in its own soil it must develop a sense of its identity; and it could only find the foundations it sought in the grace of God, not in the disaster of a Conquest that strongly resembled the Apocalypse. For Mexicans Quetzalcóatl was the instrument of a change in spiritual status, a change that imparted to the creole consciousness the energy necessary a century and a half later to throw off the colonial yoke and restore politically that "Empire of Anahuac" which connoisseurs of "antiquities" like Sigüenza y Góngora had earlier brought back from spiritual death. If they had not first appropriated the Indian past, the creoles could never have taken the Mexican nation's future into their own hands.

The Dissertation on Saint Thomas-Quetzalcóatl of the Dominican Mier (1813)

The political potential of Saint Thomas of America only became clear a century later in the writings of the Dominican of Monterrey, Fray Servando Teresa de Mier. If Saint Thomas Quetzalcóatl appeared in the second half of the seventeenth century to be America's sheet anchor, its best and surest hope, the reasons were still essentially spiritual. The eschatological hope of the first Franciscans, the millenarian dream of an *Iglesia Indiana,* expressed by Fray Jerónimo de Mendieta, had vanished by the beginning of the reign of Phillip III. Lacking an exalted future, the "Indian church" must find a great past for itself; who could better endow it with such a past than an apostle of Christ? Thus when Duarte and Sigüenza y Góngora brought Saint Thomas-Quetzalcóatl back to life he appeared as a kind of relay horse, destined to give a fresh start to New Spain's spiritual life, totally exhausted by a strenuous century and a half of eschatological exaltation. If the "Indian church" was not in fact the New Evangelical church, like that of Jesus and the apostles, it seemed necessary to link it to the apostolic church in some fashion. The abandonment of the first hypothesis really left no other logical alternative. The role of the illuminist friars, who had played so great a part in the formation of an

American consciousness on prophetic foundations, remained vital in this second spiritual fever. Although less ambitious than the previous one, its progressive laicization was to make it a leaven of political separatism.

Fray Servando Teresa de Mier was born into the family of a former governor of Nuevo León and always insisted on being treated with the respect due a man of his quality. Throughout his *Memorias* he claims for himself the benefits and prerogatives corresponding to his noble state, to his status of a doctor of the university and a Dominican friar. An accident, the sermon which he delivered in 1794, the day of the solemn celebration of the Virgin of Guadalupe, changed his life and ended his career of preacher. Learned and quick, he perceived how fragile were the proofs of the miraculous appearance of the Virgin and (so he testified during his trial) sought to find more ancient foundations for the tradition. Mier did no more than expound the cloudy ideas of a connoisseur of Mexican antiquities, licentiate Ignacio Borunda. Mier claimed that the appearance of the Virgin on the cloak of the Indian Juan Diego when he presented himself to Bishop Zumarraga was a pious legend. According to the Dominican, the cloak belonged to Saint Thomas of Mylapore (not to the apostle Saint Thomas), who had evangelized Mexico about the sixth century. This was clearly proved, Mier insisted, by the beliefs, the rites, and the codices of the ancient Mexicans. Without denying the miraculous tradition of Guadalupe, Mier thus snatched away from the Spaniards all its benefits, claiming that the arrival of the Virgin had preceded their coming by ten centuries. The Virgin of Guadalupe, patroness of the Indians of New Spain, was traditionally opposed to the Virgen de los Remedios, invoked by the routed Conquistadors during the *Noche Triste;* if Mier's hypothesis of a pre-Hispanic evangelization were accepted, it would undermine the principal—indeed the only—juridical foundation of the Conquest, Spain's evangelical mission. Given the fervent loyalty of Mexicans (creoles as well as Indians) to Guadalupe and their hatred for the *gachupines,* the complete spiritual autonomy promised them by Mier's dual hypothesis threatened to heat Mexican minds to the point where they might demand political autonomy. Mier's daring theory undermined the foundation of the Spanish title to America and simultaneously affirmed God's special grace to Mexico, thereby freeing her from Spanish messianic tutelage. Much later, in 1822, summarizing what had been his intent to the Constituent Congress in which he sat as deputy, Mier declared: "I preached that America, which was not a greater sinner than the rest of the world, had its place in the economy of the redemption of mankind."[32]

Mier had consulted all the authors who dealt before him with the problem of pre-Hispanic evangelization; he cited the study of Sigüenza y Góngora (which he had not read) and that "of a Portuguese Jesuit of Manila" who was doubtless Manuel Duarte. (Fray Servando's comments tend to confirm my hypothesis that Sigüenza y Góngora's essay was lost and that the texts published by Ramírez were materials collected by Duarte.) Significantly, Mier published his *Dissertation on the Preaching of the Evangel in America Before the Conquest* as an appendix to the *Historia de la Revolución de Nueva Espana, antiguamente Anahuac*,[33] published in London (where Mier lived in exile) in 1813. Previous writings on the subject had spoken of the evangelization of America "in the time of the apostles." The new wording reveals a different perspective. Reference to "the time of the apostles" placed the accent on the mission entrusted to the apostles by Christ and the theological difficulty of excluding America from that original evangelization. On the other hand, Mier (who identified Quetzalcóatl, Viracocha, and the like with a Saint Thomas of the sixth century, and not with the apostle) referred to the Conquest, meaning that for him the important point was that the ancient Mexicans, like the modern ones, had received the immediate grace of revelation and not a mediated, tardy grace with the Spaniards acting as mediators, as the people chosen by God to bring the Light to the gentiles of the New World. The date of the first evangelization was unimportant; the important thing was that it took place *before the Conquest*.

The thesis of the evangelization of New Spain "anciently Anahuac," by Saint Thomas, was in preestablished harmony with the uncertainty of the liberators of New Spain about the name that their new country should bear; after having wavered between "Anahuac" and "Mexico," they chose the second; in both cases there is a clear wish to reknit the thread of a history interrupted by the Conquest. The *Disertación* (more explicitly than the *Apologia del Dr. Mier,* in which he justifies his position on the connected problem of Guadalupe) is composed of an interpretive part and a critical part; the second part is the most interesting. His major thesis will not stand up under modern scientific examination. It may be summed up with this statement of the author: "It is a remarkable thing that all Mexican mythology can be explained by its Christian foundation, once one has translated 'Quetzalcóatl' by Saint Thomas."[34] Although Mier's use of linguistic arguments to prove the identity of the ancient Mexican beliefs with Christianity gives the appearance of novelty, he had borrowed the method in part from the licentiate Ignacio Borunda, author of a *Clave general de geroglíficos americanos*.[35] We know that Borunda inspired Mier's sermon of 1794 on Guadalupe. By skillful symbolic interpretations of the Mexican codices and glyphs, Mier introduced Christ, the Virgin, the

Trinity, and all the saints of Paradise (and Paradise itself!) into the Mexican and Maya religions.

Boturini had already employed this interpretation when he wrote: "The glorious Apostle Saint Thomas, whom the Indians metaphorically call Quetzalcóatl, that is, 'Plumed Serpent.' "[36] Mier went farther and attributed to Spanish blindness the error of foisting on the Mexicans the idolatrous cult of the serpent (with its Christian connotation of a diabolic symbol): "That is why Mexico has been made to appear the most serpentine and snaky land in the world."[37] He developed this charge: "I repeat that the Spaniards and the missionaries, who saw the devil everywhere, have bedeviled everything unconscionably; seeking to collect the rites and beliefs of the different provinces after they had burned the libraries, they got their information from the stupid multitude (who today would also give a diabolic picture of our Catholic beliefs) and so concocted an incredible mishmash."[38] It is clear what Fray Servando, creole friar and Mexican aristocrat, is about: he is indicting the methods of the missionaries and subjecting to critical revision the history of the ancient Mexicans as it had been written by the Spanish religious (*gachupines*) before him. Two causes had contributed to the failure to comprehend the early Christianity of the Mexican Indians: ill will and ignorance. "The Spaniards were intent on creating devils and even insisted on seeing Greek and Roman gods in Mexico."[39] Mier nowhere mentions Sahagún, who could be charged with this offense; was he afraid to take on this formidable adversary? Or was he ignorant of his work? Very likely, but Mier's dislike for the Franciscans repeatedly manifests itself. On the other hand, he often exalts the Dominicans, his coreligionists, and especially Las Casas. In his defense of the Indians, and by his contribution to the "Black Legend" of the Conquest, Mier appears in some respects a belated continuator of the work of the bishop of Chiapas. Curiously enough, this aristocrat, related to a colonial governor, exalts the Indians or rather the Indian past; a Dominican, he indicts the Hispanic missionary record. The reason is that Mier's hatred for the *gachupines* had come to dominate every other feeling. Mier reproached Clavijero for his lack of boldness and sincerity on the subject of pre-Hispanic evangelization, a thesis which Clavijero secretly approved, according to Mier. It should be noted that in the eighteenth century the creoles came to form the overwhelming majority in the American religious orders (this had been the case with the Dominicans of New Spain since the second half of the seventeenth century) and resented the rule which required "alternation" with the *gachupines*.

The conflict between Spaniards and American Spaniards, which arose together with the first creole generation about 1550, had become acute by the end of the eighteenth century, due to causes which I have already discussed. Mier, persecuted for propounding a historical hypothesis which appeared dangerous to Spanish authority (specifically to Archbishop Haro y Peralta), expressed the creole revolt in historical terms.[40] He denounced the falsification of the past of his American *patria* as the fruit of reasons of state and baseness. Reviewing the history of the question, he explained the difficulties that his coreligionists, Antonio de Remesal and Agustin Dávila Padilla, had encountered in publishing their works by their favorable posture toward the thesis of an apostolic evangelization of Mexico. As for the Jesuit Acosta, "He attributes everything to the teaching of the devil, who, he says, wanted to ape God. The devil, if you please, had nothing better to do than make crosses and teach the catechism!"[41] For the rest, Acosta, in *De procuranda Indorum salute*, had shown that he did not believe all this; opportunism made him later pretend, in his *Historia*, that he supported the thesis of "diabolical parody." In reality, according to Mier, Acosta was convinced that the Mexicans had preserved the memory of an ancient evangelization, as shown by Moctezuma's remarks to Cortés. "For this reason and many others, Acosta says again and again that the way was open for introducing the Gospel into America without effusion of blood."[42] Apparently contradicting himself, but really complementing what went before, Mier wrote: "All the rites and all the history of the Mexicans so clearly allude to rites and to passages of the Old and the New Testament that the Spanish authors comment on it at every step." What follows is even more interesting: "The migration of the Mexicans to Anahuac is so identical with that of the people of Israel in the desert that in the first edition of Torquemada's work this passage was suppressed, and the editor of the second edition had to engage in all kinds of circumlocutions to restore it to the second edition."[43] The facts seem to support Fray Servando here, for the editor of the second edition of Torquemada's work, after many circumlocutions, published the chapter on "The Journey Made by the Mexican Indians, Resembling That of the People of Israel," but ascribed it to Fray Gregorio García, who had expressed "the same idea, but more briefly."[44]

   The fear of creole heresies was not entirely unjustified at the end of the sixteenth century and in the seventeenth century, as shown by the trial of Fray Francisco de la Cruz in Peru. Fear for territorial security played a large part in the struggle against heresy. Letters to royal confessors were filled with insinuations that illuminist friars (Spaniards at first) might launch an American messianic movement (a "reply" to the Spanish messianism) and incite the Indians against the Spanish administration. Later the illuminists became fewer, but the patriotic creoles never ceased to trouble the Spanish government. Everything in the Indian pre-Conquest past that might make the Indians appear a chosen people, must be erased from the histories. Hence the seizures of manuscripts in the sixteenth century and the persecution of Mier in the eighteenth century. Mier, accused of heresy, in reality was feared because of his American patriotism. To proclaim that the separatists of the Indies were heretics, was a consistent Spanish tactic. The insistence on silence was greater than ever in the twilight years of the eighteenth century when the whole world was in revolution; the national past of the American viceroyalties must remain buried under the ashes. Mier has the virtue of denouncing official hypocrisy, of showing in a political light a problem that to some extent had always been a political one: "What a pity that fear prevented men from giving pertinent information on this point to the learned Baron de Humboldt, and that the Baron, who gave the world such a magnificent edition of the antiquities of Mexico and the history of Quetzalcóatl, should have copied literally the mistakes of the old missionaries and wasted his splendid erudition in looking for a snake-worshiping people to compare with the Mexicans!"[45] Mier wrote his *Disertación* to redress the wrong done to the history of his country. "I, who have carefully studied Mexican mythology, find that Torquemada, like all the Spanish authors, talks nonsense. . . . Therefore, I enter without fear the serpent's jaws that formed the entrance into the temple of Quetzalcóatl."[46] Mier tamed the serpent and denounced the swindle that Spanish reasons of state had imposed for two and a half centuries.

Such, at least, was Fray Servando's conception of his role. I have said that his thesis cannot stand examination. But given the world system of Fray Servando—a world outlook which remained metaphysically the same as that of his forerunners, the missionary friars—his interpretation of Mexican mythology was just as consistent as theirs. Either the Indians had been idolaters, as Sahagún had seen them, and in that case the analogies with Christianity were diabolical parodies; or they had been converted before the arrival of the Spaniards, and their Christianity had later been perverted. Mier's research, his studies of the Oriental Jews which led him to identify Quetzalcóatl with a Hellenized Jew, Saint Thomas of Mylapore, make his thesis appear more coherent (if not more convincing) than that of the early Franciscan missionaries, considered in the light of their common system of ideas. Today we know that neither of these theses is tenable. But the overlap of revelation, Scripture, and imperial policy as late as the beginning of the nineteenth century reveals the spiritual chasm that separated Spain (even after Charles III) from contemporary Europe. The whole

Hispanic world including America, which had just begun to read Rousseau and Bentham, was still ready to dispute about the exile of the people of Israel. From these disputes, perhaps as much as from Rousseau's *Contrat Social,* Mexican independence, symbolized by Hidalgo brandishing the banner of Guadalupe, was born. The fact of the joint publication of the *Revolución de la Nueva España* and the *Disertación* on Quetzalcóatl is very significant. The revolution was not made so much in the name of "new ideas" as in that of old principles, like those of that "Constitution" of colonial Mexico whose application Mier demanded, and which was constructed from the Laws of the Indies. Since the Western world was founded on the Catholic religion, it was vital for the flowering of Mexican national sentiment (and American patriotic feeling in general) that Quetzalcóatl should have been a Christian missionary—but not a Spaniard. Mier had the political intelligence to feel this necessity; his persecutors were perceptive enough to sense the danger that his views posed to Spanish rule over New Spain. These facts reveal a continuity between the first hypotheses relative to America's past and the great nineteenth-century movements of independence. The important thing about those revolutions is not their ideological dress but their atavistic passions. Quetzalcóatl was less fortunate than Guadalupe (as Bolivar well understood); like the "Queen of Independence," his name could have been a rallying point for the soldiers of Independence. Nevertheless, the history of his politico-literary vicissitudes blends with that of Mexican and, in a larger sense, American patriotic feeling from the Conquest to Independence and even beyond, for the driving forces and goals of Mexican national consciousness have remained fundamentally the same.

Saint James of Compostela and Saint Thomas of the New World

Among the Spanish conquistadors, some, like Bernal Díaz del Castillo, had denied seeing the apostle Saint James galloping through the clouds and brandishing the flaming sword that put the Indians to rout. The wars of Conquest in Mexico and elsewhere in America, like those of the Spanish *Reconquista,* took place under the sign of the "Lord Saint James." No apostle was better qualified to be patron of the most ambitious enterprise of conversion in the history of Christendom since apostolic times. In a response of July 24, on the eve of the "Day of the Apostle," Pope Calixtus had written "in the second tone [of the plain chant], Jesus called Saint James and Saint John by the name of Boanerges, which means 'sons of the thunder.' Just as a clap of thunder makes the whole earth shake, so the whole world trembles at their voices. . . ."[47]

The discoverers and conquerors of America were such devotees of the patron of Spain and of the Virgin Mary that the Mexican Indians took "Santiago y María" for the dual principle of their religion, *Ome teotl.* The Dominican chronicler Remesal wrote that the Indians did not know "whether Saint James was a man or woman."[48] The syncretic aspiration worked through both meanings, and in the present case it favored the development of the cult of Saint James among the Indians. In Mexico the apostle seems to have appeared in the first battles fought in Tabasco by Cortés, if we may believe Gómara, Cortés's chronicler, who writes: "All said that thrice they saw a gray spotted horse fighting at our side against the Indians. . . . and that it was Saint James, our patron."[49] Saint James appears to have also intervened in the battle of Otumba in Jalisco to aid Núño de Guzmán, at Querétaro, in New Mexico at Guadalajara, and (what is most remarkable) he seems to have taken part in the famous massacre at the great temple of Mexico-Tenochtitlan, when Alvarado ordered the slaughter of the unarmed Mexican nobility, engaged in ritual dances. If the military intervention of Saint James at first made him appear to the Indians as a terrifying divinity, with the return of peace he was incorporated in the popular *mitotes* or dances as a result of the introduction of the festivals of "Moors and Christians." Undoubtedly one of the most original manifestations of the cult of Saint James in Mexico is the dance "of the Saints James." R. Heliodoro Valle and Robert Ricard have shed light on the syncretic religious phenomena connected with the acclimatization of the festivals of the "Moors and Christians" in Mexico; in these festivals the apostle Saint James plays the role of protagonist. Yet the warrior Saint James was capable of sudden awakening from his sleep when historical conditions were propitious. One of the most significant military interventions of the saint, cited by Heliodore Valle, is that at Janitsio, where the apostle came to the help of Tarascan Indians besieged by loyalist troops during the battles of the War of Independence. Recalling that Michoacán was the starting point of Hidalgo's rebellion, we may see in this event a symbol of spiritual liberation. The reversal of the role of Saint James, transformed into an ally of the Indians in a war of liberation against the *gachupines,* is a sign of the transfer of Spain's sacred power to New Spain. The spiritual rooting of the most Spanish of Spanish saints in Mexico signals the completion of a general process of assimilation of the cultural values of the colonizing people. Decolonization became possible the moment the principal tutelary divinities changed residence, making a divine migration from the old sites of pilgrimage to new ones. The "translation" of the Virgin Mary to the hill of Tepeyac is doubtless richest in national implications but is far from being the only one. The Indian who, dancing to the sound of his ritual Aztec *teponaxtli,* incarnates the "Lord Saint James" at the foot of the pyramids of Teotihuacan, leads a religious life that is not materially different from that of his forebears, who occasionally incarnated Quetzalcóatl or some other divinity of the ancient Mexican pantheon. The ritual dress has changed, but the Nahuatl dialogue in its ambiguity and the oath—free from all ambiguity—reveal a permanent spiritual attitude, which is the most important aspect.

If the cult of Saint Thomas-Quetzalcóatl never became truly popular in New Spain, the competing cult of Saint James was partly the cause. Writing about the alleged preaching of Saint Thomas, whom the Indians called Quetzalcóatl, Fray Servando Teresa de Mier commented: "I was not surprised by this preaching, for I had heard about it from infancy from the mouth of my learned father. All that I have since learned has confirmed its existence and I do not believe a single cultured American does not know about it or doubts it."[50] Mier's statement suggests that it was a belief widely held by cultured creoles (*sabios; instruidos*), but that it enjoyed little popularity among the mass of the people. The controversy about the evangelization of America by the apostle Saint Thomas, begun at the end of the sixteenth century by the theologians, was continued by the historians and eventually came before the supreme tribunal of Spanish and Spanish American historiography, the Real Academia de la Historia, at the end of the eighteenth century. This, to be sure, was an accident, the result of the inquisitorial trial of Fray Servando, which had to do with the cult of Guadalupe. The authorities moved against Mier because he had tried to revise the Guadalupan tradition and carried the debate to the public in a sermon that he preached in the cathedral. We note that the sensitive point was not Saint Thomas-Quetzalcóatl, whom Mier had skillfully linked to the Virgin of Guadalupe in his argumentation, but the Virgin alone. However, it was in the form of a hypothesis of the evangelization of Mexico by the apostle Saint Thomas that Mier best expressed the Mexican claim of supernatural equality with Spain. In his *Apologia* he writes: "I saw that the *patria* gained thereby an apostle, a glory to which all lands aspire, especially Spain, which is but a handful of earth, yet must have no less than three apostles of the first class."[51] (He refers to Saint James, Saint Paul, and Saint Peter.) Here the debate focuses on the true issue: the capture of the sacred power from whose seats (the sites of apparitions or sacred relics) radiated a charismatic power that could be translated into military and political power. Mier himself confirmed this interpretation when, seeking to win J. B. Muñoz and Traggia to his side, he attributed to the latter this comment, addressed to the Academia de la Historia: "I assure you, gentlemen, that if we Spaniards could supply for the preaching of

Saint James in Spain one-tenth of the proofs that the Americans have for the preaching of Saint Thomas in America, we would proclaim our victory."[52]

Nations, as Mier also wrote, "dispute over their apostles," and Spain, which claimed three apostles for herself alone, refused to grant America (one-third of the world) a single apostle, the doubting Saint Thomas; this, for the Dominican, was a most revolting manifestation of *gachupín* injustice. There seemed to be no danger to Spain in promoting the cult of Saint James in America (this was only apparently so, as we saw above), but to allow the development of an American apostle proper, all the more American because in popular belief he merged with one of the most important divinities of the pagan pantheon, Quetzalcóatl, would have been a political mistake for the Spanish Crown. One of the most distinguished representatives of that Crown in New Spain, Bishop Palafox, had ordered the destruction of the surviving statues of Mexican divinities in his diocese of Puebla—a town situated hard by Cholula, the holy city of Quetzalcóatl; he had also ordered the removal of coats of arms bearing the Aztec eagle. The possession of a native apostle, rooted in Scripture on the one hand and in the legendary tradition of the Toltecs on the other, would have been a trump card in the hands of the heroes who played for the destiny of renascent Anahuac, the New "Phoenix of the West." Fray Servando was not, properly speaking, one of those illuminist friars which New Spain produced in such plenty, but he must have sensed the potential virtues, even in politics, which a fully Mexican apostle like Saint Thomas-Quetzalcóatl must have. Thus we see emerge under his pen, like a resurgence of the cosmic struggle between Quetzalcóatl and Texcatlipoca, the symbolic combat of the native gods against the foreign gods: Saint James, champion of Spain, against Saint Thomas, champion of Mexico.

The *Apologia del Dr. Mier,* which blends in part with the apologia for Saint Thomas-Quetzalcóatl, presents two principal aspects. One aspect does not differ perceptibly from the *Dissertation,* whose arguments in favor of the evangelization of Mexico by the apostle it restates in more diffuse fashion. But its other aspect, that of a critique of the Spanish pious traditions, merits our close attention. In Part 3, I shall have occasion to review Mier's critique of the Marian traditions; here I consider only what he has to say concerning the apostle Saint James. In the *Relation about What Happened in Europe to Dr. Mier,* the Dominican relates that the apparition of the Virgin to Saint James at Pilar de Zaragoza was only a belief of the Aragonese common people, and he adds: "Not only was it denied by Benedict XIV and by Natal Alexander, and disputed by Ferraras and by the innumerable authors who deny the preaching of Saint James in Spain, but the academicians of history tell me that it is absolutely untenable. 'I have in my possession,' said to me Doctor Traggia, an Aragonese and the ecclesiastical chronicler of Aragon, 'the oldest document bearing on the subject, and it dates from the fourteenth century.'"[53] To Fray Servando his arguments in favor of the evangelization of America by Saint Thomas seemed all the stronger because proofs of the evangelization of Spain by Saint James appeared so weak. If the latter were considered sufficient for Spain, a fortiori the much more numerous indications of Saint Thomas's presence in America (the famous footprints) should be admissible evidence. In the fragility of one hagiographic tradition, Mier found proof of the strength of another hagiographic tradition which, in fact, was only slightly weaker. In reality the essence of the question was the fact that all nations disputed possesssion of the Apostles, and that New Spain refused to accept the unequal division which gave three to Old Spain ("a handful of earth") and refused even one to New Spain. The part played in the historiography of Mexico (and of the Indies in general) by the theme of the evangelization of Saint Thomas is an important aspect of the dialogue which began in the first colonial decades between Spain and her American viceroyalties. With Mier, precursor of and actor in the Mexican independence movement, the dialogue become clearly vindicatory in tone; there is a transition from hagiographic legend to polemic. But the continuity with the past—a past that goes back well before the Conquest—is total.

The obstacles to the authenticity of the tradition of Saint James in Spain and the controversies that it inspired prefigured the resistance to the tradition of Saint Thomas in America. One has but to read the apologetic treatise published in 1609 by the illustrious Jesuit historian Juan de Mariana, *De adventu B. Jacobi Apostoli in Hispaniam*, to be convinced of the fact. The titles of the chapters alone are eloquent: chapter 5, "Arguments against the Coming of Saint James to Spain"; Chapter 6, "The Above Arguments are Breached."[54] For the apostle of Spain, as for the apostle of America, exegetic and theological difficulties had arisen. Mariana had invoked the Acts of the Apostles in support of a universal evangelization during the lifetimes of the apostles.[55] One objection to the evangelization of Spain by the apostle seemed decisive, the agelong silence of historians down to Pope Calixtus II, who had written in the tenth century the original *Liber Sancti Jacobi*. To this argument, that it was extraordinary that an event of such importance should have been passed over in silence, Mariana replied that doubtless men had not previously known where the relics of the saint were, that this was not a unique case, that many cults which had obscure origins later attained a great popularity, as witness the Guadalupe of Extremadura and the sanctuary of Montserrat in Catalonia. Thus the Jesuit claimed not to be surprised at a historio-graphic silence of almost ten centuries: "I am not surprised that si-lence should have surrounded the coming of the apostle. . . ."[56] We know that this phase of occultation of relics lasts at least one century, occurring in all known cases; we might call it a law of incubation of beliefs. In the last analysis, the principal arguments advanced by Mariana in support of the evangelization of Saint James were based on authority. Three or four popes (*trium aut quator*)—it was not known for sure—accepted the tradition; Saint Braulius attested to it, and, finally, "the authority of Saint Isidore [of Seville] confirms it."[57]

A creole of Lima, Pedro de Peralta y Barnuevo, restated the argu-ments of Mariana with more conviction in his *History of Spain Vindi-cated,* which appeared in 1730. They were accompanied by reflections which I find very informative. The work bears the subtitle: *Wherein is Established with Irrefutable Arguments the Coming of the Apostle Saint James, the Apparition of Our Lady to the Saint at Pilar de Zaragoza, and the Transla-tion of His Holy Body.*[58] This apologist for the history of Spain (the first of a series of such defenders in the eighteenth century) naively ex-plains to us in his preface how difficult is the transmutation of a devout belief into a rational proof. "But I do not know whether, subjecting the devotion to study, truth can be made proof."[59] With this preliminary warning, we can begin to consider the "irrefutable" arguments of the coming into Spain of "Lord Saint James." The first is this: if nothing seemed to happen between the last Cantabrian War and the establishment of the Gothic empire, it was because "the Faith had to be a prelude to Empire," for Spain "was a celestial monarchy before becoming a terrestrial monarchy."[60] Here we have a peninsu-lar model of the *Monarchia Indiana,* the "celestial monarchy." All na-tions are proud of their illustrious men, asserts Peralta y Barnueva; they should be all the prouder of possessing an apostle of Christ. Spain would be content with possessing Saint Paul, if he were really her own, but he had preached a little in every part of the Roman Empire, whereas Saint James was her exclusive possession. The proof was in a Mozarabic missal, inspired by Saint Isadore of Seville and decreed by the Fourth Council of Toledo, wherein "Saint James is placed at the right hand of the Lord, with John, representing Asia, on the left, and Saint James representing Spain."[61] To the authority of Saint Isidore, one can add with Peralta that of Saint Julian of Toledo, of the Beatus of Liebana, of several venerable foreigners, and above all the great devotion of Pope Calixtus II to Saint James. Calixtus informs us that Saint James had chosen seven disciples in Galicia to accompany him to Jerusalem. This is probably the origin of the popular legend of "seven brother saints," which still lives in our time. We may also note the tradition of the prodigious imprints of Saint James' staff, of his thighs, or of his feet, in the region of Cape Finisterre, at Pastoriza.[62] Thus the vestiges of the passage of Saint James through Spain prefigure the traces of Saint Thomas in America. Peralta y Barnuevo, a faithful disciple of Mariana, recalls the reply of his predecessor to a major objection: the omission of Saint James by Spanish chroniclers before the tenth century. "Since the fact was so well known, they judged that an event which was on everybody's lips had no need of literary monuments."[63] Thus all arguments were good to support the tradition of the evangelization of Saint James; the silence of historians had little weight in the face of the popular faith, the miracles produced by the relics, and the authority of saints and popes.

Peralta y Barnuevo made a naive avowal of the utility of the cult of Saint James. "Because this privilege incites to devotion and that devotion in turn renders the patronage efficacious. . . . Spain possesses his holy body and thus is conscious of possessing a part of Heaven, and together with his sepulcher it possesses an urn filled with all the graces."[64] One could not better describe this race for the supernatural treasure, the "urn filled with all the graces," to which all the nations of the Hispanic world gave themselves up. The evangelization of Spain by Saint James (and the apostle's relics, above all) and the evangelization of America by Saint Thomas satisfied the collective aspiration to possess "a part of Heaven." As Américo Castro has written: "While Europeans reflected, Spaniards cast themselves into the abyss of their faith. . . . And all Iberian America shares this same mode of existence."[65]

The apologists for Saint Thomas of America, and Fray Servando Teresa de Mier, in the first place, had only to search the apologetical literature about Saint James of Compostela to find the arguments they needed. The physical traces in the form of footprints in stone may have come from the Celtic substratum of Galicia, or probably from even more distant points in time and space. The absence of contemporary documents was explained by the systematic and thoughtless destruction of native codices by the first missionaries who, like Zumárraga in Mexico, "bedeviled everything." As for religious authorities, Father Ruiz de Montoya invoked that of Santo Toribio de Mogrovejo, who had gone on a pilgrimage in search of traces of Saint Thomas in a village of the province of Chachapoyas, in Peru. Not only were the apologetical problems and the hagiographic materials the same, but the religious-patriotic climate was the same in Spain and New Spain. In his reply to Marmontel and to Cornelius de Pauw,

Reflexiones imparciales, Juan de Nuix y Perpiñá wrote in 1783: "The Spanish missionaries were the Apostles chosen by the Lord to announce the Gospel in those unknown lands."[66]

The issue was which nation was to be the new chosen people, or at least had received a more abundant grace from heaven. Nothing more natural than that Fray Servando, conscious of the competition with Spain, should have seen the advantage of enriching the defense of Saint Thomas-Quetzalcóatl with a Marian episode. The idea he developed in his famous sermon of 1794, which made the image of Guadalupe date from the time of the apostle Saint Thomas, was directly inspired by the Iberian model, which had associated the prodigious image of Mary venerated at Pilar de Zaragoza with the evangelization of Saint James. If Mier had been able to persuade his audience and the archbishop of Mexico City, above all, the way would have been opened for Mexico's conquest of complete equality with Spain in divine grace. There is a profound affinity between the role played by the apostle of Galicia in the formation of Spanish national consciousness and that of Saint Thomas-Quetzalcóatl in the awakening of Mexican national sentiment. It is explained by the fact that the latter was partly inspired by the former; but more secret affinities united them. One is surprised that a man like Borunda, with his esoteric knowledge of the past, did not note and gloat over them. Contemplating the Milky Way and asking himself what its mysterious significance could be, the Emperor Charlemagne had a vision of the apostle Saint James, who said to him: "The starry road which you saw in the sky signifies that you must go from these lands as far as Galicia with a great army to liberate my road and my country. . . . After you all the peoples, from sea to sea, will go on pilgrimage."[67] Now, one of the Mexican traditions least open to the charge of influence by Iberian syncretism presented Quetzalcóatl as the son of a major divinity of the Aztec pantheon, Mixcóatl, the "Serpent of Stars" or the Milky Way (a paternity which may have some relation with the final metamorphosis of Quetzalcóatl, the "Lord of the Night," or the Morning Star). Saint James and Saint Thomas, united in the New Testament tradition and in the evolution of the Spanish and Mexican national consciousness, are also associated on the primary level of stellar symbolism, the common property of our culture, born in the Mediterranean Near East, and of Aztec culture, heir to the Olmec-Maya astrology.

A creole of Lima, Antonio de León Pinelo, offers an example of the preoccupation with proving that the West was the new "East." Seeking to reconcile his faith in an "American Paradise" with revealed truth, he recalled that Moses had written his description of the earthly paradise while he was in exile in the desert to which he had led the people of God. Although Moses had placed his paradise in the East, León Pinelo did not regard this statement as incompatible with his own claim that Paradise was in America; it sufficed to make a simple calculation of longitude: "One can state with all geographic precision that Mexico was in the eastern hemisphere in relation to Moses when he was writing in the Sinai."[68] If the grass was always green on the "road of Saint Thomas," the American prolongation of the "road of Saint James," it was because the star which had arisen in the East of the Judaic eschatology had accomplished in sixteen centuries its revolution to the West, the new "North Star" of Christian hope.[69]

11 Epilogue: The "Four Hundred" Modern Quetzalcóatls

The mentality which inspired the Spanish missionaries to recognize the "hidden Jews" of Scripture in the Indians of Amazonia and Carthaginian monuments in the ruins of Tiahuanaco remained the same during the next three centuries. Only this changed, that whereas in the sixteenth century the assimilation of American cultural phenomena to the spiritual patrimony of the Mediterranean West found its guarantee in revealed truth, in the nineteenth century the beginning of studies on the Indo-Europeans and the vogue of Egyptology gave a pseudo-scientific dress to the traditional Eurocentrism. Under the title of Viracocha, Bochica, Quetzalcóhualt, Brasseur de Bourbourg revealed the analogies of the Inca, Colombian, and Mexican gods and assimilated all three to the "hieroglyphical personage of Thoth who serves to express, according to Eckstein, the rudiments of the literary corpus of most ancient Egypt."[1] The movement toward the Indo-European sources is characteristic of the end of the nineteenth century. This new mode of linking the New World to the Old completed and prolonged the historical annexation that followed the Columbian discovery. The *being* of America thus remained limited to its *being for* the Europeans.[2] The New World, even in its ancient, pre-Columbian being, owed its culture and its most important beliefs to the Old World. Although America had won its political independence at the beginning of the nineteenth century, it had not yet escaped from its colonial status.

All these hypotheses, whose scientific value it would be very easy to criticize, reveal the same permanent tendency of the European intellect to deny the autochthonous character of the cultures of the New World. The identification of the principal divine civilizer of the Indians, Quetzalcóatl (and his American variants) with an apostle of Christ, later with a medieval friar, was but one aspect of a general interpretation of the history of mankind which assigned a secondary place to America. Works tending to prove the exogenous character of American beliefs from the most remote times multiplied; after the

Histoire légendaire de la Nouvelle-Espagne rapprochée de la source indo-européenne (1874) of H. de Charencey, there appeared in London, in 1882, *Indian Myths or Legends, Traditions, and Symbols of the Aborigines of America Compared with Those of Other Countries Including Hindostan, Egypt, Persia, Assyria and China*, by Russel-Emerson. In 1896 E. Beauvois published the *Pratiques et institutions religieuses d'origine chrétienne chez les Mexicains du Moyen Age*.³ Ten years later Charencey published at Caen *Yama, Djemschid et Quetzalcóatl*.

It may cause more surprise that new metamorphoses of the pseudo-scientific myth of Quetzalcóatl continue to appear today. From the essay of José Díaz Bolio, *La Serpiente emplumada*,⁴ which reveals a disturbing ophidian mania, to that of Dr. Diaz Infante, *Quetzalcóatl (Ensayo psicoanalítico del mito nahua)*,⁵ in which the author analyzes the personality of the hero "in the light of the Oedipus Complex" (p. 19), Quetzalcóatl has recently assumed the most unlikely forms. Even the ideological sequelae of Nazism have touched him in a book entitled *Ich fand den Weisen Gott*, whose author preferred to hide his identity under a pseudonym.⁶

In Mexico City itself, amid the mediocre run of buildings erected with the assistance of the Social Security Administration, a statue of monumental proportions⁷ (vaguely inspired by the monolith preserved at Castillo de Teayo, in the state of Veracruz) officially assigns to Quetzalcóatl a role promising a reign of justice and prosperity, a role he has never lost in the popular mind. The same attitude inspired the proposal of a revolutionary minister to replace Father Christmas (who is the Saint Nicholas of Germanic lands in Mexico) with his Mexican homologue, Quetzalcóatl.

But together with the Promethean Quetzalcóatl who gave the Indian his life and his techniques, there also existed a Quetzalcóatl who was the god of thieves, and he, like the "four hundred rabbits" (*centzon totochtin*) of the Aztec legend, has multiplied almost endlessly and continues to pillage the huts (*jacales*) of the peons; some day history will tell whether those who today hide behind the effigy of Quetzalcóatl still strike two blows with the forearm of a woman who died in childbirth (as Sahagún informs us),⁸ or if they have invented other narcotics to put their victims to sleep before they rob them. The secular image of a lost Golden Age, Quetzalcóatl remains the ambiguous symbol of the frustrated hopes of modern Mexico.

Part 3

Guadalupe, or the New Epiphany

12 Holy Mary and Tonantzin

Tonantzin, Mother-Goddess of the Mexicans

In the first book of his *Historia general,* which deals with the divinities of the ancient Mexicans, Sahagún devotes chapters 6 to 8 to the goddesses. He devotes the first chapter to Tonantzin because he considers her the most important of all. "The first of these goddesses was called Cihuacóatl, which means the wife of the Serpent; they also called her Tonantzin, which means our mother."[1] Sahagún, so well informed about other divinities, has little to tell about Tonantzin's attributes. "They [the Indians] said that this goddess had a sinister influence, for she brought poverty, abasement, and suffering . . . ; they also said that she had a cradle on her back, as if she carried her son in it."[2] Sahagún also reports that the ancient Mexicans had the custom of celebrating very solemn sacrifices at three or four places on or near hills. He further says that "one of those places is here in Mexico City, on a hill called Tepeacac . . . , where they had a temple consecrated to the mother of the gods, called Tonantzin, which means 'our mother' . . . and people came from afar to celebrate these sacrifices."[3] This account is confirmed (or borrowed from Sahagún) by Fray Juan de Torquemada, who writes: "In another place, one league to the north of Mexico City, they [the Indians] celebrated a feast of another goddess, called *Tonan,* which means 'Our Mother.' She was the divinity for whom they felt the greatest devotion when our brethren [the Franciscans] came to this country; innumerable crowds came from a hundred leagues around to celebrate the feast days of this goddess."[4] In the eighteenth century, the Jesuit Clavijero, listing the divinities of the ancient Mexicans, gave this information about Tonantzin: "Her name signifies 'Our Mother,' and I do not doubt that she was the same as the goddess Centeotl, of whom I have already told. Tonantzin had a temple on a hill one league north of Mexico City, and her feasts were attended by an immense concourse of people and many sacrifices."[5] Thus the missionaries agree on essential points: Tonantzin was a major divinity, her principal shrine was on the hill of Tepeyac, one league north of Mexico City, and people came from all parts of the country to celebrate her feasts.

We note, however, that Sahagún identifies Tonantzin with the goddess Cihuacóatl, while Clavijero assures us that she was Centeotl. Several reasons dispose me in favor of Sahagún, a very careful investigator closer in time to the pre-Hispanic past. The decisive reason is that Sahagún identifies Cihuacóatl as the principal goddess of the ancient Mexicans and twice affirms "they called her Tonantzin," "Our Mother," a name especially fitting for the most important goddess. Moreover, the Franciscan describes Tonantzin and specifies that "the finery in which this woman was decked was white,"[6] which corresponds exactly with the description of the goddess Cihuacóatl in the history of the Dominican Durán: "The goddess Cihuacóatl was clad in woman's garb—skirt, blouse, and mantle—that was all white."[7] Given the importance of colors in the religious symbolism of the ancient Mexicans, it is most unlikely that two like but different divinities were both dressed in white. Finally, since Sahagún and Durán represent two different but equally important traditions in the historiography of ancient Mexico, the convergence of their testimony is a powerful argument.

Unfortunately, Durán does not say that Cihuacóatl was also called Tonantzin. Sahagún, however, gives the following details about Cihuacóatl-Tonantzin: she would vanish while in a crowd of women, leaving behind the cradle of her child, leaving also "a piece of flint carved to make a spear point with which they put to death the victims of their sacrifices."[8] This corresponds completely with what Durán reports: "The diabolical priests of this temple . . . , seeing that eight days had passed without human sacrifices, looked for a child's cradle and placed in it the stone knife with which they performed their sacrifices and which they called 'the son of Cihuacóatl.'"[9] Durán also writes that the festival of Cihuacóatl was *huey tecuilhuitl,* the ninth feast of the calendar, that is, "the great feast of the lords"; and that "they called this goddess Cihuacóatl," the sister of Huitzilopochtli, "the great god of Mexcio-Tenochtitlan."[10] Sahagún tells concerning the feast of *huey tecuilhuitl* that "they celebrated this feast in honor of the goddess called Xilonen";[11] and Durán explains: "Twenty days before this feast they bought a slave, purified her, and dressed her in the same manner as the stone idol (Cihuacóatl)—all in white with her white mantle. Thus dressed, she represented the goddess. . . . The Indians called this woman Xilonen from the day of her purification to the day of her sacrifice."[12] The name "Tonantzin" designated Cihuacóatl in the same way that "Our Lady" designates the Virgin Mary in the Christian religion; Xilonen (the goddess of the *Xilotes,* the tender ears of corn), was the name of the goddess Cihuacóatl in her provisional incarnation, somewhat like Jesus being the incarnation of one of the elements of the Holy Trinity, the Son. We may therefore accept Sahagún's statement that *huey tecuilhuitl* was the feast of Xilonen. But we also discern here, thanks to Durán, who raises a corner of the veil, one of the mysteries of the Mexican religion. The goddess Cihuacóatl, "which means the wife of the Serpent,"[13] is also called Tonantzin, and is identified with Xilonen in a certain context, the feast of *huey tecuilhuitl*. She is also Centeotl, according to Sahagún's Indian informants; according to the same sources, Teteoinan, the mother of the gods, or of the Mexicans, also wore a white shirt. It appears, too, that Xilonen wore the same ornaments as Chicomecóatl, goddess of subsistence, and we note the similar ritual finery of Chalmecacihuatl, patroness of Chalma, sister of Yactecuhtli (one of the invocations of Quetzalcóatl) and Tonantzin. Among the fragmentary indications provided by Sahagún's informants about the attributes of the divinities, we read the following concise and categorical statement: "Cihuacóatl: the mother of the gods; the mother of the gods, the same thing; the white woman, the same thing."[14] We could lengthen this chain by adding Toci, mother of the gods, and Citlalicue, the goddess with the skirt of stars.

As Jacques Soustelle has shown, these divinities are simultaneously identical and different, and there is "a reciprocal imbrication" or overlap of the different aspects of the mother-goddess. After Jacques Soustelle's study, *La pensée cosmologique des anciens Mexicains*, the most penetrating analysis of the ancient Mexican religion is Miguel León Portilla's *La filosofía nahuatl estudiada en sus fuentes*. I cite from this work a passage of capital importance to our subject:

Line 18 (from the manuscript of 1558)
As soon as the divinity called Quilaztli—who is Cihuacóatl—arrived, she ground the men into paste and placed it in a precious bowl.

Quilaztli, who (as the text indicates) is the same as Cihuacóatl, appears here as the partner of Quetzalcóatl. . . . The pair Quetzalcóatl-Cihuacóatl, who invented man at Tamoanchan, is but a new aspect of Ometecuhtli-Omecihuatl, the couple to which the title of "inventor of men" (Teyocayani) was given.[15]

Thus, according to León-Portilla, the couple Quetzalcóatl-Cihuacóatl was one of the representations of the dual principle Ometeotl, the source of life and all things. This dual principle also found a reflection in the institutions of ancient Mexico. "Their Tlacatecuhtli, or king, is the representative of Quetzalcóatl, while his lieutenant or 'coadjutor,' as the chroniclers call him, received the title of Cihuacóatl."[16] In this

dense forest of symbols, we make out a continual regrouping of the
different mother-goddesses and goddesses of fertility about one of
their figures. Take Tonantzin as the axis, and beside her appears the
figure (often doubled again) of Quetzalcóatl. One of the fundamental
couples of the Mexican pantheon, or rather one of the dominant
expressions (especially in the minds of the ruling elite) of the universal creative principle, is Tonantzin-Quetzalcóatl, whose creole avatars
are equally inseparable. From pre-Columbian times they appear
linked together as the two faces, male and female, of the primary
creative principle.

The fact that Durán saw in Cihuacóatl the patroness of Xochimilco
no more affects the argument than the patronage of the Virgin of
Pilar over Zaragoza prevents the Virgin Mary and the Immaculate
Conception from having an immense spiritual importance for universal Christianity, apart from their meaning for the town of Zaragoza.
Even the most scholarly Spanish missionaries were incapable of seeing
the Mexican religion entire, in its living unity, for several factors
darkened their vision. To begin with, their informants accented their
accounts according to their membership in a local community.
Moreover, the classic culture of the friars made them view the antique
Roman model as the archetype of every polytheistic religion; their
adherence to Christianity and the spiritual options that that adherence implied made it impossible for them to see in a multitude of idola-
tries a coherent religion culminating in a divine creative principle.
When I say that Durán may have erred in making Cihuacóatl the particular goddess of Xochimilco, I only mean that he may have been partly
wrong. No doubt Cihuacóatl was, as the Dominican thought, the tutelary goddess of the Xochimilco, but this is not the essential thing. Quetzalcóatl similarly appeared to the chroniclers as the protective divinity
of Cholula, but this local role by no means exhausted his religious significance. Once again the analogy with the Virgin of Pilar or any other
Hispanic cult comes to mind; the line of division between the highest
spirituality and idolatry (in the strict sense) appears in Christianity just
as in the Mexican religion. The importance of the sanctuaries is primordial; on the topographic base of the sanctuaries, the process of syncretism between the great divinities of ancient Mexico and the saints of
Christianity worked itself out. The most notable example is precisely
that of the hill of Tepeyac, first a place of pilgrimage and sanctuary of
Tonantzin-Cihuacóatl and later of Our Lady of Guadalupe.

Just as the Christians built their first churches with the rubble and
the columns of the ancient pagan temples, so they often borrowed
pagan customs for their own cult purposes. Thus they preserved
Druid or Iberian places of pilgrimage, substituting a Christian

sanctuary for a pagan image. The missionaries of Mexico engaged in a process of spontaneous reinterpretation with numerous precedents. Let me recall the case of the Iberian Marian cult, the example of Our Lady of Battles, the Virgin of Covadonga. When the Infante Pelayo took refuge in the grotto where he was cornered by the Moors, a sanctuary was already there, and we know that the waters which gush from this flow into a river called Deva or Diva, the name of the mother-goddess of the Celts. If Covadonga derives from *cova dominica,* the identity of the *Domina* ("Lady") originally must have been as ambiguous as was that of Tonantzin-Guadalupe.

The evangelization of America and, in the present case, of Mexico, carried on this tradition. Indeed, in the constitutions of the first Council of Lima, assembled in 1552, we read the following: "We order that all the cult idols and edifices found in the villages where Christian Indians reside be burned and destroyed, and if the site is suitable, a church or at least a cross should be planted there."[17] This missionary policy, given legislative force in Lima, was also applied in Mexico, as Sahagún and Torquemada testify. The latter writes: "Wishing to remedy this great evil, our brethren, who were the first to gather in the grapes of these wild vines and to prune them . . . decided to build a church in the place called Tonantzin, near Mexico City, a temple to the very Holy Virgin, who is Our Lady and Our Mother."[18] The intention of the missionaries, as expressed by Torquemada, is perfectly clear; they wanted to send the pilgrims to Our Lady, the Virgin "who is Our Lady and Our Mother," to substitute Christ's mother, mother of mankind, whose redemption she permitted, for the mother-goddess of the ancient Mexicans.

If one remembers that the Virgin Mary was traditionally described as the "new Eve," Sahagún's comments become even more significant: "This goddess is called Cihuacóatl, which means, 'the wife of the Serpent,' and they also called her Tonantzin, which means 'Our Lady.'

"These two indications seem to reveal that this goddess is our Mother Eve, who was misled by the Serpent, and that the Indians had a knowledge of what took place between Mother Eve and the Serpent."[19] This profound error of the most illustrious historian of ancient Mexico is doubly instructive. It reveals a mind held captive by biblical tradition, a mind that could not interpret "Our Mother" as being other than Eve and for which the serpent must be a symbol of the Devil. To the contrary, we know, particularly as a result of the rediscovery of Nahuatl manuscripts, published and commented by A. M. Garibay and León-Portilla, that in ancient Mexico the serpent was a religious symbol. Sahagún's error is interesting from another point of view; it contradicts his belief, which he states unequivocally elsewhere in his work, that the ancient Mexicans had never been evangelized before the arrival of the Franciscans. Now, a belief in a pristine apostolic evangelization of the Indians was all that was needed to identify Tonantzin, not with the old, but with the new Eve, Mary. No doubt such phenomena are not the result of conscious, deliberate thought processes, but they suggest one possible source of a future syncretism. Another, more certain, source indicated by Sahagún derives from philology: "Now that the Church of Our Lady of Guadalupe has been built, the Indians also call her Tonantzin, on the pretext that the preachers call Our Lady, the Mother of God, 'Tonantzin'. . . . This is an abuse which should be stopped, for the true name of the Mother of God, Our Lady, is not Tonantzin but 'God' and 'nantzin' (*Dios-nantzin*). To me this looks very much like a satanic invention to palliate idolatry by playing on the ambiguity of this name Tonantzin. The Indians today, as in the old days, come from afar to visit this Tonantzin, and to me this cult seems very suspect, for there are everywhere numerous churches consecrated to Our Lady, but they do not go there, preferring to come from afar to this Tonantzin, as in the past."[20] The Franciscan's lucid comment confirms the sincerity of his professed design: to describe the ancient forms of the Mexican religion in order to assist in its extirpation.

Sahagún's position in this specific case typifies the attitude of the first Franciscan missionaries toward syncretism. Sahagún advocated a total break with the polytheist beliefs, for he believed that all efforts at assimilation introduced ambiguities utilized by the Evil One for his own ends. In an appendix devoted to "superstitions," Sahagún cites other examples, such as that of Toci, "which means our grandmother. . . . They give this name to Saint Anne, with this pretext: since the preachers say that Saint Anne is the grandmother of Jesus Christ, she must be the grandmother of all Christians."[21] Here he is discussing a sanctuary near Tlaxcala, but the process is the same, and Sahagún adds: "The people who come to the feast of Toci, as in the old days, claim they do so from devotion for Saint Anne, but since the name of Toci is equivocal and the Indians respect their traditions, there is good reason to believe they come to worship their ancient Toci, and not from affection for the new cult."[22] (A Frenchman involuntarily recalls Saint Anne d'Auray, whose solemn feast antedated the Christianization of Britanny.) The uncompromising severity of the Franciscan pioneers sheds a new light on the origins of the cult of the Virgin of Tepyac; it sets the phenomenon within a larger syncretic framework, in which the cult of Tezcatlipoca, another major divinity of the Mexican pantheon (we recall his duel with Quetzalcóatl, with its cosmic symbolism), had its own place, with Tezcatlipoca assimilated to Saint John the Baptist. Sahagún, who had acquired a profound knowledge of the native religion and the Nahuatl language, criticized newly arrived clergy (it is uncertain whether he referred to Jesuits or secular clergy) for contributing unknowingly to the rebirth of idolatry.

Sahagún wrote the appendix on "superstitions" in 1576, four years after the arrival of the first Jesuits and the start of the magistracy of Archbishop Moya de Contreras, who gradually transferred control of the Indian missions from the regular to the secular clergy. At this date Sahagún takes a decided position with regard to the cult of Guadalupe: "It is clear that in their hearts the common people who go there on pilgrimages are moved only by their ancient religion."[23] Denying the cult's syncretic character, he believes the Indian show of Christian piety is all a sham. "To me this looks very much like a satanic invention to palliate idolatry by playing on the ambiguity of this name Tonantzin."[24] Each term must be understood here in its primary sense: satanic "invention" means an invention of Satan and to "palliate" means to veil, as if with a pallium; "ambiguity" expresses the equivocal (opposed to "univocal") character of "Tonantzin," designating "Our Mother" in the ancient religion and "Our Lady" in the new one. But a name, or a false meaning, does not suffice to explain the survival of a belief, nor the flowering of a new, indisputably syncretic belief, the cult of Our Lady of Guadalupe of Tepeyac. It is time for me to evoke Our Lady of Guadalupe of Estremadura, whose image the conquistadors of Mexico and their chief, Hernán Cortés, ardently venerated. Cortés himself, I may note in passing, was a native of Medellin, a town of Estremadura near the sanctuary of las Villuercas.

Our Lady of Guadalupe of Estremadura,
Protectress of Iberian Christianity

The new Tonantzin or, as Sahagún would have said, "Dios-nantzin," worshipped on the hill of Tepeyac, was known to Spaniards by the more familiar name of Guadalupe. Controversy still surrounds the origin and meaning of this name. Scholars generally agree, however, that it contains the Arabic radical *quad,* of frequent occurrence in peninsular toponymy (Guadalquivir, Guadiana, Guadalete, etc.), used to designate streams and rivers (*oued*); there is little doubt on this point. On the other hand, the suffix has long been interpreted as of Latin origin—*lupum,* the wolf, whence "river of wolves." But the association of an Arabic radical and a learned Latin suffix (the normal development of Castilian popular speech produced the modern form *lobo*) appears unlikely, and philological inquiry (*al* is the Arabic article) and a quick reconnaisance of the site persuaded me that "quad al upe" signifies rather *rio oculto*, that is, a river flowing between high banks. In this instance, the Virgin received the name of the sanctuary where she is venerated, in the heart of an eastern sierra of Estremadura (the sierra of Villuercas); according to tradition, this sanctuary was founded after a prodigious apparition of Mary. This tradition, is well established by a series of fourteenth- and fifteenth-century accounts, written by Jeronymite religious who had charge of the sanctuary from 1389 to 1835. Aside from the intrinsic interest of the early chronicles of Guadalupe, which deserve to be published in toto (in the same spirit that the Bollandists collected the lives of the saints, even though apocryphal) for the light that they shed on the origins of the Marian cult in Western Europe, these chronicles contribute to a better understanding of the "prodigious apparition of Mary" on the hill of Tepeyac.

The studies of Fray Arcangel Barrado Manzano, in particular, have saved me a long research effort. The interested reader may consult the introduction to his edition of the *Crónica del Monasterio de Guadalupe*, the work of a Jeronymite monk who died in 1484, Father Alonso de la Rambla. Thanks to the existence of a group of authentic and richly informative manuscripts, all aspects of the miraculous tradition have come down to us. Although the classic work is the *Historia de Nra. Sra. de Guadalupe* of Father Germán Rubio,the most intensive study, I believe, is that of Father Barrado Manzano, *Libro de la invención de Santa María de Guadalupe;*[25] I should note, however, that Father Rubio offers a modernized version of the most ancient manuscript, which reports the legendary history of "the dark lady of Villuercas," the image venerated at the sanctuary of Guadalupe. Later manuscripts derive from this first manuscript or reproduce it. I borrow from Father Barrado M. this chronological table of the sources:

1. *Codex written before 1400*, missing.
2. *Codex 555 of the Archivo Histórico Nacional*, written in 1440.
3. *Codex of Father Alonso de la Rambla* (1484).
4. *Codex 344 of the Archivo Histórico Nacional*, written in 1500.
5. *Codex of Father Diego de Ecija* (died 1534).
6. *Codex of Father Juan Herrera, in the Library of the Escorial, IV-a-10*, written in 1535.

The third and fifth codices were published by A. Barrado M.; the sixth was analyzed by him in his edition of the fifth codex, and the second and third were studied in his introduction to the third codex, so that all the manuscripts except the missing pre-1400 codex have been published or commented by Father Barrado M.

Having familiarized myself with the published manuscripts, I examined the unpublished ones, particularly the oldest available text, that of 1440, and the fourth codex, that of 1500. The codex of 1440 is a little parchment notebook of eighty sheets; folios five to eight are of particular interest because they contain the essentials of the tradition. I shall indicate below some variants presented by *Codex 344*, which is clearly posterior; these variants do not fundamentally change the tradition, but embellish it according to a familiar pattern.

Instead of summarizing its contents, I prefer to give a partial translation of the Codex of 1440 which will preserve the naive flavor of the original account (fol. 6r): "Wherein is told how Our Lady, the Virgin Mary, appeared to a shepherd as he watched his cows and ordered him to go home, call the priests and other people, and return to dig at the place where she was, where they would find a statue of the Virgin.

"After the sword of the Moor had passed through almost all Spain, it pleased God, Our Lord, to comfort the Christians so they might regain the courage they had lost. Thus [the apparition of the Virgin Mary] gave them new courage."[26] This simple beginning transports us to the customary milieu of these pious legends: a pious image hidden in the mountain; an apparition, witnessed by a shepherd, coming at a time when the Christians were in dire need of a manifestation of God and his supernatural grace. The Virgin, mother of Jesus, appears as intercessor between God and men. The narrator goes on to record the miraculous event with admirable simplicity (fol. 6v): "At the time when King Alfonso reigned over Spain, Our Lady, the Holy Virgin Mary, appeared to a shepherd in the mountains of Guadalupe.... She said to this shepherd: 'Have no fear, for I am the Mother of God, through whom mankind will be redeemed...' (fol. 7v). The shepherd came home, found his wife in tears, and said to her: 'Why do you weep?' She replied, 'Your son is dead,' and he said: 'Have no care, for I dedicate him to Holy Mary of Guadalupe, that she may bring him back to life and health.'... Immediately the young man rose up sound and well; he said to his father: 'Father, hasten; let us go to Holy Mary of Guadalupe," at which all who were present marvelled. This shepherd went to find the priests and told them... that the miracles to be worked by the Virgin would cause many pilgrims from many regions to come to her sanctuary, and that a large village would arise in that great mountain. As soon as the priests and other people heard that, they set to work."[27] This pious legend is typical of the legends circulating in the medieval West, especially in the Iberian Peninsula. The Virgin's choice of a humble shepherd to be the messenger of her grace is an obligatory feature of the genre. The resuscitated son, consecrated to the future sanctuary of the Virgin, places the seal of authenticity on the apparition. The

Virgin herself prophetically announces the future rise of the village. It only remained for the priests and laymen of Caceres to set out for the sierra of Guadalupe and disinter the holy image, which they hasten to do after hearing the blessed shepherd with the predestined name, Gil Cordero ("lamb"), and witnessing the resurrection of his son.

Actually, it is doubtful whether a prophet was needed to foresee the flowering of the Marian cult at Guadalupe, the construction of an abbey with a village growing up about it, and the occurrence of miracles or at least a belief in miracles that would attract pilgrims. One could cite numerous examples of places of pilgrimage with similar origins which prospered from the Middle Ages down to the nineteenth century. The account I have just transcribed of the prodigious event—the oldest account known—was composed at least a century after the origin of the sanctuary of Guadalupe. When it was written by a Jeronymite religious of the convent of Guadalupe, the temple, the convent, the village, the miracles, the pilgrims were no longer a prophetic vision but a daily reality, or at least an image of that reality capable of inspiring popular fervor. That is how this version of the origins or the "invention" of Holy Mary of Guadalupe—to use the term employed by her fifth chronicler, Father Ecija, who died in 1534—was popularized and established. For the rest, I believe the Codex of 1440 should be regarded as a piece of pious propaganda. It is entirely possible the shepherd Gil, searching for a stray cow, accidentally found a cave obstructed by a rock and, hoping to find treasure, made his way inside with the help of comrades. This required no miracle. Was the holy image already in the cave? Was it introduced by some pious hand in order to be discovered shortly thereafter? It would take daring to attempt to solve these problems. Again, perhaps the shepherd Gil Cordero never existed.

According to the same Codex of 1440, the origin of the Dark Virgin, with the child, was as follows (fol. 5v): "At that time (in the eighth century) all the Christians fled from Seville. Among them were some saintly priests who took with them the statue of Our Lady, Holy Mary . . . , and in these mountains these priests dug a cave that they surrounded with large gravestones; inside they placed the statue of Our Lady, Holy Mary, together with a small bell and a reliquary containing a writing which told how this statue of Holy Mary had been offered at Rome to the Archbishop of Seville, Saint Leander, by the Doctor of the Church, Saint Gregory."[28] Codex 344 presents a slight variation from the above account; it relates that the relics of Saint Fulgencio were also found in the cave and that the bell only sounded matins.

Here, even more than in the account of the prodigies, we are surrounded by legends. It is entirely possible that Sevillian priests, fleeing the Almohade invasion, decided to protect certain relics against profanation by taking them in their flight across the mountainous part of eastern Estremadura. In most pious traditions of the Christian West, relics are discovered after a period of concealment designed to save them from profanation. It is more difficult to believe the story that the Sevillian priests dug a cave instead of utlizing natural recesses and then indicated the place to would-be pillagers by laying down great stones like "gravestones." As for the supposed deposit of a museographic note, describing the origin of the dark statue and its history for the use of indiscreet visitors—this sounds like pure fantasy. I conclude that if the historical note in question ever existed, like the account of the apparitions, it was composed later by some pious Jeronymite of the convent of Guadalupe. As for the bell which sounded matins of itself, all I can say is that the folklore of the Peninsula (especially of Galicia) is replete with analogous examples down to the twentieth century.

Even before its prodigious reapparition, the statue of the Virgin with child, notable for its dark color—a "black Virgin"—and its Byzantine aspect, had a history filled with legend. It was supposedly carved by the evangelist Saint Luke, buried in Byzantium (during its first disappearance), and brought to Rome by Pope Saint Gregory the Great. There the Virgin—not yet the Virgin of Guadalupe—was carried in procession and worked a miracle by expelling a plague. Later, another epidemic having desolated the ancient Hispalis, Pope Saint Gregory presented the sacred image to Leander, archbishop of Seville, who used it to gain the same relief. What should we make of all this? It is almost certain that the image is a Byzantine work, probably of the first centuries A.D. (the rich ornaments with which it is decked out do not allow a complete examination). This presumption, founded on artistic criteria, seems to be confirmed by recent analysis of the material, which is cedar, a wood widely used in the Mediterranean world, but doubtless much rarer in Western Europe in the period under consideration. The saint's chisel, the statue's disappearance in Byzantium, the bonds of amity between Saint Gregory the Great and Archbishop Saint Leander, are so many dubious circumstances whose role in the tradition was to reinforce the sacred power of the holy image. In the race for relics and miracles to which medieval Christians devoted themselves, pious invention compensated for the shortage of authentic relics. Only thus could each region boast, like the province of Caceres, of having received a prodigious boon from Heaven, at a time which must have seemed so opportune to the later chronicler: "After the sword of the Moor had passed through almost all Spain, it pleased God, Our Lord, to comfort the Christians. . . . "[29]

Subsequently, in 1340, prefiguring the action of Philip II with regard to the Escorial, King Alfonso XI ordered the construction of the Gothic church and the priory as a thanksgiving for the victory of Salado; then, in 1389, King Juan I assigned to the Jeronymite order the care of the sanctuary. After the cardinal-regent Cisneros, came Cortés, Pizarro, Andrea Doria, Francisco de Borja, to prostrate themselves at the feet of the Virgin of Guadalupe. Among the monastery's relics and ornaments one can still admire the golden scorpion which the conqueror of Mexico offered to the Virgin as an ex-voto, after being healed of a scorpion's sting. Until the nineteenth century the monastery was one of the richest in Europe; consequently many Spaniards, religious or laymen, simple devotees or historians, regarded Our Lady of Guadalupe of Mexico as a copy (*un transunto*) of the holy image of Estremadura and nothing more, since all went back to the legendary history of "the dark Lady of las Villuercas," the work of Saint Luke's chisel. That tradition, at any rate, is contained in an anonymous manuscript: "Gregory the Great sent Saint Leander this statue of the Virgin, Mother of Our Lord and our Mother, which he kept in his oratory, because it was said that it had been carved by Saint Luke."[30] This detail has its own importance, for it links the Spanish Guadalupe cult to the apostolic cults which developed in Western Europe, as A. Dupront has shown, in competition with the pilgrimages to Jerusalem. The causes of this geographical shift, which required a millennium to complete, included the problem of distance, the practical difficulties of travel to a Holy Land dominated by the "Turks," and the menace of Barbary pirates who scoured the seas. The great Crusades ultimately failed to solve the problem. But the decisive reason for the development of centers of pilgrimage in Spain, and in Europe generally, was the profound tendency of the religious consciousness to sink its cult roots in native soil.

The Arab chronicler Iban Hayyan wrote in the eleventh century that the sanctuary of Saint James at Compostela was as holy for the Christians as the Kaaba at Mecca was for the Moslems. By the middle of the fourteenth century, however, that situation had changed. Saint James of Compostela was probably the principal center of sacral gravity of that spiritual "Holy Empire" which survived the dismemberment of Charlemagne's empire. But the progress of the Reconquista by the Christian kingdoms of the Peninsula brought in its train a migration of centers of pilgrimage, so that the principal hearth of Iberian religiosity tended to draw near the geographical—one could even say geometrical—center of the Peninsula. It has been said that "Guadalupe is the history of Spain from the battle of Salado until the construction of the Escorial";[31] that is, from 1340 to 1561. The erection of a specifically Hispanic religious hearth was, so to speak, the consecration of the great cleavage between Spain and the other regions of Western Europe—a cleavage which would culminate in Spain's cultural isolation.

América Castro has justly drawn attention to the historic importance of the role of a typically Spanish order, the Jeronymites. The history of this order (poorly studied from a nonmonastic point of view) almost blends with that of the monastery of Guadalupe and, still later, with that of San Lorenzo of the Escorial. In his catalog of the Jeronymite monasteries of Spain, the prior of Guadalupe, Fray Gabriel de Talavera, writing in 1597, singled out four for special citation: San Bartolomé de Lupiana, Nuestra Señora de Guadalupe, Yuste, and San Lorenzo el Real (the Escorial), in the order of their creation. Noting that these successive foundations took place by a process of breakaway, since Guadalupe was founded by friars from Lupiana, and the Escorial and Yuste by religious from Guadalupe (with the prior of Guadalupe himself departing for the Escorial), we perceive an underlying spiritual continuity. Another aspect attracts our attention: the close link between Spanish dynastic history and Jeronymite monastic history. On October 29, 1389, King Juan I founded the Jeronymite priory of Guadalupe, to which he sent Fray Fernando Yañez with thirty friars of Lupiana. Yuste, to which Charles V retired in 1557, was founded in 1408, and it was the Jeronymites of Guadalupe who were called upon to create the new monastery. When Philip II undertook to fulfill the vow he had made at the battle of Saint Quentin to build a monastery to Saint Lorenzo the martyr, it was to the friars of Guadalupe, again, that he turned for help in bringing his devout enterprise to a successful conclusion.

But Guadalupe (and later the Escorial) was not simply a kind of small royal retreat. América Castro notes that cryptojudaic ceremonies had been celebrated in this principal sanctuary of Spanish Catholicism. The history of Guadalupe is linked to the history of inquisitorial persecution of judaizers. Its links with political history are even closer—one could even call them constitutional—for the priory was founded as a thanksgiving for the victory of Salado. In this connection, we note that the copper lamp belonging to the Turkish admiral captured at Lepanto still hangs in the nave of Guadalupe's church. Among the holy image's wonder-working actions, a statistically important place must be assigned to cases of miraculous liberation of Christian prisoners of the Moors and the rescue of sailors from shipwreck. The course of the alliance of the monastery with the Castilian dynasty did not always run smooth. In the regency of Cardinal Cisneros, who sought to limit the monastery's territorial expansion, the Jeronymites instituted two suits against the great reformer, who levied annual taxes of a thousand maravedis upon them in 1508. Perhaps the most critical event in the relations between the friars and the monarchy was the great national crisis of the revolt of the Comuneros in 1521. Although we know more about the role of a Franciscan of Caceres, Fray Juan de Torres, in a Comunero movement in Estremadura, it seems certain that the friars of the Guadalupe monastery regarded with sympathy the movement of regional resistance to the claims of the young foreign sovereign Charles I of Spain (Charles V of the Holy Roman Empire).

When, a score of years later, Christopher Columbus returned from his first voyage to the New World, the cult of Guadalupe was at its zenith; her name was given to one of the lesser Antilles (Guadalupe), and the first American natives to set foot on Spanish soil were baptized there under the auspices of royal godparents. The severe but instructive judgment of the Franciscan Father Germán Rubio in his classic history of Guadalupe calls attention to an aspect which is central to the problem of the origins of the Mexican image of Guadalupe: "As a result of the universal devotion to Our Lady, there appeared in Spain, Portugal, America, and other places a great number of sanctuaries erected in her honor, and they would have multiplied infinitely if, moved by sordid jealousy, the Jeronymites of Guadalupe (in Estremadura) had not opposed it with all their power, from fear of the injury that these sanctuaries might do the holy mother house, to which alms flowed in a constant stream."[32]

American "Mariolatry"

For the Mexican creoles, the "prodigious image" of Tepeyac was a supreme favor that Mary had done the Mexican people, and *Non fecit taliter omni nationi* ("He did not do the like for any other nation").[33] Viewed from this perspective, Our Lady of Guadalupe is only the prolongation of a Western, purely Christian tradition; she takes her place among a series of images of the Virgin that were reputed to have accomplished miracles or prodigies in other American lands as well. The study of R. Vargas Ugarte, *Historia del culto de María en Ibero-America,* offers an almost complete catalog of the sanctuaries dedicated to the Virgin Mary in Latin America, under her different invocations. This author cites a work listing for Mexico alone 1,756 toponyms invoking the Virgin Mary. The analysis is helpful for our subject, for Guadalupe comes first, with 256 invocations, as opposed to only 21 for Remedios.

The task of analyzing these figures would take too long and offers little interest; even if not rigorously correct, the relations they express speak for themselves. Among the different invocations of the cult to the Virgin Mary, Guadalupe today is clearly the most widespread. On the other hand, the Virgin of the _Noche Triste,_ Remedios, now appears to have lost favor, as befits the _gachupina_ in a Mexico that is spiritually mestizo.

According to a pious legend, told by the Jesuit Florencia, in the last quarter of the seventeenth century the miraculously healed uncle of the Indian Juan Diego was charged by the apparition to say to Bishop Zumárraga "that when he (Zumárraga) built her temple and placed there her miraculous statue, he should call her Holy Mary Virgin of Guadalupe."[34] This appellation is not incompatible with the Woman of the Book of Revelation; medieval iconography already confounded the two images. Although certain exegetes distinguished the one from the other, others, like Joachim of Floris (whose influence on the missionaries of Mexico was important, as we know) deliberately interpreted Revelation 12 in an amphibiological manner: the Woman is the church of the hermits and the monks, who will return to build the spiritual church, but she is also Mary, mother of Christ, symbol of the church, the mother of all. Modern exegesis tends to reject the assimilation of the Woman of Revelation to the Virgin Mary. But it appears that this assimilation was general in Hispanic America, indeed throughout Western Christendom. Consider these apostrophes to the Virgin in a Marian litany cited by Vargas Ugarte, and attributed by some to Saint Toribio de Mogrovejo:

> _Luminare coeli_
> _Pulchra ut luna_
> _ut sol electa_

> [Light of Heaven
> Beautiful as the Moon
> As unique as the Sun.]

The phrases could be applied to the image of Tepeyac without any difficulty. At the same time, as the image of the Virgin Mary, Guadalupe became the object of official and public devotion in New Spain.

Under this aspect the cult of Guadalupe, so specifically Mexican, formed part of a vaster phenomenon, the Marian cult, of which it represented a particular regional example. It is not possible, within the limits of this book, to undertake a general study of the Marian cult, even limited to Latin America. Within those continental limits, the work of Vargas Ugarte provides all the information we need to form certain conclusions. To begin with, we note the amplitude of the phenomenon in the lands that emerged from the old Spanish and Portuguese empires. Each country placed itself under the protection of the national image of the Virgin: Guadalupe in Mexico; the Virgin of Luján in Argentina; Our Lady of Gualpulo in Ecuador; Our Lady of Copacabana in old Peru (which included present-day Bolivia); Nuestra Señora de las Mercedes in modern Peru; Nuestra Señora de Caacupe in Paraguay. In fact, numerous cities of Latin America bear one of the names of the Virgin and are placed under her protection, for example, Our Lady of La Paz, capital of Bolivia. The development of the Marian cult in America appears to have several causes. Doubtless the first historic reason is the widespread cult of Mary among the leaders of conquering expeditions, who came from Estremadura or other Iberian provinces. The most famous examples are the brothers Pizarro, natives of Trujillo, and, in the case of Mexico, Hernán Cortés, who came from Medellin. The first Christian images given the Indians were Saint James, who appeared to them as a formidable god of war and of thunder, and the Virgin Mary, whose appearance, by contrast, must have consoled the vanquished. This introduction of the Marian cult into the Indies was soon reinforced by the arrival of the first missionaries, especially the Franciscan religious, who were especially devoted to the Virgin Mary.

Thus, the *Iglesia Indiana*, of which the Franciscan Jerónimo de Mendieta dreamed, first bore the visage of Mary. By the last quarter of the sixteenth century the millenarian fever had subsided, yet the cult of the Virgin Mary enjoyed a new upsurge. The Jesuits placed a special stress on the Immaculate Conception, and the Marian brotherhoods which they created contributed mightily to the growth of temples and of the cult itself. But the Franciscans had anticipated the Jesuits in moving in that direction. The Third Mexican Provincial Council, assembled in 1585, declared the feast of the Immaculate Conception obligatory, on pain of mortal sin. In Spain and its empire the cult of the *Inmaculada* assumed the proportions of a national interest; a junta of the Immaculate Conception, created at the instance of the Spanish monarchy, met from time to time between 1616 and 1770 with a view to securing promulgation of the dogma of the Immaculate Conception. This junta did not disappear until about 1820.

In the eighteenth century, the cult of the *Inmaculada* reached its apogee in the Hispanic world (as did the cult of Guadalupe in Mexico) but the papacy dragged its feet and reached no conclusion. The junta had especially sought to obtain in 1665 "that the Pope institute the feast of the Patronage of the Very Holy Virgin Mary over Spain and her possessions."[35] This precedent is interesting and suggests the climate in which the Mexican creoles of the next century fought for recognition of "the universal patronage" of Guadalupe of Tepeyac. To the "Spanish challenge," represented at this date by the Virgin of Pilar rather than by the Guadalupe of Estremadura, there was added in the New World the "Peruvian challenge," for Saint Rose of Lima was then recognized as the "Universal Patroness" of the Indies. The extraordinary upsurge of the Marian cult in general and of the Immaculate Conception in particular is partly explained by the climate of the Catholic Counter-Reformation (after the Council of Trent), whose great champions were the Jesuits. The new Protestant confessions had kept their distance with regard to the cult of Mary. The eschatological expectancy of the mendicant orders, in particular, followed by the anguish of sin (which had an enduring influence on Lutheranism) found in Mary the Immaculate a sheet anchor. The Virgin, the only mortal to escape the universal stain of the line of Adam, carried the promise of redemption. Applying a kind of dialectic to the impenetrable designs of God, the religious, like Sahagún, concluded that where sin had abounded more than elsewhere (among the Indians held in the bondage of idolatry for centuries) grace should henceforth abound. Mestizos and creoles, treated with the same scorn as the Indians by the *gachupines*, felt the weight of centuries of idolatry and mortal sin. The Virgin Mary brought them grace and dignity in the form of "prodigious" apparitions, almost all of which occurred in the last quarter of the sixteenth century and the first quarter of the seventeenth. Thus the Mother of Christ came to signify the salvation of the New World, a world chosen to be the site of a renewed Christendom—renewed even if not completely new, for on that point the climate of opinion had changed. The cult of Mary appeared more and more inseparable from the cult of the Immaculate Conception, well before the proclamation of the dogma by the sovereign pontiff.

The American legends of the "apparitions" bear a curious resemblance to each other. In substance, they are borrowings from the European Middle Ages; nevertheless, they are profoundly American. The shepherd of the Spanish traditions is replaced by an Indian. We see immediately the advantage of this indigenous version. The Indians rediscovered in the new religion the mother-goddess of their old faith. (I have already noted Sahagún's semantic reservations on this point.) In Peru, the same phenomena developed with the Virgin of Copacabana; the Indians spontaneously gave the Virgin the name of Pachamama, the mother-goddess, mother of the peoples. For the rest, these images of the Virgin had brown Indian skins and were promptly styled *inditas* ("Indian women"). The great popularity that these images, miraculous or not (some were not proclaimed to be such) immediately gained among the Indians is largely explained by factors I have already discussed. Much more complex, on the other hand, are the causes of the relative abandonment by the creoles of the first American images of Mary, such as that of Remedios.

No doubt the antagonism between the creoles and the peninsular-born Spaniards who came as officials to the Indies must have played a large role in this abandonment. The Spaniards rendered homage to the traditional images of Mary, that is to say, to replicas of those which existed in Spain, in their native provinces. Moreover, many must have felt repugnance at the idea of mingling with the *Indiada*, the multitude of Indian devotees of Guadalupe, for example. The creoles, of Spanish stock but born in the New World must have shared this repugnance, but how could they be insensible to the prodigies which designated their *patria* as the chosen home of the Virgin Mary! Creoles, mestizos, and Indians of New Spain soon found themselves gathered under the banner of Guadalupe; the process must have been at least well under way by the time Archbishop Montúfar began his famous inquiry into Guadalupe in 1556. The skepticism of the *gachupines* with regard to the apparitions only strengthened the unity of the American devotees and effaced the caste differences that separated them, bringing them together, united by the same religious and national fervor, in a common front against the agents of peninsular domination.

The charisma with which the Mexicans believed themselves endowed by the "apparitions" of the Virgin Mary at Tepeyac, which transformed their country into a "Western Paradise," is not a unique example; it simply happens to be the one richest in sociopolitical implications. Peru, Ecuador, Colombia, and other provinces were strewn with sanctuaries of the Virgin Mary that were so many centers of regional spirit. We also observe a certain process of gemination or duplication, notably in the case of Guadalupe. Her image was copied and transported to other places. Long before the papacy recognized—not without hesitation and mental reservations—the patronage of Mary of Guadalupe over all Mexico in the middle of the eighteenth century, churches, convents, and *colegios* had been placed under her patronage in the principal towns of New Spain. The same happened with the Virgin of Copacabana in Peru, and the great Spanish dramatist Pedro Calderón de la Barca even wrote a sacramental *auto* entitled *La aurora en Copacabana,* in which, in the manner of medieval allegories, idolatry appears on the stage and yields her place in the hearts of the Indians to Mary the Immaculate. The resemblances and differences between the two traditions, that of Guadalupe in New Spain and that of Copacabana in Peru, are very instructive. Both assigned to an Indian the role of initiating the cult, and this fact, it seems, was the principal cause of their later notable development.

By contrast with the image of Guadalupe, claimed to be miraculous, that of the Virgin of Copacabana had a purely human origin, according to the tradition; it was supposedly sculptured by an Indian, Tito Yupanqui, native of a village situated on the banks of Lake Titicaca, called Copacabana from the name of an Inca idol who had his sanctuary there. Here, as in the case of Tepeyac (the ancient sanctuary of Tonantzin), we find the new religion appropriating an ancient pagan center of pilgrimage. The apparition of the Virgin of Copacabana came after the creation of her effigy and brought confirmation of the divine will that the new sanctuary should prosper. In both cases—in the case of Juan Diego for Guadalupe and that of Tito Yupanqui for Copacabana—the Indian origin was clearly more important than the prodigious origin of the image. This autochtonous aspect of the cult of purely American images of the Virgin was of capital importance; it was one of the ways in which the sentiment of American patriotism could find more or less conscious expression at a time of pervasive distrust of the Spanish monarchy and fear of its capacity for repression. The creole cult of Indian images of the Virgin is an aspect of a larger phenomenon, the creole elite's imaginative rehabilitation of the Indian past, which in turn implied the need for revision of the official historiography of the Spanish Conquest.

We may provisionally conclude, therefore, that the cult of Guadalupe, although specifically Mexican in content, presents a broadly American configuration. The comparisons I have made with the Virgin of Copacabana in Peru are only especially choice examples. We observe that the Virgin of Guápulo, in Ecuador, was a replica of the Guadalupe of Estremadura, a Virgin with child, and was transported with great pomp from Quito (where she had first been installed by a confraternity of merchants) to Guápulo, a village of Chibcha Indians, probably in 1587. This image, like that of Guadalupe, was carried in procession throughout the colonial period at times of great public calamities, and multitudes of Indians made pilgrimages to her sanctuary. The Virgin of Caacupe of Paraguay (like that of Copacabana) had allegedly been sculptured by an Indian who, threatened with death, had invoked the aid of the Virgin and vowed to carve her image from the trunk of the tree that concealed

him from a troop of savage Indians of the Mbya tribe. Compared with
these images, the image of Guadalupe retrospectively appears as the
one best qualified to inspire ardent devotion in her followers. She had
the advantage of having a supernatural origin, and the initiator of her
cult was a humble village Indian chosen by the Virgin Mary (who
appeared to him five times in succession!) as her mediator with the
archbishop. These were facts calculated to purge of sin that sinful
land that ancient Mexico was supposed to have been. Such a striking
manifestation of the grace of Mary was, as it were, a collective baptism
of the people of New Spain, incarnated for the occasion in one of its
humblest representatives, the Indian Juan Diego, a neophyte converted by the Franciscans. In that movement of conversion, sanctified
by prodigies, the Virgin Mary took a decisive part, with her ambiguous personality, compounded of the Woman of Revelation, an-
nouncer of the Parousia, and the Mother of Christ, intercessor for
mankind with God. In that double sense, Guadalupe indisputably
prolonged the European Marian tradition; this was well understood
by the Spaniards who, having first rejected Guadalupe as doubtful
and apocryphal, later sought to appropriate her for themselves. That
effort continues in our own time when Guadalupe is described as
"Queen of *Hispanidad*," a notion that doubtless reflects political designs rather than spiritual fervor.

13   The Infancy of Guadalupe

The Name and the Image: Troubling Contradictions

Why does the image of the Virgin Mary venerated near Mexico City on the hill of Tepeyac (called by the creoles *Tepeaquilla*), an image so different from that of Guadalupe of Estremadura, bear her name? Historians have often asked that embarrassing question, without giving a satisfactory answer. Since Guadalupe was a toponym, its transfer to New Spain, to a place which already had a name long associated with the site of a religious sanctuary, appears an enigma. The solution offered by Father Vargas Ugarte in his classic history of the Marian cult in Hispanic America cannot satisfy a critical spirit. Let the reader judge for himself: "One must conclude that the name was given by a kind of association of ideas, understandable under the circumstances, or, more likely, because that was the Virgin's wish when she appeared."[1] If we dismiss the second solution, clearly the product of an act of faith, and turn to the first solution proposed by the learned Jesuit, we discern a possible avenue of investigation. Although the Jeronymites did not participate directly in the conversion of Mexico, the image of the Virgin of Guadalupe of Estremadura commanded the loyalty of the conquistadors. This was due to her role as symbol of Hispanic Christianity in its struggle against the Moslems and, by a process of association, in the wars against the pagans of the New World. Let me again recall that Gómora regarded the American conquests as a natural prolongation of the *Reconquista*. Moreover, the regional origins of Cortés and many of his companions, who were *extremeños* like him, inevitably favored the development in New Spain of the cult of an image of the Virgin, the honor of Estremadura. On this eminently propitious soil was to sprout the new Mexican cult of a Virgin of Guadalupe who presented, however, the disconcerting peculiarity of being completely different from her presumed peninsular model.

Sixteenth-century witnesses who could shed light on the origins of the image of Tepeyac were few in number, and all clearly of later date

231

than 1531, regarded by the devout since 1648 as the date of the apparitions. To the best of my knowledge, the oldest testimony is that of a creole interrogated in the course of an inquiry ordered by Archbishop Montúfar in 1556 after the Franciscan provincial, Fray Francisco de Bustamante, had delivered a sermon against Guadalupe. This witness attributed to the Franciscan the following comment, which he must have made in his sermon: "To say to the Indians now, that an image painted by an Indian worked miracles, would cause great turmoil among them."[2] This is an interesting piece of evidence, although it does not answer the question of the iconographic model of the image of Tepeyac. We know that about the same time an Indian by the name of Marcos had a great reputation as a painter. It is not at all unlikely, therefore, that an Indian painted the image of Tepyac. The later testimony of Dávilla Padilla concerning the Indian custom of hanging pious images made of flowers on church walls tends to strengthen this possibility. The testimony of the Franciscan Alonso de la Rea, almost exactly contemporary with the first Guadalupan "gospel" of Miguel Sánchez, deals with the Tarascans of Michoacán and images of Christ, but may help to illuminate the origin of the "prodigious" effigy of Tepeyac. La Rea writes of the Tarascans: "They are such good painters, possessing such delicacy and elegance of style, that all the churches of this province are ornamented with paintings on cloth and wood made by Indian painters; they are not at all inferior to the painters of Rome."[3] Readers familiar with the specimens of pre-Columbian art which fill our museums know that the Franciscan chronicler does not exaggerate. We know, then, that it was a custom in New Spain (in particular, but not exclusively, in Michoacán), to hang images painted by Indians on church walls. In addition to painted images (lienzos) and images made of flowers, examples of the ancient art of featherwork were displayed; apropos of this last art, La Rea makes a point with which every student of post-Conquest Mexican religious art will agree: "Although the Franciscans naturally gave the design of the image to the Tarascans, the fineness of touch which distinguishes the work was contributed by the Indians."[4] La Rea and Dávilla Padilla indirectly tend to confirm the statement of their predecessor Bustamante with regard to the Indian origin of the image of Tepeyac; it is the work of an Indian artist, evidently based on a model of European origin.

A decade after Bishop Montúfar's inquiry, judging by the fact that Bernal Díaz del Castillo finished his history in 1568, the chronicler of the Conquest referred to "the holy house of Our Lady of Guadalupe at Tepeaquilla, where Gonzalo de Sandoval established his camp when we captured Tenochtitlan."[5] Although this passage from the *Historia verdadera* sheds no light on the origin of the image, it offers a clue to the probable origin of the name of Guadalupe, for it associates the headquarters of a captain of the Conquest with the sanctuary of the Virgin Mary. It does not say that Sandoval was a devotee of Guadalupe or that he placed her protective image there, but this would follow from what we know, from the chronicles of the Conquest, about the religious behavior of the Spanish conquerors of America. To be sure, this is only a hypothesis. We must now turn to the only explicit document on the subject (aside from the record of Montúfar's inquiry), a letter of Viceroy Martin Enríquez, dated September 25, 1575: "They gave this statue the name of Our Lady of Guadalupe, saying that she resembled the image of the monastery of Guadalupe of Spain."[6] These are the viceroy's words; they are quite inapplicable to the known image of Tepeyac. We have no reason to suppose that Viceroy Enríquez wrote carelessly; for the rest, it is difficult to see what interest he could have in falsifying the truth. The date of his letter (September 25) is an additional indication in favor of the Estremaduran origin of the image of Tepeyac.

We recall that the feast of Guadalupe of Estremadura was celebrated on September 8 and that as late as 1600 the cathedral chapter of Mexico City decided that the Nativity of the Virgin would be celebrated September 10 at the chapel of Guadalupe de Tepeyac, because that was her invocation. I have not been able to determine exactly when the feast of the Mexican Guadalupe was moved from September 8 or 10 to December 12 (the present date); but one is struck by the parallelism of the change of the calendar and the change in the image. Both reveal an intention to establish a distance vis-à-vis the mother image and her cult, to distinguish totally the Mexican Guadalupe from the Guadalupe of Estremadura, whose name alone was preserved. All that we know for certain is that the substitution of the image took place after 1575 and the change of the feast day calendar after 1600. There are good reasons to believe that these two decisive stages in the Mexicanization of a cult so specifically tied to the conquistadors coincided more or less with the publication of the book of Miguel Sánchez, which, by attaching the image of Tepeyac to the prophetic vision of John in Revelation, gave the cult a universal dimension.

A question naturally arises: why did the Indians, or the creoles, their religious guides, feel so early the need to distinguish their Guadalupe from that of Estremadura? The question is important, for the event correlates with the birth of a tradition of "apparitions" whose raison d'être was that same desire to establish a distance vis-à-vis Spain, as well as the desire to be geographically closer to the site of miracles, thereby relieving pilgrims from having to make the "great voyage" (Gómez Moreno) to a distant sanctuary. To attempt to answer that question is the very object of this book. Let me begin by saying that the change of images was the first forward step of Mexican national consciousness.

But we must seek immediate causes and commence our inquiry on a more modest level, that of devout practice and the religious-commercial life of Christian sanctuaries in the sixteenth century. A recent publication by the Franciscan Fray Arturo Álvarez is helpful; it is his edition of the travel diary of a Jeronymite religious of Guadalupe, Fray Diego de Ocaña, who traveled in South America between 1599 and 1605. His mission was contemporaneous with the official recognition of the cult of Guadalupe of Mexico City. On arrival at Potosí, the famous Peruvian mining center of Peru, Fray Diego wrote down a naive account of his mission. "With much zeal I set about painting in oils, something I had never done in my life . . . and the Very Holy Virgin guided my brush so that I drew such a perfect image, of the same size as that of Spain, that the whole city was transported with devout fervor. During that time I sent Monsignor the Bishop of Charcas a copy of the *cédula* of the king our lord, together with a request for authorization to collect alms and memberships in the confraternity of Our Lady of Guadalupe, both in this city and throughout the bishopric; he promptly gave his permission, for he comes from Estremadura and is a very devout subject of Our Lady."[7] Here we see how the export of the art of illumination (which was the glory of the monastery of Estremadura), aided by the regional solidarity between the religious and the bishop, resulted in the creation at Potosí (an ideal place for the collection of alms!) of a secondary sanctuary of Guadalupe of Estremadura. By such initiatives the Spanish Jeronymites, absent from the work of conversion, which had been entrusted to the mendicant orders, secured through the establishment of Marian confraternities a spiritual influence and a promising source of revenues in the New World. Undoubtedly this was the object of the mission entrusted to Fray Diego de Ocaña; listen to his reflections on the September day that saw the installation of his image of Guadalupe, a large illuminated drawing: "At that moment we set up a counter at the door of the church. . . . And I began to enroll in the confraternity all who wished to enroll, and by this means in eight days I amassed four thousand silver pesos. But if I had not painted that image of the Virgin, I would not have collected 4000 reales . . ., and if I had not painted that image, as soon as I left the place, the whole business would have collapsed. . . . I must complain of the negligence of the convent of Guadalupe, which failed to send me certain things for which I asked, especially the engravings, for if I had had twenty or thirty thousand engravings [of the Virgin of Guadalupe] on the table in front of me, I could have disposed of them all, for everyone would have wanted one for his room; and the least I could have gotten for an engraving was a silver peso, which is worth eight reales."[8]

I suspect that if another Jeronymite, one as zealous and able as Diego de Ocaña, had been sent to Mexico City and tried to make profits for the mother house of the nascent cult of Tepeyac, he would have encountered strong creole hostility. A royal *cédula* was explicit on this point: alms collected by means of replicas must be paid to the original image. The substitution for the pristine image of Tepeyac of the image which has since conquered the whole Hispanic world probably resulted from the desire to keep the alms in New Spain; the change in the feast calendar and the development of a tradition of "apparitions" in which an Indian convert played the leading role were due at least in part to the same cause. I am the more inclined to adopt this explanation because the silence of the old historians on this point, their very embarrassment, suggests motives which could hardly be avowed in so devout a question.

Some verification of this hypothesis is provided by an eighteenth-century writer, Fray Francisco de San José, former prior of Guadalupe de Estremadura. In his *Historia universal de la primitiva y milagrosa Imagen de Nuestra Señora de Guadalupe,* Fray Francisco sought by every possible means to attach the image of Tepeyac, which was then gaining recognition and importance, to the Spanish sanctuary. This apologist accepted the Mexican tradition of the Virgin's "apparitions," but claimed to see in an image of the Virgin in the choir of the basilica of Estremadura the model of the image of Tepeyac. But he made no effort to explain the choice of such a marginal model, disposing of the question with a reference to the inscrutable designs of Providence: "When the Virgin resolved to give the name of Guadalupe to her effigy of Mexico City, why would she have it copied from that of the choir of our basilica, and not from the famous, very ancient, and very noble bearer of that appelation? This pertains to the designs of God, which we must not try to fathom, but only venerate humbly."[9] Despite his avoidance of the troublesome problem of motives, Fray Francisco's discussion has the value of putting us on the track of a possible origin of the new image of Guadalupe. The image of the choir does present striking similarities with the Guadalupe of Tepeyac. In this connection, Father Germán Rubio observes that "neither the crown nor the canopy that complete her today are original and rather mask certain details that accentuate the resemblance with the Mexican Guadalupe."[10]

If we accept the explanation that I find most plausible for the substitution of the image of Tepeyac, we immediately perceive the cleverness of the maneuver: replace the "universal" Guadalupe with an image of Mary also housed in the famous monastery and, to foil any possible effort at annexation by the Jeronymites of Spain, modify this secondary image in one, very visible point. The Virgin of the choir is a Virgin with child, that of Tepeyac is the traditional *inmaculada*. Let me also note that one of the antiphonals of the choir of Guadalupe of Estremadura, dating from the fifteenth century, is illustrated with illuminated drawings that include an *inmaculada* who could have served as model for that of Tepeyac. For the rest, there is nothing unusual about the image. That of the choir of the monastery of Estremadura dates from 1499; there is another, painted on wooden doors separating the parish church from the enclosure of the convent of the nuns of St. Clare of Moguer (province of Huelva), dating from the same epoch and also resembling the image of Tepeyac, both in its composition and its symbolic attributes.

The problem of the original image of Guadalupe of Tepeyac—the image that disappeared—and of the present image is inseparable from the general question of artisan manufacture of pious images in the monastery of the Sierra de las Villuercas and of their diffusion. Fray Arturo Álvarez reminds us that Queen Isabella had charged the Jeronymites of Estremadura with illuminating her *Flos Sanctorum;* and visitors to the monastery can still admire the eighty-nine codices illuminated by the old monks. The complaints of Fray Diego de Ocaña at Potosí prove that the friars printed or drew with brushes replicas of the sacred image, in considerable quantities if not on an industrial scale. We must distinguish the engravings destined for individual devotion in a room, from the effigies designed for sanctuaries and the like; we know less about the latter. Fray Francisco de San José informs us in his *Historia* that "the very noble town of Jerez de la Frontera possesses a statue of the Mother of God which bears the name of Our Lady of Guadalupe," but he disputes the local tradition that makes it go back to the time of King Alfonso the Wise, for, he writes, Guadalupe appeared in 1284 in the sierra de las Villuercas, forty years after the death of King Alfonso the Wise.[11] We note that the Guadalupe of Jerez was deposited in the church of Saint Luke, doubtless because of the tradition that attributed the original statue to the apostle Saint Luke. This replica of the dark Virgin de las Villuercas is not the only one in Spain. There is another several leagues from the town of Ubeda (province of Jaen), of which she is patroness; each year, in May, she is carried in procession; the tradition of her apparition is in all respects analogous to that of las Villuercas. The architecture and the plan of the hermitage which houses the holy image suggests that it was occupied by some religious at the period of its construction, which may go back to the end of the fifteenth century.

The rise of secondary centers of the cult of the Virgin of Guadalupe of the province of Caceres and its polarization around these centers seems to be explained by the need of pilgrims from the cities to make the journey out to the sanctuary and back home on foot, between daybreak and nightfall. In any case, that condition was satisfied by the sanctuary of Ubeda, of Mexico City, and the sanctuary of Manila, contemporary with that of Mexico City. An Augustinian in the Philippines, Fray Gaspar de San Martín, informs us in his *Conquistas de las Islas Philipinas,* published at the end of the seventeenth century, that "In 1601, from devotion for the Miraculous Image that is venerated in Spain under the invocation of Guadalupe, there was brought from this kingdom [Spain] a statue, copied from and closely resembling that which is venerated in Estremadura, and a church and a convent were built in a dry and rocky sierra, two leagues from the town of Manila, upstream from the river Passig."[12]

The existence—before or contemporary with the image of Tepeyac—of outlying sanctuaries of Our Lady of Guadalupe that depended on the mother house materially (through provision of a copy of the original statue sculptured in the workshops attached to the monastery of Guadalupe) and spiritually (due to the fidelity of the copy, which required the transfer of legacies and alms to Estremadura), suggest that the original image of Guadalupe of Tepeyac was also a statue (*imagen de bulto*) imported from Spain. The English traveler Miles Phillips described it in 1582 as a life-size statue of gilded silver. That the question of legacies and alms formed the background of the change that took place in the first half of the seventeenth century both in the sacred calendar and in the miraculous tradition (it was not miraculous before) of the Guadalupe of Tepeyac is further confirmed by the official *Historia univeral* of Father Francisco de San José. This author, who wrote in 1743, could not avoid mention of the matter of alms, still pending under Philip V. After admitting that "Divine mercy has been very liberal to the Mexicans," he added that "Mexicans who on their deathbeds wish to favor the Mother of God of Guadalupe, whom they call *la Extremeña,* to distinguish her from the Mexican Virgin, leave a certain sum of money to our Holy House, by a legacy binding on all testators . . . and although diverse opinions have been expressed in recent years on the subject of these obligatory

legacies, our Catholic monarch decreed by a royal decree of 1700 that
these legacies must pass to our sanctuary."[13] Thus nothing escaped
the reach of colonial exploitation; to the royal fifth (*quinto*) and all the
extraordinary contributions (*donativos*) with which the Mexicans were
taxed, were added the drain of legacies and alms made obligatory by a
royal decree of 1736. Under these conditions, it is clear why the
Guadalupe de Tepeyac could know no peace until she had changed
her appearance and become beyond the shadow of a doubt the "little
Indian" (*Indita*) born of popular devotion.

Guadalupe, Apple of Discord between the Archbishop of Mexico and the Franciscans (1556)

Some years before Fray Bernardino de Sahagún recorded in his *Historia general* his grave doubts about the cult of Guadalupe, another
Franciscan voice was raised to denounce the new cult. In a sermon
delivered on September 8, 1556, on the occasion of the Nativity of the
Virgin, Father Fray Francisco de Bustamante publicly protested in the
presence of the civil authorities against the new and already popular
cult of the image of the Virgin Mary of Guadalupe, whose very name
he disputed, "to which they have given the title of Guadalupe."[14] The
autograph manuscript of the sermon has not been preserved; we
know its contents from the record of an inquiry ordered by the archbishop of Mexico City, Fray Alonso de Montúfar, whom the preacher
did not hesitate to criticize. One of the reasons for the obscurity of the
origins of Guadalupe is the fact that she was the stake in a quarrel
between the most powerful of the mendicant orders in New Spain and
the secular clergy or, more precisely, an archbishop who, succeeding a
Franciscan, Zumárraga, sought to diminish the hitherto undisputed
sway of the missionary friars. Archbishop Montúfar favored the new
cult, while the Franciscan provincial denounced its pernicious effects.
It will be recalled that from the first the Franciscans had practiced a
policy of decisive break with the Indian beliefs; the Franciscan
pioneers believed the danger of confusion of the mythical figure of
Tonantzin with the Virgin Mary had to be avoided at all cost. Franciscan hostility to the new cult was all the stronger because their
forerunners may have instituted the cult of the Virgin of Tepeyac in
order to combat the old cult of Tonantzin, venerated in this same
place.

Father Bustamante's protest illuminates the Erasmian purity of the
Franciscan faith in Mexico at a time when Erasmianism had already
come under violent attack in the Peninsula. The religious passionately

affirmed that "nothing was better calculated to keep the Indians from becoming good Christians than the cult of Our Lady of Guadalupe. Ever since their conversion they have been told they should not believe in idols, but only in God and Our Lady. . . . To tell them now that an image painted by an Indian could work miracles will utterly confuse them and tear up the vine that has been planted. Other cults like that of Our Lady of Loreto had great foundations, so it is astounding to see the cult of Guadalupe arise without the least foundation."[15] This appeal to an essential Christianity, free from all idolatry, struck a chord that would shortly cease to sound in New Spain. We observe that no mention was made on this occasion of a "prodigious apparition" of the holy image, only of its miraculous intercession. Had there then existed a tradition similar to the eighteenth-century tradition of an "apparition" of the Virgin, Father Bustamante would have certainly mentioned it, in order to attack it. But he does not allude to it, expressly stating that the Virgin of Guadalupe of Tepeyac had been painted by an Indian. Another witness declared that he had heard "that the religious had sought to make the natives understand that Our Lady was not God" and "that, if the present situation was not remedied, he [Bustamante] would forever renounce preaching to the Indians." A third witness attributed to the Franciscan the comment that "a hundred lashes should have been given to the first person who said that this image of Guadalupe performed miracles."[16]

The vigor of the Franciscan protest is explained by their belief that to tolerate the new cult "would be the ruin of the missionary effort."[17] When we recall that Fray Bernardino de Sahagún wrote his *Historia general* in order to instruct curates of Indian parishes how they might discover ancient religious practices hidden under Catholic ritual, the fear that the new cult inspired in the Franciscans is understandable. Guadalupe-Tonantzin, female image of the universal dual principle, must inevitably appear to the Indians as "God." From this initial ambiguity was to arise the Mexican cult of Guadalupe, an original form of Christianity in which the Virgin Mary, in her Immaculate Conception, is Mexican. Thus the Franciscan pioneers sensed, with remarkable clairvoyance, that the sudden rise of the cult of Tepeyac was the beginning of an effort to demolish the "Indian Church" which they had tried to erect in Mexico. This explains the favor which the secular clergy accorded to the new cult, whose success would signify a repudiation of the Franciscan pioneers and diminish their ascendancy over the Indians as well as the creoles. Beneath the rivalry between the regulars, founders of the *Iglesia indiana,* and the seculars who sought to supplant them, we perceive a struggle between two conceptions of

European Christianity. One, of Erasmian inspiration, distrusted images and cults; the other would dominate the Counter-Reformation and assign a large place to the sacraments, to frequent communion, to the display of cults. Arriving in Mexico in 1572—only a few years after Fray Francisco's sermon—the Jesuits were the chief artisans of this metamorphosis of the "Indian Church," which became ever more "creole." In sacred eloquence as in architecture—in the construction of ephemeral triumphal arches and temples built for the ages—a baroque luxuriance carried along pell-mell antique heroes and the gods of Mexican polytheism in a euhemeristic optimism that was the very opposite of the "rupture" with the ancient beliefs upheld by the Franciscan founders.

But in 1556 they alone foresaw the dangers presented to the purity of the faith of their Indian converts by the cult which would ruin their missionary effort. Considerations of morality and a parochial spirit influenced the partisans of the new cult. One of the witnesses questioned in the course of the inquiry ordered by the archbishop testified: "He is of opinion that this cult should be favored and promoted, the more because no other cult in this country is so popular. Thanks to this holy fervor, many people have stopped going into the woods according to the former custom of the country. They have abandoned this and similar pleasures and now go where they find only the pure pleasure of pious contemplation, just as in Madrid they go to the convent of our Lady of Antocha."[18] Readers who have walked of a Sunday in the park of Chapultepec will immediately understand the reference to walking in the woods and "similar pleasures" of Mexican life in those distant times. A distinguished contemporary, Zumárraga, first bishop of Mexico City, had denounced in his *Doctrine breve* those "profane festivals." Guadalupe gave a providential purpose and a pious justification to the Sunday promenades of the Mexicans. It also endowed the capital of New Spain, rival of Madrid, with its own shrine. From the first, the cult of Guadalupe thus figured as a source of prestige for Mexico City in its incipient rivalry with the capital of spain, a rivalry which in the eighteenth century assumed the form of an attitude of superiority on the part of Mexican creoles. A less laudable motive (if we may believe the angry Bustamante) animated Bishop Montúfar; this was his concern for the alms and legacies that the cult of Guadalupe must inevitably bring in; if this was really the archbishop's hope, the future was to prove him right. Clearly, faith played a small part in all this. The devotees seem to have been chiefly attracted by the image's "miraculous reputation" and brought their sick children to be healed: "He said that he went to Our

Lady of Guadalupe because he had a daughter sick with the cough."[19] But a decisive factor in the success of the new cult among the Indians (aside from the topographic coincidence with the sanctuary of Toci, denounced by Sahagún), was the "Indian" character of the image. On this point, at least, there was agreement on the part of the devotees of Guadalupe and the enemies of an equivocal cult.

One of the witnesses expressly recalled Bustamante's comment: "Because it was a painting made by Marcos, an Indian painter."[20] Bernal Díaz del Castillo cites a certain Marcos de Aquino as one of three celebrated Indian painters of Mexico City at that period. But the image of Guadalupe of Mexico does not present any typical Indian feature, except, perhaps, for the trait that distinguishes it from its probable model at the shrine of Estremadura—the absence of the child Jesus. The very name of Guadalupe which may have been assigned to it on this account was disputed by another Franciscan of Mexico City, Fray Alonso de Santiago, who said, according to one witness: "it should not have been called Our Lady 'of Guadalupe,' but 'of Tepeaca' or 'Tepeaquilla,' because Our Lady of Guadalupe in Spain has that name because the village itself is named 'Guadalupe.'"[21]

This is the essential content of the oldest authentic document regarding the Mexican cult of the image of Tepeyac. In his sermon Father Bustamante described the cult as *nueva,* "new"; this meant that he did not regard it as a creation of the first missionaries.[22] The vigor of the Franciscan protest suggests that the vigilant religious would not have waited for years to denounce a cult they regarded as so harmful to their Indian converts. The expression applied by Father Bustamante to the image of Tepeyac—"painted the day before by an Indian"—confirms the recent origin of the image in 1556. In the 1550s, news of miraculous healings inspired a sharp upswing of support for the cult of the Virgin of Tepeyac.

Such, in its broad lines, is the early history of the Mexican cult of Guadalupe. What I said before concerning the Marian cults in Hispanic America and especially about Our Lady of Copacabana supports the testimony of the documents of 1556. The image of Tepeyac and the initial upsurge of the Indian and Creole cult present traits typical of the principal manifestations of the Marian cult in the New World. However, the emergence of the Mexican cult of Guadalupe appears a precocious phenomenon by comparison with similar cults in South America. (Peru, invaded ten years later than Mexico, then ravaged by civil wars and Gonzalo Pizarro's revolt, displays retarded development in all fields.) An intense early evangelization, a vigorous urban colonization, and a native population issued from a powerful empire are some of the factors that help to explain the prior appearance of an original Marian cult in New Spain.

The "Invention" of Guadalupe by the Bachiller Sánchez: The Woman of Revelation (1648)

A Spanish friar, Father Diego de Ecija, had written, probably in the first quarter of the sixteenth century, the *Libro de la invención de Santa María de Guadalupe*. This Jeronymite had a rival in the person of the Mexican *bachiller* Miguel Sánchez, who published in 1648 a work entitled *Imagen de la Virgen María Madre de Dios de Guadalupe milagrosamente aparecida en México*.[23] About a century separated the two books, the first of which dealt with the Virgin of Estremadura, the second with the Virgin of Tepeyac. Yet, *mutatis mutandis*, the process of "invention" was the same in both cases. In both more than a century separates the traditional date of the apparition from the oldest known written account of the tradition. It was in 1531 that the "prodigious image" of Guadalupe (Miguel Sánchez was the first to describe it as prodigious) is supposed to have appeared in Mexico. Between 1556 and 1648, one may suppose, the Franciscans had either abandoned their opposition to the cult, or popular fervor had overwhelmed their resistance. Then, too, the Franciscans had become "creolized," as the Augustinian Calancha attests for Peru and the *visitador* Fray Alonso Ponce for New Spain, in 1584. We recall that the cult had been officially encouraged by Bishop Montúfar, who founded the first basilica of Guadalupe in 1555; this provoked the scandal described above. The death of the last Franciscan pioneers (Motolinia in 1569, Olmos in 1571), the arrival of the first Jesuits in 1572, the accession of Archbishop Pedro Moya de Contreras that same year, had renewed the spiritual climate of New Spain. Although Father Sahagún lived until 1590, the manuscripts of his *Historia* had been confiscated in 1577, and the Third Mexican Provincial Council, assembled in 1585, had consecrated the preeminence of the archbishop and the bishops over the mendicant orders. The Jesuits, who more and more took over the evangelizing mission of the Franciscan pioneers, were much more receptive to those religious manifestations which the Franciscans had described as idolatrous. Finally, the curates come from Spain were accustomed to local cults of the Virgin Mary, with their accompanying advantages for the clergy, and naturally encouraged the cult of an "image" of Guadalupe, even if she was "Indian."

There is every reason to suppose, therefore, that the Guadalupan fervor of the Indians (who doubtless saw the old Toci beneath the features of the Virgin Mary) and of the creoles who wanted to have their own patroness, with roots in the soil of their new *patria,* increased after 1556. In his letter of 1575, Viceroy Martín Enriquez noted the existence about 1555 of the chapel of Guadalupe of Tepeyac and declared that "the cult began to grow because a cattle dealer let it be known that he had regained his health by making a pilgrimage to this chapel."[24] This corroborates the testimony of Fray Francisco de Bustamante, twenty years earlier. In 1585, Fray Alonso Ponce reported in his famous *Viaje* that the Spaniards (he doubtless meant Spaniards and creoles as opposed to mestizos and Indians) journeyed to the basilica of Guadalupe, at Tepeyac, to attend mass said by a priest apparently attached to the chapel of Guadalupe. The acts of the ecclesiastical chapter of Mexico City, assembled August 29, 1600, declare that on September 10 the Nativity of the Virgin would be celebrated "at the chapel of Guadalupe, because it is under her invocation." We recall that September 8 was the feast day of Guadalupe of Estremadura. The Mexico City chapter still viewed the chapel of Tepeyac as one shrine of the Virgin Mary among others in New Spain; there is no reference to the "prodigious" character of the image. In a work of Marian devotion published in 1621 by the Mercedarian Fray Luis de Cisneros, the cult of Guadalupe of Tepeyac is simply mentioned in vague terms as old, "dating almost from the conquest of the country."[25] But at that date the 1550s may have seemed like that distant period when Mexico, or at least the valley of Mexico, was conquered and colonized. Although the Dominican Martín de León in 1611 revived Sahagún's arguments against the cult of Guadalupe, the archbishopric had nevertheless continued to encourage it since Montúfar's time, and in 1622 Archbishop Juan de la Serna consecrated a new basilica of Guadalupe at Tepeyac.

Before the *bachiller* Miguel Sánchez, no one had explicitly referred to an "apparition" of the image of Tepeyac. Father Cuevas cites a passage from Suárez de Peralta, whose work cannot be later than 1589, but it is not convincing. The creole chronicler, probably a devotee of Our Lady of Guadalupe, wrote regarding a visit of the viceroy to the shrine: "This is a very holy image which is found two leagues from Mexico City and has performed many miracles"[26] (something we already knew from Montúfar's inquiry), and added laconically: "She appeared among the rocks and the whole country is devoted to her."[27] Since Suárez de Peralta left New Spain in 1570, Father Cuevas concluded that by that date, at latest, the tradition of the apparitions of Tepeyac had been generally accepted in New Spain. But if I interpret correctly the citation from Suárez de Peralta, it means the following.

1. On his arrival in Mexico, Viceroy Martín Enríquez paid a visit to

Tepeyac. This information is interesting, for in the sequel all viceroys and archbishops of Mexico City would profess an ostensible devotion for the image of Tepeyac as a primary condition for enjoying the confidence of the Mexican people.

2. The reputation which Guadalupe had acquired in 1556 for its miraculous cures had lost none of its force, but quite the contrary; the single cure had become "many miracles."

3. The cult of Guadalupe had spread throughout the region (the valley of Mexico).

There is nothing that we do not already know or that could not be reasonably foreseen on the basis of the facts furnished by Montúfar's inquiry. All of Father Cuevas' arguments in favor of an "apparition" is founded in this phrase: "she appeared among the rocks." Now, we know from all later Guadalupan literature that mention of the apparition was always followed by a train of adverbs, usually the qualifiers "prodigiously and miraculously." If Suárez de Peralta thought that the image of Tepeyac had appeared miraculously, he would have certainly stressed the fact and would not have been content with a dry and almost furtive reference; he would not have given prominence to the "many miracles" (healings), petty therapeutic miracles by comparison with the *Mariophany* of Tepeyac presented by a later tradition. Moreover, a considerable number of images of the Virgin Mary venerated in Spain had "appeared," that is, had been discovered by devotees. I might cite the example of Guadalupe of Estremadura, whose ties to the Mexican Guadalupe I have shown. One could also cite the case of the Virgin of Montserrat, in Catalonia, and many others.

Between the "discovery" of the image of Tepeyac (in this respect comparable to that of Remedios, a little statue found on a maguey plant by a Christian cacique) to which Suárez de Peralta refers, and which seems to reflect popular belief about 1570, and the "Apparition" championed by Miguel Sánchez in 1648, almost eighty years went by. In 1556 no witness had mentioned such a miraculous apparition, not even a "discovery" of the image of Tepeyac "among the creoles." In 1570, possibly, more likely in 1587, the date at which Suárez de Peralta wrote, the idea of a discovery of Guadalupe "among the rocks" of Tepeyac was expressed for the first time, by a Mexican creole who had lived in Spain for seventeen years. Suárez de Peralta thus had every opportunity for learning the tradition of the original Guadalupe, discovered in the hollow of a rock in a sierra of Estremadura. Here are hints of a possible contamination of the nascent Mexican tradition by an already established Spanish tradition.

The "invention" of the Mexican Guadalupan tradition was the work of Miguel Sánchez, a famous preacher and theologian, in a book entitled *Image of the Virgin Mary, Mother of God, of Guadalupe, Celebrated in Her History by the Prophecy of Chapter Twelve of Revelation.*[28] Let me recall the first lines of Revelation 12, which immediately call to mind the image of Guadalupe of Tepeyac as the plastic expression of the Woman of the Apocalypse:

> And there appeared a great wonder in heaven; a woman clothed with the sun, and the moon under her feet, and upon her head a crown of twelve stars. . . .

The "prodigious" image venerated on the hill of Tepeyac is truly a woman "clothed with the sun"; a crescent moon is under her feet. She no longer has a crown of stars, but did at least until the nineteenth century, and her numerous ancient Mexican replicas are crowned. Doubtless this crown may be interpreted as that of the Virgin Mary, "Queen of Heaven"; nevertheless, the very abundant Guadalupan iconography presents a series of features borrowed from the Woman of the Apocalypse. In this respect, verse 14 of Revelation 12 offers a valuable clue:

> And to the woman were given two wings of a great eagle, that she might fly into the wilderness, into her place, where she is nourished for a time, and times, and half a time, from the face of the serpent."

Readers will easily recognize here the symbolism of the Aztec tradition, in which the eagle triumphs over the serpent.

As concerns the lunar symbolism in Guadalupan iconography, we must distinguish the lunar epiphanies so characteristic of the Indian religions from the Easter moon with its train of antique symbols assimilated by Christianity, notably by Saint Paul and Saint Ambrose. Doubtless the crescent moon of Guadalupe owed much more to the ancient European and Near Eastern tradition than to the Mexican past.

Francisco de la Maza cites his prefatory note of the *bachiller* Jerónimo de Valladolid to the book of the Jesuit Florencia: "The Woman of Revelation appeared as a supernatural sign of the birth and flowering of the primitive Church of Europe; and Guadalupe appeared as the supernatural sign of the beginnings and progress of the primitive Church of our America."[29]

Revelation—at least Revelation 12—was thus transformed by a daring exegesis into what might be called a Mexican prophecy.

In the prefatory approbation of *The Translation of the Church to Guadalupe* (1748), we read: "In Chapter 12 of Revelation, which so truthfully describes the miraculous apparition of our Lady of

Guadalupe, following the evangelist's ecstatic vision of this prodigy, the celestial woman. . . ."[30] In the essay of the *bachiller* Sánchez the Mexican Guadalupan tradition first appears with the features that have remained peculiarly its own down to our time—the prophetic roots and the patriotic implications that constitute its originality.[31] Francisco de la Maza's analysis of the subject excuses me from duplicating his effort. I resume my inquiry where Maza leaves off, when he writes: "Miguel Sánchez accepts the Guadalupan tradition and develops it by providing it with a theological foundation, without which it would have remained a formless legend."[32] Of the tradition which may have inspired the *bachiller,* the "first evangelist of Guadalupe," we know only those aspects on which Montúfar's inquiry throws light. We must conclude, therefore, either that Miguel Sánchez invented almost the whole tradition, or else that it grew up in the course of the years—a little less than a century—that separate Bustamante's protest from the apologia of Sánchez.

The first hypothesis is most unlikely, although enemies of the apparition have advanced it. These critics base themselves on the letter addressed to Miguel Sánchez by Luis Lazo de la Vega, "vicar of the holy chapel of Guadalupe," after he had read his book. The vicar of Guadalupe wrote, in effect: "All my predecessors and I have been slumbering Adams, though all the while we possessed this new Eve in the paradise of her Mexican Guadalupe."[33] To be sure, this is a disturbing admission; it suggests that the priests attached to the service of the basilica of Guadalupe since its foundation, which went back to 1622, had been unaware of the tradition of the "apparitions" and the "prodigious image," until the publication of Miguel Sánchez' book in 1648. However, we must place this statement in its context and make allowance for hyperbole. Lazo de la Vega (a new Saint Paul following the evangelist Sánchez) writes immediately after: "But now I have the privilege of being Adam awakened to see her in the image and in the account of your *History:* to see her entire, yet in her different aspects, in the prodigy of the miracle, in the event of her Apparition, in the mysteries that her painting signifies. . . . Truly, I could say what Adam said."[34]

In the context of a letter of thanks to the author, who had offered his book to him, this is nothing more, I believe, than a hyperbolic eulogy of a devotee of Guadalupe, such as a priest devoted to her image of Tepeyac must have been. At the start of his letter Lazo de la Vega wrote: "to me, entrusted with the sovereign relic of the miraculous Image of the Virgin Mary, whom the angels alone merit to have for their companion, that they might serve her."[35] Thus, even before having read Miguel Sánchez, Lazo de la Vega knew that he served "a relic" and a "miraculous image"; what he found in Miguel Sánchez was an ordering (*formada*) of the elements of the tradition, clarity in its exposition (*compuesta*), and above all a deciphering of the Guadalupan symbol in the light of Revelation 12, which conferred a new patriotic and transcendent significance upon the *Mariophany*, or new epiphany of Tepeyac.

Miguel Sánchez ordered and interpreted, or rather "deciphered," the factual or anecdotal elements of the miraculous tradition of Guadalupe in the light of Scripture, but where did he find them? We cannot avoid this question, once we agree that the contribution of the *bachiller* Sánchez was exegetic rather than documentary. Had it been otherwise, his book would certainly have provoked a scandal, as always happened when someone tampered with a pious tradition. It is at least plausible, as Francisco de la Maza believes, that Sánchez borrowed his edifying account of the successive "apparitions" of Mary from their depiction in the already numerous ex-votos of the basilica and, one might add, from oral tradition. Francisco de la Maza has shed light on the links between the *bachiller* Sánchez and the vicar Lazo de la Vega. One year later Lazo de la Vega published, in Nahuatl, a version of the pious legend for the use of the Indians: *Huey Tlamahuicoltica omonexiti in ilhuicac Tlatoca cihuapilli Santa Maria,— Iotlaconantzin Guadalupe in nican huei altepenahuac Mexico itocayocan Tepeyacac.*[36]

This book has given rise to controversy; for some, like Joaquín García Icazbalceta, it represents an adaptation for a more naive public of the exegetic audacities of *bachiller* Sánchez; others see it as a borrowing from an older Indian chronicle, the work of a certain Antonio Valeriano. Again I refer the reader to the study of Francisco de la Maza, who dismisses this hypothesis. We have already studied a comparable problem, that of the group of histories by Fray Diego Durán, Juan de Tovar, and Tezozomoc, who, according to certain authors, derived from a common source (called *Crónica X* by Robert Barlow), an Indian chronicle. In the case of Lazo de la Vega, we observe that in his preface he declares three times that he wrote down the miraculous tradition in Nahuatl and protests his insufficient knowledge of that language: "Would that I had enough mastery of that fiery Nahuatl language to describe the great miracle of her apparition to those poor natives."[37] In the absense of valid reasons for charging Lazo de la Vega with a literary hoax, I assume that he is the author of *Huey Tlamahuicoltica;* if a hoax had taken place, its most likely object would have been to pass the book off as a native work.

It appears that the first effort to base the Guadalupan tradition on native Nahuatl sources was the much later effort of Boturini, who devoted the last chapters (24–26) of his *Catálogo del Museo Histórico Indiano* to Guadalupe. The catalog ends with this profession of faith: *Laus Deo, et Virgini Guadalupensi per infinita saeculorum saecula. Amen.* ("Praise be to God, and to the Virgin of Guadalupe, for ever and ever. Amen.")

Boturini affirms that the history of Lazo de la Vega "is not and cannot be the work of that author" but gives no reasons for this categorical statement. He intended to prove that its author was Antonio Valeriano or some other Indian, a student of the colegio "of Santiago Tlatelolco, a contemporary of the miracle of those apparitions."[38] Unfortunately, the history of Our Lady of Guadalupe which Boturini proposed to write and in which he intended to prove all he had affirmed in his *Catálogo* never saw the light of day, as a result of the confiscation of his library and his expulsion from New Spain. One cannot seriously believe that the Roman *cavaliere* made up out of whole cloth the Guadalupan manuscripts in Nahuatl of which he gives a list and a very succinct analysis in his *Catálogo.* There is the less reason to doubt the existence of these documents because an illustrious son of Puebla, Mariano Fernández de Echeverría y Veitia, who inherited Boturini's writings, utilized them in preparing his own version of the miraculous tradition of Guadalupe; but Boturini and Veitia wrote at the end of the eighteenth century.

The Patriotic Significance of Guadalupe

The question of the authenticity of the missing Nahuatl sources mentioned by Boturini to buttress the Guadalupan tradition is not really very important from the viewpoint of this book. For the historian of Mexico, Guadalupe "appeared" not so much in 1531, the date given by the pious tradition, nor even in 1556, when Montúfar's inquiry confirmed the existence of a new cult, but above all in 1648 and 1649. The two Guadalupan essays of Miguel Sánchez and Lazo de la Vega appeared a year apart. The two books could pass for two more of the many works of devotion published in New Spain in that period. But they had a special meaning, at least in the long run, for they were the first step toward recognition of Guadalupe as the Mexican national symbol. We noted above the strong impression made on Lazo de la Vega by Miguel Sánchez's Guadalupan essay: Lazo de la Vega found it a true revelation. If a priest devoted to Guadalupe, serving in her basilica of Tepeyac, had been a "slumbering Adam" until the day he read the book, it was because that book metamorphosed the "miraculous reputation" of the image of Tepeyac into a transcendent event.

What was the contribution of Miguel Sánchez to the oral tradition and its naive depiction in the ex-votos? Most important of all, he gave it prophetic roots whose eschatological significance would fully emerge a century later, when the millenarian fever was reborn. Over the bridge thus thrown between Tepeyac and the Revelation of John, the eighteenth-century preachers, followed by the nineteenth-century revolutionaries would boldly advance. But for the moment let us stay in that seventeeth-century milieu in which creole New Spain searches for its destiny in Scripture. The first chapter of Sánchez's book makes the title, which already mentions the prophecy of Revelation 12, more explicit: "Prophetic Original of the Holy Image Piously Foreseen by the Evangelist Saint John, in Chapter Twelve of Revelation."[39] Thus, according to Sánchez, the first to "see," prophetically, the celestial original of Guadalupe was the apostle Saint John, for his description of the Woman of the Apocalypse corresponds to the image of Tepeyac. Basing himself on Saint Augustine, for whom the most faithful image of God in this world was that of the Virgin Mary, the author went on to affirm that Guadalupe, "so miraculous by reason of the circumstances of her apparition, and so revered in this land," is the most perfect replica of the Virgin.[40] He deduced this conclusion with the aid of syllogisms. "It follows, then (for I have always loved the syllogistic style of the logicians) . . . that God executed his admirable design in this Mexican land, conquered for such glorious ends, gained in order that a most divine image might appear here."[41] Make no mistake, these words signified a true revolution.

To be sure, the creole *bachiller* compared the king of Spain to the sun, but he also invoked the authority of the prophet David in Psalm 47 in support of his opinion that if Mary lived on Mount Zion, "we can rightly give the same name to the hill of Guadalupe."[42] If Tepeyac is a new Mount Zion, it is because the "translation" of the Virgin Mary to her shrine of Guadalupe, which a century later became the subject of a famous sermon, is already an accepted idea. Moreover, Mary "showed herself to Juan Diego just as Rebecca showed herself to her son Jacob."[43] Behold the humble Indian convert transformed into Jacob's rival. Again, the strong woman of Proverbs "very clearly prophesied the Virgin Mary in her domain of Guadalupe, where she founded her chapel."[44] One problem confronted the devout *bachiller:* the Virgen de los Remedios, an inevitable rival of Guadalupe whose tradition circulated in print (in a work by Juan de Grijalva) since 1624. Why should the Virgin Mary not have chosen her image "of the Remedies," so near the sick Indian's house, to restore him to health? The example of Ruth and Naomi offered the apologist a compromise solution. Naomi being a "creole of Bethlehem," Ruth had come from her country of Moab to accompany Naomi. Just so the Virgen de los

Remedios, "who came from Spain in the company of the conquistadors," was as worthy of veneration as the new Naomi, "the creole Virgin of Guadalupe, who appeared in Mexico."[45] The devotees of Remedios thus had no reason to complain about the votaries of Guadalupe. What is remarkable here is the identification of Mexican reality with the Holy Land and the prophetic books. We recognize here those *conceptos predicables* of which Father Antonio Vieira was then the master in the Luso-Brazilian world, conceits in which text and sensuous reality became interchangeable. In the eighteenth century the Dominican Mier would poke fun at the fantasies of the preacher Sánchez.

Miguel Sánchez went so far as to claim that the image of Guadalupe was "the first creole woman, a native of this land."[46] On the prophetic level, historic time is abolished. Guadalupe has been Mexican, *criolla,* for all time—was it not her that John saw at Patmos? As for the Mexican creoles, descendants of Spaniards but born in the land of Anahuac, they are nothing less than "sons of the Virgin of Guadalupe" (*hijos de la Virgen de Guadalupe*). For Miguel Sánchez all shrines of the Virgin Mary resemble each other except one, Tepeyac, "a new paradise, set aside, sure, and protected."[47] The myth of the "Western Paradise," principally known through a later work by one of New Spain's greatest authors, Carlos de Sigüenza y Góngora, received a solid foundation. Later Sor Juana Inés de la Cruz and Sigüenza y Góngora, followed by the preachers of the eighteenth century, would only have to gloss, develop, and embellish this prophetic and idyllic vision of the Mexican creole *patria,* preserved by Guadalupe from all evils (the dragon of Revelation). Miguel Sánchez thus emerges as the true founder of the Mexican *patria,* for on the exegetic bases which he constructed in the mid-seventeenth century that *patria* would flower until she won her political independence under the banner of Guadalupe. From the day the Mexicans began to regard themselves as a chosen people, they were potentially liberated from Spanish tutelage.

Was Miguel Sánchez simply a devotee of Guadalupe who knew Scripture better than a multitude of others, or was he a patriot conscious of the subversive potential of his pious book? If we assume the latter, we must view as base or hypocritical the passage devoted to the "Catholic Sun of the Spains" which illuminated Mexico, thanks to the Conquest. This would be unfair. Miguel Sánchez' interpretation of Psalm 61 makes Spain the sun and Mexico the moon; this is fully in the tradition of historico-allegorical exegesis. To make Miguel Sánchez a premature Mexican revolutionary would be an anachronism. But he was certainly a creole patriot, fully conscious of being one, as the final address of his book on Guadalupe attests: "I have written it for my *patria,* for my friends and comrades, for the citizens of this new world."[48] It was the Mexican *patria* which inspired the *bachiller* to write his devout book. A final apostrophe to the apostle Saint John (willy-nilly become a creole apologist) made clear that the book was written to promote: "the honor of Mexico City . . . the glory of all the faithful who live in this New World."[49] The apocalyptic seal affixed by Miguel Sánchez to his *patria*'s historic destiny simultaneously charged it with a messianic expectation and conferred on its people the honor of being a chosen people. More particularly, the exegetic daring of the creole *bachiller* demolished the traditional idea that the Spaniards, a new chosen people, had been designated by providence to bring the Gospel to the gentiles of the New World. Sánchez had deduced "by syllogism," we recall, that the conquest of Mexico, the land of God, "gained in order that a most divine image might appear here," had been accomplished for "glorious ends."[50] This was nothing less than a Copernican revolution.

Sánchez had advanced a new providential interpretation of the Conquest that was incompatible with the prevailing one. Although the Spanish conquistadors still appear as instruments of God, they no longer have the leading role, which has devolved upon the first creole woman, the Virgin of Guadalupe. Consequently the historiography of the Conquest must be revised. More, the pre-Conquest Indian past, and even the history of Christendom as it marched toward its consummation, that is, the providential unfolding of the history of humanity, on which the Guadalupan interpretation of the apocalyptic vision of John cast a new light, must also be revised. Along the road that Miguel Sánchez had opened up, coming creole generations were to march, without questioning the prophetic and patriotic revelations of the spiritual father of the Mexican nation.

Were Sánchez' immediate contemporaries conscious of the importance of his book? Did they calculate that the revelation of a bond between the messianic hopes of Christendom and the creole cult of Guadalupe would make Mexico a new Holy Land and its inhabitants a new chosen people? At least some understood it, like a certain substitute professor of the Prime chair in theology at the university and "prebendary of the holy metropolitan Church of Mexico City."[51] Breaking with the custom of compliment in verse, he wrote a letter by way of a preface to Miguel Sánchez' essay. This Doctor Francisco de Siles declared that he spoke for all his compatriots: "I speak and write in the name of the whole *patria,* which received your history as the letters patent of its grandeur."[52] Clearly, Sánchez' history is the "letters patent" of Mexican grandeur, that is, a document which conferred a title of nobility or a royal favor, but it was God himself who granted that favor. What the king had so parsimoniously doled out to the creoles, God lavished upon them through the intercession of the Virgin Mary in her prodigious image of Tepeyac. What would the "letters patent" of the Spanish king henceforth mean to the Mexicans? Sánchez and the writer of the preface are careful not to spell out the point but their readers would have no difficulty in grasping it for themselves. Recall that Cortés himself had to beg for royal "favors," that he was one of the very few conquistadors to obtain a title of *marqués*, that he was quickly stripped of his governing powers, that his *marquesado* and the privileges attached to it were disputed and amputated. All the literature of the viceroyalty, civil and religious, echoes the grievances of the creoles—whether descendants of conquistadors or not—disappointed in their ambition for revenues and honors, power and dignity. Miguel Sánchez supplied them with a dazzling metaphysical compensation, "for you have introduced into the sacred asylum of the divine Virgin Mary all who were born in this country," as Doctor Siles writes; *el sagrado,* in other words the inviolable asylum where Guadalupe, "a new Esther, our chief and queen,"[53] will protect the Mexicans from all attacks. Let me note in passing that Guadalupe appears here for the first time as "Queen of the Mexicans," a notion which was to have a large historical future.

The history of Guadalupe as told by Sánchez, wrote Doctor Siles, ensured that in the future "all our compatriots, like others, will have letters and legal powers . . . that will serve all who are born in this New World as letters of credence, safe-conduct, and security in every part of the world."[54] We see here a reflection of creole rivalry with peninsular Spaniards, the *gachupines,* who landed in New Spain knowing nothing of the country and its inhabitants (whom they took a priori for barbarians), but provided by the king and the Council of the Indies with "legal powers" (*provisiones selladas*), always bearing a seal, which they used for their protection and advancement. By raising the competition to the supernatural level, Miguel Sánchez made it possible for his compatriots to triumph "magically" over the *gachupines,* those "others" to whom Doctor Siles refers in veiled terms.

Henceforth the Mexican creoles would be provided, like those "others," with letters and powers. Since the king had not wished to grant them, God himself had performed that act of grace. Guadalupe would be forever and ever, *saecula saeculorum,* the "letters patent" which ennobled the Mexican people. We should not underestimate the role of Doctor Siles in the formation of Mexican national consciousness, for he formulated more clearly and boldly than Miguel

Sánchez himself the consequences for his *patria* of the *bachiller*'s lucu-brations. Later, become principal canon of the cathedral of Mexico City, Doctor Francisco de Siles wrote the Holy See in 1663 to solicit from the Congregation of Rites a special office on December 12 in honor of Guadalupe. He thus initiated a series of representations to the Holy See which did not gain their object until 1754. Siles had attached to his letter a copy of Miguel Sánchez' pious history. The failure of this initiative stimulated the later publication of Guadalu-pan apologias, notably the books of Becerra Tanco and Father Floren-cia. More immediately, Canon Siles took the initiative of launching a new inquiry into the Guadalupan tradition which yielded the *Infor-maciones* of 1666, gathered one century after the inquiry of Bishop Montúfar.

14

The Dispute
of the Apparitions

The Little War of the Supernatural Coats of Arms

Although the royalty of Guadalupe was recognized in New Spain before its acknowledgment in Rome and Madrid, even there its supremacy was not accepted without a struggle. When we attempt to retrace the stages of evolution of the Mexican Guadalupan cult, two dates emerge as especially important. The year 1629, first of all; then it was, as Father Florencia recalls, that the sacred image, carried in procession from Tepeyac to Mexico City, delivered the capital from the menace of floods. Guadalupe was then proclaimed the city's "principal protectress" against inundations. Remembering that from Aztec times Mexico-Tenochtitlan lived under the shadow of this seasonal threat (repeated almost every September), we can understand how deeply felt were the prayers and vows designed to avert it. Mexico City had been slowly won from the lagoons; the Aztec emperors had begun important drainage works which were continued by Cortés, later by Porfirio Díaz. It is an age-old problem which modern technology has not completely solved. For seventeenth-century Mexicans, only divine intervention could dam up the floods. In 1629, by displaying its efficacy in a desperate situation, the image of Tepeyac achieved supremacy over the other protective effigies of the city.

Although flooding was the most ancient scourge of Mexico City, since the Spanish Conquest a new periodic scourge brought death to a considerable portion of the population, notably the Indians; this was the scourge of epidemics (*pestes*). The most destructive came in 1545, from 1576 to 1579, and in 1595 in the valley of Mexico; in the course of the seventeenth century several attacked different regions of New Spain; an epidemic of measles caused great ravages between 1725 and 1728. Worse in one sense than the floods—which it often followed—by reason of its unexpected appearance and mysterious origin, the plague (*cocoliztli*) inspired a feeling of helplessness and terror; collective conjuration of supernatural powers appeared to be the only possible remedy. According to the Jesuit Alegre, in his *Historia,* the epidemic of 1736 caused at least 40,000 deaths in Mexico City (the city had 150,000 inhabitants at most at that date). Prayers were invoked to save the country and not just Mexico City, for the epidemic was even more destructive at Puebla and Querétaro; images of the great biblical cataclysms and the catastrophic end of the Aztec suns must have obsessed the population, whether Indian or creole.

It was in this end-of-the-world atmosphere that the image of Guadalupe of Tepeyac displayed its therapeutic efficacy (well known from the beginnings of the cult) on a scale that promoted her at once from protectress of her individual devotees to savior of the social body as a whole. The aspiration for salvation, not in the beyond but in this life first of all, the thirst for survival, was the true oath of allegiance of all Mexicans to the protective image of Guadalupe. This solemn oath, taken by the municipal magistrates and the civil and ecclesiastical chapters in the name of the whole Mexican nation, united in a common destiny, had an importance for the unity of Mexico comparable to that of the Federation of 1790 for the unity of revolutionary France. At Mexico City in 1737, a sacred bond was created between all Mexicans, who acknowledged themselves to be "serfs of Guadalupe"; according to religious usage, this gesture of the civil community meant that its members consecrated their lives to the image of Tepeyac in recognition of her redeeming prodigy, her victory over the epidemic that was a perfect replica of the victory over the Beast of the Apocalypse. Henceforth Mexican art and literature would be an interminable act of thanks, a protean and baroque collective ex-voto in which the ritual dances (*mitotes*) of the Indians and the legacies of the mineowners (*mineros*), the sermons of the religious and the theses of the theologians, the masterpieces of the painters and the architects, the thousand products of the popular crafts and even of the confectioner's shop celebrated the image of Guadalupe and its pious legend.

To understand how Guadalupe became the Mexican national emblem at the time of the Wars of Independence we must review the previous stages of Guadalupan iconography. I call the reader's attention to the seventh plate of Francisco de la Maza's *El guadalupanismo mexicano,* where the Aztec coat-of-arms, the eagle devouring a serpent on a prickly pear plant (*nopal*) appears as a support for the image of Tepeyac.[1] The angel whose arms hold apart the ends of Mary's robe curiously rides astride the Aztec eagle. At the four corners of the tableau, medallions represent the "apparitions" of the Virgin to Juan Diego, then to Archbishop Zumárraga; the association of the Aztec eagle and the Virgin (perhaps considered dangerously syncretic) does not occur again to my knowledge. On the other hand, combination on the same cloth (or engraving) of the image of Guadalupe and the events of her prodigious manifestations, painted on medallions in the form of edifying tableaux, was to become traditional; this was the form in which the Mexican Guadalupe was popularized, first in Mexico, then in Spain and other countries of Hispanic America. One is struck by the prominent place assigned to Guadalupe in the Church Santa Prisca of Taxco, built about 1754 (the year of the pontifical bull instituting the office of December 12 in honor of Guadalupe); here Guadalupe holds the place of honor. The baroque main altar is surmounted by a retablo in the center of which a shrine contains the image of Tepeyac. A choir of chubby angels point out to the devout the shrine which they support. To the right of Guadalupe is an image of Santa Prisca, virgin and martyr; although the church is named after her, she occupies a secondary position. To the left of the transept, a second retablo representing Guadalupe, to the right a Virgin with child. On the aisles, disposed like stations of the Cross, great medallions evoke the successive "apparitions" of Guadalupe. Similar observations can be made in churches in different parts of Mexico. For example, at San Antonio, Texas, the church of the mission of Saint Joseph, founded by the blessed Antonio Margil de Jesus, still displays in the center of the tympanum, dominating an admirable baroque portal, the image of Guadalupe.

The Jesuit missionaries of California (the names of Fray Junípero Serra and Father Kino have more than one claim to fame) created a town of Guadalupe in that desert which they proposed to integrate into New Spain. Antonio Margil, an illustrious Franciscan missionary, had come out of the apostolic *colegio de Propaganda fide* of Zacatecas, placed under the invocation of Guadalupe. Founded in 1721, the colegio of Guadalupe trained more than seven hundred missionary friars; it is no exaggeration to say that the revival of missionary expansion in New Spain in the eighteenth century had its base there. Supported by a mining center like Zacatecas, with Guadalupe as its patroness, this expansion was a truly Mexican enterprise, originally the work of creole Franciscans, continued by the Jesuits, then again entrusted to Franciscans after the expulsion of the Society of Jesus.

Popular opinion certainly regarded the image of Tepeyac as the national coat of arms from the time of the Virgin's victory over the floods of 1629, but official recognition did not come until 1737, when her patronage over the capital was proclaimed. In this respect, the famous work of C. Cabrera y Quintera marks a milestone in the history of the Mexican cult of Guadalupe. It was written in 1738, the year which followed the taking of the solemn oath: *The Coat of Arms of Mexico: Celestial Protection of this very noble City, of New Spain, and almost all the New World, Holy Mary in Her Prodigious Image of Guadalupe of*

*Mexico City, who Appeared Miraculously in the Archepiscopal Palace in 1531
and Was Sworn the Principal Patroness of Mexico City the Past Year, 1537,
Amid the Anguish Inspired by the Epidemic Which, Having Especially Struck
at the Indians, Mitigated Its Fury Because of the Great Shade Cast by Mary.*[2]

This title of a work by a priest of the archdiocese of Mexico City, an
authorized spokesman of the creole archbishop J. A. de Vizarrón y
Eguiarreta, expresses the principal aspects of the Guadalupe cult at
the time when it became national. Guadalupe is presented as the
radiant coat of arms of the imperial city; her devotees already aspire
to make her the "universal Patroness" of the New World. Of the
successive apparitions, only the last is mentioned, the one which supposedly occurred in Mexico City itself, in the archepiscopal palace.
This apparition has always been controversial, even for devotees of
Guadalupe, but it was important for the first head of a Mexican national church (that resurgence of Mendieta's *Iglesia indiana*), that at its
very birth and in the presence of its first bishop, it should have received this sign of the favor of God. The miraculous intervention of
Guadalupe against the epidemic took place almost exactly two centuries after the "apparitions." This circumstance was calculated to
fascinate creole minds haunted by millenarianism and Indian minds
dominated by a cyclical conception of their history. The archbishop
therefore entrusted Cabrera y Quintana with writing a work of
Guadalupan apologetics which was published in a first edition of eight
hundred copies (a large printing, considering the number of prospec-
tive buyers and potential readers). The municipal council, which
wished to perpetuate the solemn oath of "patronage," assumed the
costs of publication. The example of the capital was soon followed by
the principal towns of New Spain, which recognized and "swore"
Guadalupe to be their "principal protectress" against the
epidemics—scourges which threatened the very existence of what was
already a community of faith but not yet a Mexican nation.

We must not lose sight of the fact, however, that in the background
of the triumphant cult of Guadalupe there was all the spiritual sedi-
ment of the cult of the Virgin in Spain and in the New World. (Father
Constantino Bayle, in his book *Santa María en Indias,* and Father Vargas Ugarte, in his *Historia del culto de María en Iberoamerica,* give a
much more complete picture of this phenomenon than my sketch in a
previous chapter). Let me recall, too, that the Jesuits of New Spain
greatly favored the cult of the rosary and the creation of Marian
confraternities, essential economic and sociological supports of the
cult of the Virgin. The confraternities were in New Spain—as they
still are in old Spain—the true cells of religious and municipal life, or
of communal life in the case of the Indian agrarian communities. The

Virgin Mary appeared from the first in the coat of arms of the New World, for her banner was the banner of Christopher Columbus. Guadalupe, become the emblem of New Spain in North America, appears retrospectively as a specific regional aspect of the image of Mary, not as an effigy on the field of azure of America's coat of arms.

Juan A. Maravall, like Weisbach, has called attention to the importance of symbolic expression in the painting born of the spiritual climate of the Catholic Counter-Reformation. Saint Ignatius Loyola attached a great importance to the imaginative activity of the senses. The moving beauty of the image of Tepeyac was an important factor in its success. The symbolic value of colors in the religious pictures of the Indians reinforced the accumulated sacred power represented by the effigy of the Virgin Mary, confounded with the Woman of Revelation. Indeed, the blue of Mary's mantle could not be distinguished from the jade blue of Quetzalcóatl, a fundamental color of the Mexican religion. The jadeite (*chalchihuitl*) from which the labret of the supreme priest was carved was blue-green in color; the Nahuatl language used a single adjective to designate the blue and the green. Even more important, from the point of view of Mexican creole spirituality, all the thought that we describe as "baroque," for want of a better term, was emblematic. The convergence in New Spain of the dying seventeenth century and the eighteenth century, of conceptism and *culteranismo* on the literary plane, on the one hand, and on the other of Jesuit religiosity, which accorded a special place in spiritual exercises to sensuous representation, conferred a new importance on the religious emblem.

A simple listing of the titles of apologetic works, sermons, or the reading of contemporary poems dedicated to Guadalupe or other pious subjects, reveals the overwhelming preponderance of the emblem. The title that Cabrera y Quintana gave his Guadalupan treatise, *Coat of Arms,* clearly stresses the emblematic intention, but one could cite many other examples: *Sacred Palladium; Polar Star; Seal of Miracles; Tree of Life; Eclipse of the Divine Sun; Flower of Miracles; Celestial Iris; Guadalupan Zodiac; New Jerusalem; Column of America.*[3] All these titles of pious works inspired by the cult of Guadalupe lend themselves easily to plastic representation. The perfect emblem as defined by Orozco y Covarrubias requires a composed figure and a legend; the image of Guadalupe lacked a legend until the inspired citation from Psalm 147 by Father Florencia which subsequently remained attached to the sacred image: "He has not done the like for any other nation." Thus by the end of the seventeenth century the Mexican national emblem had been perfected; it was perfect even from the viewpoint of the chivalric definition which distinguished the emblem from the allegory, the former evoking an exploit of the knight, who bore it on his coat of arms. The image of Guadalupe, surrounded by medallions recalling the apparitions and bearing her charismatic device, was the most radiant coat of arms to which a chivalric city could aspire. The creole utopia of the *Indian Spring* culminates in this masterpiece of renovated emblematic art.

When the emblem, a symbolic form, has a religious instead of a chivalric meaning, it easily assumes the hermetic form of a hieroglyph or an enigma. The genius of the epoch called baroque sought plastic beauty for its own sake as well as for the *concepto;* consequently we observe the luxuriant proliferation of a whole esoteric language of cabbalistic or allegorical origin about the central figures of Christian religious symbolism. I alluded to the symbiosis that took place between Mexican hieroglyphs and Christian symbols, already associated with the symbols of classic antiquity, when I discussed the work of Sigüenza y Góngora. If the Aztec eagle was confounded with the eagle of Patmos so that it could bear the Virgin Mary on its wings to Mount Tepeyac, the iconography of the apocryphal Gospels reinforced the apparent orthodoxy of the solar and selenic symbolism. We note that the star which announced the Davidic Messiah, but which also recalled one of the avatars of Quetzalcóatl, the Morning Star, was present on the doubly azure mantle of Guadalupe. It should cause no surprise that his "Immaculate Moon" conquered the "divine Sun," thanks to an enigmatic victory of the new Mexican coat of arms over the Spanish monarchy, mistress of an empire over which the sun never set. It would be valuable to establish a Mexican emblematic corpus of the seventeenth and eighteenth centuries and to attempt a typological analysis preliminary to a general deciphering. Such a study would be inseparable from an inquiry into the emblematic (and often enigmatic) expression of creole aspirations vis-à-vis Spain.

The apparition, conjoint with that of the Virgin Mary, of a being in whom some saw the angel Gabriel and others the archangel Saint Michael, inspired floods of sacred eloquence which sought to move the auditor and reader by means of a turgid style corresponding to that of contemporary sculpture: "The greatest glory of the highest celestial spirits, of the first of the greatest princes, the archseraph Lord Saint Michael, revealed in his distinguished apparition at Mexico City, at the sovereign feet of Mary, our venerated Queen of Guadalupe."[4] To the allegorical and metaphorical proliferation corresponded the flowering of the emblematic imagination. In Part 1, I gave a sketch of the multitude of pious images, often reputed to be prodigious and always considered to be capable of working miracles. In his history, the Jeronymite Fray Gabriel de Talavera, of the monastery of Guadalupe of Estremadura, had already affirmed: "It does not diminish the credit of the miracles which are told of this great Lady that they are not reported by very ancient authors."[5] The miracles worked in the recent past by the Mexican Guadalupe, like those worked by the Guadalupe of Spain, sufficed to confirm the authenticity of the tradition of her "apparitions." This doctrine also held good for the numerous images of Mary and the "holy Christs" venerated in the different dioceses of New Spain; accordingly none of the miraculous Virgins of the country was ready to yield precedence to the new star, Guadalupe, coat of arms of the capital. In Mexico City itself, four protective images of the Virgin Mary at first disputed the "Patronage," as suggested by a devotional work by an author of capital importance for our subject. This was the *Bastions of Mexico City. Historical Relation of Four Sacred and Miraculous Images of Our Lady, the Virgin Mary, Venerated Outside the City Walls, and Description of Their Temples,*[6] by M. Fernández de Echeverría y Veitia. This book was not published until 1820, in Mexico City, but must have been written before 1780, the year of the author's death. In the second half of the eighteenth century, the preeminence of Guadalupe over her rivals was no longer disputed, and it is significant that Echeverría y Veitia devoted two-thirds of his book to the Virgin of Tepeyac, barely one-third to the Virgin de los Remedios, and only seven pages each to Nuestra Señora de la Piedad and Nuestra Señora de la Bala. These last two effigies of the Virgin Mary are now forgotten by comparison with that of Guadalupe, the object of a national and even international cult, or with that of Remedios, emblem of the *gachupín* party during the Wars of Independence. Mexicans could divide their fervor between Guadalupe and Remedios. But Remedios was linked directly to a dramatic episode of the Conquest, the "Sad Night," in the course of which the fleeing Spaniards suffered a disastrous loss of life. Guadalupe, on the other hand, according to the legend, had lavished her grace on a poor Indian convert and his family. To the degree that the creoles vaguely sensed the need for a national unity of faith, Guadalupe better symbolized the common hope.

The "first evangelist" of Guadalupe, Miguel Sánchez, skillfully balanced the two images to the detriment of neither. In his *Novenas of the Virgin Mary de los Remedios and of the Virgin Mary of Guadalupe* he offers us his preparatory "spiritual meditations"; the meditation for Saturday, "Of the Choir of the Thrones," deserves summary here. It is an allegorical exegesis of Psalm 88 of David: "His throne will be like the Sun and the Moon in my presence. . . ." I gloss the two words which refer to the Virgin. The first is the throne like the moon, the conquering image of Remedios, in which are shown the properties and names of the moon: "Beauty of the night" (torch), "in the great [sad] Night," "Diana, companion of hunters," "she wished to appear in a wood," "mother of the dew," "mother of the rains, Remedy for great droughts."

The throne that is like the Sun is represented by the divine Image of Guadalupe, who is depicted in the middle of a sun. . . . "Or just as the Moon, in the form of Remedios, brings the rains in periods of drought, so the Sun of Guadalupe dries the waters in the period of floods, as she did after the greatest flood that was ever seen."[7] Allegorical exegesis was a springboard from which Miguel Sánchez vaulted to the peaks of creole syncretic spirituality: "For the apparitions of her two images the Virgin chose two neighboring hills which, ever confronting each other, contemplate each other in their glory, like the two miraculous mountains of Thabor and Hermon. . . . The two Indians, brothers in race and in their common name of John; the plant, the maguey, was the same. It was a maguey on which the image of Remedios first appeared; from the fiber of the same plant was woven the humble mantle on which was miraculously imprinted the image of Guadalupe."[8] If meditations of this kind had reached Indian ears, what echoes might they not have awakened? One Virgin appears on a maguey, another is miraculously imprinted on a cloth of maguey fiber; one brings the rains, like Tlaloc, and the other is aureoled with the sun, like Tonatiuh. Through the metamorphosis of beliefs the Mexicans rediscovered their solar emblem, obscured by the Conquest. There, perhaps, is one of the secrets of the enigmatic figure of Tepeyac.

The coat of arms of Mexico City, granted by Charles V, only recalled the exploit of the Conquest and was not a supernatural sign. In this respect another "imperial" city (an appelation conferred as a privilege on a small number of cities) of New Spain, was much more favored. The coat of arms of Puebla evoked the prophetic dream of the Franciscan bishop of Tlaxcala, Fray Julián Garcés; in that dream he saw angels surveying the terrain and delimiting the bounds of the new colony. (A *puebla* in medieval Spain was a new city, like the *bastides* of medieval France.) "La Puebla de los Angeles," born of an inspired vision, was a utopian creation, symbolically achieved beside a great sanctuary of idolatry, Cholula, the holy city of Quetzalcóatl. The creoles saw in this circumstance a design of divine providence. At the summit of the great pyramid of Quetzalcóatl, often compared to the Tower of Babel, the religious had constructed a chapel dedicated to the Virgin de los Remedios. Thus Puebla was the only city of New Spain that could dispute Mexico City's primacy in grace. When the Mexicans, by reason of the acknowledgment of the patronage of

Guadalupe over Mexico City (an example followed by other towns), replaced their chivalric coat of arms, granted by the emperor, with the emblem given by heaven, la Puebla de los Angeles felt that it had been outclassed in the order of hieroglyphic symbols. Mexico City had just secured for itself first place among the cities of New Spain in the one domain in which she had not excelled before; henceforth she was "protected, distinguished, and marked with the seal of the Most High."[9] The refusal of the master of ceremonies of the cathedral of Puebla to bend to the canonical decree issued in favor of Guadalupe "by virtue of being the elected and sworn Patroness" was only an impotent protest;[10] the "disputed patronage" could no longer be denied to Guadalupe of Tepeyac, nor, by the same token, could one question the preeminence of Mexico City, which henceforth possessed divine letters of nobility.

The Persecuted Champions of Guadalupe:
Mier's Sermon (1794)

The importance of the cult of Our Lady of Guadalupe in Mexican spiritual life, with its numerous intellectual and artistic repercussions, was only equalled by the weakness of the pious tradition's historical foundations. In this contradiction between the uncommon power of expansion of the cult of Guadalupe and the weakness of the "proofs" resides the explanation of the interminable "quarrel of Guadalupe" (which has not yet ended). This double attraction: the élan of the cult and the passionate search for its historiographic foundations, was felt almost from his landing in Mexico by a Milanese gentleman named Lorenzo Boturini Benaducci. He arrived in New Spain in February 1736, sent by the Countess of Santiesteban, descendant of Moctezuma, and one could say that the shadow of Moctezuma hung over his Mexican career. Father Díaz de la Vega wrote about him in 1783: "Among the authors I have consulted, the most favorable to the Indians is the *cavaliere* Don Lorenzo Boturini."[11] What I dare not anachronistically call his "Indianism" took the devout form appropriate to that society. He writes: "Hardly had I arrived [in Mexico] when I felt myself driven by an invincible attraction to undertake research into the prodigious miracle of the apparitions of Our Lady of Guadalupe; I discovered that its history was based on a single tradition and that it was not known where or into whose hands the written proofs of such a great prodigy had fallen."[12] His point of view remained fundamentally the same as that of his predecessors, the creole religious who had sought for traces of the apostle Saint Thomas. Men did not doubt the preaching of Saint Thomas, nor the apparitions of Guadalupe; all that was necessary was to organize a kind of race to find the documentary treasure. The codices assembled by Boturini, whose ensemble constituted the *Museo Histórico Indiano,* inspired in the unfortunate collector this reflection: "It [the Indian museum] may be considered one of the greatest treasures of the Indies."[13] To disinter the Indian past (*la gentilidad*) and provide an incontrovertible documentary foundation for the tradition of Guadalupe were two complementary aspects of a single enterprise.

But that enterprise was gravely compromised by an excess of pious zeal on the part of the *cavaliere.* Having obtained from the Holy See in 1740 the canonical authorizations necessary for a public coronation of the image of Tepeyac, Boturini did not trouble to seek authorization from the Council of the Indies. Worst of all, he had been imprudent enough to organize a collection to cover the expenses of his devout project, soliciting communities and individuals. The Conde de Fuenclara, the newly arrived viceroy, had him arrested and brought to trial. The charges against him came down to this: he was a foreigner in New Spain without permission, he had meddled indiscreetly in a Spanish national question. Guadalupe was quite literally an affair of state; the trial of Boturini in 1748 implicitly acknowledged the fact. The imprudent *cavaliere* was exiled to Spain and his documents were confiscated. To be sure, he was rehabilitated some years later and named official historiographer of the Indies, but he remains the first illustrious martyr of the Mexican Guadalupan movement.

Yet his work was useful; in addition to the salvage of numerous documents, it brought together the only manuscripts in Nahuatl relating to the "apparitions" of Guadalupe. In the *Catálogo del Museo indiano* there figures in particular the testament of the Indian cacique Francisco Verdugo Quetzalmalitzin, the most ancient documentary trace of the existence of a cult of the Virgin of Guadalupe at Tepeyac. Although the "History of Guadalupe" projected by Boturini never saw the light of day, his *Prólogo galeato* promised to supply thirty-one proofs for the tradition of the apparitions. What was new, and would establish a school, was his view of the Indian codices and hymns as historical documents worthy of faith and not simply "fables"—documents that could be used in determining the authenticity of a Christian religious tradition. In other words, Boturini qualified the Indians as witnesses regarding pious traditions, whereas their testimony was rejected in court trials, since Spanish law regarded them as minors. We note, too, that Boturini was charged with having sought to place over the crown he intended for Guadalupe some other emblem than the royal coat of arms. For all these reasons, Boturini's pious designs were resented by the Mexican authorities (and doubtless by the creoles, who did not grant him the financial support he had hoped for) as profanation by a foreign hand, no matter how well intentioned, of a national sanctuary.

Very different, in this respect, was the situation of the Dominican Fray Servando Teresa de Mier, a son of the creole aristocracy who had taken his degrees at the Royal and Pontifical University of Mexico City, a preacher who enjoyed enough of a reputation to be invited to deliver the sermon in the basilica of Tepeyac, December 12, 1794, the feast day of Guadalupe. Now, half a century after Boturini, Mier also became a victim of an indiscreet zeal in the service of Guadalupe. It is a remarkable fact that the sermon that cost Fray Servando a long exile had the same origin as the historical projects of his Milanese forerunner. Mier, like Boturini, felt the weakness of the pious tradition and sought to attach it to the Indian past so as to give it an unshakable foundation. But, being less scholarly and more speculative than Boturini, he followed the example of the licentiate Borunda in attempting an allegorical exegesis of the native hieroglyphs. The sermon in which he expounded his views on the Guadalupan tradition provoked an inquisitorial reaction on the part of Archbishop Haro y Peralta, himself a devotee of the Virgin of Tepeyac. In effect, Mier was brought before the tribunal of the Inquisition (of which his uncle had been president) and was called on to repudiate his theses. As happened to Boturini before him, and to Veitia (posthumously), his library was confiscated. Like the Milanese, several years later he was rehabilitated by the Council of the Indies. By contrast with his forerunner Boturini, Fray Bernardo was a creole like Veitia, who served as his bondsman. Veitia played a notable role in the development of the pious tradition of creole Mexico; he was denied permission to publish his manuscripts in New Spain, but they were used by Fray Servando Teresa de Mier. His *Bastions of Mexico City*,[14] which assigns the premier place to the Virgin of Guadalupe, was written in 1775 but not published until 1820, and his monumental *Historia antigua de México* did not appear until 1836.[15] Another work which might be called, by analogy with the codices of the Vatican and Rheims, the *Codex Veitia*,[16] a series of plates designed to serve as illustrations to the *Historia Antigua,* did not see the light of day until 1945. On his death, his confiscated manuscripts were sent to the royal library, where Juan Bautista Muñoz first used them. As the basis for his *Discurso histórico-crítico* against the miraculous tradition of Guadalupe, Muñoz employed Veitia's version, a cautious synthesis of previous writings. Veitia's posthumous work also included an important *Historia de la fundación de la Puebla de los Angeles* and *Tablas chronológicas para ajustar el calendario tulteca con el nuestro.* These writings constitute a veritable corpus devoted to the principal aspects of the religious and cultural history of ancient and colonial Mexico. (The last two mentioned works are in volumes 3 and 5 of the manuscripts of the Muñoz collection of the Biblioteca de la Real Academia de la Historia, in Madrid, where I consulted them.) Marcel Bataillon has rightly observed to me that a study of Veitia's works—a true crossroads of Mexican creole historiography and the Spanish critical response—would form a valuable supplement to the present work. A correspondent of the exiled Clavijero, Veitia, born in that citadel of criollismo, the bishopric of Puebla, was an apologist both for Guadalupe and Saint Thomas-Quetzalcóatl.

Mier, we know, proposed to identify the apostle Saint Thomas with the Mexican divinity Quetzalcóatl. By his own admission, the idea was not new, but he enriched it with a truly new hypothesis. Hitherto historians of the Conquest, inspired by a providential spirit, had reasoned as follows: "Not without a Providential design did the infinite Wisdom prepare the natural throne that is the hill of Cholula in this North America, that it might become the Throne of new cults and the Remedy of the afflicted. . . . Some claim that the Indians in the time of their paganism venerated there a goddess to whom they offered sacrifices."[17] Just as the pyramid of Quetzalcóatl at Cholula had been mysteriously constructed to serve as a base for the future basilica of the Virgen de los Remedios, so the shrine of Tonantzin on Mount Tepeyac, center of pilgrimages, had been a "teething ring" for Our Lady of Guadalupe. Taking a position against a historiography which still reflected the policy of "rupture" of the Franciscan pioneers and also drew inspiration from Saint Augustine, Fray Servando suggested a pure and simple assimilation of Indian polytheism into Christianity. In his *Apologia* he justified the language of his sermon: "Who was this Tzenteotinantzin or Tonantzin, whom Quetzalcóatl taught the Indians to know and who from those remote times had been venerated on the hill of Tepeyac, which was named Tonantzin after her? To know the answer it is enough to read Torquemada and Cabrera. She was a Virgin consecrated to God, in the service of the Temple, who by the will of Heaven conceived and bore—without loss of her virginity—the Lord with the Crown of Thorns or Teohuitzahuac, who partook both of human and divine nature, was born a fully grown man . . . and at birth destroyed a serpent that was pursuing his mother. . . .

"This Lord of the Crown of Thorns, whom the Indians also depicted nude, holding in his hand a cross composed of five tufts of feathers, was also called Mexi."[18] Here was damning evidence, more than enough to send Fray Servando to the stake. But in the spiritual climate of eighteenth-century New Spain the sermon might have gone unnoticed if the imprudent preacher had not attempted to revise the Guadalupan tradition.

What seemed heretical (heretical in relation to a Guadalupan orthodoxy whose customary canon law was more rigorous than the written law of the Congregation of Rites) was Mier's critical attitude toward the "apparitions." Evidently drawing inspiration from the apologetic tradition of the Virgin of Pilar (as recounted by Mariana and restated by Peralta y Barnuevo, who put the Virgin's appearance back to the time of the evangelization of Spain by the apostle Saint James), Mier got the idea of linking the evangelization of Mexico by the apostle Saint Thomas to the image of Tepeyac. But he stopped midway, for he decided that the supposedly divine *ayate,* or cloth of maguey fiber, was simply an ancient Mexican painting. Mier's use of external criticism, based on his knowledge of traditional Aztec painting technique, thus refuted the official physicians—the *proto-médicos*—who during the inquiry of 1666 had solemnly affirmed the "prodigious renovation" of the sacred image. Still later, in his *Apologia,* Fray Servando went so far as to write that "the image of the village of Tecaxic [Calixtlahuaca] is identical as a painting and as cloth with Our Lady of Guadalupe. No one claims on that account that it is painted on the cloak of an Indian, although there, too, they tell of an apparition. There were innumerable such paintings in New Spain right after the Conquest. Torquemada relates that the Indians painted many images that they brought to the churches and left there, so that new ones were found daily, and none knew who had brought them."[19] The Dominican thus demolished the principal elements of the pious tradition, offering rational explanations for all the things that the apologists of Guadalupe had tried for one and a half centuries to pass off as supernatural manifestations. Mier also noted that the Indians, unlike the creoles, continued to celebrate the feast day of Guadalupe on September 8, not December 12, and recalled that according to Torquemada "all the pious images venerated down to his time on the retablos of New Spain had been painted in back of the convent of San Francisco in the painting workshop that the Flemish lay brother Pedro of Ghent installed for the Indians."[20] The iconoclastic Mier explains everything; he was the first to write that Miguel Sánchez "invented" the tradition of the apparitions.

Strange as it may seem, Fray Servando's sole intent was to establish the cult of Guadalupe on unshakable foundations. He later boasted that he had gained the support of the official historiographer of the Indies, Juan Bautista Muñoz: "He analyzed my sermon and demonstrated that my system offered the only means of answering the arguments against the tradition of Guadalupe. . . ."[21] Fray Servando offered the Guadalupan tradition a way out of the impasse by proposing that the *ayate* of Tepeyac was not the cloak of the Indian Juan Diego but of the apostle Saint Thomas; the Archbishop of Mexico City (who spoke for all the devout, no matter what Mier might say) rejected the solution. The Dominican's inquisitorial trial remains the official record of a heretical deviation from the orthodoxy of the Mexican Guadalupan faith, the only faith jealously protected in the "New Rome," Mexico City.

The Discurso histórico-crítico *of Muñoz, the Judgment of the* Real Academia de la Historia *(1794)*

In view of the growing importance of the Mexican cult of Guadalupe, accompanied by a flood of sacred oratory and a burgeoning Guadalupan apologetical literature in New Spain, the supreme tribunal of Spanish historiography, the Real Academia de la Historia, could not remain silent on the subject without being derelict in its duty. It finally spoke through the voice of one of its members, still only an associate member (*miembro supernumerario*), but superbly qualified to assemble the necessary documentation. In 1779 Don Juan Bautista Muñoz had been charged by the Crown with writing a history of America; in order to facilitate his task, a royal order opened up to him all the public archives. Muñoz immediately undertook to inventory the Archivo de las Indias. "I have discovered a treasure; this name could well be given to a mass of original documents of every kind which were buried there, and of which nothing was known,"[22] he wrote in the first volume of his *Historia del Nuevo Mundo* (1793). This was the only published volume of a work which promised to be a monumental contribution to the historiography of the Indies, and which would have helped to dispel the heavy shadow cast on Spain's work in America by the Abbé Raynal in his *Histoire philosophique et politique . . . des Européens dans les deux Indes.*[23] Muñoz clearly defined his historical method in the prologue to his *Historia.* "The subject matter, organization, and style were left entirely to my free choice. . . ."[24] "I assumed an attitude of radical doubt with regard to all that had been published on these matters, with the firm intention of verifying the facts by reference to authentic and irrefutable documents."[25] In this same spirit, the next year he began his inquiry into the Mexican tradition of Guadalupe, determined, as he wrote in the prologue to the *Historia,* to bring out "all the important truths, without concealing any from regard for what the world may think."[26] As concerns his documentation on the subject, we know that a large part of it was already assembled for the purpose of writing the *Historia del*

Nuevo Mundo; the proof is in the form of manuscripts of the Muñoz collection preserved in the Academia de la Historia. In a letter dated December 29, 1783 (that is, eleven years before the reading before the Academy of the *Discurso histórico-crítico*) the archivist of Simancas wrote Muñoz to inform him of the dispatch "by special courier, of a series of documents of the archives," with express mention of "information touching Our Lady of Guadalupe of Mexico City."[27] By virtue of his historical method, his office of historiographer of the Indies, and the documents at his disposal, Juan Bautista Muñoz was certainly the best qualified man in Spain to elucidate the thorny question of the Mexican Guadalupan tradition.

The essay published in volume 5 of the *Memorias de la Real Academia de la Historia,* in 1817, with the title *Memoria sobre las apariciones y el culto de Nuestra Señora de Guadalupe de México,*[28] had been originally entitled by the author *Discurso histórico-crítico sobre las apariciones y el culto de Nra. Señora de Guadalupe de Mexico.*[29] The expression *discurso histórico-crítico* defines precisely the spirit of this communication to the Academia read by Muñoz April 18, 1794, and submitted to two reviewers especially assigned to the task before being approved by the general assembly of the Academia and finally published. The "appropbation" of the Academy, following the report of the two censors, makes the *Discurso histórico-crítico* appear to be the official expression and even (in view of the polemical atmosphere surrounding Mier's sermon) the "sentence" of a body whose mission was precisely to define and protect historiographic orthodoxy.

The *Discurso histórico-crítico* brings into play all the documents and all the major arguments that would henceforth support the "anti apparition" historiography. The author begins by distinguishing the canonical miracles (attested by Scripture or the Acts of the Apostles) that every Catholic was obliged to believe, from the miracles belief in which was left to individual judgment. Among the latter, some were altogether doubtful. "Finally, there are some which are not so groundless as the above, nor so certain as those about which one can safely pronounce a favorable judgment."[30] Muñoz then poses the question as to which of these three categories the apparitions of Our Lady of Guadalupe can be assigned, but is careful not to reply to the question at once. In its broad lines, the argument of Muñoz runs as follows.

1. He takes for his basis of discussion the relation of Fernández de Echeverría y Veitia, which he regards as the most representative contemporary synthesis of all that had been published on the apparitions. "This relation of Veitia is analogous in substance to that which Licentiate Miguel Sánchez, the first historian of those apparitions, published in the middle of the last century, to that which the *bachiller* Luis

Becerra Tanco, professor of languages and mathematics, wrote in 1666, and to the histories of the same tenor written by the celebrated Don Carlos de Sigüenza y Góngora, his imitator Gemelli Carreri, Father Francisco de Florencia, Don Cayetano Cabrera, and some others."[31]

Muñoz thus listed three of the four "evangelists" of Guadalupe; he only omitted the author who diffused the tradition in Nahuatl, Lazo de la Vega or whoever wrote the *Huey tlamahuicoltica*.

2. He cites against the tradition of the apparitions the contemporary and subsequent historiographic silence on the subject. "The silence of Father Torquemada is especially weighty evidence. . . . One could say the same of the silence of Father Luis de Cisneros." As for the relation copied by Alva Ixtlilxochitl, according to Sigüenza y Góngora, "Let it be brought to light."[32]

3. Muñoz cites unpublished documents, earlier than all those advanced by the supporters of the "apparitions" (he suspects that all these documents were fabricated after the publication of Miguel Sánchez' work, for the good of the cause.)

The new documents, so often cited at the time and since, are the letter of Viceroy Martín Enríquez, dated September 25, 1575, and the passage from the *Historia General* of Sahagún (then unpublished), concerning the sanctuary of Tonantzin of Tepeyac.

With the aid of these irrefutable documents, Muñoz unmasks Miguel Cabrera, who cited Sahagún incorrectly, and denies all authenticity to the testament of Juana Martín, which Boturini regarded as "a document of the greatest importance."[33]

4. Thus faked documents played a part in the genesis of the Mexican Guadalupan tradition, according to Muñoz, who sought to reconstruct the spiritual climate in which the pious legend appeared. This is the most valuable part of this little manuscript notebook of some twenty pages: "This is the way in which fables are born, and in similar ways they grow and take shape. A painter, let us say, represented Our Lady of Guadalupe on her hill of Tepeyac together with a devotee on his knees, praying. A simple Indian might conclude from this that the Virgin had appeared to one of her followers. Another Indian, having heard this story, passes it on as a certain fact. Rumor spreads the tale and, with the daily addition of new details, the whole legend finally emerges. This is one of the thousand ways in which this story could have arisen. . . .

"As for the time and the occasion which gave rise to the story . . . , I suspect that it was born in the Indian mind in the years 1629–1634. During this whole period the image of Guadalupe remained in the capital because of a terrible flood, and became the object of extraordinary demonstrations, which made Cabrera say that 'Mexico City broke the dikes of her devotion' . . . ; the popular fervor found expression in dances, dialogues, Indian songs in which the hitherto unknown apparitions were mentioned; copies of the image, previously very rare, multiplied infinitely."[34]

The retreat of the waters from the flooded capital caused the flowering of the miraculous roses of the image of Guadalupe. "From that marvelous flowering, I believe, was born the fruit of the apparitions. What will the Indian imagination, heated and fertilized by such enthusiasm, not produce?"[35]

5. The author then traced the progress of the cult of Guadalupe, stressing the growing prosperity of the sanctuary thanks to the influx of alms, until the erection of the new collegiate church of Guadalupe by Archbishop Rubio y Salinas in 1749. "The whole edifice cost 482 thousand pesos, collected in the form of alms."[36]

Muñoz also observed that the heirs of the principal donor, Andrés de Palencia, gave an additional 293,000 pesos, and added, "This sum and its accumulated interest formed a capital of 527,832 pesos, which the king took, and its interest at 5% was assigned to the royal ninths of the tithes of the dioceses of Mexico City and Puebla de los Angeles."[37]

Note the considerable wealth of the Mexican sanctuary of Guadalupe, the lion's share that went to the king, and the effort to maintain an equilibrium between the archbishopric of Mexico City, hitherto the only beneficiary of the cult of Guadalupe, and the bishopric of Puebla, doubly injured, but which at last rallied to the national cult.

6. The official historian of the Indies diplomatically concluded that the cult of Guadalupe is "a very reasonable and just cult, with which individual opinion on the subject of the apparitions has nothing to do."[38]

It is interesting to note that Juan Bautista Muñoz at Madrid and Fray Servando Teresa de Mier at Mexico City, only several months apart, without any exchange of documents, reached identical conclusions about the fragility of the Guadalupan tradition. But Fray Servando was a creole friar who shared with his brethren the aspiration of endowing his *patria* with a holy place and a complementary relic, signs of divine favor. That is why he sought in Borunda's cloudy speculations the means of refashioning the pious tradition, in order to strengthen it. We know the sequel: the scandal of the devotees, the exile of Fray Servando. . . . Now, the Dominican informs us in his *Memorias* that Borunda had written on Mexican antiquities at the invitation of the Academia de la Historia, which may have taken this initiative at the instigation of Muñoz, aware of his own inadequate knowledge of the Mexican past and the significance of the codices, as he himself modestly observes. In his *Apologia* Mier cited as a weighty argument in favor of his heretical theses the fact that "the chronicler [J. B. Muñoz] composed an elegant dissertation in which he undertook to show the history of Guadalupe is a fable."[39] But the milieus and audiences of Fray Servando and J. B. Muñoz were as different as could be. The academicians applauded the luminous argumentation of the historiographer of the Indies. The devotees of Guadalupe and the archbishop of Mexico City rose in indignation against the all-too-ingenious preacher. This meaningful coincidence shows that in 1794 the subject of the Mexican cult of Guadalupe was in the air on both Atlantic shores, in Spain and in New Spain. One could even say, more precisely, that concern with the Mexican Guadalupan tradition, whether for or against, was an aspect of the agelong dialogue between creoles and Spaniards, in the last phase of the colonial domination.

Forty Years of Polemic:
Mexican Replies to Muñoz

The controversy whose high points were the sermon of Fray Servando and the *Discurso* of Muñoz had its repercussions. On the eve of Independence the Mexican creoles picked up the gauntlet thrown down by Muñoz; their spokesman was an Oratorian friar of Mexico City who wrote a *Defensa guadalupana . . . contra la disertación de D. Juan Bautista Muñoz.*[40] This was in 1819, and the reply may seem belated, but it is likely that the essay of Muñoz was not known in Mexico City before its publication, in 1817, in the Academia de la Historia's *Memorias,* whose real appearance was certainly later than the year that volume 5 bears. The author of the *Defensa* did not refute Muñoz point by point (he would have been at a loss for an answer) but resorted to the argument of Florencia: the force of tradition. He also invoked the "very numerous and irrefutable documents" of the apologists. He skillfully attacked Muñoz on what was clearly his weak point, Mexican antiquities; creoles had invoked this argument, "knowledge of the country," against the *gachupines* since the sixteenth century. "If Don Juan Bautista Muñoz had studied the matter with impartiality, and if he had known the language, the characters, and the ancient writing of the Mexicans, he would not have committed the error of scorning those precious documents [the pictographic codices], nor would he have let his pen run so freely on a subject so important for the whole kingdom."[41] Observe the exaltation of the written monuments of the Indian past, a constant theme in the writings of Mexican creoles since the time of Sigüenza y Góngora, and especially the charismatic feeling reflected in the claim that the whole Hispanic world addressed its prayers to the image of Tepeyac. "All the kingdoms of the Spanish Crown, yes, all in time of need and affliction, sustained by this belief, direct their prayers to Guadalupe of Tepeyac."[42] Thus we find in 1819, expressed by the pen of the Oratorian friar Manuel Gómez Marín, the essence of the argument of Father Florencia in 1668: tradition and national interest.

However, the debate was not closed, and twenty-two years after Mexican Independence another adversary accepted the challenge thrown down by Muñoz, the challenge of Madrid. Licentiate Carlos María de Bustamante, one of the official historians of Mexico at the time, published in 1843 *The Apparition of Guadalupe at Mexico City, Vindicated from the Defects Attributed to It by Dr. Don Juan Bautista Muñoz in the Dissertation That He Read in the Academia Real de La Historia of Madrid*.[43] Bustamante's refutation naturally reflected the separation from Spain that had taken place since the publication of the essay of Father Gómez Marín. In the manner of Mier in the *Historia de la Revolución de Nueva España*, Bustamante denounced the colonial historiography, claiming that fear of reprisal had kept it from telling the truth. In view of the tribulations which Sahagún's *Historia* had suffered, what credit could be given to it? If Torquemada had not spoken of the apparitions of Guadalupe, it was because he was constrained, like his contemporaries, potential victims of *gachupín* tyranny, to practice self-censure. For Bustamante the first and decisive proof is this: "We know that Jesus Christ, the second celestial Adam, was tied so closely in all respects to the second Eve, Mary His mother, . . . that he did not wish to retire to the side of His Father, nor enter into His Glory, without having left his most holy mother commended to the recently born Church."[44] Did Bustamante really believe in the cogency of so general an argument? It is difficult to say, but his contemporary Lorenzo de Zavala, speaking of his *Cuadro Histórico*, called it "a farrago of false, absurd, and ridiculous statements."[45]

For Bustamante then, the historiographic silence of the century and more that followed the apparitions of 1531 is to be explained by colonial oppression. The rest of his discourse reveals how much his ideas owed to Mier. Recalling that the Virgin Mary had served as guardian of the apostles, notably of Saint James in Spain, he added: "Who knows what Mary may have done for Thomas, if it is true that this apostle was charged with spreading the Light in the East Indies?"[46] To which Bustamante appended this footnote: "Today there is not the slightest doubt that the Gospel was announced in our America to the ancient Indians by an apostle, shown by Father Mier to have been Saint Thomas, known by the name of Quetzalcóatl."[47]

There follows an account of the gift of Quetzalcóatl's ritual finery to Cortés and of the Conqueror's ruse, accompanied by a reflection that reveals the contemporary climate of opinion: "A criminal, ridiculous illusion, [the identification of Cortés with Quetzalcóatl], without which Moctezuma would have never received him nor made presents to him; but for that illusion, the Spanish army would probably never have penetrated the interior."[48] For the space of a moment, in the imagination of the author and his readers, the Conquest itself has been abolished, the Spaniards driven into the sea; treachery alone could have given them victory over the Mexicans. The atmosphere of open war which then characterized Spanish-Mexican relations inspired a new revision of the historiography of the Conquest, as shown by other contemporary Guadalupan documents. The *Manifiesto de la junta guadalupana,* published in 1831, on the occasion of the tricentenary of the "apparitions," contained a *Disertación histórico-crítica sobre la aparición,*[49] (again by Bustamante) whose title was borrowed from Muñoz. In this "Dissertation" Bustamante recalled that in 1829 he had published Book 12 of Sahagún, "a small work which I published to show the cruelties of the Spaniards, and to make the Mexicans understand that the fate of Cortés' victims awaited them if the Spanish expedition which was then being prepared and which landed the following year at Tampico, under the orders of General Isidro Barradas, succeeded in penetrating the country."[50] In an *Informe crítico-legal . . . para el reconocimiento de la Imagen de Nra. Señora de Guadalupe,*[51] ordered by the chapter of the cathedral of Mexico City, in 1835, we also read: "The Spaniards trace everything back to Spain . . . without reflecting on the essential difference between image and image, overlooking the fact that the Mexican image is *original.*"[52] The following year, 1836, appeared *El gran día de México* (its date, December 10, reveals at once that it has to do with the apparitions of the Virgin of Guadalupe). Here we read that Mary wished in 1531 "to console that afflicted people [the Indians]. . . . The Archbishop, Don Fray Juan de Zumárraga, was obliged to conceal the event, lest it become a new motive of persecution of the unhappy people who had received [that gift]."[53] Clearly, Spanish cruelty and the oppression that reigned in Mexico were the only reasons for the absence of authentic testimony for the "apparitions" of Guadalupe. In the critical years during which Mexicans lived under the threat of a military reconquest by the Spaniards (the dispatch of Count Calderón de la Barca as the first ambassador of Spain in 1840 marked the beginning of a detente), the polemic concerning the apparitions of Guadalupe initiated half a century before by Juan Bautista Muñoz was still one of the forms of the creole challenge to Spain.

15   Guadalupe, a Mexican National Emblem

The Burgeoning of the Sanctuary (Tepeyac)
and of the Cult (1555–1831)

In 1555 Archbishop Montúfar founded the first basilica of
Guadalupe, a modest structure, for not until 1609 was the first "temple in vaulted masonry" built at Tepeyac. Construction of this new
sanctuary was made possible by a public subscription, evidence that
the cult of Guadalupe of Tepeyac already had enough devotees to
collect the funds necessary to build an edifice at a time when an
upsurge of construction in Mexico City mobilized the available work
force and inevitably brought a sharp rise in construction costs. We also
know that the first chapel (*hermita*) was built with the contributions of
devotees. According to a document cited by Father Cuevas, by 1570
the basilica already had "six or eight thousand pesos in revenue." The
temple, whose first stone was laid in 1609, was finished thirteen years
later, and the sacred image was installed there by Archbishop Juan de
la Serna, in 1622. Since the multitude of pilgrims constantly grew, and
the cult of Guadalupe held an ever more official place in the life of
New Spain, it was decided in 1694 to undertake the construction of a
new basilica, larger than its predecessor. This is the present structure,
which is threatened with ruin as a result of the sinking of the ground.
This church measures 77 meters in length, 37 meters in width, and 30
meters in height; these facts give us an idea of its size relative to that of
the cathedral of Mexico City and the other cathedrals of New Spain.
The first basilica, called "of the Indians," housed the venerated image
during the period of construction of the present temple, which was
built on the exact site of its predecessor (reminding us of the ancient
Mexican ritual practice of constructing new pyramids over the old
ones).
    Beginning in 1694—or, in any case, in 1709—the sanctuary of Te-
peyac thus was distinguished from other Marian sanctuaries in New
Spain by the size of its basilica, which made it comparable to a provincial cathedral, situated outside Mexico City. Robles, in his *Diario,*

reports that in 1675 (almost twenty years before the establishment of the new collegiate church) "work was begun on the highway to Our Lady of Guadalupe . . . ; along the way are fifteen chapels corresponding to the fifteen mysteries of the Rosary."[1] This entry shows the importance that the viceroy must have attached to the sanctuary of Tepeyac, to link it to Mexico City by a highway with fifteen chapels. The same entry tells us that the cult of Guadalupe was associated with the cult of the rosary, Dominican in its origin but later become a typical aspect of Jesuit religiosity. December 12, 1678, feast day of the image, "water ran into the holy water basin of Guadalupe by order of his Excellency and at his expense."[2] Robles reports that on Sunday, August 1, 1694, construction of the new basilica having begun, "the curates of Saint Francis began to collect alms for the construction of the church of Our Lady of Guadalupe; the first gift was of 50,000 pesos given by Don Pedro Ruiz de Castañeda, a rich merchant, and by licentiate Don Ventura Medina, curate, both creoles."[3] The most venerable convent of Mexico City appealed to the devout to supplement the large initial sum donated by two benefactors, both creoles, as Robles is careful to point out. Robles obviously wanted to make clear that the cult of Guadalupe was the property of his creole countrymen, implicitly distinguished from the *gachupines*.

To this material flowering—the construction of ever larger and more sumptuous basilicas, three being built in a century and a half, and an access highway from Mexico City—naturally corresponded the growing brilliance of the sacred feast days and the marks of official devotion. In October 1603 the corregidor of Mexico City "said that, as the town council knows, the Marques and his lady have requested the presentation of two plays [*comedias*] at Guadalupe, and to this end he [the corregidor] contracted with Velásquez and his troupe that they should twice appear in the chapel of Guadalupe and there give the plays for their Excellencies. The price agreed on was two hundred gold pesos."[4] We have some indications that Tepeyac early became a place where devotees went to meditate at critical junctures in their lives. Guijo reports that in 1661 the duke of Albuquerque, the departing viceroy who had been subjected to a severe *juicio de residencia* "left this town on Saturday, March 26, at 2 P.M., amid all this unpleasantness, for the chapel of Guadalupe; the viceroy, his wife, and some courtiers accompanied him on this journey."[5] It also seems that it became an established custom at the viceregal court to go out as far as Tepeyac to meet distinguished guests and to accompany them, on their departure, as far as the basilica of Guadalupe. Robles writes in his *Diario* that December 29, 1681, "Monsignor the Bishop of Michoacán entered Guadalupe in the afternoon, and the city council

[of Mexico City] went to see and receive him, but he had already left
the church when they arrived."[6] When the viceroy, Conde de Galve,
left for Spain on May 10, 1698, "the Audiencia, the tribunals, and the
new viceroy accompanied him as far as Our Lady of Guadalupe."[7]
Again, on January 25, 1702, "the Oidores and many other persons
went to Guadalupe to visit the President of Guatemala, who is there to
make a novena to Our Lady before continuing his journey, and he did
not come to Mexico City so as to avoid having to pay official visits."[8] A
future asylum for all Christendom on the day of judgment, Tepeyac
was also a refuge from tribulations, the place for saying farewell to
viceroys who had come to the end of their terms of office, and a kind
of celestial embassy, enjoying the privilege of extraterritoriality about
a league and half to the north of the capital. This character of Tepeyac
is confirmed by another fact cited by Guijo in his *Diario*: "Thursday,
July 22, 1660, died Garcí Tello de Sandoval, former corregidor of this
city; he had been suspended from office June of last year; he died
leaving many debts, and his wife brought his body to the chapel of
Guadalupe, where he was buried the same day."[9]

Thus Tepeyac had become a sacred asylum for the dead as well as
the living, and a place of retreat for notables; the highway built in
1675 was, as it were, a grand drive which ended at the viceregal palace
and a triumphal avenue leading to Mexico City. These were so many
semiprofane marks of devotion.

The accumulation of sacred power represented by the image of
Guadalupe early inspired great pilgrimages and other mass cult manifestations. The pilgrimages of twentieth-century Indians to Tepeyac
give some idea of the vast encampments that arose on the approaches
to the sanctuary in past centuries, seasonal migrations that began at
the approach of September 8 in colonial times and probably December 12 after Independence. The collective manifestations of the
Indian faith—the *mitotes* of Indians ornamented with feathers, dancing with wooden bells attached to their ankles and wrists; the sacramental plays in Nahuatl, imitating the mystery plays introduced by
the missionaries, and representing the apparitions of Guadalupe to
Juan Diego—composed a colorful fresco that continued the sacred
dances of the ancient polytheism and the Christian mysteries of
medieval Spain. Indian faith continued to express itself in Aztec
ritual; the devotee burned incense (copal) in a little clay vase and
offered flowers or ears of maize to the holy image; he joined to these
immemorial gestures the signs of the cross and the genuflections of
Catholic ritual. The devotee regarded his prayer, in the case of a
Marian litany, as a conjuration; it was normally accompanied by a
prayer requesting the Virgin's bounty. In exchange for his offering,

the Indian sought to make the divine spirit intervene in his favor; failure of the prayer to achieve its purpose might cause the devotee to grow angry and curse the sacred image. That the traditional belief in Tonantzin of Indian pilgrims to Tepeyac remained basically the same is attested by Sahagún in the sixteenth century, by Torquemada in the seventeenth century, by Fray Servando Teresa de Mier in the eighteenth century. Explicit testimony by the archepiscopal authority confirms that the nature of the cult of the Indian pilgrims of Tepeyac was not "ambiguous," as it has often been described, but clearly foreign to Christianity. In 1753 Archbishop Rubio y Salinas declared that he had created schools in his diocese for the teaching of Spanish to the Indians in compliance with the law, but he depicted the situation, basing himself on a report presented by the abbot and the canons of the collegiate church of Guadalupe, as follows: "Among the Indians who frequently come to the sanctuary and to the collegiate church of Guadalupe, a great number are completely ignorant of Castilian. . . . That may be the reason why these Indians do not ask for the sacraments and stay away from the sermons . . . and since at the collegiate church there are no clergy who know the native languages, the Indians frequently leave, because they can find no outlet for their devotion."[10]

The Spanish name of "Guadalupe" was still unknown to the majority of the Indian pilgrims to Tepeyac—whether they spoke Nahuatl, the language of the majority, Otomí, or some other tongue—in the mid-eighteenth century, at the very time when the Holy See gave an indirect acknowledgment of the tradition of the apparitions of Tepeyac, a tradition whose most solid foundations were the Nahuatl documents cited by Becerra Tanco, and especially by Boturini. For the Roman doctors it was but one more image of Mary the Immaculate, for the Spaniards it was a copy of the Guadalupe of Estremadura, but in the eyes of the Indians it was the mother-goddess of the Aztecs, Tonantzin, who had always dwelled at Tepeyac.

One would like to know the ethnic composition of the solemn procession of December 12, which Robles briefly mentions. "Monday the eleventh, in the afternoon, the procession of Our Lady of Guadalupe left from the convent de la Merced." He has more to tell about the end of the feast days at Tepeyac, December 31: "On the 31st the cupola of the new church of Our Lady of Guadalupe was completed; the Indians lit many fires and two plays were staged, and there was a feast with a mass sung as a thanksgiving."[11] This was in 1702, and by that date the cult of Guadalupe had been a completely official cult (and not simply a popular Indian cult) for almost half a century. The year 1703 was marked by a Guadalupan festival at Mexico City, in one of the most famous convents of the capital: "Wednesday, December 12, there was celebrated at the convent de la Merced with great pomp the feast of Our Lady of Guadalupe and the dedication of her cloister; a great many people attended."[12] The diary of Antonio de Robles, licentiate in canon law, commissary of the Inquisition, is lacking in warmth; it is little more than a series of dry notations of deaths and civil or ecclesiastical news. Robles mentions Remedios much more often than Guadalupe; the latter cult, popular in origin, is mentioned in his journal only when it has official recognition. Robles was chary of adjectives and expressions of surprise; this lends a special weight to his reference to the "great solemnity" and the great concourse of people on that December 12, 1703. Perhaps a baroque and detailed account of the event lies in some archival repository. Other evidence of the contemporary popularity of Guadalupe is provided by the testamentary executors of Andrés de Palencia, who wrote the Council of the Indies in 1717 that "they could not overlook the fact that the sanctuary of Our Lady of Guadalupe was the principal center of devotion, not only of Mexico City, but of all the kingdoms of New Spain, and that while the edifice was imposing and sumptuous, its revenues were as meager as the number of its priests and the amount of their prebends."[13]

A more personal form of devotion was that of numerous creoles, clergy, and laymen. The Jesuit Florencia lovingly described the effigy of Guadalupe: "I feel as if heart and soul strain to rush out to look at her, and look again, and love tenderly."[14] In the atmosphere in which American baroque art flourished, this outburst should cause no surprise; piety and the divine mysteries were diffused by plastic beauty and the enigmatic agency of religious symbolism. However, Florencia was a devotee rather than an inspired exegete, and it was the modest visage, the inexpressible serenity of the Virgin of Tepeyac, that touched his heart. We may also regard as a typical—if extreme—case of Guadalupan devotion the story told by Father Isidoro Felix de Espinosa about his teacher Fray Francisco Frutos (a Franciscan of San Diego). The example of Father Frutos is all the more significant because he was not creole; it testifies to the fascination that the image of Tepeyac exerted on men's minds, independently of the patriotic-charismatic sentiment that was mingled with this influence in the case of the Mexicans.

Fray Francisco Frutos had come from the convent of San Diego de Alcalá, in Castile; Felix de Espinosa informs us that he was a great reader of Saint Teresa de Ávila, of Juan de la Cruz, and of the Venerable María de la Antigua. He felt a great devotion for Our Lady of Guadalupe of Tepeyac. Having suffered an intestinal occlusion, he was regarded by physicians as being in a desperate state, and decided to make a pilgrimage to Guadalupe. Contrary to all expectations, he was cured after several days, "so that the physicians acknowledged it was a miraculous cure."[15] The object of the miracle immediately went on foot from the convent De Propaganda Fide of Santa Cruz de Querétaro, where he then was, to the sanctuary of Tepeyac. There he had the excellent painter Juan Correa execute an exact replica of "the image painted by the angels with flowers," with himself standing in prayer beside the artist, the traditional attitude of donors on the re-tablos. He also had a miniature of the image painted on a cockleshell which he always kept on his person. He would show this image to others, asking them to recite the rosary and sing litanies before it. Having returned to his convent, Fray Francisco sought and obtained permission to place in the church a copy of Guadalupe, of the same size as the original, and daily celebrated mass in front of the sacred image. He went about the country asking for alms of candles to decorate the altar of Guadalupe, and "people gladly gave them for he told them it was for the sake of 'good grandmother Guadalupe' [*la abuelita*]."[16] This account sheds light on the forms assumed by the cult among religious and laymen; it also reveals that by the mid-eighteenth century the cult of Guadalupe had become country-wide.

Father Frutos became an active propagandist for the image of Guadalupe. Felix de Espinosa reports that he collected copies of the sacred effigy and "wanted every home to have this image of Our Lady"; if he did not find one, he openly complained, "Why is the good little grandmother Guadalupe not here?"[17] (The descriptive phrase *abuelita* may be a Spanish translation of *tonantzin*, a term which Father Frutos may have used for Our Lady when speaking to Indians.) When he died (shortly after the arrival of Fray Antonio Margil as guardian of his convent) a great light appeared in the sky, according to his biographer. He died with his eyes fixed on the image of Guadalupe and called on Holy Mary with his last breath. This edifying end at the age of forty-six shows how hagiographic traditions and miraculous images played into each other's hands. The life of Father Frutos, devoted to Guadalupe, served the expansion of the cult of Tepeyac; reciprocally, the prodigies worked in his favor by the sacred image were the first steps in the development of a hagiographic legend which could have led to his ultimate beatification.

The cult of Guadalupe raised the Mexican creoles to a pitch of exaltation comparable in Spanish religious history to that of the Spaniards who in the great days of the Road of Saint James proposed to transfer the capital of the church from Rome to the tomb of the apostle at Compostela in Galicia. *The Translation of the Church to*

Guadalupe[18] was preached by the Jesuit Carranza in that same city of Querétaro where, some years earlier, the Franciscan Frutos (if Miguel Sánchez was the Saint John of Guadalupe, Frutos was her local Saint Paul) had spread the Guadalupan Good Word, authenticated by the miracle which answered his appeal to God.

When, a half-century later, Mexican independence was won under the banner of Guadalupe, she was again consecrated Protectress of Mexico. The project of a medal to be struck and issued to reward the winners of "the secular games in honor of the miraculous apparition of our Lady of Guadalupe," organized on the occasion of Guadalupe's tricentenary in 1831, exactly ten years after the winning of Independence, reads as follows:

> The prizes could consist of engraved medals . . . On the obverse America could be represented as a young woman dressed in the manner of the ancient Indian nobles, pointing with her right hand to the image of Our Lady of Guadalupe descending from the sky, and with the left to broken chains, bars of precious metal, and a cornucopia lavishing every kind of fruit upon the earth. The upper part could display this motto: *Cunctis Prætiosior illa,* which means in Castilian "None compares with her." The reverse could display this inscription: "Mexico—To her divine Protectress—María de Guadalupe—For three centuries of benefits—In the year 1831."[19]

Guadalupe, Queen of the Mexicans

The conquest of Mexican religious life in the eighteenth century by the cult of the "prodigious image" of Tepeyac had secondary effects in most aspects of social life. One of the most ordinary of those effects, in a sense, yet very significant, was the vogue of Guadalupe as a given name in New Spain (and later in independent Mexico, down to the present). It appears (although intensive research in surviving parish archives would be necessary to confirm it) that the given name of Guadalupe (given to men as well as women) did not appear in New Spain before the second half of the eighteenth century, that is, long after Our Lady of Guadalupe had been sworn patroness of Mexico City against floods and the work of Miguel Sánchez had certified the legend of the "apparitions." Sor Juana Inés de la Cruz mentions a "Doña María de Guadalupe Alencastre," but she was a lady of the viceroy's court, probably born in Spain, who belonged to a noble peninsular family and was therefore baptized with the name of Guadalupe of Estremadura. That was in the middle of the seventeenth century. Mier indirectly reveals that it was fashionable in

Mexico City at the end of the eighteenth century to name one's daughter "Guadalupe"; criticizing a *gachupín* for pretending to love Mexico, he wrote: "This bandit of a Branciforte named his daughter 'Guadalupe' for this reason, but no sooner had he returned to Spain than he changed her name."[20]

Whatever the truth of Mier's charge, this is evidence of social pressure in favor of the given name "Guadalupe." At that period, in the Hispanic world, the choice of a given name was a religious act; to name a child "Guadalupe" was equivalent to devoting her to that sacred image; it created a bond of allegiance and protection. The choosing of the name "Guadalupe" by a person taking religious vows is still more persuasive, from this point of view; I can cite at least one, preserved in the title of a sermon of a canon of Guadalajara. On January 15, 1797, a certain Doña Juana María Josefa Sánchez Lenero took the veil in the Dominican convent of Santa María de las Gracias de Guadalajara, under the name of Sor Juana María de Guadalupe. This case is completely analogous to that of the many religious who at the same period in New Spain took the religious name "Francis Xavier" or of the nuns who, like Sor Juana Inés de la Cruz, born Juana de Asbaje, chose the name of "Santa Inés," the object of a widespread cult.

The "Guadalupenization" of New Spain extended to toponyms. In his *Diccionario geográfico-histórico de las Indias Occidentales o América,* published in Madrid in 1787, Alcedo mentions under the rubric "Guadalupe" (besides the island of the Lesser Antilles) fifteen towns or villages and two rivers. Unfortunately he does not indicate the precise origin of each appellation, or the date. (A history of the names of Mexican villages, or rather of their changes of name, could shed light on the *intrahistory* of Mexico; only our ineptitude prevents us from seeing its visible signs.) The majority of Guadalupes listed by Alcedo (he must have overlooked some) were in New Spain. A Guadalupe of Peru, in the bishopric of Trujillo, owed its name to the image of Estremadura; another in New Granada and a third in the island of Guadeloupe are certainly linked to the peninsular cult. The cases of two villages in the Jesuit missions of Ecuador are more difficult; I lean toward the Mexican Guadalupe as the origin of their names. Finally, there is a Guadalupe in the state of Pernambuco in Brazil which may be connected with a secondary Portuguese sanctuary situated in the Alentejo.

We may safely conclude that of the villages of the Indies which bore the name of Guadalupe at the end of the eighteenth century, two-thirds owed that name to the Mexican image of Guadalupe. Among these, seven were mission villages of New Spain, two were Jesuit mission villages of South America; at the head of the list comes Guadalupe of Tepeyac, which grew up beside the sanctuary. The meaning of the Jesuit apostolate in California, in the Tarahumara, and in Sinaloa, like that of the Franciscan missions of New Mexico and New Biscay, is confirmed here by toponymy. The majority of these villages had been recently formed when Alcedo composed his gazeteer; they were as old as the missionary beginnings in the North and West, that is, as old as the cult of Tepeyac itself. The first villages renamed by the Spaniards in the years following the Conquest all had a double name which associated the Nahuatl toponymy with the name of the Catholic saint chosen as patron, for example San Juan Guelache, San Pedro Guelatao, Santiago de Gueyapa, and so on. The name "Guadalupe," given by the Jesuit and Franciscan missionaries in the seventeenth and eighteenth centuries to the villages they founded in regions usually occupied by nomadic Indians, attested to the patronage of Our Lady of Guadalupe over the missionary enterprise and taught the converts the name of an image in whose guise the Virgin Mary had chosen to appear in order to reveal to the Mexican Indians that she had become their eminent protectress. For those fishers of souls, the missionaries, Guadalupe was a sign of divine grace dispensed to the new converts and therefore to the missionaries, a sign that was doubly meaningful.

Altogether different was the origin of the name of the village that had naturally developed in the shadow of the sanctuary, on which its existence totally depended. The village of Guadalupe, situated on the approaches to Tepeyac, could have no other name; human will did not enter into the choice of that name, as was the case with the missionary villages. It is interesting to see the impression this village made on Alcedo, a guards colonel, about 1785, at the apogee of enthusiasm for Guadalupe. "This same name is borne by a village of New Spain, situated in the jurisdiction of Mexico City, on an arid hill, celebrated for its magnificent temple and the sanctuary of Our Lady of Guadalupe, who appeared to the Mexican Indian Juan Diego, in 1531, painted on an *ayate* or cloak; this temple is of beautiful construction and very richly endowed, because it is the favorite cult of the whole kingdom; the population of this village consists of sixty Spanish and mestizo families, and one hundred Indian families; it is situated one league from Mexico City and is connected with the city by a paved highway one *vara* high."[21]

Alcedo remembered the aridity of the site, the date of the apparitions according to the tradition diffused by the abundant Guadalupan aplogetic literature, the popularity of the cult—"the favorite cult of the whole kingdom." He describes precisely the highway leading from

Mexico City to Tepeyac and extolls the architectural beauty and wealth of the new basilica. His most valuable contribution is his account of the ethnic composition of the village of Guadalupe, where the three principal groups of contemporary Mexican society were represented. Alcedo (herein he displays his *gachupín* character) unfortunately does not distinguish mestizos from creoles, but at that date there must have been more mestizos than pure-blooded Spaniards in the village of Guadalupe. The numerical proportions of the inhabitants of white or mestizo descent, on the one hand, and the Indians, on the other, illustrate the fact that the Virgin had appeared to an Indian and that "the Indian nation" felt itself most favored. Indians naturally composed the great majority in villages of pre-Conquest origin, but its inhabitants must have chosen to come to a village like Guadalupe of Tepeyac, which had arisen in an arid desert as a socioeconomic derivate of the sanctuary and a by-product of the cult. The number of Indian families was almost double that of white and mestizo families, 110 to 60.

This observation calls our attention to the Indian, one might say "indigenist," aspect of the cult of Our Lady of Guadalupe. This aspect appears with special clarity in the *Memorias piadosas de la nación Indiana, recogidas de varios autores* by the Franciscan Díaz de la Vega.[22] These memoirs, contemporary with Alcedo's *Diccionario,* were composed in 1782 and remain unpublished to this day. The author does not say who were the "various authors" from whom he borrowed his pious legends, but it is easy to surmise who they were. Some, whom he cites occasionally, were chroniclers charged with writing the history of their religious province, others were devout apologists. But these authors, like Father Díaz de la Vega himself, had drawn the material of the pious traditions (directly or indirectly) from Indian hymns and religious plays. The hymns were the repository of the collective Indian memory, which preserved only those past events charged with eschatological significance on the level of the ethnic group. That is why the "pious memoirs" contain at least as many apparitions of the Virgin Mary as there were Indian tribes in Central Mexico. Chapter 5 is devoted to the "Very Special Grace of Heaven to the Indian Nation, in the Form of the Prodigious Apparition of Holy Mary in Her Celestial Image of Guadalupe."[23] Our Lady of Guadalupe became tutelary divinity of the "Mexican" (Aztec) Indians in a period which could be called "the Sun of Mary," thereby adopting the traditional native chronology in order to permit the integration of the Aztecs into the new transcendent order. The mythical image of Guadalupe played the same role in the Indian mind of the ancient Tenochca as was played by the image of the eponymic hero Tenoch during the "Sun of

Huitzilopochtli," the last Aztec sun before the Spanish Conquest. To be sure, the Virgin had "appeared," according to another legend, in her image of Ocotlan, to a Tlaxcalan Indian; she had also "appeared," in her aspect of Remedios, to an Otomí Indian.

Thus the three ethnic groups whose history had most profoundly marked the pre-Columbian history of central Mexico—the old rural Otomí population base, the Mexican conquerors, the unvanquished Tlaxcalans—were endowed by legend with a protective image of the Virgin Mary. Meanwhile, the Most Holy Cross of Querétaro guaranteed the Chichimecs the benefits of divine grace, while the Cross of Tepic assured a like favor to the Tarascans. Forty years before Father Díaz de la Vega composed his book, licentiate Mota y Padilla had written: "Although the whole world may envy Mexico City its good fortune in having the appearance of a Sign as great as Holy Mary, who protects it, the Sign which casts its shade over Nueva Galicia and protects it is also a very great Sign; both are signs of great good fortune."[24] The *signs* of divine grace must also be equally distributed among the diverse Indian ethnic groups of Mexico, and the Indians had to rejoice thereat, as they were invited to do by Father Díaz de la Vega: "Let the Indians in general, in all their nations, rejoice and rejoice again, for in the capacity of Holy Mary's chosen children they will have her special protection, promised at Tepeyac, at Ocotlan, at Otoncapulco."[25] Mythical invention carried the concern with symmetry and equality among the different ethnic groups so far that the "three Indians to whom Mary wished to consign in turn her most high designs, the first glorious witnesses of her appearance at Mexico City and of her discovery at Ocotlan and at Otoncapulco,"[26] were all named John. I have already noted the fascination exerted on religious minds by the homonymy between John the Evangelist, Juan Diego (the Indian witness of the apparitions of Tepeyac), and the archbishop of Mexico City, the Franciscan Juan de Zumárraga. In the eighteenth century the "Juans" became a pleiad of visionaries of Mary. Onomastic esotericism went hand in hand with that of chronology. What should one think of the fact that the archangel Saint Michael had appeared to a Tlaxcalan Indian in 1531, the exact year of the apparitions of the Virgin at Tepeyac? This other privileged neophyte was not simply called Juan, like the others, but Juan Diego, like the Juan Diego of Tepeyac. One is seized with a kind of vertigo observing this game of musical chairs of supernatural signs, which are repeated with a rigorous and disconcerting symmetry from one sanctuary to another.

In the background of this esotericism of names and numbers lurk ancient tribal rivalries, as Father Díaz de la Vega unconsciously confirms: "Chapter 6: Holy Mary appears to another Juan Diego in the Province of Tlaxcala." Since this duplication of Juan Diego of Tepeyac was calculated to surprise even contemporary readers, the Franciscan writer gave the reasons for this occurrence. "The very noble and fortunate province of Tlaxcala being the first on whose horizon rose the divine Sun of Jesus Christ . . . , it was inevitable that from the very dawn of Christianity the beneficial influence of its very pure mother, Mary, the most holy dawn, should shine resplendent in order to ennoble the province of Tlaxcala by her eminent protection."[27] The Tlaxcalans, allies of Cortés who greatly aided in the Spanish capture of Mexico-Tenochtitlan, had been almost from the first on the side of the conquerors. By virtue of that fact, they could not have been treated worse in the distribution of divine favors than the vanquished of the Conquest, their agelong enemies, the Mexicans or Mexica.

This brief incursion into the pious traditions of most direct Indian origin deepens our understanding of the local rivalry between Mexico City and Puebla (the latter being inseparable from Tlaxcala, the first seat of its bishopric); their competition on the emblematic level of coats of arms had its roots in the Mexican intertribal past. We may say that all the phenomena that determined the spiritual evolution of New Spain and its social history in general emanated more or less directly from the Indians. Even in Humboldt's time the Indians constituted almost half of the population of New Spain; their ancestral beliefs were the seedbed, so to speak, in which the creole cults germinated. However, Guadalupe, image of the Virgin Mary, fully belongs to the great spiritual flood of Marian devotion which washed over Western Christendom from the beginning of the seventeenth century. If we seem to find the influence of hieroglyphic writing in the association of the prickly pear (*nopalli*), the glyph of Mexico-Tenochtitlan, with the effigy of the Virgin, what shall we say of the contemporary Parisian prints which depicted Mary on the bark of Lutetia—the coat of arms of Paris? Under all skies the roads of heraldry and emblematics have crisscrossed because of the inherent limitations of symbolic writing and the mythifying invention.

The cult of Our Lady of Guadalupe of Tepeyac owed part of its great importance in New Spain to its identification with the Immaculate Conception. The slow canonical progress of the doctrine from the time of its approval by Pope Sixtus IV in 1476, and the prolonged efforts of the Spanish monarchy to secure papal promulgation of a dogma and the institution of a rite of the first class, not achieved until the time of Leo XIII, reveal the true eschatological significance of the image of Guadalupe. Karl Rahner has penned a phrase that illuminates the whole history of the Marian cult: "the human person we call Mary is, as it were, the point in the history of Salvation on which the saving radiance of the living God falls perpendicularly, the point whence it extends to all mankind."

A creole preacher, Father Baltasar de Arizmendi (a discalced Franciscan), expressed the eschatological significance of the Mexican Guadalupe cult most explicitly in a sermon pronounced at Guanajuato in 1797: "For this is certain, that if, by a decree of providence a new sky, a new earth, and new creatures were to appear in this New World, that event could only be deferred until the day that Mary came to visit us."[28] This Marian virtue of being the dispenser of all graces flows naturally from her place, not in the human order, nor even in that of grace, but in the hypostatic order which infinitely surpasses the two others. Let a modern theologian speak on this point: "Mary, by virtue of her divine maternity, is part of the hypostatic order, she is an indispensable element—in the actual economy of divine Providence—in the Incarnation of the Word and the Salvation of mankind."[29]

It was the incarnation of the Word and the salvation of mankind that was at stake in the cult of Guadalupe; listen to the Jesuit Francisco Javier Carranza: "Saint Matthew counts fourteen generations from Abraham to David; from David to the transmigration of Babylon another fourteen generations; from the transmigration of Babylon to the birth of Christ fourteen more generations. . . . The Word appeared in roses on the fourteenth day of the acute fever of Juan Bernardino, whose miraculous healing was the second testimony of that marvelous apparition. What had been allegory, here was made reality. There she appeared to a whole world, here to a single part of the world. . . . The Word, incarnate in order to establish the eternity of His Kingdom, healed the perilous sickness of fourteen centuries in order to found the permanence of His Church. Our Lady of Guadalupe, almost two centuries after her apparition, healed the perilous plague of *matlazahuatl* that had raged for fourteen centuries."[30]

Here is a complete explanation of the "mariophany" of Mount Tepeyac: in the economy of salvation the miracle of Guadalupe appeared as the second incarnation of the divine Word. The Mexican patriotic and charismatic sentiment also had its roots here, for we have read (Father Carranza's audience heard those words on December 12, 1748): "Here it was made reality." The orator spoke ontologically, not by way of metaphor. Whereas in the first Incarnation, that of Jesus, the Word had come to redeem mankind, this second Incarnation, that of Mary at Tepeyac, only brought salvation to fortunate Mexico City. Who could deny that the Mexican Guadalupan cult was a resurgence of the call of Abraham? I have already called attention to the creole ambition to see the New Jerusalem in Mexico City; I cited Ita y Parra: "The Indian [*Indiana*, meaning the creoles and Indians] nation eclipses and surpasses not only Israel but all the nations of the world."[31] A modern Catholic theologian, probably unfamiliar with Mexican religious history, thus defines the call of Abraham: "The call of Abraham is a totally new intervention of God. . . . As King and Lord of all the earth he singles out among all the peoples of the earth a people to be His holy property and royal domain. . . . Thanks to this call, Israel, a backward people in other respects, excells by far all other peoples. Israel alone is elevated to that height."[32] The text of this resumé could be applied without a change of meaning to the spiritual history of Mexico; simply replace Abraham by Guadalupe and Israel by Mexico.

Again, Ita y Parra writes: "Mary entire belongs to the Americans, and by a mysterious reciprocity, all Americans are consecrated to Mary."[33]

All the manifestations of the Mexican cult of Guadalupe flow as if from a single source from the *call of Guadalupe*. Guadalupe, both *queen* and *mother* of the Mexicans; in the first case they are the "slaves" of Mary, in the second her "sons." These are the two ways of the perfect consecration to Mary, according to Saint Louis Marie Grignon de Monfort: "It consists in giving oneself completely, like a slave, to Mary and to Jesus through Her, and in doing everything by Mary, with Mary, in Mary, and for Mary."[34]

The Mexicans were a people "consecrated to Mary of Guadalupe" in the two ways of the Marian cult. They had but to recite the litany of Our Lady of Loreto, in the descending order of creatures, mentally replacing Loreto by Guadalupe:

> Queen of the Angels
> Queen of the Patriarchs
> Queen of the Prophets
> Queen of the Apostles
> Queen of the Martyrs
> Queen of those who confess her faith
> Queen of the Virgins
> Queen of all the saints
> Queen conceived without sin
> Queen raised to Heaven
> Queen of the Most Holy Rosary
> Queen of Peace
> and finally "Queen of the Mexicans"

I have emphasized that Guadalupe was first of all "mother of the Indians": "My clemency full of love and the pity I have for the natives," Father Díaz de la Vega has her say.[35] The Mexican creoles claimed their part of the grace dispensed to the *nación indiana*. The semantic evolution of the name "Mexican," which we studied in Clavijero, reflects an effort at appropriation of the *mexicayotl*— "Mexicanness"—by the minority of European origin. Although Guadalupe was the mediator between God and men, between God and the Mexicans, her mediation did not stop there. She was mediator between the king and the "Americans," as Ita y Parra also said. This role, which could be called "political," was less important than the spiritual current which ran through a society as divided as was that of New Spain. A Virgin with an olive complexion who first appeared to an Indian, Guadalupe made creoles, mestizos, and Indians a single people united by the same charismatic faith. The dialogue of the cultures did not really come alive (going beyond questions of rights and interests) until the moment when the Guadalupan apologetic became its principal subject. All the Mexican champions who, in the name of the Mexican *patria,* took up the challenge thrown down by Spain and by all Europe were great devotees of Guadalupe: Sigüenza y Góngora and Florencia in the seventeenth century; Eguiara y Egurén, Clavijero, Mier in the eighteenth century; Lizardi (*El Pensador Mexicano*) in the nineteenth. We noted the polemic unleashed by the rash judgment of Dean Martí, of Valencia, answered by the *Bibliotheca* of Eguiara. The charge of "American inferiority" leveled by Cornelius de Pauw provoked the reply of the ex-Jesuit Clavijero. The *Discurso histórico-crítico* of Juan Bautista Muñoz, who had criticized the central theme of creole religiosity, the cult of Guadalupe, brought an uninterrupted series of creole counterattacks from 1794 to 1843. Medina informs us that the *Defensa guadalupana* of the Oratorian friar Gómez Marín, a mediocre refutation of Muñoz, sold for six reales in the shop of Don Alejandro Valdés at Mexico City. This Guadalupan propaganda tract was thus within the reach of every purse and was one form of the muted struggle waged by Mexican patriots against Spain in 1819–20.

Guadalupe naturally became the banner of the insurgents when Hidalgo issued the "cry of Dolores" in 1810. Ten years earlier, a group of conspirators were called *Los Guadalupes,* and from the proceedings of their trial, we learn that these young men, without means, really incapable of posing a threat to the political security of the viceroyalty, entrusted their subversive enterprise to Our Lady of Guadalupe. One of them, a goldsmith, had fashioned an insignia, "explaining that the hole in the form of a crescent moon was designed to receive the image of Our Lady of Guadalupe."[36] They failed; but in the hour of triumph of the armies of Independence, the "sentiments of the nation" had already received unequivocal expression: "Let a constitutional law establish the celebration of December 12 in all the villages as a feast day consecrated to the Patroness of our Liberty, Holy Mary of Guadalupe."

Let me also recall the proclamation of Morelos, requiring that "every man above the age of ten carry in his hat a cockade with the national colors, namely, white and blue, a device consisting of a ribbon or band, of cloth or paper, which will proclaim him a devotee of the image of Guadalupe, soldier and defender of her cult."[37]

Thus, on March 11, 1813, from the camp of Ometepec, an order was launched that affirmed the spiritual permanence of the real Mexico against the legal Mexico (New Spain). Guadalupe had become the standard of a political struggle. This metamorphosis was achieved unknown to the devout patriots, who believed that the last times— called in a new language "the Day of Glory"—had arrived. But did not this *gloria*, borrowed directly from the French Revolution, have a more remote source, the same Judeo-Christian source as the Woman of the Apocalypse? That same woman who bestrides the dragon in the book of Beatus of Liebana and who, for her devotees of medieval Spain, trampled underfoot the half moon of threatening Islam, translated to a distant Mexico, symbolized the church and the *patria* battling against a mythical Antichrist, Napoleon Bonaparte, whose agents the *gachupines* appeared to be. The choice of Mary's colors as the national colors, and of Guadalupe as symbol of the national unity, consecrating the patriot blood that had been shed, was a consequence of her agelong role as protectress of Mexico. The first President of the Mexican Republic bore the predestined name of Guadalupe Victoria.

All had begun with the *sign* that Guadalupe had given to the Mexicans, the sign of the *bachiller* Miguel Sánchez to his compatriots, whose meaning Canon Siles had been the first to grasp in the month of June 1648 and which was to be transmitted and repeated endlessly in the course of the centuries by Mexican hands.

Signum: Sign, Miracle, Standard, Image, Seal, Goal,[38]

Miguel Sánchez had written, in that emblematic language which invites glossing. Like the *Names of Christ* of the blessed Luis de León, the *names of Guadalupe* have significance for the exegete. I do not believe I betray the hopes of the bachiller Sánchez or historical truth when I hazard the following interpretation:

Sign: password of the Mexican patriotic conspiracy.
Miracle: The miracle of accomplished national unity.

Standard: Standard of the Wars of Independence.
Image: Image of the Mexican people.
Seal: Indelible seal of the two cultures confronting a third culture.
Goal: The historical salvation of the Mexican people, the mysterious goal of the Guadalupan cult.

The Old and the New Guadalupe before History

The key item in the dossier composed by Canon Siles and transmitted by him to the Congregation of Rites was the documentary record of the inquiry of 1666. In fact, this dossier did not reach Rome, for the canon of Seville, Mateo de Bicunia, who had been charged with presenting the petition, died before he could accomplish his mission. This circumstance alone would explain its failure, but the creole Jesuit Francisco de Florencia exposed the canonical difficulties of the problem in his famous work, *La Estrella del Norte de México . . . Nuestra Señora de Guadalupe,* of 1688. The resumé given by Florencia makes unnecessary a detailed analysis: "The inquiry was very conclusive and very complete. Although eyewitnesses could not be found, because one hundred and thirty-five years had elapsed since the event, there were eight native witnesses who gave hearsay testimony of the miracle, obtained from contemporaries who had known Juan Diego, Juan Bernardino, and Monsignor Bishop Fray Juan de Zumárraga, the principal personages in that miraculous apparition. . . . And the deposition of Licentiate Luis Becerra Tanco cites four Spanish witnesses, three of whom were priests and the fourth an interpreter for the ecclesiastical Indian court, who had known witnesses of the miracle. . . . It therefore appears that the inquiry was perfectly proper."[39]

Father Florencia's argument seems to come down to the Latin aphorism: *Traditio est, nihil amplius quaeras* ("It is tradition, therefore ask nothing more"). Florencia sought to demonstrate the authenticity of the pious tradition by its effects: "The fact that this is a universal and well-established tradition, the influx of people to the sanctuary from all Mexico City who come to invoke Our Lady through her holy image of Guadalupe, the devotion and veneration accorded to the image, the sumptuous temple that was built sixty-six years ago, the very valuable gifts and offerings, the favors received by her intercession, the miracles that the Most Holy Virgin has worked: these are tangible proofs."[40] As for documentary proofs, the *Sufragio* of Luis Becerra Tanco, which accompanied the file drawn up by Siles in 1666, seemed to him sufficient.

Modern methods of historical inquiry do not consider oral tradition admissible evidence when it comes to establishing facts. This explains the clear-cut position of the Mexican scholar Joaquín García Icazbalceta, who regarded the statements under oath of creole priests and notables questioned in 1666 as indications of senility. The scholar who may be regarded as the founder of the history of colonial Mexico cited by way of refutation the silence of Archbishop Zumárraga, the principal witness of the miracle, according to the pious tradition, and the general silence of Mexican apologists like Bernardo de Balbuena, who, writing at the beginning of the seventeenth century, mentions all the sanctuaries and cults of any importance in Mexico City without breathing a word about the Guadalupe of Tepeyac. The writings of Sahagún, of Torquemada, and the inquiry of Montúfar, above all, fatally undermined the tradition. The ambiguity of Florencia's proof arises from the fact that he considered the devout consensus conclusive evidence. But the consensus only proves the existence of a cult, not the miraculous origin of its object. The resistance of the Congregation of Rites, it seems, stemmed not so much from the suspect character of the proofs assembled by the inquiry, as from administrative concern with avoiding a precedent. One gathers this from a letter of Cardinal Rospillozi, cited and summarized by Florencia: "[there is] a very sage rule, observed both by the sovereign pontiff and the Congregation of Rites, not to canonize the miraculous images with which Christendom abounds, for if one creates a precedent, one cannot say no to all the others."[41]

Explaining its position, the papal response called attention to certain aspects of the cult of Guadalupe at Tepeyac which shed light on its enigmatic image. The Mexicans had requested a canonical prayer (*rezo propio*) on December 12, the date of the apparition, according to tradition. This date of December 12 being the fourth day of the octave of the Immaculate Conception, the Congregation of Rites replied: "Since the image was of the Conception and the apparition took place during one day of her octave, it seemed unnecessary to give her a canonical prayer separate from that which the Church made to Our Lady on that day."[42] In short, Rome regarded the Mexican Guadalupe as a replica, one among many such in the Hispanic world, of the *Inmaculada*. As a consolation to Canon Siles, a brief granted a "plenary indulgence for that day";[43] unfortunately, the pontifical brief had replaced the date of December 12 with that of September 12.

This lapse of the Congregation of Rites tends to confirm that at the end of the eighteenth century Rome still regarded the Guadalupe of Mexico City as a replica of the Guadalupe of Estremadura, whose feast day came in September (September 8). The reasons that Florencia advanced to explain this "error" (probably intentional) of the Congregation of Rites, while unconvincing, do shed light on the question of the change of the calendar in the cult of Guadalupe at Tepeyac. The Jesuit attributed the error to the fact that "someone must have read that the feast day of Our Lady is held in September, as is in fact that case, and must have confused the feast day of September (celebrated at that time because the holy image is patroness against the floods of Mexico City, and September is the month when the danger of flooding is greatest and it was in that month that the memorable inundation of 1629 took place, on which occasion the holy image of Guadalupe was brought to Mexico City to combat it) with December 12, the date on which the miraculous apparition is celebrated because it took place on December 12."[44]

This makes quite clear that the original image of Tepeyac was copied from the Guadalupe of Estremadura, whose feast day coincided providentially with the period of great rains in the valley of Mexico. The intercession of Guadalupe had proven efficacious, notably in the course of the terrible floods of 1629. That this circumstance was present in the memory of the Mexican creoles thirty-five years later is certain; it is much less likely that it was known in Rome. At the time when Florencia wrote his essay the two feast days of Guadalupe were in competition: the original feast day of September 12, a heritage from the Guadalupe of Estremadura, reinforced by the cycle of rains (important in the beliefs of Mexican polytheism and a source of periodic anguish for the creoles of Mexico City) and the new feast day of December 12, which the apologists for the apparition sought to make prevail. Had the date of December 12 been made an obligatory feast day by the Congregration of Rites, it would have crowned the process of "Mexicanization" of the image of Tepeyac, which would thus have broken its calendrical ties (after breaking its iconographic connection) with the Spanish Guadalupe. The office of December 12, for the rest, would have implicitly confirmed the "apparition," happily situated in the octave of the Immaculate Conception, then a flowering cult in Hispanic Christendom. Finally, those roses of December of which the image of Tepeyac was composed, admirably symbolized the situation of the *Indiada*—the Indian masses—left in such desperate plight by defeat, and saved by Mary's redeeming grace.

The cult of Guadalupe of Estremadura had developed in a comparable historical climate, according to tradition. Moreover, the miracles of the Guadalupe of Manila, reported by Fray Gaspar de San Agustín in his *Conquistas de las islas Philipinas* (1698), cited previously, have in common with those of the Virgin of Tepeyac that they benefited the natives of Luzon. Although the image of Manila was not reputed to be miraculous, like that of Tepeyac, it had the fame of producing healing miracles, among others the resurrection of a Tagalog child one year old. In a contemporary relation we find the following account of the history of the origins of the image of Guadalupe of Manila:

At first, in 1601, this beautiful church was dedicated to Our Lady de las Gracias, a wooden statue very similar to that which is venerated in Estremadura of Spain under the same invocation.

After three years , in 1604, at the request of the Spaniards who then lived in Manila, the name of Our Lady de las Gracias was changed to that of Our Lady of Guadalupe, in order that the Philippines might have a church dedicated to the Queen of Heaven and Earth in her image of New Spain, so venerated and so rich in offerings.[45]

The role of the Augustinians in this transfer of the image of Tepeyac to the Philippines (the Philippines were under the jurisdiction of the religious provinces of New Spain), was certainly decisive. But it is doubtful that the reference is to the Guadalupe of Tepeyac. More likely it is to the Guadalupe of Estremadura, especially since in those years there was discovered in a river of the island of Luzon a replica of *Nra. Sra de la Pena de Francia,* another brown (*morenica*) Virgin venerated in Estremadura. The extraordinary flowering of the cult of Guadalupe of Mexico in the eighteenth century would lead to a refashioning of the Philippine tradition, understandable in view of the fact that the islands were a religious, administrative, and economic annex of New Spain.

What is noteworthy, in any case, is the substitution of one image of the Virgin Mary for another, with the new one soon proving its greater efficacy by means of miracles. The possibility of a transfer of the sacred virtues of the original Guadalupe of Villuercas (Caccres) to its copies was an essential aspect of the cult and of the pilgrimages. Father Francisco de San José in his previously cited *Historia* (1743) of the first image of Guadalupe (that of Estremadura), writes: "She appears as miraculous in her copies as in the original image . . . , and innumerable prodigies are said to have been performed by the medals, and portraits on cloth and paper, of the Virgin of Guadalupe. I could cite many such cases."[46] The religious added that in this respect the Virgin resembled the sun, which communicated its light to the objects on which it shone. Recalling the importance of lunar symbolism in the Mexican image of Guadalupe, one could translate the symbolic relations between the sun of Guadalupe of Villuercas and the moon of Guadalupe of Tepeyac into astronomical phenomena. From this point of view, the Mexican tradition of the "apparitions" becomes unnecessary to explain the miracles of Tepeyac.

Although the terms of the bull *Non est equidem* (1754) were cautiously phrased with regard to the authenticity of the apparitions of Guadalupe—"It is reported that in 1531 a miraculously painted image of the Mother of God appeared in Mexico City"—it nevertheless made up for the defeat of 1666. Florencia's tract, *La Estrella del Norte de México* (1688), had a decisive effect on the history of the Mexican cult of Guadalupe. The Jesuit also devoted an essay to the rival image of Remedios, but it was *La Estrella del Norte* that was republished in 1741, in Spain, after the death of Father Florencia, perhaps at the initiative of another great Mexican creole devotee of Mary, Francisco Javier Lazcano. The latter himself published at Venice a treatise *De principatu Marianae gratiae,* and at Rome an essay, *Brevis notitia Apparitionis mirabilis B. Mariae Virginis de Guadalupe,* the first in 1755 and the latter in 1756; these dates coincide with the pontifical recognition of the patronage of Guadalupe over New Spain. In his book Florencia had advised concerning the approach to be made to the Congregation of Rites;[47] It seems that the eighteenth-century Jesuits profited by his counsels.

In reality, the dossier of the Guadalupe of Tepeyac must have seemed to Rome no worse and no better than any other of its kind. One is struck by the similarity with that of the Guadalupe of Estremadura as presented a little more than a century before by the prior of the Jeronymite monastery of Villuercas, Fray Gabriel de Talavera. The arguments he advanced in favor of the authenticity of the Villuercas tradition are identical with those the Jesuit Florencia used to support the Mexican tradition:

GUADALUPE DE LAS VILLUERCAS (Spain)	GUADALUPE OF TEPEYAC (New Spain)
Image	
Sculptured by the Apostle Luke. Miraculous preservation.	Painted by the angel Gabriel. The "continuous miracle" of its preservation.
Site of the Apparition	
A mountain, among rocks, near a river with steep banks.	A hill, among rocks, near a spring.
Circumstances of the Apparition	
Incredulity of the clergy of the provincial capital.	Incredulity of the clergy of the capital.
Repetition of the apparition, the Virgin's wish to have her sanctuary established at the site of the apparition.	Repetition of the apparition, the Virgin's wish to have her sanctuary established at the site of the apparition.
Resurrection of a close relative of the witness of the apparition.	Resurrection of a close relative of a witness of the apparition.
Enlightenment of the clergy, who organize a procession and inaugurate the sanctuary.	Enlightenment of the archbishop; he installs the image in a new sanctuary.

Immediate massive popular support.	Massive popular support (especially among the Indians).
A time of disarray for the Christian community after the Moslem invasion.	A time of disarray for Indian converts after the Spanish Conquest, followed by great epidemics.

Development of the Cult

Historiographic silence from 1322, the presumed date of the apparition, until 1440, date of the first Guadalupan apologetic manuscript.	Historiographic silence from 1531, presumed date of the apparition, to 1648, date of the first Guadalupan apologetic work.
Foundation of the monastery of Guadalupe in 1340 by King Alfonso XI as a thanksgiving for the victory of Salado over the Moors.	Construction of the first sanctuary of Tepeyac, by public subscription, eighty years. after the date of the apparition according to the tradition (1609).
Our Lady of Guadalupe de las Villuercas is the most favored sanctuary of the peninsula, from Alfonso XI to the Catholic kings, reaching its apogee at the end of the Reconquista and during the conquest of America —end of the fifteenth and beginning of the sixteenth centuries.	Our Lady of Guadalupe of Tepeyac is sworn "principal Patroness" of Mexico City two centuries after the apparition (1737). Pontifical recognition of the Guadalupan tradition and the "universal Patronage" of Guadalupe over all Mexico (from 1754).
Multiplication of healing miracles in the beginning, then a role of supernatural protection with respect to the national community (Reconquest).	Multiplication of healing miracles in favor of Indians, at first, then the salvation of the entire community (floods 1629; epidemic 1737).

Father Talavera devotes a whole dissertation to proving the force of tradition in general. "We know the credit that the Church gives to custom, the importance that Saint Paul assigns to it, and what authority it enjoys among the learned."[48] Pope Julius II had issued a bull recognizing the sanctuary of Our Lady of Loreto, without other proof than tradition. "We may therefore say that in this case, which is public knowledge, the unanimous voice of the people is the voice of God."[49] Since the oral tradition had continued uninterruptedly, historiographic silence did not weaken the force of the pious legend; the author invoked the precedent of the Gospels, whose originals were lost but whose copies did not lose any of their authority on that account. Fray Alonso de Oropesa, prior of Guadalupe, caused the first relation to be written in 1455. Then "was composed the famous history of Guadalupe; and its authors acknowledged that they had taken it from ancient books, written at a time when there still lived many witnesses of the miracles and prodigies of its wonderful discovery."[50] According to Father Talavera, if there had been deception on the part of the first friar-historian, the surviving witnesses would have denounced the fraud and the tradition would have immediately lost its support. If the contemporaries of the miracle did not record it in writing, it was because of the well-known Spanish carelessness, "some being busy with the trade of war, others with government, and others wrapped up in their own affairs." The most ancient documents had disappeared "in the disorder that wars engender."[51] What remained as final proof was the "universal devotion," confirmed by innumerable miracles.

One of the most astounding miracles, perhaps, was "the preservation of the holy image for more than six centuries in a damp site situated near the river."[52] This fact recalls (or prefigures) "the spontaneous restoration" of the image of Tepeyac, duly attested by painters and physicians, the subject of Miguel Cabrera's book.[53] The miraculous preservation of sacred images, far from being a special attribute of the divine *ayate* of Tepeyac, seems to be a cliché of pious traditions. In his *Journey to Covadonga,* Ambrosio de Morales, a priest sent to the sanctuary by King Philip to inquire into the tradition, wrote: "It is said that this church was founded by King Alfonso the Chaste, and that it has remained miraculously in the same state ever since, without any decay of its wood."[54] Morales was skeptical and saw "clear signs of new construction"; but he accompanied his doubt with the reflection, which recalls Father Talavera: "God can perform the greatest miracles." Reverence for the divine power is the common denominator of Morales's incredulity and Talavera's credulity. When he reports the discovery of an image of the *Ecce homo* at Zebu by a soldier who was digging the foundations for his house, Fray Gaspar de San Agustín describes the event as a "miraculous discovery," and accompanies his account with this reflection: "A very holy image of an *Ecce homo* has been found, a wooden sculpture very well preserved for having lain so many years in such a place."[55]

Another trait common to the image of Villuercas and that of Tepeyac: the humble condition of the witness of the "apparition" —a shepherd in Spain, an Indian *macehual* or peasant in Mexico. Thanks to the lowly state of the elect, the grace received touched the entire community. For the same reason the priests of Caceres, and

Archbishop Zumárraga, later on, were incredulous; the Virgin herself had to intervene to gain recognition of the prodigy and construction of the basilica at the new place of pilgrimage; such, at least, is the tradition. I shall not dwell on the topographic constants (distance from the city, height, a nearby fountain or river), but I must stress the popular character of all these traditions. Come from the people, pronounced by the voices of friars who had issued from the people, the pious legends (the Marian legends in particular) encountered the resistance of learned bishops who found them suspect. Later, the fame of the miracles causing new miracles to occur, the state could not disavow a cult which attracted pilgrims and had no option but to try to attach the meaning of a sanctuary that was above all chthonic to the universal transcendence of Christianity. The pontifical refusal to acknowledge the miraculous origin of any particular local image was inspired by a desire to maintain the link which united all the cults to one Catholic cult of the Virgin Mary in her Immaculate Conception.

The fact that the image of Tepeyac was painted, not sculptured, did not make it unique; Fray Diego de Ocaña, the friar sent from the monastery of Estremadura to South America, in 1602 painted for the cathedral of Sucre a replica of the Guadalupe de las Villuercas "on cloth," and proclaimed that "there is not another image of this kind in the whole world, for the painting is so splendid that it dazzles all who see it." It may be recalled that the Jeronymite, by his own admission, had only vague notions of the technique of illumination, for he adds that "I, too, was stupefied at my own talent . . . evidently due to the aid of the Most Holy Virgin of Guadalupe."[56] The rapture of devotees before the superhuman beauty of the image was analogous to that which pilgrims felt at the sight of the Guadalupe of Tepeyac. Only a supernatural intervention could explain such beauty. A Mexican tableau of the eighteenth century represented the Holy Spirit painting the image of Tepeyac; one author attributes the tableau to the archangel Saint Michael, another to Gabriel. . . . The most ardent enthusiasts affirmed that the Virgin Mary herself, on her own initiative, had imprinted her image on the *tilma* or cloak of the Indian convert Juan Diego. The precedent of the marble column on which the Virgin had appeared, at Zaragoza, before the eyes of the apostle Saint James authorized a new self-portrait of Mary at Mexico City.

In all respects—the anecdotal details of the pious legend, the topographic conditions of the sanctuary, the "spontaneous" popular origin of the cult, the resistance of the church, the historiographic silence of more than a century, the belated flowering of an apologetical literature, the growing influx of pilgrims—the cult of Tepeyac appears to be a repetition of the cult of Estremadura. This does not mean that the former should be considered a simple reflection of the latter. We can only say that in the case of two peoples, inhabiting the same spiritual world, comparable historical ordeals, threatening the existence of the community, inspired the rise of analogous mythical responses at an interval of more than two centuries. The historian also notes the fact of emigration from the old places of pilgrimage; to the extent that they promise salvation to the community, the gods are found accompanying men in their migrations. To New Spain, with the delay of more than a century that is normal in the transfer of a holy place, came the "New Guadalupe," like a reserve of spiritual oxygen needed by the new society to affirm its identity and stimulate its development. Considering, as A. Dupront notes, that it took a thousand years and several fruitless crusades to achieve the transfer of the holy places from Palestine to Western Europe (specifically to Santiago de Compostela), we observe, beginning in the seventeenth century in America, an acceleration of history, at least of those spiritual processes that serve as beacons marking its course.

16   Epilogue:
        Guadalupe Today

Guadalupe Today

The essential problem remains the problem of what was early described as the Mexican "Mariophany." The term is appropriate, for it truly describes a new epiphany. Because the image of Guadalupe has been interpreted as a new epiphany ever since the *Historia* of Miguel Sánchez, published in 1648, it inspired a large devout literature from that time down to the nineteenth century, with a belated resurgence in the twentieth century, marked especially by the publication of the *Album guadalupano del IV centenario* of the Jesuit Father Mariano Cuevas, in 1931. Drawing inspiration from Marc Bloch, I may express my position as follows: the question is not whether the image of Our Lady of Guadalupe, venerated on Mount Tepeyac, is the result of a miracle or the work of a native artist. "The problem is to understand how it happened that so many men believed and still believe"[1] (in a Mexico in which there triumphed a revolution of positivist inspiration, followed by a revolution under Marxist influence) in the miraculous character of the image of Tepeyac.

The cult of Guadalupe is the central theme of the history of creole consciousness or Mexican patriotism. Every study of that subject must inevitably lead to that cult or take it as its point of departure.

The Mexican Mariophany I regard as a *patriotic epiphany* in which one of the most permanent currents of Christianity, the cult of Mary the Immaculate, and one of the fundamental beliefs of the ancient Mexican religion, the dual principle, converge. This phenomenon illuminates the history of the Mexican people in the degree that, within a certain ethic and a system of thought which is no longer that of our times, it was, in the happy phrase of Francisco de la Maza, the "mirror" of the national consciousness. For Maza "the cult of Guadalupe and baroque art are the only authentic creations of the Mexican past."[2] The cult of Guadalupe was the spiritual aspect of the protest against the colonial regime. Well before Justo Sierra and Antonio Caso, there appeared in Mexican history the permanent search for identity, for *Mexicanidad*. Since the sixteenth century this passionate quest for the national soul (the *Mexicayotl* of the ancients) has been inseparable from a thirst for the acquisition of grace and the miracles that are its manifestation; thus, much later, Justo Sierra wanted to "mexicanize knowledge,"[3] that is, science, that grace of positivist times. At different moments of Mexican history, the mirror of the national consciousness has been called Saint Thomas-Quetzalcóatl, Tonantzin-Guadalupe, or by some other name. The first corresponds to the hour of the primitive evangelization, and its mission was to free the Indians, in a way, form a Christianity which they were not yet ready to accept, but above all from sixteen centuries of spiritual darkness which delivered them bound hand and foot to the Enemy of mankind. The identification of Quetzalcóatl with Saint Thomas amounted to *mexicanizing Christianity*, to paraphrase Justo Sierra. The relatively belated upsurge of the cult of Guadalupe (it took more than a century after the supposed apparition of 1531 for the first "gospel" of Guadalupe to appear) coincided, we have seen, with the favor that the cult of the Immaculate Conception then enjoyed. Here again, it was a question of *mexicanizing the Immaculate Conception*. In both cases, the collective aspiration tended toward the universal through the national, toward the recognition of national dignity in the concert of nations. Centuries before Samuel Ramos, Mexico elaborated at each moment of its history a philosophy that was the expression of the "circumstance," in the sense in which Ortega y Gasset has defined that word. The development of the civic cult of the young forebear (*joven abuelo*) Cuauhtémoc played the same role after the triumph of the Mexican revolution, at a time when an indigenist current rehabilitated the Indian, regarded as the nucleus of Mexicanidad. In this connection, Alfonso Reyes has rightly cited the poetess Victoria Ocampo: our ancestors, she wrote, felt themselves to be "possessors of a soul without a passport";[4] the expression suggests a constant of Mexican history. The Mexican creoles manifested a fervent and possessive attachment for the Virgin Mary in her prodigious image of Guadalupe, "this celestial treasure" (*este Celestial Tesoro*), for she was the "passport" of their sinful souls and their subjugated *patria*.

In the age of speed, Guadalupe has become the tutelary image of the truck driver and the airplane pilot. Placed on the dashboard of all the taxis of Mexico City, accompanied by the eloquent motto "Holy Virgin, protect me!" the protective image is watched over by a little red light that has replaced the candles of yesteryear. Her "Universal patronage," diversified and enlarged together with the empire of techniques, now extends to the new perils of the twentieth century.

17   Perspectives

The Spains and Beyond

The central phenomenon of the formation of Mexican national consciousness may be called the *dialogue of the cultures*. Its effects are
visible throughout the history of New Spain, but it is necessary to
distinguish its different levels. On the technological level, it is composed of exchanges and loans; for example, the European image of
the Virgin of Guadalupe was painted on a coarse tissue of agave fiber
(*ayatl*), which was used by the Indians to make cloaks (*tilmatli*). On the
level of beliefs the question clearly is more complex, but we find here
the same kind of exchanges: reinterpretation of Tonantzin; the
creole challenge to Spain through the cult of Guadalupe of Tepeyac;
imitation of the apologetic of Saint James of Compostela by creole
apologists for Saint Thomas-Quetzalcóatl. In the latter case, the creole
spirit resorts to conscious imitation of Spain. The Mexican wish to
break with Spain does not prevent mimicry with respect to the
Spanish language and beliefs. At the very height of the controversies
which opposed Eguiara y Egurén to Dean Martí, and Juan Bautista
Muñoz to several Mexican authors, the dialogue between Hispanic
culture and Aztec culture continued without interruption. The creation of new mythical images associating Iberian contributions with
Amerindian hieroglyphic signs was the most profound form of this
symbiosis. The enigmatic expression of hybrid myths in creole
emblematic language represents the maximum interiorization of the
fusion of cultures; indeed, the existence of new myths and their original expression is the birth certificate of a new culture. But if Mexican
civilization appeared early, issuing from that violent effort which
Wigberto Jiménez Moreno has described,[1] the two mother cultures
continued to express themselves, each in its own language. Mexican
pictographic expression was transformed and enriched with hieroglyphs of a new kind, a necessary consequence of the need to express
Christian symbols and concepts. The studies of Joaquín Galarza on
the devices used to express Christian symbolism in the post-Conquest

codices give a good idea of the syncretic richness of those documents. We know less about the evolution undergone by the ritual songs and dances of the Mexican Indians, songs and dances which retain to the present the most characteristic means of expression of their faith. But we are not much better informed about the borrowing of creole sacred eloquence from Spanish conceptism, carried to abusive extremes by Fray Gerundio de Campazas.

The remodeling of the Mexican pious traditions according to the traditional patterns of Iberian hagiography, the directions borrowed by the Mexican wait for the Second Coming, indisputably show New Spain's complete integration in the Hispanic *vividura* or "mode of being." The very trait which distinguishes New Spain's spiritual life, the resurgence of the call of Abraham in the new form of the *call of Guadalupe,* is clearly a loan from a Hispano-Portuguese Christianity saturated over long centuries with Judaism.[2] A study of the mentality or general history of New Spain would not be correctly oriented if it did not center on the existence of intimate and permanent bonds with Spain. In effect, it was from Spain that Mexico drew its substance; if the Spaniards abusively exploited the productive forces, the mineral and agricultural resources of Mexico, it was Spain—however unwillingly—that made Mexico a nation. The very style of the Mexican War of Independence was that of the Spanish War of Independence. Who knows whether the Mexicans would have taken arms to liberate themselves from Spanish tutelage if the Spanish people—the *gachupines*—had not offered an example (which was also a challenge) by rising up against the French invaders? An analysis of Spanish revolutionary literature and the proclamations of the Mexican liberators reveals a striking similarity of ideas. Here is a rich field for study in which the marriage of the Enlightenment with the Judeo-Christian heritage could teach us much about the origins of the ideologies of progress and their links to the messianic wait. The methods of Sperber and Guiraud (to which A. Dupront has drawn the attention of historians),[3] furnish valuable tools for research of this nature.

We would oversimplify Mexcian reality if we reduced the dialogue of the cultures to an exchange between the ancient dominant Aztec culture and the new dominant Hispanic culture. Rich and very new studies could be made of Michoacán. Far from the radiant center of Mexico City, the Tarascans, who maintained their freedom from the Aztec domination, developed an original culture and beliefs in the marginal zone which they occupied, a zone which, we know, played a decisive role in the Wars of Independence. I have called attention more than once to the important role of the Tlaxcalan tribe, composing almost the whole population of the diocese of Puebla. Blacks and mulattoes also created in Mexico, as in other regions of America, an embryonic counterculture of which the diary of Robles offers at least some evidence.[4] However, these are regional phenomena whose effects on the formation of the Mexican nation have been limited or occasional. The orientation of New Spain's spiritual life and the development of Mexican national consciousness have been above all regional variants of the evolution of the Hispanic world.

The most remarkable example of this is the apologetic literature about Saint Thomas-Quetzalcóatl. The apostolic evangelization of the Indians was supposed to have made "old Christians" (*cristianos viejos*) of them and to have washed them clean from that new original sin invented by the Christian communities of Spain, the sin of being "new Christians." By an easy analogy the Indians were more or less expressly assimilated to the Jews and Moors. Their protectors, the missionary friars, knew only one way of saving the Indians from the indignity of those second-class subjects of the king of Castile: to prove the apostolic conversion of the New World. This effort differed not at all from the "false chronicles" (*falsos cronicones*) composed in the same period by apologists for the Granadan Moriscos and the Jews converted by force. In a society in which individuals adorned themselves with borrowed genealogies attesting to their "purity of blood" (the only way of recovering social dignity and gaining access to honors), the ethnic groups regarded as "ignoble" also resorted to able historians to compose for them a past of "old Christians."[5] The skepticism of the official Spanish historiographers was the first challenge thrown down to the creole apologists. To deny the identity of Quetzalcóatl with the apostle Saint Thomas, to deny the authenticity of the apparitions of the Virgin Mary at Tepeyac, were so many ways of reducing the Indians (and the Creoles after them) to the ignoble state of infidels and idolaters. Consequently the aspiration to dignity (*dignificación*) became a constant in the Hispanic-American societies. It survived long after Independence, as proved by the success in Argentina of Peronist *Justicialismo*, whose slogan was: "Peron keeps his word, Evita gives you back your dignity (*Peron cumple, Evita dignifica*)." The thirst for justice also blended with the hope for the coming of Christ or its Mexican variant, the reign of Guadalupe or that of Quetzalcóatl (the first pointing to the future, the second to the past).[6]

The great spiritual currents which flowed across Western Christendom between the end of the sixteenth and the nineteenth centuries (not to speak of the twentieth century when Spanish emigration played a capital ideological role in Mexico) reached Mexico by way of Spain. To begin with, the climate of the marvelous in which the conquerors of the New World were bathed was directly inherited from the great Crusades or rather their spiritual aftermath, above all the crusading spirit which was to mark so profoundly the Western church. The creole charismatic spirit had its roots in that moment; the Conquistadors, like the crusaders before them, felt themselves to be God's chosen. In an anonymous relation of the Crusades which Émile Brehier published, we see saints mounted on white horses coming to the aid of crusaders against the Turks, several centuries before Saint James, killer of Moors (*Santiago matamoros*) came to put the Indians to rout. I need not again stress the importance of the spirit of poverty which on the part of the "Twelve" went hand in hand with the expectation of the Second Coming. The Indies were simultaneously the last refuge of the feudal spirit of the Peninsula and of the spirit of evangelical renovation of the mendicant orders—a spirit soon to become suspect in Spain. A utopian Spain in its beginnings, New Spain would remain such until and even after her political independence; and her constant rivalry with Spain, nourished by the debate relative to Quetzalcóatl and Guadalupe, was due above all to the Mexican feeling that their *patria* was a promised land.

If the Second Coming was the permanent horizon of Mexican spirituality, by the joint effect of Christian eschatology since the evangelical renovation and Judaic messianism, the new Mexican cosmogonic space was totally tributary to the Crusades. After the fall of Jerusalem, Western religiosity assumed forms that were after a fashion compensatory: pilgrimages, the cult of relics.[7] Here was an astounding fact: the mythical Orient set in motion, beginning a slow revolution toward the Ultima Thule. One of the first stations of the New Jersalem took place at Santiago de Compostela, heart of Western Christendom during the centuries when it was reborn after suffering the heavy defeat of the Crusades and passing the cape of the first millennium. The conquest of America was like a new departure of the youthful forces of Europe on a new crusade, this time to the West. It was as if, having failed to reconquer and retain the historical Jerusalem, the nephews of the Crusaders had departed (knights errant in search "of the divine," Saint Teresa de Ávila would have said) to build a New Jerusalem at the antipodes of the Old. This supernatural adventure was authenticated by signs, in the first place the apparition of the Virgin Mary at Tepeyac, which promoted the Mexican sanctuary to the rank of a new, sacred North Star of Hispanic Christendom.

History as Hermeneutics and as Catharsis

The history written in the Christian West from the time of Gregory of Tours down to the French Revolution was essentially derived from the economy of salvation. A document like the *Tablas chronológicas* of J. E. Nieremberg, published at the end of the eighteenth century, makes this fact quite clear for the Hispanic world.[8] The *Historia de España vindicada* (previously cited), following Mariana's *Historia,* organizes the events of Spanish history in their relation to the Incarnation and assigns a capital importance to events which had an eschatological importance, like the preaching of the Apostle Saint James in the Iberian peninsula, the apparition of the Virgin Mary at Pilar de Zaragoza, the discovery of the relics of the apostle. The Christian menology completed this vision of the Hispanic past. These characteristics of historiography had been fixed long before, for they flowed from Revelation itself. "Canticle of glory, history took its place in the immense liturgy which the monasteries offered as an example of perfect life and displayed as a prefiguration of celestial joys. Finally, history made it possible to discern more clearly, within the framework of time, the roads of humanity on the march toward salvation. . . . Holy Scripture, which is no other than history, described it as a progressive ascent in three Times."[9] These lines by George Duby, dealing with the friar-historians of the eleventh century, could be applied without change to the historiography of the Indies.

Two competing currents of historical hermeneutics confronted each other throughout the history of New Spain. The providential historiography of the Conquest, of which the work of Acosta and that of Solórzano Pereira offer good examples, presented this conquest as a holy act reserved by providence for the elect of God, for Columbus and Cortés above all, but also for the Spaniards in general (indeed, for the Aragonese in particular). As Robert B. Tate clearly saw, "the political rise of Spain was accompanied by a flowering of mythological history."[10] To this providential vision the Mexican creoles, with the help of sermons or tracts of Guadalupan apologetics, opposed another providential vision. According to the latter, the Conquest was realized to permit the new incarnation of the Word at Tepeyac; consequently, the elect were not the Spaniards but the Indians and the creole restorers of the ancient Mexican splendor. The whole historical problem was thus reduced to a question of exegesis, which explains the constant preoccupation of the historiographers with chronology. The Last Times, the climax of humanity's supernatural adventure, have always been anxiously awaited as the moment when the gates of glory would open, but also awaited with a sacred terror. History had for its object to reassure the nations on this point; the surest means was to persuade them that they were the elect of God. Hence the esoteric jugglings with coincidences of dates and numbers with which the pious and hagiographic literature of New Spain is so replete. The

search—one is tempted to say "tracking down"—of the visible *signs* of
divine grace, promise of the glory to come, was one of the essential
objects of history. The history of Israel had the value of an archetype
and of providing a model for historical writing. The facts of contemporary history were routinely illuminated by one or another episode
of sacred history. Each national history was viewed as a reflection of
the history of Israel, the more so because each region of Hispanic
Christendom felt itself called to a Covenant. The controversies among
Spanish and creole historians of the New World would seem vain were
they not constantly illuminated by their eschatological background.
That is why I first planned to retain as the subtitle of this work *Eschatology and History,* before adopting the more explicit title of *The
Formation of Mexican National Consciousness.*[11] It was by seeking to impose a new providential version of its history that New Spain defeated
Spain in the lists of hermeneutics, achieving its spiritual emancipation, the necessary prelude to its political independence.

But if Mexican historiography was in its origins a sacred hermeneutics, it was at the same time a catharsis. I have already observed that
the image of its past that a society gives itself is more revealing of the
state of its consciousness than the utopian formulation of the future to
which that society aspires. In reality, the two aspects are complementary, but the cathartic vision is more intelligible for the historian. The
image of the national future reveals shortcomings: the Mexican creole
aspired to *dignity.* The image of the national past is not the product of
unrestrained imagination; it must take into account the reality preserved by the chronicles and in the given case the pictographic codices
and manuscript commentaries of the missionary friars or their native
students. In order to fulfill satisfactorily its function of catharsis, history must sort out the facts of the chronicles. Thus we have seen the
Spanish chroniclers (*gachupines*) describe with complacence the
human sacrifices and ritual sprees (*borracheras*) of the Aztec religion,
while creole authors compared the Mexican *tlatoani* with the emperors
of ancient Rome and denounced the treachery of Cortés, which they
considered the only cause of the Mexican defeat.[12] Omission or, contrariwise, a prolix insistence, are the most obvious techniques of a
history designed to dress up a dead fatherland. There are more subtle
means which one cannot even describe as techniques, for the historians undoubtedly were unconscious of using them. Themselves
members of the society of New Spain, they were but mediators between the vision of a past already haloed with an epic and marvelous
light in the early chronicles, and readers avid to read the confirmation
of their charismatic certitude. That is why history sometimes appears
as an incident in the triumphal discourse of the pious literature,

sometimes as an Indianist apologia. The latter is meaningful only as a function of a hermeneutic: the Indians are part of the line of Adam, they were converted by an apostle, their prophets had announced the Conquest, their converts received *signs* of God's favor. In the free universe of a history which drew its substance from Scripture rather than from the national past, the creole creative fantasy could take a brilliant revenge over the *gachupines*, protected as it was by the double rampart of historical "truth" and the truth of Scripture. Hermeneutic on both the creole and the Spanish sides, the historiography of the Indies was above all a liberating catharsis for the American creoles. It was in historiographic discourse that the dialogue of the cultures appeared most prominently.

Suggestions for an "Introhistoric" History of Mexico[13]

The present study does not claim to exhaust the material offered by the two subjects of Quetzalcóatl and Guadalupe. In reality they have only been a means of illuminating Mexican history, approached from a religious point of view. To achieve the wish expressed by Alfonso Reyes[14] would have required a large anthropological inquiry that only a number of teams of investigators could have carried out. Here I have indicated enough landmarks to prove the primordial importance of religious beliefs in the formation of the Mexican nation. If there was not, properly speaking, a Mexican *geographic space* that from the first defined the natural borders of modern Mexico, there existed, on the other hand, a *sacred space* whose existence ordered the national potentialities of the societies of New Spain as a field of forces. Study of the profound continuities which characterize the development, flowering, and decline of the great national mythic images reveals the slow processes of social transformation of New Spain. Correlatively, the jolts of a history so often troubled by natural disasters and political upheavals more than once contributed to a sudden upsurge of national consciousness. The importance of seismic, epidemic, or political accidents in the history of a society varies according to the interpretation of those events that is offered to men or that they spontaneously forge for themselves. A study of reactions to an event in New Spain can be attempted on the base of the dispersed evidence which has been preserved. Javier Ocampo has successfully carried out an effort of this kind for the period of Independence; I have sketched a portrait of the Mexican public response to a decisive crisis, the expulsion of the Jesuits. The history of what Alfonso Reyes somewhat romantically called the "national soul" (*alma nacional*) of Mexico, remains to be written. I have only sought to show that the avatars of the myth of

Quetzalcóatl in the creole apologetics, and the cult of Guadalupe, have been among the most characteristic aspects of this Mexican "national soul" in the process of formation, from the sixteenth to the twentieth century. But other mythical figures, other beliefs, would reveal the same texture. Each sanctuary could be the object of a study in depth, beginning with that of Tepeyac, which I have only sketched, nothing more. The Christ of Chalma, the Cross of Tepic, the Virgin of Ocotlan, and so on, are so many regional components of the formation of a Mexican national consciousness, whose affirmation required the integration of an extraordinary ethnic diversity.

There is truly the heart of the problem. If it is true, as Roger Bastide has written, that "all folklore is a symbolic mediation between individuals and groups, and between groups,"[15] Mexican folklore, studied in all possible ways (inquisitorial archives of Mexico City, whose surface I have only skimmed; research on the spot, still very fragmentary) is the choice terrain of the ethnohistorian. I may cite here, giving it the broadest possible meaning, the judgment of Claude Lévi-Strauss: "Every work of history is impregnated with ethnology."[16] The notion of cultural challenge, whose importance has been revealed in sociology in connection with the study of Afro-American cultures, underlies the phenomena which I have described as syncretic. The substitutions and reinterpretations of beliefs borrowed from the dominant culture by the dominated culture in the last analysis represent efforts at salvaging the latter. The cult of Tonantzin was prolonged for centuries in the shelter of a sanctuary of the Virgin Mary.

Side by side with the permanence of sanctuaries and the revitalization of mythical images in a new religious context, we observe the creative activity of the collective memory. A popular genre like the *corrido* (poetry most often composed of octosyllables like the Spanish *romance* of which it is the American offshoot), the epic and lyrical breath of the Mexican nation, would yield to us, together with its original flavor, the fears and aspirations of the "national soul," if we hasten to sound-record it (as well as prepare a printed corpus) before it is extinguished in its turn.[17] One could say, imitating Melville Herskovits, that one of the essential aspects of the Mexican national consciousness has been "The Myth of the Indian Past."[18] The image of the pre-Columbian Indian is inseparable from the signs of the grace which he was supposed to have received in apostolic times (the evangelization of Saint Thomas-Quetzalcóatl) or after the Spanish Conquest (apparitions of the Virgin of Guadalupe, of Ocotlan; the miraculous cross of Tepic, and the like). The history of the birth and the evolution of a mythical image of the Indian, resulting from a creole reinterpretation of the native pictographic codices (preserved in the pictographic codices and the hymns) is a possible guideline for a history of the Mexican nation. I have tried to show the importance of authors like Sigüenza y Góngora and Clavijero (who had already drawn the attention of Mexican historians in this respect) from that point of view, but the inquiry should be enlarged beyond the authors to take in the collective consciousness. What Guijo thought of the Indians in his *Diary*, how the Indian appeared to such and such a witness in a trial, to a missionary friar in a given region, to Bishop Palafox, are so many valuable clues. The correlative question, that of the origin of the American Indians, whose spiritual implications at the beginning of the seventeenth century I have already suggested, continued to be the object of publications and controversies, in Europe and in the Americas, into the nineteenth century—not to speak of the twentieth. This vast question deserves to be reexamined.

There is one question whose importance has yet not been recognized, as far as I can tell: the study of emblematic expression. I have barely broached the subject in reference to the titles and the images of the Guadalupan apologetic literature and the coat of arms of Mexico City. The Mexican cults of protective images (cults that were both religious and patriotic) were expressed, on their highest level of elaboration, through the voices of preachers. It is not enough to speak of baroque exuberance, of bombast and incoherence; I have tried to show that we have to do with an original mode of expression, a *language*.[19] Whether we like it or not, the enigmatic language of the preachers is the language in which the Mexican national claims were first formulated. The mingling of mythological images from classic antiquity, from the Mexican past, and from the biblical tradition, according to the principles of the conceptism then at its height in Spain, formed the texture of a language whose semantic content remains to be discovered. Mexican baroque writings cannot be dissociated from the contemporary plastic expression of the same religious-patriotic sentiments and in particular from a heraldry renewed according to the needs of a pious and hagiographic apologetics.

In a different form, the popular ex-votos were the naive language of devotion in New Spain; they have already formed the object of studies in Mexico, but each passing year makes more difficult the discovery of an ex-voto of indisputable authenticity. Beside these immobile testimonies, we must make a large place for dramatic representations of pious inspiration and the hymns (*cantares*) accompanied by dances. The borrowing of gestural or musical discourse from Hispanic culture, itself often born of the fusion of different borrowings (from Celtiberian, Arabo-Maghrebian, Visigothic, Latin, Judaic sources) rarely takes place without semantic changes; the same is true of Amerindian components, taken over apparently intact.[20]

New studies can enlarge our understanding of the history of New Spain, but they would remain incomplete if they were not prolonged toward modern Mexico. The study of Jean Meyer, *La Cristiada I. La guerra de los cristeros* (Siglo XXI, 1973), is a contribution of great interest to the history of Mexican national consciousness, whose evolution from the sixteenth to the nineteenth century I attempted to illuminate. Beginning with the period of Independence, we observe a change in the image of Guadalupe; from the protectress against epidemics that she had chiefly been, she becomes the "goddess of victory" and liberty. Thus each historical moment is capable of giving a sacred "recharge" to a pious image, by endowing it with a new power adapted to new aspirations. This enrichment was contained in the notion of a "universal Patronage," that is, one that was polyvalent and not specifically limited to floods and epidemics. Later, by a sort of shift of attributions, the Virgin of Guadalupe will appear as the symbol of the Conservative party, the Liberal party having sought, so to speak, to substitute the magical effect of an ideology of progress for the sacred power of the prodigious image. The tenacious hold of the cult of Guadalupe in a Mexico that is profoundly de-Christianized (at least in its urban milieu) deserves the attention of students of religious sociology. No less interesting is the question of the profound meaning, from the point of view of the national consciousness, of the Quetzalcóatl myth as a literary theme. The poets in particular have been fascinated by this mythical image of the Indian past: besides Mexicans like García Pimentel, Agustí Bartra, Carlos Fuentes,[21] we find the Chilean poetess Gabriela Mistral and D. H. Lawrence.[22] Without seeking to anticipate the conclusions of a study that may cast a surer light on the "Mexican soul," that is, on Mexican society, I may observe that the literary renaissance of Quetzalcóatl is contemporaneous with the rise of the indigenist movement in the 1920s and 30s.

If we accept the judgment of a psychologist of penetrating vision, according to whom, "The history of cultures is summed up in the process of the creation of mythical images, their dogmatization, and their destruction,"[23] we must admit that the viceregal culture inherited from New Spain is breathing its last in modern Mexico. Some day Guadalupe will become an extinct star, like the moon, with which she is associated; it would be fascinating to study the emergence of the mythical image that will replace her. Quetzalcóatl, by contrast, more closely linked to Mexican polytheism, and now detached from his temporary twin, Saint Thomas, seems to have a better chance of a future sacred "recharge" in a laicized society like that of present-day

Mexico. If the myth of Quetzalcóatl has retained its vitality throughout its successive avatars, in colonial and independent Mexico alike, it
is because he is the symbolic expression of the Indian past which the
creole consciousness sought to revive from its ashes so as to build
upon it the claim of Mexican independence. Evoking the origins of
the Mexican revolution, José Vasconcelos wrote that "Quetzalcóatl-
Madero won a victory without precedent."[24] After Madero, the Mexican people believed that it saw in Quetzalcóatl-Cárdenas the new incarnation of the Indian messiah come from the depths of the ages, a
Phoenix who is reborn with each new "sun" from the ashes of the
preceding sun. Like the aspiration for justice, Quetzalcóatl is im-
perishable; no sooner has he been driven away or, like Madero, assas-
sinated by a modern Tezcatlipoca, than he is ready to be reincarnated
in the form of a new political chief. Mexico is simultaneously a sacred
space, the land of the "children of Guadalupe," and, in time, a nostalgic yearning for the lost paradise of Quetzalcóatl, a floating myth ever
ready to alight on the Elect.

Notes

A Historian's Profession of Faith

1. Wilhelm Mühlmann, *Messianismes révolutionnaires du tiers monde*, Paris, Gallimard, 1968 (original ed., *Chiliasmus und nativismus*, Berlin, 1961).

2. Francisco de la Maza, *El guadalupanismo mexicano*, Mexico City, 1953.

3. Marc Bloch, *Apologie pour l'histoire ou métier d'historien* (1941), Paris, 1959 (3d ed.), p. 101.

4. Fray Servando Teresa de Mier [José Guerra], *Historia de la revolución de Nueva España, antiguamente Anáhuac*, London, 1813 (repr. Mexico City, 1922).

5. José M. Cuevas *Album histórico guadalupano del IV centenario*, Mexico City, 1930, p. 229.

6. George Dumézil, *Mythe et Épopée. L'idéologie des trois fonctions dans les épopées des peuples indo-européens*, Paris, Gallimard, 1968.

7. Claude Lévi-Strauss, *Anthropologie structurale*, Paris, Plon, 1958; *Magie et religion*, pp. 227–55.

8. Marcel Bataillon and Edmundo O'Gorman, *Dos concepciones de la tarea histórica con motivo del descubrimiento de América*, Mexico City, 1955 (Bataillon's letter to O'Gorman, p. 96).

9. Américo Castro, *La realidad histórica de España*, Mexico City, 1962 (enlarged ed.), pp. 109–10 and 117ff.

10. Charles Morazé, *La logique de l'histoire*, Paris, Gallimard, 1967.

11. Bloch, *Apologie pour l'histoire*, p. 7.

12. The present work is a revised and condensed version of a doctoral dissertation (*thèse de doctorat d'État*) presented to the University of Paris with the title *Quetzalcóatl et Guadalupe, Eschatologie et histoire au Mexique*, Bibliothèque de la Sorbonne W 1971 (52), 1–4 (4 vols.), 932 pp. + tables, index, maps, and illustrations.

Chapter 1

1. Juan de Solórzano Pereira, *Política Indiana*, Madrid, 1648, p. 244a.

2. Pedro de Bolívar y de la Redonda, *Memorial, informe y discurso legal, histórico y político al Rey Nuestro Señor en su Real Consejo de Cámara de las Indias, en favor de los Españoles, que en ellas nacen, estudian y sirven, para que sean preferidos en todas las provisiones eclesiásticas, y seculares, que para aquellas partes se hiciesen*, Madrid, 1667.

3. Dr. Juan de Cárdenas, *Problemas y secretos maravillosos de las Indias*, Mexico City, 1591, p. 177r.

4. Gemelli Carreri, *Viaje a la Nueva España (México a fines del siglo XVIII)*, preface by Fernando B. Sandoval, 2 vols. Mexico City, 1955, II, 232.

5. Fray Agustín de Vetancurt, *Teatro mexicano, Descripción breve de los sucessos exemplares de la Nueva España* (Mexico City, 1696), 4 vols., Madrid, 1960, II, 305–6.

Chapter 2

1. Gemelli Carreri, *Viaje a la Nueva España*, I, 45.
2. Ibid.
3. "Provisión . . . año de 1530," in *Cedulario indiano*, ed. by Diego de Encinas (Madrid, 1596), p. 135.

Chapter 3

1. *Libro primero de votos de la Inquisición de México (1573–1600)*, Mexico City, 1949, Appendix: "Instrucciones del cardenal D. Diego de Espinoza a los Inquisidores de México, agosto de 1570"; "rubr. 34: Item, se os advierte que por virtud de nuestros poderes no habeis de proceder contra los indios del dicho vuestro distrito. . . ." p. 297.
2. *Procesos de Indios idólatras y hechiceros, Publicaciones del Archivo General de la Nación*, vol. III, Mexico City, 1912. "Proceso del Santo Oficio contra Martín Ucelo, indio, por idólatra y hechicero," pp. 17–51.
3. Ibid., p. 29.
4. Ibid., p. 31.
5. Ibid., pp. 22–23.
6. Ibid., p. 58.
7. Ibid., p. 178.
8. *Libro primero de votos*, pp. 129–30.
9. Ibid., p. 269.
10. Ibid.
11. Ibid., p. 270.
12. J. Toribio Medina, *Historia del Tribunal del Santo Oficio de la Inquisición en México*, Mexico City, 1952, ed. by J. Jiménez Rueda, p. 259b.
    1. There shall be no tributes or taxes and contracts shall be free of duty;
    2. He grants freedom to all slaves;
    3. He promises rewards to the descendants of conquistadors and their sons;
    4. The right of presentation to the bishops, and the grant of prebends and benefices shall pertain to him;
    5. Indian parishes shall be returned to the religious and will be theirs in perpetuity;
    6. He promises to create titles of nobility and grandees in this kingdom;
    7. He promises to assign revenues to the convents;
    8. He promises to give dowries each year to one hundred maidens; he ends with a long protestation of the great service that he renders to God and this realm by throwing off the tyrannical yoke of the kings of Spain. . . .
13. Ibid., pp. 325–26. "Edicto del Tribunal de la Inquisición de Nueva España, de 26 de febrero, año de 1735." "They say he has made many prophecies, among them that the Antichrist has certainly been born, that the Day of Judgment is very near, but first the evil world must end and the good begin."

Chapter 4

1. Robert Ricard, *La "Conquête spirituelle" du Mexique. Essai sur l'apostolat et les méthodes missionaires des ordres mendicants en Nouvelle-Espagne, de 1523–24 a 1572*, Paris, Institut d'Ethnologie, 1933.
2. *Divini abbatis Joachim Liber Concordie Novi ac Veteris Testamenti, nunc primo impressus et in lucem editus, opere equidem divinum ac aliorum fere omnium tractatum suorum fundamentale, divinorum eloquiorum obscura elucidens, archana referans necnon eorundem curiosis*

sitibundisque mentibus non minus satietatem afferens. Venice, 1519.

3. Joachim of Floris, *Liber introductorius in expositionem in Apocalipsim, in L'Évangile éternel,* first French translation preceded by a biography by Emmanuel Aegerter, Paris, Rieder, 1928, vol. ii, p. 96.

4. Ibid., p. 50.

5. Ibid., p. 111.

6. Ibid., p. 92.

7. Ibid., pp. 117–18.

8. Ibid., p. 106.

9. Fray Bernardino de Sahagún, *Historia General de las cosas de la Nueva España,* 4 vols. Mexico City, Porrua, 1956, I, 90, 95.

10. Francisco López de Gómora, *Hispania Victrix, Primera y segunda parte de la historia general de las Indias* . . . (hereafter cited as *Historia general de las Indias*), in *Historiadores primitvos de Indias,* biblioteca de Autores Españoles, Madrid (hereafter cited as BAE), vol. XXII, p. 156.

11. Códice 55, Madrid, Archivo Histórico Nacional, fol. 6r.

12. Gómora, *Historia general de las Indias,* p. 156.

13. Gregorio García, *Orígen de los indios del Nuevo Mundo, e Indias occidentales, averiguado con discurso de opiniones por el Padre Presentado Fray Gregorio García de la Orden de Predicadores,* book I, ch. i, Valencia, 1607.

14. Ibid., n.35.

15. Ibid., ch. iii, p. 2.

16. Ibid., ch. viii.

17. Ibid., book II, ch. i, p. 4.

18. Ibid., n.17.

19. Ibid., ch. ii.

20. Ibid., n.19.

21. Ibid.

22. Ibid., book III, ch. i.

23. Ibid., ch. ii.

24. Ibid., n.23.

25. Ibid.

26. Ibid., "Proemio al lector."

27. Sahagún, *Historia General,* IV, 18.

28. Fray Antonio de la Calancha, *Crónica moralizada de la Orden de San Agustín en el Perú,* Barcelona, 1639, p. 311.

29. Ibid., p. 312.

30. Ibid., n.29.

31. Francisco de Florencia, SJ, *Historia de la Provincia de la Compañía de Jesús de Nueva España,* Mexico City, 1694; idem, "Parecer que dio el M. R. P. Francisco de Vera . . .," in ibid.; Joshua II, 14, 15.

32. Florencia, *Historia,* book I, ch. i.

33. Pedro S. de Achútegui, SJ, *La universalidad del conocimiento de Dios en los paganos según los primeros teólogos de Compañía de Jesús (1534–1648),* part II, "Extensión e interpretación que dan nuestros autores al texto Rom. I, 18–23 y Sap. I, 31–9, en relación con la universalidad del conocimiento de Dios en los paganos," Consejo Superior de Investigaciones Científicas, Delegación de Roma, 1951.

34. Solorzano Pereira, *Política indiana,* p. 20b.

35. Ibid., p. 30a.

36. Ibid., p. 29b.

37. Ibid., p. 29a.

Chapter 5

1. Fray Jerónimo de Mendieta, OFM, *Historia Eclesiástica Indiana* (1596), Introduction by J. García Icazbalceta, Mexico City, 1945.
2. Bernardo de Balbuena, *Siglo de Oro y grandeza Mejicana,* Real Academia Española, Madrid, 1831, p. 37.
3. Ibid., p. 60.
4. Ibid., p. 35.
5. Ibid., p. 59.
6. Ibid.
7. Ibid., p. 65.
8. Ibid., p. 54.
9. Ibid., pp. 54–55.
10. Ibid., p. 79.
11. Ibid., p. 55.
12. Ibid., pp. 61, 65.
13. Carlos de Sigüenza y Góngora, *Primavera Indiana,* Mexico City, 1945, p. 41.
14. Ibid., p. 31.
15. Ibid., p. 19.
16. W. Jiménez Moreno, *Estudios de historia colonial,* Mexico City, 1958, p. 128.
17. Sigüenza y Góngora, *Teatro de virtudes políticas . . . ,* Medina, 1216.
18. Sigüenza y Góngora, *Piedad heroyca de Don Fernando Cortés,* Jaime Delgado, ed., Madrid, 1960, p. 57.
19. Sigüenza y Góngora, *Paraíso Occidental,* Mexico City, 1648, pp. 47–48.
20. Sigüenza y Göngora, *Alboroto y motín de México del 8 de junio de 1692,* ed. Irving A. Leonard, Mexico City, 1932, p. 65.
21. Ibid.
22. Sor Juana Inés de la Cruz, *Los empeños de una casa,* Jornada Ia, esc. IIa, verses 321–32, in *Obras completas,* ed. Mendez Plancarte, 4 vols., Mexico City, 1951–57, IV, 37–38.
23. Ibid., pp. 43–44.
24. Ibid., p. 44.
25. Gemelli Carreri, *Viaje a la Nueva España,* I, 45.
26. Sor Juana Inés de la Cruz, *El Divino Narcisco,* scene I, in *Obras completas,* vol. iii.
27. Francisco Bramón, *Los sirgueros de la Virgen sin original pecado* (1620), Mexico City, 1943, pp. 109–11.
28. Robert Ricard, *Une poetesse mexicaine du XVIIe siècle, Sor Juana Ines de la Cruz,* Paris, 1954, IIe leçon.
29. Ibid., p. 38.
30. Sor Juana Inés de la Cruz, *Obras completas,* III, 107.
31. Ibid., p. 143.
32. J. T. Medina, *Imprenta en Mexico,* no. 4, 310.
33. Sor Juana Inés de la Cruz, *Obras completas,* II, 182.
34. *Fama y obras pósthumas del Fénix de México,* Madrid, 1714, p. 39.

Chapter 6

1. 1746, Medina 3752.
2. 1729, Medina 3098.
3. 1733, Medina 3296.
4. 1738, Medina 3510.
5. 1743, Medina 3653, 3654.

6. 1746, Medina 3785.
7. 1749, Medina 3953.
8. 1750, Medina 4001.
9. 1751, Medina 4058.
10. 1753, Medina 4111.
11. 1758, Medina 4464, 1759, 4542.
12. 1756, Medina 4352.
13. Medina 4033.
14. Francisco Javier Alegre, *Historia de la Provincia de la Compañía de Jesús de Nueva España*, ed. E. J. Burrus and F. Zubillaga, 4 vols., IV, 379–80, Rome, 1956–1960.
15. 1741, Medina 3566.
16. 1742, Medina 3606.
17. 1750, Medina 3991.
18. B. F. de Ita y Parra, *El círculo del amor*, 1747 (New York Public Library microfilms, Medina 3837).
19. Fr. Agustín de Bengoechea, *La Gloria de María, 15 de mayo de 1768*, Mexico City, Zúñiga y Ontiveros, 1768 (John Carter Brown Library microfilms, Medina 5224).
20. *Compendio breve de las indulgencias y jubileos . . . de Nuestra Santíssima Madre la Virgen María de la Merced*, Mexico City, Joseph Bernardo de Hogal, 1731.
21. 1739, Medina 3552.
22. Ita y Parra, *El círculo del amor.*
23. 1749, Medina 3931.
24. 1735, Medina 3381.
25. Medina 3742, John Carter Brown Library, HA-M 51–19.
26. Medina 4474.
27. 1749, Medina 3931.
28. *R. P. F. Thomae/Malvenda setabitani ord. Praedicatorum/Sacrae Theologiae Magistri/de Antichristo/Tomus Primus/in quo Antichristi Praecursores, adventus . . . Lugduni,/MDCXLVII*, ed. princ. Rome, 1604 (Biblioteca Nacional, Madrid, 3/24 801).
29. 1749, Medina 3931, "Parecer . . ." (New York Public Library).
30. 1749, Medina 3931, "Aprobación. . . ."
31. Medina 3641.
32. 1750, Medina 4029.
33. Ibid., n.32.
34. 1731, Medina 4147.
35. 1753, Medina 4147.
36. Francisco de la Maza, *El guadalupanismo mexicano*, Mexico City, 1953, p. 107.
37. 1735, Medina 3381.
38. 1750, Medina 3391.
39. Fr. Manuel de Bocanegra y Cantabrana (*El círculo del amor*, 1746, "Parecer . . ."): "A Jesuit swan sang its glories, so that this second Rome might not lack its Virgil."
40. 1758, Medina 4487.
41. Bocanegra y Cantobrana, *El círculo del amor.*
42. Alexander von Humboldt, *Essai politique sur le royaume de la Nouvelle-Espagne*, 5 vols., Paris, 1811, II, 11, 13.
43. Fray Servando Teresa de Mier, "Relación de lo que sucedió en Europa al Dr. Mier," in *Memorias*, Mexico City, 1946, vol. II, writes: "In Spain and Europe generally there is no devotion for our Virgin of Guadalupe; all they love is hard cash [*pesos duros*]" (p. 198).
44. Códice de 1440, Archivo Histórico Nacional, Madrid, cod. no. 555, fol. 6r.
45. Francisco Xavier Carranza, SJ, *La transmigración de la Iglesia a Guadalupe*, Mexico City, 1749, p. 24 (Medina 3931).

Chapter 7

1. Beatriz Ramírez Camacho, "Breve relación sobre la expulsión de los jesuitas de Nueva España," *Boletín del Archivo General de la Nación,* II series, vol. VII, no. 4, Mexico City, 1966, p. 885.

2. J. T. Medina, *Imprenta en Mexico,* vol. v, no. 3, 885.

3. Ramírez Camacho, "Breve relación," p. 883.

4. Ibid., pp. 883–84.

5. Ernest J. Burrus, "A Diary of Exiled Philippine Jesuits (1769–1770)." *Archivum Historicum Societatis Iesu,* vol. XX, 1951, p. 298.

6. Ibid., p. 299.

7. *Charles II et les jésuites de ses états d'Europe et d'Amérique en 1767. Documents inédits publiés par le P. Auguste Carayon (SJ),* Paris, 1868, p. 374.

8. Ibid., p. 377.

9. Ibid., pp. 377–78.

10. Ibid., p. 380.

11. Ibid., p. 381.

12. Miguel Batllori, SJ, *El abate Viscardo. Historia y mito de la intervención de los jesuitas en la independencia de Hispano-américa,* Caracas, 1953.

13. These causes are not well understood but are linked to the disfavor into which the Society fell in several European courts. The expulsions of the Jesuits from the king-doms of Spain, Portugal, and France came only a few years apart; shortly afterward the pope himself decreed the dissolution of the Society of Jesus.

In the specific case of the Indies and especially of Mexico, it seems that the influence of the Jesuits over the creole elite of the towns and the Indians of the missions was regarded as an obstacle to the autocratic reformist program of an enlightened despot like Charles III. Conflicts of authority were frequent between the military entrusted with the *presidios* and the missionaries of the "Internal Provinces" whose security was a constant source of concern to the viceroys in the seventeenth and eighteenth centuries. Finally, their able management of vast domains (real estate in the towns and haciendas in the most prosperous rural regions) had made the Society the leading capitalist company of New Spain.

14. Miguel Batllori, SJ, *La cultura hispano-italiana de los jesuitas expulsos,* Madrid, 1966, p. 578.

15. Francisco Javier Clavijero, *Historia antigua de México,* 4 vols., Mexico City, 1958, I, 1–4. See Jacques Lafaye, "Conciencia nacional y conciencia étnica en la Nueva España," in *Acts of the IVth International Congress of Mexican Studies* (UCLA, California), 1973.

16. Clavijero, *Historia antigua de México,* I, p. 7. Compare J. José de Eguiara y Egurén, *Biblioteca Mexicana,* ed. A. Millares Carlo, Mexico City, 1944, "Prólogo XX": "It should be understood that the persons I call 'Mexicans' are those who were born in America, unless I expressly say that they were born of Indian parents" (p. 211).

17. *Colección de obras y opúsculos . . . de Nuestra Señora de Guadalupe,* Madrid, 1785, p. 798.

18. Clavijero, *Historia antigua de México,* III, 291–93.

19. Batllori, *La cultura hispano-italiana,* p. 577.

20. *Der Teutsche Merkur,* Weimar, July 1786, vol. 1, "Des Herrn Abts Clavigero Abhandlung . . . ," pp. 3–52; August 1786, pp. 154–81; October 1786, pp. 44–57.

21. Humboldt, *Essai politique,* I, 217.

22. Manuel Payno, *Compendio de la historia de México para el uso de los establecimientos de Instrucción pública de la República Mexicana* (7th ed.), Mexico City, 1883, pp. 120–21.

23. "Bosquejo de la anarquía de América . . . ," Biblioteca Nacional, Madrid, MS 3 049.

24. Lorenzo de Zavala, *Ensayo histórico sobre las revoluciones de Nueva España,* Mexico City, 1949, p. 71.

25. Ernesto de la Torre Villar, *La constitución de Apatzingan y los creadores del Estado mexicano,* Mexico City, 1964, Document 10—"Proclama del cura Hidalgo a la nación mexicana" (1810), pp. 203–4.

26. Ibid., Document 3, p. 112.

27. Ibid., p. 131.

28. Zavala, *Ensayo histórico,* p. 63.

29. Xavier Tavera Alfaro, *Dos etapas de la Independencia (Documentos),* Universidad Michoacana de San Nicolás de Hidalgo, 1966, "Discurso pronunciado por Morelos en la apertura del congreso de Chilpancingo, 14 de septiembre de 1813," p. 49.

30. Ibid., p. 50.

31. Ibid., p. 52.

32. Torre Villar, *La constitución de Apatzingan,* n.7, Document 74, p. 358.

33. Tavera Alfaro, *Dos etapas de la Independencia,* p. 54, n.27.

34. E. Lemoine Villicana, "Zitacuaro, Chilpancingo y Apatzingan, tres grandes momentos de la insurgencia mexicana," *Boletín del Archivo General de la Nación,* II Series, vol. IV, no. 3, Mexico City, 1963, pp. 711–30; Villar, *Constitución de Apatzingan,* article 65.

35. Lemoine Villicana, "Zitacuaro, Chilpancingo y Apatzingan," p. 600.

36. Tavera Alfaro, *Dos etapas de la independencia,* "Decreto del Tribunal de Inquisición," p. 108.

37. Ibid., "Respuesta al capítulo 10," pp. 105, 115.

38. Ibid.

39. Ruth Wold, *El "Diario de México," primer cotidiano de Nueva España,* Madrid, 1970, p. 168.

40. E. Lemoine Villicana, "Apoteosis de los mártires de la guerra de Independencia Mexicana en 1823," *Boletín del Archivo General de la Nación,* II Series, vol. VI, no. 2, Mexico City, 1965, p. 239.

41. Carlos María de Bustamante, *Diario histórico de México (16 de septiembre de 1823),* Mexico City, 1896, vol. I, cited in Lemoine Villicana, "Apoteosis de los mártires," p. 228.

42. Humboldt, *Essai politique,* II, 304.

43. Javier Ocampo, *Las ideas de un día (El pueblo mexicano ante la consumación de su Independencia),* Mexico City, 1969, p. 82.

44. Ibid., p. 87.

45. Fray Cesáreo de Armellada, OFM, *La causa indígena americana en las Cortes de Cádiz,* Madrid, 1959, p. 86.

46. Mier, *Historia de la Revolución,* London, 1813, vol. II, p. 285.

47. Ibid., p. 318.

48. Ibid. Fray Servando deplored the abolition of the Inquisition, whose victim he had been, for he attributed all his difficulties to the *gachupín* archbishop of Mexico City. He wrote: "Consider what is happening to Spain because they have put out the fires of the Inquisition" (ibid., p. 320).

49. Mier, *Memorias,* vol. II, , pp. 15, 139.

50. Mier, "Apología del Doctor Mier," in his *Memorias,* vol. I, p. 19.

51. Mier, *Historia de la Revolución,* vol. II, p. 320.

52. Mier, "Carta a Don Miguel Ramos Arizpe, chantre de Puebla," May 14, 1823, University of Texas Library, MS 1319, no. 629.

Chapter 8

1. Motolinia, *Memoriales,* ed. Luis García Pimentel, Mexico City, 1903, p. 67.
2. Ibid., p. 68.
3. Ibid.
4. Ibid., "Epístola proemial," p. 13.
5. Ibid.
6. Ibid., p. 81.
7. Ibid., p. 77.
8. Ibid., p. 54.
9. Ibid., p. 56.
10. Ibid., p. 57.
11. Motolinia, *Historia de los Indios de la Nueva España* (1956 ed.), pp. 9–10. But we find a contradictory statement in the *Memorials,* "Epístola proemial," p. 13.
12. Fray Jerónimo Román y Zamora, *Repúblicas de Indias* (1575), Madrid, 2 vols., 1897, I, 170. Román had borrowed this information from Las Casas, *Apologética historia . . .* (BAE, vol. CVI, p. 140a).
13. The principal sanctuaries (archaeological sites) of Quetzalcóatl in Mexico:

> Calixtlahuaca (State of Mexico)
> Teayo (Veracruz)
> Cholula (Tlaxcala)
> Coatepec Chalco (Mexico)
> Ecatepec (Mexico)
> Tenayuca (Mexico)
> Teotihuacan (Mexico)
> Tepoztlan (Morelos)
> Toluca (Mexico)
> Tula (Hidalgo)
> Xochicalco (Morelos)

14. Sahagún, *Historia general,* I, 279.
15. Ibid., p. 291.
16. Ibid., II, 330–31.
17. Ibid., III, 188.
18. Ibid., I, 45.
19. Ibid., p. 90.
20. Ibid., III, 358.
21. Ibid., p. 359
22. *Histoyre du Mechique,* ed. E. de Jonghe, in *Journal de la Société des Américanistes,* n.s., vol. II, no. 1, Paris, 1905, p. 35.
23. Ibid.
24. Ibid., p. 36.
25. Ibid., p. 37.
26. Ibid.
27. Ibid., p. 38.

Chapter 9

1. Sahagún, *Historia general,* I, 90.
2. Bernal Díaz del Castillo, *Historia verdadera de la conquista de la Nueva España,* ed. J. Ramírez Cabañas, 2 vols., Mexico City, 1966, I, 266.

3. Hernán Cortés, *Cartas de relación,* "Segunda Carta" (BAE, vol. XXII, p. 30a and b) and also the first speech of Moctezuma (ibid., p. 25b).

4. Sahagún, *Historia general,* IV, 86.

5. Fray Diego Durán, OP, *Historia de las Indias,* 2 vols. and atlas, Mexico City, 1867–80, II, 118.

6. Sahagún, *Historia general,* IV, 25.

7. Codex Vaticanus 37–38, fig. 9, commentary.

8. Fray Bartolomé de Las Casas, OP, *Historia de las Indias,* book I, ch. x (BAE, vol. XCV, p. 41b).

9. Sahagún, *Historia general,* IV, 23–24.

10. Las Casas, *Apologética historia,* ch. cxxii (BAE, vol. CV, p. 425a).

11. Codex Vaticanus 37–38, fig. 9, commentary.

12. Díaz del Castillo, *Historia verdadera,* I, 48.

13. Diego Lopez Cogolludo, OFM, *Historia de Yucatan* (1688), Mexico City, 1957, pp. 95–96, 99.

14. Sahagún, *Historia general,* III, 358–59.

15. *Codex Telleriano remensis,* fifth *Tercena, Cielo, caña,* p. 24.

16. Codex Vaticanus 37–38, fig. 21, p. 22.

17. Durán, *Historia de las Indias,* I, 18.

18. Ibid., II, 71.

19. Ibid., p. 72.

20. Ibid., p. 118.

21. Ibid.

22. Ibid., p. 73.

23. Ibid., I, 73.

24. Ibid.

25. Ibid.

26. Las Casas, *Apologética historia,* ch. cxxii (BAE, vol. CV, p. 424a and b).

27. Durán, *Historia de las Indias,* II, ch. lxxix.

28. Ibid., p. 75.

29. Ibid., p. 76.

30. Ibid.

31. Ibid., Introduction of A. M. Garibay, I, 13–15.

32. Ibid., 1.

33. Ibid., 18.

34. Joaquín García Icazbalceta, *Don Fray Juan de Zumárraga,* 4 vols., Mexico City, 1947, IV, 89–95.

35. *Manuscrit Tovar. Origines et croyances des Indiens du Mexique,* ed. Jacques Lafaye, Collection UNESCO d'oeuvres représentatives, Akademische Druk und Verlagsanstalt, Graz, 1972, p. 69.

36. Ibid., p. 70.

37. Ibid., p. 73.

38. Ibid.

39. Durán, *Historia de las Indias,* II, 73.

40. *Manuscrit Tovar,* p. 73.

41. Ibid.

42. Ibid.

43. José de Acosta, SJ, *Historia natural y moral de las Indias* (BAE, vol. LXXIII, p. 231): "All is shown in the form of paintings in the Mexican annals. This book is in Rome, deposited in the Vatican Library, where a Father of our Society, who had come from Mexico, saw it with other histories and explained their meaning to the librarian of

His Holiness. The librarian was much pleased to understand this book, which he had never been able to understand."

44. *Codex Telleriano remensis,* p. 22.
45. Ibid., p. 23.
46. Ibid., p. 26.
47. Ibid., p. 23.
48. Ibid., p. 24.
49. Codex Vaticanus, 37–38, pl. XXI.
50. Ibid., pl. VII, verso.
51. Ibid., pl. IX, verso.
52. Ibid., pl. IX.
53. Acosta, *Historia natural,* p. 25b.
54. Ibid., p. 26a.
55. Ibid., p. 150b.
56. Ibid., p. 236a.
57. Ibid., p. 246b.
58. Ibid., p. 237b.
59. Ibid.
60. *Cedulario indiano,* book I, p. 23.
61. Las Casas, *Historia de las Indias,* ch. i (BAE, vol. XCV, p. 19b).
62. Las Casas, *Apologética historia,* ch. cxxvii (BAE, vol. CV, p. 438a).
63. Fray Juan de Torquemada, *Monarquía Indiana,* 3 vols., (Madrid, 1723), I, 162: "They had a great feast, and at this feast they slew and sacrificed these 1,200 Cuetlaxte-cans, which greatly rejoiced the demon Quetzalcóhuatl."
64. Ibid., p. 255.
65. Ibid., p. 281.
66. Ibid., II, 50.
67. Ibid., II, 49.
68. Ibid., I, 380.
69. Ibid., II, 222–23.
70. Ibid., I, p. 255.
71. Ibid.
72. Ibid., II, 48.
73. Ibid., I, 381.
74. Ibid., p. 380.
75. Ibid.
76. Ibid., II, 48.
77. Ibid., p. 50.
78. Ibid., pp. 79–80.

Chapter 10

1. Alfonso Vath, SJ, "P. F. Antonio Caballero de Santa Maria über die Mission der Jesuiten und anderer Orden in China," *Archivum Historicum Societatis Iesu,* anni I, July–December, Rome, 1932.
2. *Sinica Franciscana,* "Ad Claras Aquas," Florence, 1933, vol. II, part iv, p. 206.
3. Ibid, p. 790.
4. Ibid., vol. I, "De cultu post Diluvium," p. 544.
5. Mylapore has since become a district of the modern town of Madras, a great port on the Coromandel coast.
6. Marco Polo, *La description du monde,* Paris, 1955, pp. 264–66.

7. Saint Paul, cited by Jean de Léry, *Histoire d'un voyage fait en la terre de Brésil,* 1957, p. 343, and Psalm 19, Matthew 28.

8. Marcel Bataillon, course taught at the Collège de France in 1952–53, unpublished manuscript (cf. Annuaire du Collège de France, 1953), pp. 277–86.

9. *Monumenta Brasiliae Societatis Iesu,* vol. I (1538–53), p. 117.

10. Saint Ignatius Loyola, "Autobiografía," in *Obras completas,* Biblioteca de Autores Cristianos, Madrid, 1952, p. 59.

11. *Monumenta Brasiliae Societatis Iesu,* book V, ch. i, n.18.

12. Ibid., p. 154.

13. Ibid., p. 389.

14. Claude d'Abbeville, Capuc., *Histoire de la mission . . . en l'île de Maragnan,* Paris, 1614 (repr. by Alfred Métraux and Jacques Lafaye, Graz, 1963), p. 70r.

15. Ibid., "Histoire d'un certain personnage qui se disait descendu du Ciel," pp. 76–78.

16. Giuseppe Rosso, "Nicoló Mascardi Missionario Gesuita esploratore del Cile e della Patagonia (1624–1674)," *Archivum Historicum Societatis Iesu,* anno XIX, fasc. 37–38, Rome, 1950, p. 57.

17. García, *Origen de los Indios,* "Proemio al lector."

18. Jean de Léry, *Voyage fait en la terre de Brésil* (Geneva, 1957), Paris 1957, p. 343.

19. Calancha, *Crónica moralizada,* p. 312.

20. Fray Gregorio García, *Predicación del Evangelio en el Nuevo Mundo viviendo los Apóstoles,* Baeza, 1625.

21. Calancha, *Crónica moralizada,* p. 312.

22. Ibid., p. 311.

23. Ibid., p. 312, n.14.

24. Menasseh Ben Israel, *Origen de los Americanos, esto es esperanza de Israel* (Amsterdam, 1650), Madrid, 1881, pp. 30, 41, and ch. xx., *passim.*

25. Calancha, *Crónica moralizada,* p. 316.

26. Cédula of King Philip II to the viceroy of New Spain, April 22, 1577.

27. Nicolás León, *Bibliografía mexicana del siglo XVIII,* Mexico City, 1902–8, "Pluma rica," p. 506.

28. Ibid., p. 514.

29. Lorenzo Boturini Benaducci, "Catálogo del Museo Histórico Indiano," in *Idea de una nueva historia general de la América septentrional,* Mexico City, 1871, p. 283.

30. León, *Bibliografía mexicana,* "El Apóstol Santo Tomás," p. 525.

31. Ibid., p. 500.

32. "Discurso de Fr. S. T. de Mier al formular la protesta de lay como diputado en el primer Congreso constituyente, July 15, 1822," in Edmundo O'Gorman, *Fray Servando Teresa de Mier,* Mexico City, 1945.

33. Mier. *Historia de la Revolución.*

34. Mier, "Disertación," in León, *Bibliografía mexicana,* p. 548.

35. Ignacio Borunda, *Clave general de geroglíficos americanos,* in León, *Bibliografía mexicana,* pp. 196–351.

36. Boturini, *Historia General de la América Septentrional, por el caballero Lorenzo Boturini Benaducci,* Madrid, 1948, p. 352.

37. Mier, "Disertación," in León, *Bibliografía mexicana,* p. 544.

38. Ibid., p. 556.

39. Ibid.

40. *Escritos inéditos del Dr. Mier,* Mexico, 1944, "Manifiesto apologético del Dr. Mier," p. 140: "The preaching and prophecies of Saint Thomas concerning the coming of people of his religion from the East—people who would become masters of all—is the true key to the Conquest of both Americas, and as long as this is not accepted as the true

foundation of the Conquest, men will continue to write absurdities and follies about it."

41. Mier, "Disertación," in León, *Bibliografía mexicana,* p. 539.

42. Ibid., p. 556.

43. Ibid.

44. Torquemada, *Monarquía Indiana,* "Proemio a esta segunda impresión de la Monarquía Indiana," p. 4.

45. Mier, "Disertación," in León, *Bibliografía mexicana,* p. 543.

46. Ibid., p. 544.

47. *Liber Sancti Jacobi (Codex Calixtinus),* Santiago de Compostela, 1951, p. 259.

48. Antonio de Remesal, OP, *Historia de la Provincia de San Vicente de Chiapa y Guatemala,* Madrid, 1619, p. 2.

49. Francisco López de Gómara, *Historia de la conquista de la Nueva España,* p. 309b.

50. Mier, *Memorias,* Mexico City, 2 vols., 1946, I, 5.

51. Ibid., p. 8.

52. Ibid., pp. 270–71.

53. Ibid., pp. 156–57.

54. *Ioannis Marianae e Societatis Iesu Tractatu VII. I De Adventu B. Jacobi Apostoli in Hispania,* Coloniae Agrippinae, 1609, p. 9b.

55. Ibid.

56. Ibid., p. 11*a:* "De adventu Apostoli siluisse non miror, nullus enim nostrorum illius etatis historicus extat."

57. Ibid., chs. xi, xiv.

58. Pedro de Peralta y Barnuevo, *Historia de España vindicada,* Lima, 1730.

59. Ibid., "Prólogo."

60. Ibid.

61. Ibid., p. 683ff.

62. Ramón Otero Pedrayo, *Historia de Galiza,* 2 vols., Buenos Aires, 1962, I, 363, 365.

63. Peralta y Barnuevo, *Historia de España vindicada,* p. 700.

64. Ibid., p. 396.

65. Américo Castro, *Santiago de España,* Buenos Aires, 1958, pp. 135–37.

66. Juan de Nuix y Perpiñá, *Reflexiones imparciales sobre la humanidad de los españoles en Indias,* Cervera, 1783, "Reflexión quinta," p. 499.

67. *Codex Calixtinus,* p. 408.

68. Antonio de León Pinelo, *El Paraíso en el Nuevo Mundo,* 2 vols., Lima, 1943, I, 330.

69. Antonio Ruiz de Montoya, SJ, *Conquista espiritual... del Paraguay, Paraná, Uruguay y Tape,* Bilbao, 1892, ch. xxii.

Chapter 11

1. Brasseur de Bourbourg, *Relation des choses de Yucatan,* Lyon-Madrid, 1864, p. 105.

2. Luis Villoro, *La Revolución de Independencia,* Mexico City, 1953, ch. iii.

3. E. Beauvois, "Pratiques et institutions religieuses d'origine chrétienne chez les Mexicains du Moyen-Age," *Revue des Questions Scientifiques,* July–October 1896, 2d series, vol. X, Louvain, 1896.

4. José Díaz Bolio, *La Serpiente emplumada—eje de culturas,* Merida, Yucatan, 1957.

5. Fernando Díaz Infante, *Quetzalcóatl (Ensayo psicoanalítico del mito nahua),* Xalapa, 1963. See, for an essay of the same tendency, Jorge Carrión, "Ruta psicológica de Quetzalcóatl," *Cuadernos americanos,* no. 5, September–October 1949, vol. VIII, pp. 98–112.

6. Pierre Honoré (pseud.), *Ich fand den weissen Gott,* Frankfurt am Main, 1962 (French ed., *J'ai découvert le Dieu blanc d'Amérique,* Paris, 1962).

7. In *Política*, vol. I, no. 8, August 15, 1960, México.
8. Sahagún, *Historia general*, I, 358.

Chapter 12

1. Sahagún, *Historia general*, I, 46.
2. Ibid.
3. Ibid., III, 352.
4. Torquemada, *Monarquía Indiana*, II, 245*b*.
5. Clavijero, *Historia antigua de México*, II, 82.
6. Sahagún, *Historia general*, III, 352–54.
7. Durán, *Historia de las Indias*, ed. A. M. Garibay K., 2 vols., Mexico City, 1967, I, 125.
8. Sahagún, *Historia general*, I, 46.
9. Durán, *Historia de las Indias*, I, 130.
10. Ibid., pp. 126, 131.
11. Sahagún, *Historia general*, I, 118.
12. Durán, *Historia de las Indias*, I, pp. 126–27.
13. Sahagún, *Historia general*, I, 46.
14. Miguel León-Portilla, *Ritos, sacerdotes y atavíos de los dioses*, Mexico City, 1958, pp. 156–58.

> *ciua covatl: in nantzin in teteu*
> *teteuinnan: idem*
> *Iztac ciuat: idem*

15. Miguel León-Portilla, *La filosofía nahuatl estudiada en sus fuentes*, Mexico City, 1959, p. 184.
16. Ibid., n.13.
17. Francisco Mateos, SJ, "Constituciones para indios del primer concilio limense," *Missionalia Hispanica*, vol. VII, no. 19, 1950, p. 554.
18. Torquemada, *Monarquía Indiana*, II, 245b and 246a.
19. Sahagún, *Historia general*, I, 46.
20. Ibid.. III, 352.
21. Ibid., p. 353.
22. Ibid.
23. Ibid., p. 354.
24. Ibid., p. 352.
25. The sanctuary of Estremadura, abandoned by the Jeronymites in 1835, was not again entrusted to religious (Franciscans) until 1908. It is regrettable that the manuscripts relating to the *Milagros de Nra. Sra de Guadalupe*, anterior to 1564, which are preserved there, are not accessible to researchers, although their existence is attested to by the *Guía de fuentes para la historia de Ibero-America* (vol. II, p. 528), published in 1966 under the auspices of Unesco and the International Council of Archives.
26. P. Diego de Ecija, *Libro de la invención de Santa María de Guadalupe*, ed., Fr. A Barrado Manzano, OFM, Caceres, 1953.
27. Codice 555, Madrid, Archivo Histórico Nacional, fol. 6r–8r.
28. Ibid., fol. 5v.
29. Ibid., fol. 6r.
30. "Manuscrito 1176," Madrid, Biblioteca Nacional, fol. 2v.
31. *Monasterio de Guadalupe*, vol. VI, February 1922. no. 121, p. 27.
32. Fray Germán Rubio, OFM, *Historia de Nra. Sra. de Guadalupe*, Barcelona, 1926, pp. 223–24.

33. A citation from Psalm 147, originally quoted by Francisco de Florencia and again by the pope in 1756.

34. Francisco de Florencia, SJ, *Historia de la milagrosa imagen de María Stma. de Guadalupe, escrita en el siglo XVII* . . . , Guadalajara, 1895, p. 26.

35. *Archivo Ibero-Americano,* Vol. XV, January-June 1955, nos. 57–58 (special issue on the subject of the *Inmaculada),* p. 626ff. On July 7, 1664, the brief *Quae inter praeclara* gave a canonical character to the office and mass of the *Immaculada, con octava;* this represented a partial success for the junta.

Chapter 13

1. Rubén Vargas Ugarte, SJ, *Historia del culto de María en Iberoamerica,* 2d ed., Buenos Aires, 1947, p. 189.

2. "Información del Excmo. Sr. Montúfar," 1556, Ms, fol. 5r, Archivo de Cabildo de la Catedral de México.

3. Alonso de la Rea, OFM, *Crónica de la Orden de N. Seráfico P. S. Francisco . . . de Mechoacan en la Nueva España,* Mexico City, 1643, ch. ix, "Del ingenio del Tarasco, de la eminencia en sus obras. . . ."

4. Ibid.

5. Díaz del Castillo, *Historia verdadera* (BAE, vol. XXVI, pp. 311b–312a).

6. *Cartas de Indias,* Madrid, ed. del Ministerio de Fomento, p. 310; Francisco de la Maza, *El Guadalupanismo mexicano,* Mexico City, 1953, p. 14: "With all due respect for tradition, I believe the reason why the image was called Guadalupe is that originally an image of the Virgin of Guadalupe of Estremadura was installed in the hermitage."

7. Fray Diego de Ocaña, Jeron., *Un viaje por la América,* Madrid, 1969, p. 168.

8. Ibid., p. 175.

9. Fray Francisco de San Joseph, Jeron., *Historia universal de la primitiva y milagrosa Imágen de Nuestra Señora de Guadalupe,* Madrid, 1743, p. 146a.

10. Rubio, *Historia de Nra. Sra. de Guadalupe,* pp. 228–29.

11. Francisco de San Joseph, *Historia universal,* p. 131a.

12. Fray Gaspar de San Agustín, August., *Conquistas de las islas Philipinas: la temporal por las armas del señor don Phelipe segundo el prudente; y la espiritual, por los religiosos del orden de Nuestro Padre San Augustín,* Madrid, 1698, p. 498b.

13. Francisco de San Joseph, *Historia universal,* pp. 147b–148a.

14. Fray A. de Montúfar, *Información . . . Investigación Histórica y documental* (1st ed., Mexico City, 1888–1890), Mexico City, 1952, p. 92.

15. Ibid.

16. Ibid., p. 135.

17. Ibid.

18. Ibid., p. 129.

19. Ibid., p. 131.

20. Ibid., p. 123.

21. Ibid., p. 121.

22. Ibid., p. 135.

23. Miguel Sánchez, *Imagen de la Virgen María Madre de Dios de Guadalupe milagrosamente aparecida en México,* Mexico City, 1648.

24. *Cartas de Indias,* p. 36.

25. Fray Luis de Cisneros, *Historia de Nuestra Señora de los Remedios,* Mexico City, 1621.

26. Cuevas, *Album Histórico guadalupano,* p. 84.

27. Ibid.

28. Sánchez, *Imagen de la Virgen María.*

29. Francisco de la Maza, *El Guadalupanismo mexicano*, p. 62.

30. Carranza, *La transmigración*, Medina 3931.

31. Sánchez, *Imagen de la Virgen María*.

32. Francisco de la Maza, *El Guadalupanismo mexicano*, p. 50.

33. Luis Lazo de la Vega, "Carta al Autor," in Sánchez, *Imagen de la Virgen María*, p. 38.

34. Ibid., p. 38.

35. Ibid., p. 37.

36. Lazo de la Vega, *Huey Tlamahuicoltica*, (Mexico City, 1649), ed. Primo Feliciano Velázquez, Mexico City, 1926.

37. Ibid., p. 23.

38. Boturini Benaducci, "Catálogo del Museo Histórico Indiano," p. 312.

39. Sánchez, *Imagen de la Virgen María*, title page and pp. 41–46.

40. Ibid., p. 49.

41. Ibid.

42. Ibid., p. 181.

43. Ibid., p. 184.

44. Ibid., p. 194.

45. Ibid., p. 195.

46. Ibid.

47. Ibid., p. 206.

48. Ibid., p. 209.

49. Ibid., p. 214.

50. Ibid., p. 49.

51. Ibid., Francisco de Siles, "Dedic. a M. Sánchez," p. 31.

52. Ibid., p. 32.

53. Ibid., p. 33.

54. Ibid., p. 34.

Chapter 14

1. Francisco de la Maza, *El Guadalupanismo mexicano*, pl. 7.

2. Cayetano Cabrera y Quintero, *Escudo de armas de México*, Mexico City, 1746 (Medina 3752). It is significant that this apologist for the Guadalupan tradition also endorsed the tradition of an apostolic evangelization of Mexico by Saint Thomas, whom he described (in his dedication to King Charles III) as the "original Conquistador of these realms."

3. Medina, *Imprenta en México*, passim. (I have prepared a bibliography of Our Lady of Guadalupe, from 1648 to 1831, which will appear separately, accompanied by a study of the symbolism and an effort at formal analysis of the Guadalupan literature.)

4. Fray Antonio Claudio de Villegas, OP, *La mayor gloria del máximo de los celestiales espíritus, del primero de los mayores príncipes, el archiseraphin Sr. San Miguel, Declarada en su Insigne Aparición en México a las Soberanas plantas de María Nuestra Reyna, que se venera en Guadalupe*, Mexico City, 1751 (Medina 4064).

5. Fray Gabriel de Talavera, Jeron., *Historia de Nuestra Señora de Guadalupe*, Toledo, 1597, p. 461.

6. M. Fernández de Echeverría y Veitia, "Baluartes de México. Relación histórica de las cuatro sagradas y milagrosas Imágenes de Nuestra Señora la Virgen María, que se veneran en sus extramuros, y descripción de sus templos.," Manuscritos de América, no. 375, signatura 27 75, Biblioteca de Palacio, Madrid; Palau, *Manual del Librero hispano-americano*, no. 88423.

7. Miguel Sánchez, *Novenas de la Virgen María* . . . *de los Remedios y Guadalupe* (1665), in *Colección de obras y opúsculos pertenecientes a la milagrosa aparición de la bellísima imagen de nuestra Señora de Guadalupe que se venera en su santuario extramuros de México, reimpresas todas juntas,* Madrid, 1785, pp. 241–43.

8. Ibid., pp. 170–71, n.7.

9. Matías de la Mota y Padilla, *Historia de la Conquista del Reino de la Nueva Galicia* (1742), Guadalajara-Mexico City, 1920, p. 258.

10. A. Bera Cercada [C. Cabrera y Quintero], *El patronato disputado, Disertación apologética, por el voto, elección, y juramento de Patrona, a María Santísima, venerada en su Imagen de Guadalupe de México, e invalidado para negarle el rezo del común (que a título de Patrona electa, y jurada, según el decreto de la Sagrada Congregación de ritos se le ha dado en esta Metrópoli), por el Br. Don Juan Pablo Zetina Infante, Mro. de ceremonias en la Catedral de Puebla, en el singularísimo dictamen, y parecer, que sin pedírselo dió en aquella y quiso extender a esta ciudad, a corregir al que le pareció arrojo de esta Metropolitana* . . . , Mexico City, 1741 (Medina 3566).

11. Fray Joseph Díaz de la Vega, OFM, "Memorias piadosas de la nación indiana recogidas de varios autores . . . , año de 1782," ch. viii, fol. 62, in Colección Boturini, signatura A/153, 9/4886, Academia de la Historia, Madrid.

12. Boturini Benaducci, *Idea de una nueva historia general de la América Septentrional,* Madrid, 1746, dedication to the king.

13 Ibid.

14. Manuscritos de América, Biblioteca de Palacio, Madrid, no. 375 in J. D. Bordona, *Manuscritos de América* (Madrid, 1935).

15. Colección Múñoz, MS A/31, Real Academia de la Historia, Madrid.

16. Manuscritos de América, Biblioteca Palacio, Madrid, no. 371 in J. D. Bordona. *Manuscritos de América.*

17. Fray Francisco de Ajofrin, Capuc., "Alocución sobre la imagen de Nuestra Señora de los Remedios, venerada en un cerro de la ciudad de Cholula, a dos leguas de la Puebla de los Angeles" (n.d.), in J. D. Bordona, *Manuscritos de América,* signatura 20 419 33, Biblioteca Nacional, Madrid; and Luis Becerra Tanco, *Felicidad de México en el principio, y milagrosa origen, que tubo el santuario de la Virgen María N. Señora de Guadalupe, extramuros* . . . , Mexico City, 1675 (develops the idea that the Virgin drove away the Tonantzin) (Medina 1121).

18. Mier, "Apología del Dr. Mier," *Memorias,* I, 37–38.

19. Ibid., p. 49.

20. Ibid., p. 65.

21. Ibid., p. 273.

22. Juan Bautista Múñoz, *Historia del Nuevo Mundo,* vol. I, Madrid, 1793, Prologue, p. iv.

23. Guillaume Thomas Raynal, *Histoire philosophique et politique des établissements et du commerce des Européens dans les deux Indes,* Amsterdam, 1770 (seventeen editions between 1770 and 1786, the majority at Amsterdam, The Hague, and Geneva).

24. Múñoz, *Historia,* p. ii.

25. Ibid., p. v.

26. Ibid., p. xxvi.

27. "Carta de Larranga á d. Juan Bautista Múñoz . . . Simancas 29 de Diz^bre de 1783," Colección Múñoz, vol. 91, MS A/118 9/4853, fol. 138, Real Academia de la Historia, Madrid, *Catálogo de la Colección Múñoz,* vol. II, p. 455.

28. "Memoria sobre las apariciones y el culto de Nuestra Señora de Guadalupe de México. Leída en la Real Academia de la Historia por su individuo supernumerario Don Juan Bautista Múñoz," *Memorias de la Real Academia de la Historia,* vol. V, Madrid, 1817, pp. 205–24.

29. "Discurso histórico-crítico sobre las apariciones y el culto de Na. Señora de

Guadalupe de México, trabajado y leído en la Real Academia de la Historia por su individuo supernumerario D. Juan Bautista Muñoz 18 abril 1794," MS 11/8235, Real Academia de la Historia, Madrid.

30. Muñoz, *Memoria,* p. 206.

31. Ibid., p. 211.

32. Ibid., pp. 212–13.

33. Ibid., p. 219.

34. Ibid., pp. 219–20.

35. Ibid., p. 220.

36. Ibid., p. 222.

37. Ibid., p. 224.

38. Ibid.

39. Mier, *Memorias,* I, 19.

40. Manuel Gómez Marín, *Defensa Guadalupana escrita por el P. Dr. y Mtro, Manuel Gómez Marín, presbítero del Oratorio de S. Felipe Neri de Méjico, contra la disertación de D. Juan Bautista Muñoz,* México, 1819 (The University of Texas Library, G. 265).

41. Ibid., "Corolario," pp. 54–55.

42. Ibid.

43. Carlos María de Bustamante, *La Aparición guadalupana de México, vindicada de los defectos que le atribuye el Dr. Juan Bautista Muñoz en la Disertación que leyó en la Academia de la Historia de Madrid en 18 de abril de 1794,* Mexico City, 1843 (The University of Texas Library, G. 265).

44. Ibid., pp. 65–66.

45. Lorenzo de Zavala, *Umbral de la Independencia,* Mexico City 1949, p. 11.

46. Bustamante, *La Aparición guadalupana,* p. 66.

47. Ibid.

48. Ibid.

49. *Manifesto de la Junta guadalupana a los Mexicanos, y disertación histórico-crítica sobre la aparición de Nuestra Señora en Tepeyac: escrita por el Licenciado Don Carlos Maria de Bustamante, diputado al Congreso de la Unión, por el Estado libre de Oaxaca,* Mexico City, 1831 (The University of Texas Library, G. 265).

50. Ibid., p. 11.

51. *Informe crítico-legal, dado al muy ilustre y venerable cabildo de la Santa Iglesia Metropolitana de México, por los comisionados que nombró para el reconocimiento de la Imagen de Nra. Sra. de Guadalupe de la Iglesia de San Francisco, pintada sobre las tablas de la mesa del Illmo. Sr. Obispo D. Fr. Juan de Zumárraga,* Mexico City, 1835 (The University of Texas Library, G. 265).

52. Ibid., p. 10.

53. *El gran día de México, 10 de diciembre de 1836* (anonymous) (The University of Texas Library, G. 265).

Chapter 15

1. Antonio de Robles, *Diario de sucesos notables (1655–1703),* Mexico City, 3 vols., 1946, I, 189.

2. Ibid., p. 254.

3. Ibid., II, 308.

4. *Actas de Cabildo de México,* vol. XV, p. 250.

5. Gregorio M. de Guijo, *Diario,* Mexico City, 2 vols. 1953, II, 145.

6. Robles, *Diario,* I, 307.

7. Ibid., III, 45.

8. Ibid., III, 196; see also the entry for November 22 of the same year (1702):

"Wednesday, the 22nd, in the morning, the Lord Archbishop went to Guadalupe; the viceroy came the same day, and they dined together; His Lordship gave the dinner, which was served in the house of La Sosa, and more than thirty Indians brought it to Guadalupe" (p. 238).

9. Guijo, *Diario*, II, 136.

10. "El arzobispo . . . informa por medio del escrito adjunto que el abad y Canónigo de la Colegiata de Nra. Sra. de Guadalupe le presentaron . . . ; de ver la mitad de los canónigos y racioneros instruidos en la lengua de los Indios, que alli concurren,'" Mexico City, November 28, 1753 (Mexico City, MS 2607, Archivo General de Indias, Seville).

11. Robles, *Diario*, III, 245, 250.

12. Ibid., p. 303.

13. "Manda de Don Andrés de Palencia para fundar en México un convento de Religiosas Agustinas de Sta. Monica o un Colegio en el santuario de Na. Sa. de Guadalupe—en 17 febrero de 1717.—El Consejo se conformó con la Colegiata" (Manuscritos de América, signatura 195 12, fol. 368 r-v, Biblioteca Nacional, Madrid). "Noticias de la ciudad México·. . ." (Memorias de México, vol. XIX, MS A/135 9/4870, Academia de la Historia, Madrid): "A noble and pious gentleman, Don Andrés de Palencia, died in Mexico City in 1707, leaving in his testament 100,000 pesos . . ." (fol. 50 v). King Philip V decided on October 26, 1708, to assign this legacy to the collegiate church of Guadalupe. The Holy See delayed issuance of the necessary bulls until February 9, 1725.

14. Francisco de Florencia, SJ, *La Estrella del Norte*, Guadalajara, 1895 (cited by Francisco de la Maza, *El Guadalupanismo*, p. 65).

15. Fray Isidro Félix de Espinosa, OFM, *Chrónica apostólica seráphica de todos los colegios de Propaganda Fide de esta Nueva España*, part I, Mexico City, 1746, p. 296b.

16. Ibid., p. 297b.

17. Ibid.

18. Carranza, *La transmigración*, Medina 3931.

19. "Convite a los mexicanos para unos juegos seculares en honor de la milagrosa aparición de Ntra. Sra. de Guadalupe, 1831." Manuscritos de América, sign. 20427, Biblioteca Nacional, Madrid.

20. Mier, *Memorias*, II, 197.

21. Antonio de Alcedo, *Diccionario geográfico-histórico de las Indias Occidentales o América . . . escrito por el Coronel Don Antonio de Alcedo, Capitán de Reales Guardias Españolas*. Madrid, Manuel González, 1787, pp. 251–53.

22. Díaz de la Vega, "Memorias piadosas," fol.

23. Ibid.

24. Mota Padilla, *Historia de la Conquista*, p. 258a.

25. Díaz de la Vega, "Memorias piadosas," fol. 49.

26. Ibid.: "Premia Dios la humildad, y sencilles de la Nación Indiana en la parcialidad de los Otomites con la Aparición de Nuestra Señora de los Remedios, y su inbención feliz" (fol. 48ff.).

27. Ibid.: "Apareze María Santissima, a otro Yndio, Juan Diego, en la Prov. de Tlaxcalan y honra a la Nación Indiana, con su celestial Ymagen de Ocotlan" (fol. 40ff.).

28. Fray Baltasar de Arizmendi, "Sermones en las festividades de María Santísima predicados en diversos lugares," vol. I, fol. 440, Manuscritos de América, sign. 124 59, Biblioteca Nacional, Madrid.

29. Antonio Royo Marín, OP, *La Virgen María. Teología y espiritualidad marianas*, Madrid, 1968, p. 71.

30. Carranza, *La transmigración*, p. 4.

31. Ita y Parra, *El círculo del amor*.

32. Henricus Renckens, *Creación, paraíso y pecado original* (original ed., The Hague, 1960) Madrid, 1969, p. 41.

33. Ita y Parra, *El círculo del amor.*

34. Saint Louis Marie Grignon de Montfort, *Traité de la véritable dévotion a la Sainte Vierge*, (beginning of the seventeenth century), cited by A. Marín, *La Virgen María*, pp. 367, 398.

35. Díaz de la Vega, "Memorias Piadosas," ch. vi: "... celestial Ymagen de Ocotlan."

36. *Autos formados con motivo de la conjuración intentada en la Ciudad de México por Criollos contra los Europeos*, October 27, 1800 (Consejo, leg. 21 061, no. 458, fol. 25, Archivo Histórico Nacional, Madrid).

37. "Sentimientos de la Nación," *Boletín del Archivo General de la Nación*, II series, vol. IV, no. 3, Mexico City, 1963 (n.p.); "Proclama de D. José María Morelos, II de marzo de 1813," in *Album Histórico Guadalupano del IV Centenario*, Mexico City, 1930, p. 229.

38. Sánchez, *Imagen de la Virgen María*, pp. 117-30. See also Vetancurt, *Teatro Mexicano*, III, 351: "fué [Juan Diego] al Señor Obispo, que para certificarse le pidió *señal* volvió Juan Diego ... diciendo que ... le pedía *señal* cierta para su crédito ... la Señora [Guadalupe] dándole por *señas* aquellas flores. ..."

39. Florencia, *La Estrella del Norte*, p. 70.

40. Ibid., p. 77.

41. Ibid., p. 71.

42. Ibid.

43. Ibid., p. 72.

44. Ibid.

45. Gaspar de San Agustín, *Conquistas de las islas Philipinas*, p. 948b.

46. Francisco de San José, Jeron., *Historia universal de la primitiva y milagrosa imagen de Nuestra Señora de Guadalupe*, p. 130a.

47. Florencia, *La Estrella del Norte*, ch. xii: "Pero advierto, que si esta materia se hubiese de reproducir en Roma, sea yendo persona de por acá, inteligentte, que la trate con empeño y viveza" (p. 73).

48. Talavera, *Historia de Nuestra Señora de Guadalupe*, p. 325.

49. Ibid., p. 333.

50. Ibid., p. 336.

51. Ibid., pp. 340, 344.

52. Ibid., p. 355.

53. Miguel Cabrera, *Maravilla americana, y conjunto de raras maravillas, observadas con la dirección de las reglas de el arte de la pintura en la prodigiosa imagen de Nuestra Señora de Guadalupe de México por Don Miguel Cabrera, pintor*, Mexico City, 1756.

54. Ambrosio de Morales, *Viage ... por orden del Rey D. Phelipe II a los Reynos de León, Galicia y principado de Asturias, para reconocer las reliquias de Santos, sepulcros reales, y libros manuscritos de las cathedrales, y monasterios*, Madrid, A. Marín, 1765 (in Appendix to Luis Menéndez Pidal, *La cueva de Covadonga*, Oviedo, 1958, p. 111).

55. Gaspar de San Agustín, *Conquistas de las islas Philipinas*, p. 273.

56. Fray Diego de Ocaña, *Viaje por la América meridional (1599–1606)*, Madrid, 1969, p. 354.

Chapter 16

1. Bloch, *Apologie pour l'histoire*, p. 5.

2. Francisco de la Maza, *El guadalupanismo mexicano*, p. 9.

3. Justo Sierra, "Discurso inaugural de la Universidad de México" (1910), in *Obras completas*, Mexico City, 1948, vol. V, pp. 447–62.

4. Alfonso Reyes, "Notas sobre la inteligencia americana," in *Obras completas*, vol. XI, Mexico City, 1960, p. 89.

Chapter 17

1. Wigberto Jiménez Moreno and A. García Ruiz, *Historia de México, una síntesis*, Mexico City, 1962, p. 31.

2. Jacques Lafaye, "Le Messie dans le monde iberique: aperçu," *Mélanges de la Casa de Velázquez*, vol. VII, 1971, pp. 163–85.

3. A. Dupront, "Langage et histoire," XIIIe Congrès international des Sciences historiques, Moscow, 1970, p. 48ff.

4. Robles, *Diario* III, 228.

5. Antonio Domínguez Ortiz, *La clase social de los conversos en Castilla en la edad moderna*, Madrid, 1955, p. 214ff.

6. Jacques Lafaye, "L'utopie mexicaine," *Diogène*, no. 78, April–June 1972, pp. 20–39.

7. Paul Alphandéry and A. Dupront, *La Chrétienté et l'idée de croisade*, Paris, 1954.

8. Juan E. Nieremberg, *Tablas chronológicas . . . de los descubrimientos, conquistas*, Zaragoza, 1676.

9. Georges Duby, *Adolescence de la chrétienté occidentale*, Geneva, 1967, pp. 181–82.

10. Robert B. Tate, *Ensayos sobre la historiografía peninsular del siglo XV*, Madrid, 1970, p. 28.

11. Jacques Lafaye, *Quetzalcóatl et Guadalupe, Eschatologie et histoire au Mexique*.

12. Clavijero, *Historia antigua*, passim.

13. Miguel de Unamuno, "En torno al casticismo," in *Ensayos*, Madrid, 1945, vol. I, pp. 40–49.

14. Alfonso Reyes, *La X en la frente*, Mexico City, 1952, pp. 87–88.

15. Roger Bastide, "État actuel et perspectives d'avenir des recherches afroaméricaines," *Journal de la Société des Américanistes*, vol. LVIII, Paris, 1971, p. 26.

16. Claude Lévi-Strauss, *L'Anthropologie structurale*, Paris, 1958, p. 31.

17. A. María y Campos, *La Revolución mexicana a través de los corridos populares*, 3 vols., Mexico City, 1962; Vicente T. Mendoza, *Lírica narrativa de México (el corrido)*, México, 1964; *Catálogo de grabaciones del laboratorio de sonido del Museo Nacional de Antropología e Historia*, Mexico, 1968; Nicole Giron, *Heraclio Bernal: bandit, "cacique" ou précurseur de la Revolution (1855–1888)*, Paris, 1973 (thèse de IIIe cycle, Université de Paris III).

18. Melville J. Herskovits, *The Myth of the Negro Past*, New York, 1941.

19. Jacques Lafaye, *La Bibliographie dévote de Notre-Dame de Guadalupe, 1648–1831; Essai d'analyse formelle* (forthcoming).

20. Paulo de Carvalho Neto, *History of Iberoamerican Folklore (Mestizo Cultures)*, Anthropological Publications, Oosterhout, 1969.

21. M. A. Asturias, *Cuculcan, Leyendas de Guatemala*, Madrid, 1930; Alfredo Chavero, *Quetzalcóatl;* Mexico City, 1877 (play); J. García Pimentel, *El Señuelo del Sacrificio, Coloquio de la Derrota y Triunfo de Quetzalcóatl*, Mexico City, 1939 (play); E. Abreu Gómez, *Quetzalcóatl, sueño y vigilia*, Mexico City, 1947 (poetry); Agustí Bartra, *Quetzalcóatl*, Mexico City, 1960 (poetry); Ramón J. Sender, *Jubileo en el Zócalo*, Barcelona, 1966; Carlos Fuentes, *Todos los gatos son pardos*, Mexico City, 1970 (play).

22. D. H. Lawrence, *The Plumed Serpent*, New York, 1926.

23. Paul Diel, *La Divinité*, Paris, 1949, p. 18.

24. José Vasconcelos, *Ulíses criollo*, 13th ed., Mexico, 1969, p. 266.

Index